Karma and Rebirth

SUNY Series in Religious Studies
Robert C. Neville, Editor

KARMA AND REBIRTH: POST CLASSICAL DEVELOPMENTS

edited by
Ronald W. Neufeldt

State University of New York Press

Published by
State University of New York Press, Albany

Printed in the United States of America

For information, address State University of New York
Press, State University Plaza, Albany, N.Y., 12246

Library of Congress Cataloging in Publication Data
Main entry under title:

Karma and rebirth.

Papers from the Calgary Conference on Karma and
Rebirth, Post-Classical Developments, held at the
University of Calgary, Sept. 20-23, 1982.
1. Karma—Congresses. 2. Reincarnation—Congresses.
I. Neufelet, Ronald W. (Ronald Wesley), 1941-
II. Calgary Conference on Karma and Rebirth, Post-
Classical Developments (1982 : University of Calgary)
BL2015,K3K374 1986 291.2'3 84-16304
ISBN 0-87395-990-6
ISBN 0-87995-989-2 (pbk.)

for my Parents,
my First and Best Teachers

Contents

II THE BUDDHIST CONTEXT

III THE WESTERN CONTEXT

Preface

The chapters of this volume are the result of papers presented at the Calgary Conference on *Karma and Rebirth, Post-Classical Developments,* held at the University of Calgary, September 20-23, 1982. The conference was organized with the plan to publish the proceedings, and the participants were invited to present papers on specific topics for presentation at the conference and for eventual publication. The conference was a success to a great extent because of the care taken by the participants on their research and writings. I owe them much thanks for their work.

A conference such as this cannot, however, go on without financial and organizational support. Here I owe thanks to a lengthy group of individuals and organizations. Substantial grants were made by the Social Sciences and Humanities Research Council of Canada and the University of Calgary under their respective Conference Grant programs. Substantial financial support came from the Dean of the Faculty of Humanities, the Religious Studies Department, the Dean of the Faculty of Social Sciences, and the Political Science Department. Invaluable administrative support was given by the Faculty of Continuing Education and the Department of Religious Studies.

As any scholar knows, much work goes into checking, typing and correcting the manuscript. Harold Coward and Leslie Kawamura devoted many hours of editorial labour in working with the manuscript while was in India on sabbatical. For the many hours given to typing I must thank Marion Harrison and Rosanne Sullivan. Their work was indeed invaluable and appreciated highly.

Ronald Neufeldt
Associate Professor
Religious Studies Department
University of Calgary

A word concerning the use of diacriticals. These have been retained for the transliteration of Sanskrit, Pāli, Tibetan, Chinese, and Japanese terms. There are, however, exceptions to this. In the case of proper names, particularly names of figures and authors which commonly appear as English terms, diacritical marks have not been used. This applies in particular to figures of the Hindu renaissance and modern Indian authors.

Introduction

The papers in this volume were initially presented at a scholarly conference held at the University of Calgary on September 20-23, 1982. As the papers themselves demonstrate, there was throughout a keen awareness of the existence and importance of the ongoing project on karma and rebirth to be published by the University of California Press in four volumes. The numerous references to the first volume, *Karma and Rebirth In Classical Indian Traditions*, edited by Wendy Doniger O'Flaherty, underline the significance of this project.

Like the O'Flaherty volume, the papers in this volume are intended to be representative only, rather than exhaustive. Indeed, it would seem arrogant to suppose that one could ever treat such a vast subject exhaustively in a single volume. Also like the O'Flaherty volume, the papers are intended to be both descriptive and analytical. Of particular importance is the descriptive element. Karma and rebirth as important religious concepts are, like religious traditions, changing and fluid concepts. It may be, as Professor Potter argues, that there is an identifiable and constant core of ideas associated with karma and rebirth from the classical period of Indian history to the present. At the same time, however, there is change and adaptation as these concepts move into the modern period and into countries other than India. Just as it is important to trace and understand changes and adaptations in religious traditions as such, so it is important to trace and to attempt to understand the changes and adaptations which have taken place in the understanding of the concepts of karma and rebirth. For the most part, the papers are intended to be descriptive of the understanding of karma and rebirth. In this respect, each section contains papers surveying major streams of thought and papers dealing with specific movements and figures. The three papers offered as critiques are intended as an analysis of the papers in the light of classical perceptions of karma and rebirth.

In one important respect this volume differs from the University of California Press multi-volume series on karma and rebirth. This volume seeks to move beyond the Indian subcontinent, to look at the understanding of karma and rebirth not only in modern India, but also in Sri Lanka and Southeast Asia, Tibet, China, Japan, and finally the western world. This broader treatment is an attempt to underscore the fact that the subject of karma and rebirth has become more than simply an Indian, or even an Eastern subject. Indeed, karma and rebirth have become part of the religious history and therefore, the cultural fabric of the western world.

The arrangement of the sections of the book reflects the arrangement of the conference itself. There is a combination of the traditional religious categories like Hinduism and Buddhism and geographical categories. This was seen to be necessary, particularly in the discussion of developments in the West where it is not always possible to maintain the more traditional categories. For example, one would be hard put to label Rajneesh in terms of any of the great traditions. The same is true of Theosophy. And certainly a treatment of karma and rebirth in western psychology is clearly impossible in terms of the great traditions. This, of course, does not mean that one cannot identify at least some western movements as Hindu or Buddhist. Some of the papers show that this is indeed possible.

The papers in Parts I and III are similar in scope in that they deal with figures, movements, and developments in the nineteenth and twentieth centuries. Indeed a few of the papers of Part III involve contemporary developments or movements. The scope of Part II tends to be much wider. While there is reference to recent or contemporary developments, notably in the papers by Matthews and E. Dargyay, the discussion in this section also includes figures and texts as far back as the fourth century. Matthews, for example, feels compelled to provide a background from canonical teaching and the *Abhidhammattha Saṅgaha* for a discussion of modern interpreters and the *Saṅgha*. Jan begins with the ancient Chinese notion of retribution as the setting for a discussion of karma in Hui-yüan (fourth century), Tsung-mi (ninth century) and more importantly, the San Yen collection of short stories (sixteenth and seventeeth centuries). This apparent discrepancy in scope should not be taken to suggest that what is "post-classical" in the Buddhist is not "post-classical" in other contexts, although in some respects this may be the case. It does, however, raise the thorny issue of what is to be considered as post-classical in any context. Clearly this is an issue beyond the scope of this volume, for the question would result in almost as many opinions as there are scholars. This issue apart, the term "post-classical" was simply considered to be a convenient title for the papers contained in this volume.

In spite of this difference in scope, there are significant themes or ideas which connect a number of the papers just as there are peculiarities which surface from time to time setting individual papers apart from the others. A few of the more common themes are signalled by Creel in his treatment of contemporary Hindu philosophers. On the whole, he finds that the modern philosophical literature pays little attention to past formulations of karma and rebirth. This is echoed in Prebish's treatment of American Buddhism, a scene in which Prebish finds little attention paid to karma and rebirth either directly or indirectly, particularly as these concepts relate to traditional Buddhist ethics. In particular, he suggests that aspects of the five vows are changed and/or ignored, the three refuges are misunderstood or taken in a perfunctory manner, dharma teachers are not exemplary beings, meditation is trivialized or divorced from ethical action, and the *bodhisattva* vow is poorly understood.

While the modern Hindu philosophical curriculum seems to pay little attention to past formulations of karma and rebirth, Creel does point out the appearance of a number of themes—karma vs. freedom; karma as continuity rather than determinism; exclusive vs. associational views of karma; group karma; karma and modern science; and *niṣkāma karma*. These themes surface from time to time in one or more of the other papers. *Niṣkāma karma*, for example, a theme which is prominent in the modern philosophical curriculum, appears again in Williams' treatment of Vivekananda. However, here it becomes part of Vivekananda's understanding of *karma yoga* which, among other things, has to do with desireless action, or action without concern for the results. Something akin to this is also found in the treatment of Rajneesh. While not labelled *niṣkāma karma*, the emphasis which Rajneesh places on "being" is, in effect, action without concern for the results, an awareness of acts but without concern for the cultivation of good character or the popular applications of karma to social life. In this one finds an explicit rejection of at least some of the social-ethical concerns of the well-known figures of the Hindu renaissance.

Perhaps the most prominent themes are those which have to do with issues such as freedom, determinism, continuity, and science. Certainly we would expect to see these concerns in figures such as Vivekananda, Aurobindo, and Radhakrishnan. As Minor points out, both Aurobindo and Radhakrishnan are concerned with cleansing karma and rebirth of any fatalistic connotations. This is done through affirming that the world is subject to a positive or progressive evolutionary process and that karma and rebirth are the mechanism whereby growth and progress are achieved. By implication at least, such notions of progress are entertained by Vivekananda in his views of the dawning of a future golden age, although at times Vivekananda appears to give voice to somewhat fatalistic notions. As Williams points out, Vivekananda holds multiple points of view about karma and rebirth making no apparent attempt to harmonize these viewpoints. The wedding of karma and rebirth to views of progress through evolution is also a prominent part of Theosophical views. According to Neufeldt, Blavatsky proposes karma as a universal law of retribution and reward operative in the human sphere in order to further the evolutionary process, and rebirth is proposed as the continuity which is necessary for that process to go on.

The issue of karma and continuity is raised in a number of the papers in the Buddhist context but in a different way; that is, without the concern for evolution or progress. Matthews, for example, points out the Abhidhamma emphasis on karma as a continuum or process interpenetrating and spanning past, present, and future. L. Dargyay details Tsong-kha-pa's view of the karmic trace as an afteract, or a latent activity which produces fruit when the situation allows for it. Kawamura emphasizes Shinran's view of karma as a causality principle directed to understanding how the present is derived from the past.

Typical of those who place karma and rebirth within an evolutionary context is the assertion that karma and rebirth as explanations of life are supported by modern scientific, philosophic, and empirical research. Certainly this is the case with Blavatsky, Aurobindo, and Radhakrishnan, although little in the way of scientific or empirical evidence is put forward to support the assertion. Matthews reports that modern Theravāda interpreters appeal to empirical research and western philosophy to support and develop the concepts of karma and rebirth. And, Coward argues that for Transpersonal Psychology karma and rebirth theory is a useful paradigm for understanding human behavior.

A number of papers highlight a notion which Potter regards as a departure from the classical karma theory of India—namely, group karma. This is as an important consideration in Vivekananda, Aurobindo, Radhakrishnan, Jung, Blavatsky and others cited by Creel in his treatment of modern Indian philosophy. At issue is not only the idea that human beings and their actions are somehow interrelated, but also the ethical notion that one is in important ways one's brother's keeper.

Merit-making in association with karmic transfer, is raised by Miller in his treatment of the transactional tradition with reference to the contemporary guru. Potter argues that although the idea of karma transfer is foreign to classical karma theory, one can find it at least in the Puranic literature. However, he questions whether it is really implied in the business of merit-making as detailed in examples cited by Miller and Williams. Schmithausen, in his discussion of merit-making, seems to suggest that there is in the minds of Buddhists a connection between merit-making and karmic transfer at least in terms of good karma, and that such a connection might be found as far back as early Buddhist texts. Merit-making in relation to karma is also found in Matthews treatment of

Theravāda and E. Dargyay's treatment of the religious life of Sanskar. While Matthews sees merit-making as a pedagogical device used in the "little tradition" to explain abstract concepts such as karma, Dargyay maintains that making-merit to affect oneself and others in the community is that which occupies the mind of the lay Buddhist when he/she thinks about karma. Schmithausen offers the provocative insight that merit transfer is already there in early Buddhism, although it is reinterpreted in line with Buddhist ethics.

A paper which seems to stand apart, at least from the other papers of Part I, is Klostermaier's treatment of North Indian Vaiṣṇavas. Rather than relying on English materials, Klostermaier provides a summary and analysis of *Paraloka Aura Punarjanmāṅka,* a special 1969 issue of the Gitapress of Gorakhpur. Further, one finds here as Potter admits, a challenge to some of the ideas traditionally associated with the classical karma theory. The clearest case of challenge is the rejection of *mukti* as a goal. In other respects, particularly in the theme of retribution and reward, Klostermaier's "devotionalists" appear to support classical karma theory. And certainly the business of retribution and reward surfaces elsewhere. Blavatsky at times refers to karma as a "law of retribution." Jan, in his treatment of Chinese Buddhism points out how karma and rebirth were assimilated to the ancient Chinese notion of retribution so that it is thought of as affecting not only one's life and posterity but also one's future births.

The papers, in particular the critiques, emphasize a number of concerns which would bear further and more detailed study. All three critiques point out that there is both affirmation of and departure from classical karma theory. The nature and extent of both affirmation and departure requires more detailed development. Of particular importance and interest is the departure noted by both Potter and Penelhum; that is, that karma becomes simply a thesis appended to natural or other accounts of what man is made of and where civilization is going. Whether this is based on a misunderstanding of classical karma theory or not, one is forced to wonder whether, in the instances in which it becomes a mere appendage, karma theory has any future at all? Potter also points out that more needs to be done to make clear the earthy aspects or nitty-gritty details about the workings of karma and rebirth. Certainly he is correct. In some of the figures and movements represented here, one suspects that there will be no interest in the nitty-gritty details, that the concern will simply be to support the notions of karma and rebirth as valuable tools to inculcate morality, hope, responsibility, etc. In other instances, notably in Bhaktivedanta, one would expect considerable concern for the nitty-gritty details.

I

The Hindu Context

CHAPTER ONE

Contemporary Philosophical Treatments of Karma and Rebirth

AUSTIN B. CREEL

Where it all began is a question some thinkers raise in treating karma and rebirth. This conference on "Post-Classical Developments" does not come out of nowhere, and I have been musing on the particular and principal antecedent stream, the "karma conferences" in 1976, 1978, and 1980, one result of which is the volume, *Karma and Rebirth in Classical Indian Traditions*, edited by Wendy Doniger O'Flaherty.[1] To the extent that this conference may be viewed under the rubric of rebirth of earlier incarnations, I wonder if our efforts here will unfold the karma of the previous conferences or of the individual participants here assembled!

My assignment is contemporary philosophical treatments of karma (and rebirth), rather imprecisely defined as academic philosophy and the writings of other thinkers in the Hindu community who treat problems of modern intellectual life in a philosophical way. This veers away from popular religious teachers, who are vehicles of much religious transmission, and from the approaches of other important figures (e.g., Vivekananda, Aurobindo, Gandhi) who were not academicians and/or are being treated in other papers.

What is being said today about karma and rebirth? The first answer to be given is "surprisingly little." I flirted with the idea of generating a statistical report on the number of volumes with titles indicating contemporary Indian philosophy and listing tabulated data on the number of index listings of karma, *saṃsāra*, rebirth, transmigration, etc. But this would be so imprecise—surely out of keeping with the meticulous precision embodied in the doctrine of karma—if only because it might indicate poor indexing rather than neglect in treatment. Still, one notices the dearth of listings at once, and more careful study does not significantly alter the initial impression that karma and rebirth do not occupy as prominent a place in the modern Hindu philosophical curriculum as one might expect from their historical roles or from the affirmations of their continuing relevance that are so easily found. It is sustained philosophical interpretation that is in relatively short supply.

One point on which there seems to be wide agreement is that karma is basic and rebirth is derivative. M. Yamunacharya says that karma is a fact whereas reincarnation is an hypothesis; M. Hiriyanna sees transmigration as "a necessary corollary" of karma; N.K. Devaraja characterizes reincarnation as an aspect of karma; R.C. Pandeya notes that rebirth is only derived from karma, not vice-versa; Margaret Chatterjee speaks of the "attendant doctrine of rebirth."[2] With this in mind, our focus in the present paper will be on karma, with consequent relative neglect of *saṃsāra*, but this seems proportionate to the Indian philosophical scene today. In fact, in much discussion they are conjoined; a few modern writers, however, choose to sever the connection, as we shall see.

Despite the dearth of extensive systematic treatments, there is a current of affirmation of karma and rebirth, with some modifications of, and certain exceptions to past views; and to a summary of these we now turn. The first and most basic continuing emphasis is that we are what we are because of our past action, and what we will be depends on our present action. "The hand that rewards or smites you is your own," says P. Parameswara.[3] T.M.P. Mahadevan writes, "All that the theory of karma implies is that moral life is not chaos and that a man's actions in the past are responsible for his present state and that his present deeds will condition his future fortunes."[4] Margaret Chatterjee, in an article on "The Concept of Action," notes that the theory of karma affirms three things: "the potency of human action to bring about chains of consequences, the assumption that intelligibility includes the demand for justice, and the demand for a causal explanation of events (i.e., the demand that human actions, no less than natural events, be governed by law)."[5]

There is a strong and repeated stress on justice in a law-abiding universe, and in this connection one need only recall the primacy from an early period of the concept of law, expressed in the concepts of *ṛta* and *dharma* as well as karma. How else is one to explain the myriad inequalities which we observe all about us? Over and over again one finds this as a primary issue in Hindu thought about karma and rebirth; this is the key problem to which the doctrines provide an answer.[6]

A second affirmation is that understanding karma provides therapeutic knowledge; one blames oneself, not anybody else, for one's present state, and one knows that one's future will be shaped by one's own actions. This obviates bitterness toward others: "A believer in Karma never blames another for the suffering and misery overtaking him," says K.E. Parthasarathy, who describes the doctrine of karma as "an incentive to action and a source of consolation."[7] Surama Dasgupta calls the karma doctrine a "source of inspiration to mankind" and also says that the "most important contribution of *karma* is in its psychological implications," as pure actions are seen as conducive to "the infinite quest for the ideal."[8] N.K. Devaraja says that the Hindu view of karma gives man a sense of responsibility for his own lot and the assurance that "he can reshape his destiny by his own moral and spiritual effort."[9]

Karma places responsibility for the present upon each individual's past; at the same time, the future is dependent upon present behavior. Whatever one's present circumstances, the ultimate goal is available to all; in this sense the doctrine of karma may be said to be an "equal opportunity employer."

In the modern period, there is a pervasive issue of freedom in relation to the karmic process, of free will in the midst of deterministic perspectives. S. Radhakrishnan in one of the first of his published articles, "Karma and Free Will" in 1908,[10] addresses these problems, and while he has not written about karma very extensively, in this as in other matters, his perspective has been immensely influential in twentieth century philosophy in India. One is immediately conscious that writers from Radhakrishnan on, are answering charges that the karma doctrine involves a closed universe, without allowing for moral freedom. Probably such charges have for the most part missed the mark, but the modern discussion focuses principally on this issue and seems to go beyond replying to external criticism to reflect a widespread concern for the implications of modern personal and social values, where freedom has a richer connotation than simply the obverse of determinism.

The basic question that is posed is whether the doctrine of karma admits freedom: if we are the sum of our yesterdays, how can we affect our tomorrows? Hindu thinkers generally reply that our karma places us where we are but does not determine how we shall react to, or act in, the situations in which we find ourselves. For Radhakrishnan and many others, karma sets conditions but does not impose rigid limits, and in a passage much quoted by subsequent writers, he develops the analogy of a hand of cards:

> Our demand for freedom must reckon with a universe that is marked by order and regularity. Life is like a game of bridge. The cards in the game are given to us. We do not select them. They are traced to past Karma but we are free to make any call as we think fit and lead any suit. Only we are limited by the rules of the game. We are more free when we start the game than later on when the game has developed and our choices become restricted. But till the very end

there is always a choice. A good player will see possibilities which a bad one does not. The more skilled a player the more alternatives does he perceive. A good hand may be cut to pieces by unskillful play and the bad play need not be attributed to the frowns of fortune. Even though we may not like the way the cards are shuffled, we like the game and we want to play.[11]

So, for Radhakrishnan, "Karma is not so much a principle of retribution as one of continuity," and "Karma or connection with the past is not inconsistent with creative freedom."[12] Or, to quote T.M.P. Mahadevan, karma is not relentless fate, but rather "it is what man has achieved in the past; and he is answerable to it. He has acquired also certain tendencies and dispositions which make him act in one way rather than another. But he can change them in the present and shape his future according to his will."[13] N.A. Nikam writes, "The Law of Karma is based on the reality of human freedom, and it pre-supposes the notion of responsibility, and the Law does not state an unalterable necessity but a modal possibility or a conditional relativity."[14]

Most modern writers speak of karma as providing conditions or tendencies or as prescribing circumstances, rather than a more "absolutistic" view by which our total being—and not merely our placement in the world—is determined by our karma. One might call these the exclusive and the associational views of causality in karma, the former being the "absolutistic" one where karma is the exclusive cause of happenings, and the latter holding that our karma is associated with other forces which combine to form our present state. Suryanarayana Sastri notes that in the typical modern view the moral realm is made exempt from the universal validity of the causal law, in that if my actions have multiple causes, my karma being one, then the uncompromising causal link is considerably weakened if not vacated.[15] One of the ways of maintaining the "absolutistic" or exclusive view is to posit freedom as limited to our higher life,[16] a point made by many followers of Advaita Vedānta, from which perspective the spiritual is the absolute realm of freedom and the material is empirically real, with the causal law of karma pertaining to and operating in the material realm, but not in the spiritual realm. So in the 1908 article, Radhakrishnan wrote: "The universal law of *karma* has nothing to do with the *real* man, if he has once understood what he is in his *real* nature." He says that it is in the exercise of the faculty of reason that man is free.[17] S.K. Chattopadhyaya writes:

The phenomenal individual has to be understood as a configuration of the Karmic stuff, neither apart from it nor independent of it. In the causal operation of Karma it is this phenomenal individual which is continued or reproduced and not the self. The self is neither born

> nor reborn, it neither dies nor reincarnates. It is no participant in the cosmic process, is neither morally elevated nor condemned. As not belonging to the Karmic process it is not an agent, free or bound.[18]

Suryanarayana Sastri says that in Advaita Vedānta, "Man as Spirit is always free; viewing himself as nature, he is always bound."[19]

Another defense of the viability of freedom in relation to karma is in the view that the real meaning of freedom is self-determination, which is to say determination by the self and not by an external agency. On this basis, even in the absolutistic view of karma, the doctrine does not yield fatalism, since it is the self's own actions which produce effects. This is, I think, to say that if we are determined, it is by ourselves and that such self-determination is really freedom. This is a view found, for example, in the writings of S. Radhakrishnan and M. Hiriyanna, and, more recently, in the work of Balbir Singh.[20]

A modern theme related to the issue of one's karma as exclusive or as associated cause of one's present situations, is that of group karma, the idea that karma either is not limited to individuals or is operative in the interactions of individuals in various collectives. One thinks of Gandhi's attributing the Bihar earthquake to the treatment of untouchables, of Vivekananda's view of a national karma, and of B.G. Tilak's idea of group karma.[21] Modern thinkers generally pass over the link between human retribution and vast natural calamities and attend to the perception that much that affects me comes through other persons. Am I therefore my neighbor's karma-keeper? Various approaches may be noted.

Sarasvati Chennakesavan asks, when a father speculates with family funds and loses and all members of the family suffer, "whose karma is being worked out under such circumstances, or do all of them have the same karma?"[22]

Surama Dasgupta echoes many others in wanting to insist that the Hindu view of karma does not emphasize the individual to the detriment of the group:

> Though an individual is mainly responsible for his own good and bad actions, he shares at the same time the collective responsibility for the good of others and for society. . . .Social life is an organic whole; each member is tied with another in an indissoluble tie. We do not, and can never, live in an isolated manner, but are closely related to one another. . . .This sense of collective responsibility has been emphasised even more by the law of *karma*. . . .It is not merely the subjective changes of one's own or those of others that are caused by our actions, but changes in objective nature around us can also be effected by them . . . .We suffer or enjoy also in consequence of

other people's actions, and this is found to be very true in political and social spheres.[23]

Pratima Bowes notes that in the operation of the law of karma one is placed in "a certain environment" with particular psychic and physical endowments, but this environment "is not entirely a product of one's own karma, it is a joint product of the karma of countless men who interact with one another." She further writes, "a social institution being the result of the karma of many people, its limitations may inflict on a person suffering which is not the exclusive result of his own karma. . . .This social dimension of the law of karma has not received any attention in the Hindu tradition because it could make one critical of the caste system."[24]

P. Parameswara agrees that an individual cannot escape consequences of actions of other members of groups to which he belongs, and notes that for some this is said to be opposed to the essence of the idea of karma, because "the doctrine of karma treats the individual as an independent unity, that is, it makes the individual responsible only for his own Karma." Parameswara's solution: what appears to be vicarious suffering or "what falls to the lot of a person as a result (to all appearance) of other people's Karma is neither more nor less than the fruit of that person's own unexpended karma reaching him through the implementing instrumentality of those other people."[25] Balbir Singh gives a similar explanation for joint effects in natural calamities as well; people have come "to be linked together by virtue of this identity of their deeds and suffer a common fate during natural calamities or other tragedies."[26] Daya Krishna is quite emphatic that the traditional Hindu view held to the strict correlation of one's own actions as the cause of one's present state. He writes:

> The idea that one can be responsible for actions which have not been done by one's own self and that one can be redeemed by an action done by somebody else may seem positively outrageous to a sensibility which feels the individual is essentially apart from the relationship with others in which he may happen to be accidentally involved. The doctrine of *karma* in traditional Hindu thought primarily reflects this basic presupposition that it would be an immoral world indeed if one were to reap the fruits of someone else's actions. . . .Not only do one's own actions have consequences on oneself but, if the world is to be a moral world, nothing else could.[27]

On such a view, as Warren Steinkraus puts it, "One should not reap what he has not sown."[28]

A rather different instance of the manifestation of group karma today is provided by the following observation of N. Subrahmanian about the way some Hindus have interpreted their perceptions of the lack of success in secular efforts toward social reform and toward social progress. He writes:

> In a curious way secularism itself leads to a confirmation of unsecularism in Hindu India. The failure of secular effort, caused by lack of faith in secularism, still leaves behind the feeling that it is caused by the inexorable Karma and that all effort that was made to alter the *status quo* according to human plan, was most foolish and impious; the unexpected and unmitigated punishment for such impiety.[29]

I have not seen this presented as a philosophical argument, but it is interesting to note this popular appropriation of the idea of group karma. Ventures into consideration of group karma are tentative and meet considerable resistance. We should note the comment at the Second Karma Workshop that "group karma" does not translate any Indian terms.[30] Clearly this problem of the collective character of social causes is on the minds of Hindu thinkers as they reflect on the doctrine of karma.

Some note must be taken of Hindu voices which question the views of karma and/or rebirth. The most striking is provided by Swami Iswarananda whose original article in 1936 ("Does the Soul Reincarnate?") rejected rebirth on biological grounds, arguing "that the hypothesis of transmigration or reincarnation in untenable in the face of the facts of biogenesis." A second paper followed in 1947, and by 1964 these were gathered into a small book.[31] Volume 1 of the *Indian Philosophical Annual* contains the "Proceedings of the Seminar on Karma and Rebirth," convened in 1965 at Madras to consider Iswarananda's views. I hesitate to wade into this discussion, but certain features may be briefly noted. Iswarananda concludes from his study of biological processes of individualization that one cannot conceive of the manner of time in which the soul *(jīva)* could be associated with the fusion and division of cells involved in reproduction: "Biogenesis thus excludes the need as well as the possibility of a disembodied spirit entering into living or non-living matter for rebirth."[32] Iswarananda's positive point is to use biological patterns as the basis for understanding the creation of souls, and he sees this as consistent with the deeper affirmations of Vedānta teaching. He contends, "Rebirth and karma of past lives were unproved dogmas of Hinduism till yesterday, but today they are positively disproved dogmas."[33]
dogmas."[33]

Iswarananda further argues that Hindu thought in the approach to the karma theory in the past has been focused on only one of three factors which contribute to our situation, namely our own deeds, to the neglect of two others, the deeds of other selves (*jīvas*) and the forces of insentient nature.[34] He correlates with this exclusive concentration on one's own deeds the view, occasionally mentioned by others, that karma served to reinforce a certain callousness towards the needs of others, in that if everybody's situation is the result of his or her own action, it is needless and perhaps useless to try to do anything to improve another person's lot. At the same time one was encouraged to accept one's own lot and to try to improve it.[35] Iswarananda's conclusion is that what has been attributed to karma is really the work of ignorance, *avidyā*: "Your experiencing the fruits is not due to your karma but avidyā." The goal or remedy is *brahmavidya*, and this knowledge brings liberation without possibility of rebirth, the idea of which along with karma is an accretion on the real teaching of the Upaniṣads.[36]

The point of Iswarananda is one expressed by other writers: whether as an implication of the karma theory it is inappropriate, perhaps even hopeless, to attempt to ammeliorate situations of distress in the human community. Who are we to try to undo or offset the workings of karma? Iswarananda puts it thus:

> The prevalent Hindu doctrine that one's life is solely determined by one's karma and therefore one can afford to be callous toward the suffering of those around him on the plea that their lot is determined by their own karma, and therefore one need not to do anything for their welfare, has been responsible for not only the neglect of the masses in India by the aristocracies of learning, power and wealth, but also for standing as a barrier to their growth and welfare. This doctrine has served the well-to-do as a screen to hide their selfish motives of jealousy at seeing others as equal to themselves and as an engine of oppression and exploitation of the unfortunate millions who have been told that it is their own karma in their past lives that is responsible for their lot in this life; and those who held this doctrine need not contribute anything toward relieving the misery of those oppressed masses.[37]

Iswarananda sees this as the consequence of attending only to one's own actions as a causal factor, to the neglect of the roles of others and of insentient forces of nature. Not all writers state the matter so boldly. Sanat Kumar Sen raises the problem in a less bombastic manner: "the assumption of Karma may even seem to justify callousness in the face of human suffering, for if everybody's fate is the result of his own action, why should we attempt to mitigate others' miseries except on grounds of selfishness."[38] Many writers explicitly deny that such a view is entailed by the karma doctrine, appealing to the idea that present freedom to act in a morally responsible way towards human misery in all its forms is provided for rather than contradicted by the idea of karma.[39]

Others also examine what are perceived to be the consequences of the historic views of karma and/or rebirth, especially in inculcating an acceptance of the status quo that is at variance with modern aspirations for betterment, individual and social. B. Kuppuswamy, a psychologist who quotes P.V. Kane on the past role of the doctrine of karma in making men submissive, wishes to hold to beliefs about moral rewards and punishments here and now but rejects the rebirth component: "The doctrine of *karma* in so far as it asserts that one's actions in this life have a reaction on one's life here and now has a moral validity; but it has no validity when it is extended beyond one's death or to events before one's birth." Kuppuswamy graphically contrasts the fundamental rights of the Indian Constitution and the traditional utilization of karma doctrine: "While the doctrine of *karma* asserts that it is the duty of the individual to endure the sufferings as a result of his past *karma,* Article 47 casts upon the State the primary duty of 'raising the levels of nutrition and the standard of living of the people and the improvement of public health. . . ."[40] A similar point was made by Thiru N. Murugesa Mudaliar at a Madras seminar on "Traditional Hinduism and Social Development." He writes, "The benumbing factors like looking upon another man's poverty or pain as his Karma are repugnant to modern ideas like social justice."[41] Another who questions traditional thinking about karma is Sarasvati Chennakesavan: "Whatever might have been the utility of the *karma* theory in the past, it has lost its disciplinary hold amongst Hindus. With the spread of scientific and technological knowledge, an explantation for the physiological and mental inequalities so far-fetched as the *karma* theory has become unacceptable. Facts of sociological economics and social psychology combined with anthropology are able to explain inequalities that so puzzled our ancestors."[42]

Modern Hindus largely reject two of the three traditional embodiments of karma—individual ability as specified by birth, and social role as defined by birth.[43] Does spiritual status have any "residual" meaning? Acceptance of an inherited social role goes counter to the commitment to mobility in an open society; individual and social disabilities are seen as amenable to change, and whatever the role of karma, other causes are posited, such as defective economic arrangements, outmoded social customs, selfishness of powerful groups, etc. A few philosophers question the compatibility of the modern ethos and traditional thinking about karma; others seem to turn away from explicit repudiation or even affirmation, in favor of maintaining the view of a moral universe, and in favor of concentrating on an emphasis of greater interest and magnitude—karma as disinterested action.

The concept of non-attached action, *niṣkāma karma* derived from the *Bhagavad-gītā,* is at the very least the subject for a separate paper, but I conclude with this notation, because it is the dominant topic of contemporary discussion. (Karma-yoga is what one *does* find in the indexes of almost all contemporary works dealing with ethics.) Disinterested action, *niṣkāma karma,* and not the doctrines of karma and rebirth, receives paramount attention. Although many presentations indicate some linkage to this usage of karma or action or work, the opposite view is urged by G.W. Kaveeshwar in his book, *The Law of Karma.* He says he wishes to "distinguish from the outset the Law of Karma from some other views with which it is likely to be confused. One of them is the doctrine of *niṣkāma karma.* The two doctrines are different from one another. If a man is to do his duty without any consideration of the consequences, there may not remain much point in insisting that he is responsible for them. Actually, the view that one should perform voluntary actions without any regard for. . .consequences seems to me unnatural as also unwise." He also contends that this is not advocated by the *Bhagavadgītā.*[44]

This is, however, very much a minority view. The principal contemporary discussions reinterpret the doctrine of action by placing emphasis not on action but on attitudes involved in action; action has karmic consequences (which is to say, binds us to the realm of *saṃsāra* or cycle of rebirths) only if we are ourselves bound to that action by our own attachments; what is called for is not the renunciation of action but renunciation in action, or non-attached action or unselfish action. S.K. Saksena writes, "Related to this doctrine of *karma,* which provides an Indian with a practical and ready reckoner of the deeds of his life, is the corresponding theory of non-attached living (*niṣkāma-karma*) which is believed to undo what the law of *karma* does. The law of *niṣkāma-karma* is a philosophical antidote to the evil of bondage to the law of *karma.* While the law of *karma* binds the doer to the fruits of his deeds, the practice of *niṣkāma-karma* frees him from this thraldom."[45] Many parallels could be cited. Here the stress is not on the past explaining, much less limiting, the present, but on the present and a viable path for one and all for life in the world that is simultaneously conducive to spiritual progress, recognizing our different stages of development.[46] This fits well with the emphasis on the trans-karmic life of *mokṣa* by Hindu philosophers; despite a great deal of positive interest in worldly life and in various dimensions of temporal values, the goal is understood to be liberation and freedom from the realm where karma operates. But this *is* a subject for another paper.

To summarize: karma and rebirth are not ignored, but they are not central to the modern Hindu philosophical curriculum. There are a few outright challengers (and they may be the wave of the future, but they are at present distinctly in a minority category). Generally, there is a selective attention to the doctrine of karma, sloughing off past elements that involved religious sanctions for caste or which limited social and personal mobility.[47] There is repeated concentration on the idea of moral law and the requirement of reward/punishment and rebirth in a just universe. For past formulations of karma, there is substituted attention to the very modern interpretation of unselfish action or *niṣkāma karma*.

These are somewhat in the category of straws in the wind; in a very fluid philosophical environment, one should be hesitate about predicting which trend will prevail. I would simply note concerning my initial query that I did not find anybody who says that intellectual life is subject to karma.

NOTES

1. Wendy Doniger O'Flaherty, ed., *Karma and Rebirth in Classical Indian Traditions* (Berkeley: University of California Press, 1980).

2. M. Yamunacharya, "Karma and Rebirth," *Indian Philosophical Annual* 1 (1965), 66; Mysore Hiriyanna, *Essentials of Indian Philosophy* (London: George Allen & Unwin, 1949), p. 47, or *Popular Essays in Indian Philosophy* (Mysore: Kavyalaya Publishers, 1952), p. 30; Nand Kishore Devaraja, *Hinduism and Christianity* (Bombay: Asia Publishing House, 1969), p. 17; Margaret Chatterjee, "The Concept of Action," *Philosophy: Theory and Practice: Proceedings of the International Seminar on World Philosophy, Madras, Dec. 7-17, 1970, ed. T.M.P. Mahadevan (Madras: Centre for Advanced Studies in Philosophy, University of Madras, 1974), p. 16. Below we will note instances of questioning karma and rebirth; one writer who views such thinking as incompatible with basic Hindu thought and an intrusion from "outside the philosophical circle in India" is Nikunja Vihari Banerjee (The Spirit of Indian Philosophy* [New Delhi: Arnold Heinemann, 1974], pp. 11, 20, 48) but the reasons for this are not specified.

3. P. Parameswara, *Soul, Karma and Re-birth* (Bangalore: The Author, 1973), p. 171.

4. T.M.P. Mahadevan, *Whither Civilization and Other Broadcast Talks* (Madras: Central Arts Press, 1946), p. 47.

5. Margaret Chatterjee, "The Concept of Action," p. 16.

6. See M. Hiriyanna, *Essentials of Indian Philosophy*, p. 48; K. Satchidananda Murty, *The Indian Spirit*, Andhra University Series no. 76 (Waltair: Andhra University Press, 1965), p. 87; Pratima Bowes, *The Hindu Religious Tradition* (London/Boston: Routledge and Kegan Paul, 1977), p. 55; S.C. Chakravarthi, "Karma and Rebirth," *Indian Philosophical Annual* 1 (1965), 62; Anima Sen Gupta, "Karma and Rebirth," *Indian Philosophical Annual* 1 (1965), 114. Surama Dasgupta makes the significant observation in this connection, "Variety is the fundamental law of nature and should not be explained away by reference to *karma*. It is *svabhāva* or natural law that there should be difference in nature, difference in man" (*Development of Moral Philosophy in India* [Bombay: Orient Longman, 1961], p. 224). Another who questions the "inequalities-of-birth" view is Sarasvati Chennakesavan, *Concepts of Indian Philosophy* (Columbia, Mo.: South Asia Books, and New Delhi: Orient Longman, 1976), p. 223.

7. K.F. Parthasarathy, "The Law of Karma in Vedanta," *Aryan Path* 40 (Ap. 1969), 163, 164. See also S.C. Chakravarthi, "Karma and Rebirth," p. 62, M. Hiriyanna, *Indian Conception of Values* (Mysore: Kavyalaya Publishers, 1975), p. 173; A.R. Wadia, "Philosophical Implications of the Doctrine of Karma," *Philosophy East and West* 15 (1965), 152. N. Subrahmanian describes the negative effects of loss of belief in karma and rebirth today due to secularism which embodies a new view of merit based on status attained on ability and effort, not on birth; he says this increases the mental agony and misery which the karma doctrine helps assuage, and he further says that if there is too great a degree of secularization, the suicide rate will jump ("Hinduism and Secularism," *Bulletin of the Institute of Traditional Cultures, Madras* Pt. 1, 1966, p. 21). A. Javadekar considers materialism to be the only alternative to the law of karma ("Karma and Rebirth," *Indian Philosophical Annual* 1 (1965), 78. A more heroic approach is suggested by Haridas Bhattacharyya: "The orthodox doctrine of *karma* is a tough man's creed, for it throws an individual entirely upon his own moral resources to rise in the scale of values ("The Brahmanical Concept of Karma; Karma in the Ethical Sense," *A.R. Wadia: Essays in Philosophy Presented in His Honour*, ed. S. Radhakrishnan and Others [Madras: G.W. Press, 1954], p. 43).

8. Surama Dasgupta, *Development of Moral Philosophy in India*, p. 224.

9. Nand Kishore Devaraja, *Hinduism and Christianity*, p. 95.

10. Sarvepalli Radhakrishnan, "Karma and Free Will," *Modern Review* 3 (May 1908), 424-428.

11. Sarvepalli Radhakrishnan, *An Idealist View of Life* (London: George Allen & Unwin, 1932), p. 279.

12. Ibid., pp. 275, 276.

13. T.M.P. Mahadevan, "Indian Ethics and Social Practice," *Philosophy and Culture East and West: East-West Philosophy in Practical Perspective*, ed. Charles A. Moore (Honolulu: University of Hawaii Press, 1962), p. 483.

14. N.A. Nikam, *Some Concepts of Indian Culture; A Philosophical Interpretation* (Simla: Indian Institute of Advanced Study, 1967), p. 29.

15. *Collected Papers of Professor S.S. Suryanarayana Sastri* (Madras: University of Madras, 1962), p. 234. (His paper, here cited, "Karma and Fatalism" first appeared in *Philosophical Quarterly* [Amalner] 16 [1940-41], 81-88.)

16. M. Hiriyanna, *Indian Conception of Values* pp. 184-186, and *Popular Essays in Indian Philosophy*, pp. 33-34.

17. Radhakrishnan, "Karma and Free Will," p. 426.

18. S.K. Chattopadhyaya, "Karma and Rebirth: A Critique," *Proceedings of the Indian Philosophical Congress, 1965-66*, p. 29; also appears in "Proceedings of the Seminar on Karma and Rebirth," *Indian Philosophical Annual* 1 (1965), 50-55.

19. *Collected Papers of Professor S.S. Suryanarayana Sastri*, p. 165; see also p. 235.

20. S. Radhakrishnan, *Idealist View of Life*, p. 227. M. Hiriyanna, *Indian Conception of Values*, p. 173; *Essentials of Indian Philosophy*, p. 47; *Popular Essays in Indian Philosophy*, p. 30. Balbir Singh, *The Conceptual Framework of Indian Philosophy* (Delhi: Macmillan Company of India, 1976), pp. 227-228, 212. See also C. Rangalingam, "Karma and Rebirth in Saiva Devotional Literature," *Indian Philosophical Annual* 1 (1965), 41.

21. See Nilima Sharma, *Twentieth Century Indian Philosophy; Nature and Destiny of Man* (Vārānasi: Bhāratīya Vidyā Prakāsana, 1972), p. 44.

22. Sarasvati Chennakesavan, "A Critique of the Doctrine of Rebirth," *Indian Philosophical Annual* 1 (1965), 147. She also asks, "If each individual is responsible for his own karma. . .what relation, whether it be ethical or social, can there be between parents and children? Birth in a family merely becomes accidental and we cannot explain family relations."

23. Surama Dasgupta, *Development of Moral Philosophy in India*, p. 210-211. See also Thiru N. Murugesa Mudaliar, "Traditional Hinduism and Social Development: Report of a Seminar," *Bulletin of the Institute of Traditional Cultures, Madras*, Jan.-June, 1976, p. 253.

24. Pratima Bowes, *The Hindu Religious Tradition*, p. 72.

25. *Soul, Karma and Re-birth*, p. 172.

26. Balbir Singh, *The Conceptual Framework of Indian Philosophy*, p. 231.

27. Daya Krishna, *Social Philosophy, Past and Future* (Simla: Indian Institute of Advanced Study, 1968), p. 14.

28. Warren E. Steinkraus, "Some Problems in Karma," *Philosophical Quarterly* 38 (Oct. 1965), 151.

29. N. Subrahmanian, "Hinduism and Secularism," *Bulletin of the Institute of Traditional Cultures, Madras*, Pt. 2, 1966, p. 232.

30. Transcript of the Proceedings of the Second Karma Workshop, Pasadena, California, January 26-29, 1978, Mimeo., p. 11.

31. Iswarananda, *Does the Soul Reincarnate?* (Trichur: Sri Ramakrishna Ashrama, 1964), p. 13.

32. Ibid., p. 9.

33. Ibid., p. 37. Iswarananda's views are summarized in "Proceedings on the Seminar on Karma and Rebirth," *Indian Philosophical Annual* 1 (1965), 9-15. Not all papers deal with Iswarananda's views, but those who wish to reflect on the biological analogy may consult the contributions of Chari (127-137), Chennakesavan (143-147), Subramania Sastri (160-163), as well as the paper of Sen Gupta (108-116).

34. Iswarananda, *Does the Soul Reincarnate?*, pp. 44, 51.

35. Ibid., pp. 50-51.

36. Ibid., pp. 46-47, 55; see also p. 40 for his discussion of "videhamoksha, liberation without the possibility of taking up another body."

37. Ibid., 50-51.

38. Sanat Kumar Sen, "Indian Philosophy and Social Ethics," *Journal of the Indian Academy of Philosophy* 6, no. 1 (1967), 67-68.

39. See S. Gopalan, "Karma, Rebirth and the Hindu Philosophy of the Individual and Society," *Indian Philosophical Annual* 1 (1965), 153-154; he is responding to this aspect of Swami Iswarananda's work. See also Paramanheri Sundaram Sivaswamy Aiyer, *Evolution of Hindu Moral Ideals* (Calcutta: Calcutta University, 1935), p. 149.

40. B. Kuppuswamy, *Dharma and Society: A Study in Social Values* (Columbia, Mo.: South Asia Books and Delhi: Macmillan Company of India, 1977), p. 47. The quote from Kane (p. 45): "It cannot be denied that the doctrine of *karma*, instead of being a powerful means of urging all men to put in great efforts for doing good deeds and a gospel of hope, became, in the minds of many, confused with fatalism, which led men to become feeble, submissive, and

disinclined to work hard" (P.V. Kane, *History of Dharma Śāstra* [Poona: Bhandarkar Oriental Research Institute, 1962] pt. V, II: 1566). See also B. Kuppuswamy, "Karma and Punarjanṃa," *Brahmavadin* 4 (Oct. 1970), 241-254

41. Thiru N. Murugesa Mudaliar, "Traditional Hinduism and Social Development: Report of a Seminar," *Bulletin of the Institute of Traditional Cultures*, Madras, Jan. - June, 1976, p. 228.

42. Sarasvati Chennakesavan, *Concepts of Indian Philosophy*, p. 223.

43. See Pratima Bowes, *The Hindu Religious Tradition*, p. 55. Kalidas Bhattacharyya, "The Status of the Individual in Indian Metaphysics," *The Indian Mind: Essentials of Indian Philosophy and Culture*, ed. Charles A. Moore (Honolulu: East-West Center Press, University of Hawaii Press, 1967), p. 302, argues that for Sāṃkhya, and other systems, only three things are determined: "They are (1) the bodily and mental make-up and social position at the time of birth in that particular life (*jāti*), (2) the span of that life (*āyuh*), and (3) particular experiences with all the hedonic tones that they have in that life and all that is necessary as objects or direct or indirect causes of those experiences (*bhoga*)."

44. Gajanan Wasudeo Kaveeshwar, *The Law of Karma* (Poona: University of Poona, 1975), p. 1.

45. S.K. Saksena, "Relation of Philosophical Theories to the Practical Affairs of Men," *The Indian Mind* ed. Charles A. Moore, p. 34. See also Balbir Singh, *Foundations of Indian Philosophy* (New Delhi: Orient Longmans, 1971), p. 204; P. Nagaraja Rao, "Trends in Contemporary Indian Philosophy," *World Perspectives in Philosophy, Religion and Culture: Essays Presented to Professor Dhirendra Mohan Datta*, ed. Ram Jee Singh (Patna: Bharati Bhawan, 1968), p. 297; K. R. Sundararajan, "Hindu Ethics," *Hinduism*, ed. K.L. Seshagiri Rao and others, Guru Nanak Quincentenary Celebration Series (Patiala: Punjabi University, 1969), p. 41; C. Rangalingam, "Karma and Rebirth in Śaiva Devotional Literature," p. 42.

46. See Pratima Bowes, *The Hindu Religious Tradition*, pp. 78-79.

47. Note the observation of Genjun H. Sesaki that "the activity and potentiality of *karma* have been drawn attention to and re-interpreted by the contemporary Hindus to emphasize social values in Hinduism" ("Karma and Fate," *Indo-Asian Culture* 15 [Oct. 1969], 273). A more extensive conclusion about modern thinking is offered by Nilima Sharma: "The contemporary Indian philosophers do not preach the negation of empirical life and its activities for the attainment of one's ultimate goal. The liberation of the individual, according to them, does not only mean the attainment of freedom from *karma*, ignorance, birth and death, but it also means the attainment of harmony with society and it necessitates constant effort on the part of the liberated man to work for the progress and perfection of society as a whole" (*Twentieth Century Indian Philosophy*, p. 253).

CHAPTER TWO

*In Defense Of Karma And Rebirth: Evolutionary Karma**

ROBERT N. MINOR

Though the doctrines of karma and rebirth are traceable to the late Vedic period, in the modern period the challenge of alternative theories produced the most sustained efforts to defend and define the doctrines. Modern Indian thinkers, as an essential part of their apologetic writings, have defended the teachings of karma and rebirth against the attacks of missionaries, secularists, and materialists who would malign them as unreasonable, unethical, or unscientific. This has been a major part of the defense and definition of Hinduism or Vedānta as world-affirming, not oposed to a life of service to others, and embodying visions of human progress.

Two modern Indian thinkers who have identified with Vedānta, holding viewpoints believed to be essential to the Upaniṣads, and who have interpreted karma and rebirth in terms of theories of evolutionary progress in the universe and the significance of the phenomenal world, are the Indian Nationalist-turned-yogi, Sri Aurobindo (1872-1950), and the Indian philosopher-statesman, Sarvepalli Radhakrishnan (1888-1975). In the process of constructing vedantic positions, both attempted to respond to criticisms of Vedānta or Hinduism which included criticism of the teachings of karma and rebirth and their implications. They were unhappy with interpretations of the Indian tradition as non-ethical in interest, non-progressive in historical flow, and fatalistic. Instead, they said:

(1) the world is in a great evolutionary process which is not

*This investigation was partially supported by grants from the General Research Fund of the University of Kansas.

illusory but significant because it is, in some sense, an evolution traceable to the Divine itself

(2) this process is progressive, moving toward a desirable spiritual end which is a relevation of the Absolute

(3) the individual human being is to be an active part of this process

(4) the best human life is one which promotes the evolution to its ultimate goal.

These evolutionary affirmations were central to the responses given in defense and definition of karma and rebirth as follows:

(1) *Saṃsāra*, the doctrine that this process of karma and rebirth is a burden from which to flee, is incorrect. Instead karma and rebirth mean growth and education; they are positive opportunities when understood correctly.

(2) Karma and rebirth, though purposeful, are not fatalistic. There is a place for human choice in the process, though this place must be carefully delineated.

(3) Karma and rebirth are at least as scientific and rational as other explanations of the human soul's experience and more so if the concept of the universe as a progressive becoming is accepted.

For both of these thinkers the result of actions which promote growth is that very growth of soul and, in a sense, that is good karma. The process of *saṃsāra* for Aurobindo is absolute, and traditional issues of ethics and morality are relative; *saṃsāra* is not related in his thought to these issues in a direct sense. For Radhakrishnan, however, the process of *saṃsāra* is relative, not absolute, and issues of ethics are also relative. Thus the process is related more directly to ethics and morality. This paper is an exploration of karma and rebirth in Aurobindo and Radhakrishnan in terms of these issues.

EVOLUTION AS A KEY TO REALITY

Both Aurobindo and Radhakrishnan held theories of spiritual-physical evolution as a part of their world-views. Behind the physical evolution that biologists study, they saw a movement of spirit. In fact, the world process is viewed as essentially an evolution of consciousness from inconscient matter to what would some day be a universal or cosmic consciousness. This understanding provides the explanation for biological movement; explanations of evolution in terms of matter and force alone are judged inadequate.

More well known for his theory of evolution is Aurobindo.[1] Basing his thought upon insights and visions he felt he had gained through his sustained practice of Integral Yoga,[2] he concluded that an important key to reality is to be found in the fact that the Absolute is beyond distinctions of being and becoming. Actually being and becoming are eternal and not ultimately mutually exclusive. The Absolute, known by the traditional designation *saccidānanda* (being, consciousness, bliss), is simultaneously both static, unchanging being, and eternal, everchanging becoming. That one existent can simultaneously be both unchanging and changing is, of course, contradictory to logic, but since such logic is the process of a lower level of consciousness, mind, only if mind is somehow absolute in its knowing could this contradictoriness be considered fatal to the reality of such an Absolute. However, since mind for Aurobindo is a real but lower-level means of knowing on the evolutionary scale, "limited and only very indirectly and partially illumined,"[3] one must not absolutize its logic and apply that to reality at all levels.[4]

> The pure existent is then a fact and no mere concept; it is the fundamental reality. But, let us hasten to add, the movement, the energy, the becoming are also a fact, also a reality. The supreme intuition and its corresponding experience may correct the other, may go beyond, may suspend, but do not abolish it. We have therefore two fundamental facts of pure existence and of world-existence, a fact of Being, a fact of Becoming. To deny one or the other is easy; to recognize the facts of consciousness and find out their relation is the true and fruitful wisdom.[5]

Aurobindo's evidence for these transcendent claims is his experience, and in that experience he finds becoming an essential category of the Absolute, as essential as being. It is not a lower-level consciousness, except when taken out of its context which is the fact that all is *saccidānanda, Brahman,* divine.

The universe, then, is as real as the Absolute, for it is the Absolute in becoming. It is, therefore, characterized by *saccidānanda* as well: it is a manifestation of *sat,* pure existence, an evolution of *cit,* consciousness from inconscience to greater consciousness, and an expression of bliss, *ānanda,* the *līlā* or sport of the divine.

> We have started with the assertion of all existence as one Being whose essential nature is Consciousness, one Consciousness whose active nature is Force or Will; and this Being is Delight, this Consciousness is Delight, this Force or Will is Delight. Eternal and inalienable Bliss of Existence, Bliss of Consciousness, Bliss of Force or

> Will whether concentrated in itself and at rest or active and creative, this is God and this is ourselves in our essential, eternal, inalienable Bliss; active and creative, it possesses or rather becomes the delight of the play of existence, the play of consciousnes, the play of force and will. That play is the universe and that delight is the sole cause, motive and object of cosmic existence. The Divine Consciousness possesses that play and delight eternally and inalienably; our essential being, our real self which is concealed from us by the false self or mental ego, also enjoys that play and delight eternally and inalienably and cannot indeed do otherwise since it is one in being with the Divine Consciousness.[6]

This evolution of the universe is the progressive evolution of the previously involuted consciousness which is, therefore, a progressive integral revelation of the Absolute in and through the process itself.

Since this evolution as a manifestation of the becoming of *saccidānanda* must not be relegated to a lower level but understood with being, Aurobindo rejected traditional claims that the Absolute can only be designated negatively, *neti. . .neti,* not this, not that. These negative designations limit the Absolute.

> It follows that the absolute reality of the Absolute must be, not a rigid indeterminable oneness, not an infinity vacant of all that is not a pure self-existence attainable only by the exclusion of the many and the finite, but something which is beyond these definitions, beyond indeed any description either positive or negative. All affirmations and negations are expressive of its aspects, and it is through both a supreme affirmation and a supreme negation that we can arrive at the Absolute.[7]

Progress is therefore real, not anything less than that for Aurobindo. It is the progressive revelation of the Absolute, consciousness rising from less conscient to more conscient levels until the whole is the manifestation of the One and the Many, both affirmed in an integral consciousness, the Supermind itself. This means that evolution and all that is within it, including karma and rebirth, is the evolution of *saccidānanda* and absolutely significant, and that the process is to be affirmed, not denied, if one is truly in touch with the Real, if one is truly liberated.

The human being's mental stage is the evolutionary process; mind is "Nature become partly conscious of her own laws and forces,"[8] and able, therefore, to participate consciously in the process so as either to promote it or to hinder or make it more painful through egoistically affirming the temporary stage of mind in some ultimate manner. At this point the issue of a free human being enters as we shall see below. Yet, for Aurobindo, given the absolute nature of the phenomenal process, evolution is inevitable and freedom must be seen in an integral light.[9] The free human being cooperates with the process, working in a manner which promotes the process through a technique Aurobindo calls Integral Yoga.

Radhakrishnan also affirmed an evolutionary progress in the world. He gives little description of this evolution, in contrast to its central role in Aurobindo's discussions, but one finds it assumed throughout his writings. From his Master's thesis onwards, his emphasis was apologetic, denying claims that Vedānta, which for him was the essence of Hinduism,[10] taught that the world was illusory. It was most important that the world be real in some sense, for Hinduism, contrary to its critics, must be ethical in intent, and that requires a place in which to be meaningfully ethical.

His earliest writings which center on other topics, include defensive affirmations of the non-illusory nature of the world and its significance. However, his most sustained presentations begin with the article "The Vedānta Philosophy and the Doctrine of Māyā" in 1914.

> Thus, everything in the universe, instead of being dismissed as illusory, is thought to be produced by Brahman. But this principle of Brahman is recognized as immanent in the universe. It is not a corporeal presence seated on high in the heavens, but an eternal spirit manifesting itself in all things. It is not apart from the world—it is the world. The world is the product of Brahman, and, therefore, Brahman. Hence, instead of being an illusion, the world is the sole reality. There is nothing else besides it.[11]

Here his apologetic concern goes so far as to state that the world is not illusory because it is the Absolute. It therefore has a significance beyond finitude. Yet the nature of the relationship of the world and therefore the process of *saṃsāra* which is karma and rebirth, at times appears unclear in Radhakrishnan's thought because he wishes to affirm both the unity and yet the significance of the diversity. This lack of clarity is due to an inconsistent vocabulary in Radhakrishnan's many discussions of the status of the world in relationship to the Absolute, *Brahman*, centering around the term real. His actual position does not change. However, in some writings Radhakrishnan speaks of the world as real. The statement in 1914 that the world "is the sole reality," is liable to misunderstanding outside its context. The world is the manifestation of the Absolute. In its totality, he explains, the world is the spirit, but any part of the totality is only "a phase of the eternal spirit and is, therefore, not the spirit."[12] Lest one think, then, that Radhakrishnan's monism limits reality to the phenomenal world, however, Radhakrishnan in the same article describes the relationship of the world to the Absolute as an organism.

> Only the Absolute is real. We are unable to rest in any of the objects as an absolute reality, *i.e.*, a reality that does not need to be referred to anything else as its explanation. Reality, in other words, is an organism, furnished with a multiplicity of organs and manifestations of life. The true is the whole, and the untrue is the fragmentary or the limited. The finite is real in so far as it is an organic unity, organic with the whole life of the Absolute.[13]

Thus *Brahman* is spoken of in this early article as a total organism which is the sole reality. "The different parts of the organism are but differentiations of the Absolute."[14] Yet the whole organism is spoken of as real, while the parts are untrue in some sense.

In later writings Radhakrishnan speaks of the relationship of the world to the Absolute less and less in organic terms as he clarifies his own thinking on the status of the Absolute in comparison with the world. Yet—and this is the consistent element in Radhakrishnan's understanding of the nature of the world's reality throughout his thought—if the world is viewed independently of *Brahman*, it is unreal. This is found already in the 1914 article: "The inference of the unreality of the world from the sole reality of Brahman is legitimate, if the world is viewed as separate from Brahman."[15] The world, the process of evolution, is not independently real but is dependent upon the Absolute for its relative existence. In another article from this period, Radhakrishnan speaks more clearly of the world's reality as relative: "The theory does not deny the reality of the world or the individual souls in it. The plurality of individual souls and the material universe are not 'real' in the absolute sense of the word, for they are subject to change. They are only relatively real."[16] This is the sense of Radhakrishnan's usual statements about the reality of the world, becoming consistently so in his later writings. He denies that the world is illusory, but he will at times not declare that it is real, because to be real something must be a substance, that is, an unchanging reality which underlies the accidents, conceived of as changing. In this he comes to believe that he agrees with the ninth century advaitin thinker Śaṃkara, summarizing Śaṃkara's view as: "Unreal the world is, illusory it is not."[17] When the world is declared to be real, then, the word is to be understood in its relative sense. It is relatively real, or dependently real, dependent for its status on the Absolute. "This world is not an illusion; it is not nothingness, for it is willed by God and therefore is real. Its reality is radically different from the being of the Absolute-God. The Absolute alone has noncreated divine reality; all else is dependent, created reality. This is the significance of the doctrine of māayāa."[18] Radhakrishnan came to believe that Śaṃkara did not accept the illusory nature of the world either or that the world was mere appearance, but that in some sense the world is there. The exact relationship of the phenomenal becoming to the absolute, however, is not comprehensible and so is designated *māyā*, mysterious power. One cannot say how the Absolute and the phenomena are related, his later writings regularly declare.[19] Yet because of this relationship, the world and the evolutionary process are not insignificant. "There is a beginning to time as well as an end. . . .Between these two points, the beginning and the end, between the start and the finish, what happens is real and significant, not only for us but for the World-Spirit."[20] Though less than the Absolute, it is related inexplicably to the Absolute, and is therefore significant.

As it was for Aurobindo, this world process is a progressive evolution. Though the world is one of change, the change moves toward an end. "The world process is not an incessant fluctuation comparable to a surging sea. It is a movement with a direction and a goal."[21] It is on the basis of this affirmation—that the universe was driven by ideals and that it has meaning—that Radhakrishnan designated himself an idealist. "Ideal values are the dynamic forces, the driving power of the universe. The world is intelligible only as a system of ends."[22] Also, as Aurobindo did, he views this evolution as a progressive growth of consciousness.

> The dead mechanism of stones, the unconscious life of plants, the conscious life of animals and the self-conscious life of men are all parts of the Absolute and its expression at different stages. The same Absolute reveals itself in all these. The ultimate reality sleeps in the stone, breathes in the plants, feels in the animals and awakes to self-consciousness in man. It progressively manifests itself in and through these particulars.[23]

The end itself will be the realization of the universal consciousness by all, a consciousness which is *Brahman*, *ānanda*, a kingdom of free spirits the kingdom of God, *brahma-loka*.

However, unlike Aurobindo, for Radhakrishnan the evolution is less than absolutely real, for the Absolute is best described as *neti. . .neti*. The Absolute in itself is being, *Brahman*, as found in those Upaniṣadic passages which declare *Brahman* one with the true self, *ātman*. Yet somehow through *māyā* the Absolute as absolute freedom has produced one possibility of becoming—this world. The world is relatively real, and when we conceive of the Absolute in relationship to this one actualized possibility which is the cosmos, it appears to be God, a personal being, or *Īśvara*, lord, creator, sustainer, and judge of this world. But, though the term god refers to the Absolute, the conception God is the Absolute relativized. "It is impossible to detach God from the world."[24] Similarly, the world to which God relates is significant because somehow, on a relative level, it is divine. In Upaniṣadic terms, the world is both *Hiraṇya-garbha,* the world-spirit in its subtle form, and *Virāj,* the world-spirit in its gross form. [25] Viewpoints which affirm the relationship of the Absolute to the evolution speak in terms of the relatively real. They do not speak of *Brahman* in itself.

> Hindu thought is emphatic in asserting that the changes of the world do not affect the integrity of perfection, of the Absolute. Evolution and novelty do certainly exist, but they belong solely to the cosmic side of the picture, and their function is to reveal the immutable presence of an Absolute to which they add nothing. . . .When we look at the Absolute from the cosmic end, not as it is in itself, but as it is in relation to the world, the Absolute is envisaged as Isvara or personal God who guides and directs the process by His providence.[26]

For Radhakrishnan the evolution is less than absolutely real. It is a reflection of God as infinite possibility, whereas for Aurobindo the evolutionary process is absolute when seen in its context.

For Aurobindo the evolution is inevitable because it is the real becoming of the Absolute. A human being can hinder the process, promote it, or make it more painful, but the evolution will continue to its end no matter how slow or obscure that process might appear. However, for Radhakrishnan there would be too little talk of freedom in this discussion. It is important to his apologetic interest to affirm that the human being can make meaningful changes in the process. Yet he also wishes to affirm the ultimate unity of being. This causes him to declare that the process is, *in an inexplicable way,* at the behest of God. "Though there is no automatism in history, its course is not a matter of mere accident or chance. It may not disclose a plot or a rhythm; it yet has reason and sense. It is not mere chaos. . . .Progress is not inevitable. It requires to be achieved by man who grows by aspiration and effort."[27] Radhakrishnan's discussion of the non-inevitability of the process is on the relative level. In such discussions then, he speaks most often in terms of God.

> Struggle and growth are real in the life of God. Time is the essential form of the cosmic process, including moral life, and it has a meaning to God also. Life eternal which carries us beyond the limits of temporal growth may take us to the Absolute, but God is essentially bound up with the life in time. Progress may be degrading to the Absolute, but not to God, who is intensely interested in it.[28]

Thus, though the Absolute in itself has no relationship to the process,

God, a lower conception of the Absolute as relative to the world and whose relationship to the Absolute is, therefore, inexplicable except that in some way the term does refer to the Absolute, is involved in the process. On this relative level Radhakrishnan affirms that though the evolution on the whole is to reach its end, an end which cannot be completely predicted, in terms of human particulars there is freedom of choice. "The freedom of will possessed by self-conscious individuals makes possible sin and discord. They are not willed by the Divine, though they fall within His purpose."[29] It is also important to recognize, Radhakrishnan believes, that the evolution is not merely a development of potentials placed in the world at the beginning, for God, by definition, is continually, creatively involved in the process. "It is an emergence under the guidance of God, who is immanent in the process, though the goal is transcendent to it. The process of the world is not a mere unfolding of what is contained in the beginning. It is not a question of mere preformation."[30]

In the designation of *māyā* then, Radhakrishnan affirmed that the nature of the relationship of the Absolute to God is inexplicable. Though on the Absolute level there is unity, being-consciousness-bliss, on the relative level there is progress, evolution, and some human freedom. It is clear then, that unlike Aurobindo, Radhakrishnan does not give the world process an equal status with the Absolute. It is significant, however, because it is nevertheless related to the Absolute, although it is not ultimately Real.

AUROBINDO'S ABSOLUTE EVOLUTIONARY KARMA AND REBIRTH

In 1953, Aurobindo published *The Foundations of Indian Culture,* a collection of articles which had appeared in his earlier journal, *Arya,* from December 1918 through January 1921. One of the series included in *The Foundations* was entitled "A Rationalistic Critic of Indian Culture,"[31] a response to William Archer's analysis of India in *India and the Future.* Archer listed a number of problematic notions in "Hindu spirituality" which he believed must be recognized in any evaluation of British rule in India and taken into consideration when discussing British withdrawal from the subcontinent. In his assessment of the doctrine of karma and rebirth, Archer begins: "For my part, I know of only one objection to it, namely, that satisfactory evidence, or any evidence beyond the assertation of the holy texts, is entirely lacking."[32] He credits its place in Indian thought to the influence of aboriginal tribes, "for it is a concept that has occurred to the untutored savage fancy in almost every region of the world." But he finds it difficult to grant that the doctrine has value because it does not include a necessary ethical ingredient, the memory of past lives. "My memory is me; what is outside my memory is not me, in any sense that matters to me. . . ."[33] On the one hand, he believes that the doctrine of karma is less objectionable than the teachings of other religious positions—it is fairer that one have an indefinite series of lives to struggle upward to the goal rather than "one brief seed-time on earth, to be followed by a singularly disproportionate harvest of eternal bliss or pain"—yet he insists karma and rebirth are valuable only to the extent that the soul is conscious of its upward struggle. Without this consciousness, the whole scheme is robbed of its virtue.

> My point is that the doctrine is not one which testifies to any spiritual genius on the part of those who conceived and elaborated it; and that point is rather strengthened than otherwise if all their brooding on 'the holy texts' has not shown the Hindu people its insubstantiality. If the theory is an empty one, there is little proof of spiritual genius in having evolved it, and still less in having clung to it for three thousand years.[34]

Thus, on the basis of the existence of karma and rebirth in India, Archer questions the value of Hindu spirituality.

Aurobindo's response to Archer's critique of karma and rebirth is brief in *The Foundations*. His argument is basically that Archer has misunderstood the doctrine. It is true that karma and rebirth "may degenerate in a time of great national weakness, depression and misfortune [the British period, for example], into a quietistic fatalism that may extinguish the fire of the reparative endeavor."[35] However, such a fatalism is not its true form. In fact, the pessimism that is often associated with the teachings—that existence is a bondage to a succession of rebirths, a chain of karma from which the soul must escape—does not belong properly to the doctrine. Aurobindo believed this was a mistaken notion which he credited to the Buddhists.[36]

Though he referred to a specific critic in this series of articles, this was not where he attempted a thorough response and full presentation of the doctrine of karma and rebirth as he understood it. This was presented in another series of articles running simultaneously in the *Arya* and republished in 1952 as *The Problem of Rebirth*.[37]

However, these were not Aurobindo's first discussions of rebirth. A brief article was written for the *Karmayogin* in 1909, before his flight to Pondicherry, entitled "Fate and Free-Will." Though there is no reference to the critic to whom Aurobindo is responding, it appears that the common criticism that Indian thought is plagued by fatalism due to the doctrines of karma and rebirth is the occasion for this article as well. In it Aurobindo accepts the notion that karma as previous actions results in a certain individual *svabhāva*, own-being, nature, by which an individual acts. In this he anticipates his fuller discussions of karma as an expression of the law of the universe interpreted as evolutionary, though the evolution is not described in the detail of his later theories.

> Each man has a distinct nature of his own and that is his law of being which ought to guide him as an individual. But beyond and above those minor laws is the great *dharma* of the universe which provides that certain previous *karma* or action must lead to certain *karma* or results.
>
> The whole of causality may be defined as previous action leading to subsequent action, *karma* and *karmaphala*. The Hindu theory is thought and feelings, as well as actual speech or deeds, are part of *karma* and create effect. . . .[38]

Here, as in all of his later discussions, he concludes that what makes the theory of karma and rebirth non-fatalistic is not something about the process but the fact that the true Self is not caught up in it. The *ātman, puruṣa,* is above the process and, as one with the Absolute, *Brahman,* is the lord of the process, not merely its victim. A fatalistic attitude reflects only ignorance of this fact, not knowing what we really are. His later writings express this more clearly in terms of evolution itself.

In *The Problem of Rebirth* and more briefly in *The Life Divine,* the latter first appearing in the *Arya* from 1914 to 1919, [39] Aurobindo presents his most extended discussion. For modern minds, Aurobindo believes, rebirth is no longer taken for granted, as it had been in India, but is merely a theory, a speculation unproven by the tests of modern science and reason. The usual arguments which are proffered for and against it are insufficient and often futile. On one hand, the argument questioning rebirth because human beings lack memory of past births is unconvincing.

> How much do we remember of our actual lives which we are undoubtedly living at the present moment? Our memory is normally good for what is near, becomes vaguer or less comprehensive as its objects recede into the distance, farther off seizes only some salient points and, finally, for the beginning of our lives falls into a mere blankness.[40]

On the other hand, attempts to argue for rebirth on the basis of claims to memory of past lives induced through psychical means are also futile. "The mind can discover a hundred theoretical explanations for a single group of facts. Modern speculation and research have brought in this doubt to overhang all psychical theory and generalization."[41] Arguments for the theory's "simplicity, symmetry, beauty, satisfactoriness," are also uncertain as is the "ethical argument" which seeks to justify the world's justice or the Divine's manner of dealing with the world by claiming karma and rebirth as an ethically sound explanation for the inequalities of human beings in this life.[42]

Instead Aurobindo finds the most convincing basis for the theory of karma and rebirth in an evolutionary view of the universe and the consequent development of human beings. In this view the true reward for good actions is spiritual growth, not reward or punishment brought on by the mechanical reaction of the world or the approval or disapproval of a Divine Judge. Based upon his acceptance of the evolutionary theory, he believes such ideas are superficial.[43] On the basis of evolution, then, he attempts to pursuade the reader of the doctrines of karma and rebirth, arguing that on this basis it is satisfactory or just.

Science, he says, is incapable of discussing these matters. It is uninformed and infantile in its methods and abilities which are inadequate to spheres beyond the material. "And this inadequacy in extended application is very evident in her theories of heredity and evolution when she forces them beyond their safe ground of physical truth and labours to illumine by them the subtle, complex, elusive phenomena of our psychical being."[44] To add materialistic assumptions to this inadequacy is to do no more than assume an hypothesis which is unable to explain facts we already know. From the physical, how can one explain a conscious operation of the mind, a perception, emotion, thought-concept, or love, Plato's theory of ideas, Homer's *Iliad,* or a yogin's cosmic consciousness? "There is a gulf of difference here between the thing to be explained and the thing by which it is sought to explain it which cannot be filled up, however much we may admit nervous connections and psycho-physical bridges."[45] More basic than this is the inadequacy of human reason itself. Reason begins in ignorance, proceeds in ignorance by hypothesis, assumption, and theory, and then accepts as verification only that which is convincing to its ignorant position. In science and reason we get clues to the truth, but neither is able to lay hold on the reality of things.[46]

The most convincing verification for Aurobindo is spiritual experience or vision: "their full light must come by experimental knowledge and observation of the world without us and the world within."[47] Such experiences, Aurobindo believed, affirm the existence of an entity other than the physical—a soul or psychic being. Yet this does not immediately lead to the concept of rebirth. Rebirth follows in the light of these experiences and from belief in the evolution of the soul as part of an evolutionary order of existence.

> What we see of Nature and of human nature justifies this view of a birth of the individual soul from form to form until it reaches the human level of manifested consciousness which is its instrument for

> rising to yet higher levels. We see that Nature develops from stage to stage and in each stage takes up its past and transforms it into stuff of its new development.[48]

Once evolutionary theory is accepted and experience is believed to justify his views, he rejects other theories of the soul's existence on the basis of arguments from what he believes are justice and reasonableness, arguments he found unacceptable without the basic affirmation of evolution and the personal experience of the supramental. Theories which accept the existence of the individual soul without evolution involve the difficulty of positing a creature beginning in time but without an end, and of a soul inheriting a past for which it is not responsible. Theories which teach that an eternal soul has fallen from a pure state into a less than pure material existence from which the soul must redeem itself are unacceptable because this would result in a world in which most of these souls would fail to redeem themselves and because the theory lacks an explanation for the immense differences of gradation in which fallen souls find themselves.[49]

Aurobindo's theory of evolution from matter to mind and beyond, and a universal spirit which ensouls the evolution, provides for him the only just and reasonable explanation for the available data, scientific and psychic.

> A past terrestrial soul evolution sufficiently accounting for these variations and degrees of our mixed being and future soul evolution that helps us progressively to liberate the godhead of the Spirit, seem the only just and reasonable explanation of this labour of a matter-shackled soul which has attained a variable degree of humanity in the midst of a general progressive appearance of the life, mind and spirit in a material universe. Rebirth is the only possible machinery for such a soul-evolution.[50]

The evolutionary theory, then, results in a belief in rebirth, and in the process gives the concept of rebirth its meaning. In this Aurobindo does not mean to give a logically tight argument appealing to the intellect, for rebirth can be no more than a supposition for the mind. Yet Aurobindo believes that his is a better hypothesis than any other, one which must ultimately be proven by spiritual experience and effectuation. Until then, it is "a very sufficient clue for an answer to all these connected sides of the one perpetual question."[51]

To understand karma one must also interpret it in terms of the evolutionary progress of the universe and the soul. Past interpretations have fallen into two errors. The first has been the attempt to explain the supraphysical by a physical formula. In an attempt to be ethical, karma has been interpreted as a justice governing the award of happiness or misery on earth.[52] Aurobindo objects on two grounds. Granted the concern for the ethical, the belief that karma involves reward and retribution in material terms for good or evil deeds is not ethical in any exalted sense. Ethical action is that done for its own sake, for the fulfillment of *dharma*, "the right fulfillment and working of the higher nature," not action done on the basis of greed or fear.[53] Likewise, the theory confuses two different types of goods. It fails to explain the necessary connection between moral good and evil and pleasure and pain. Thus, on any rational ethical basis one should object to such an understanding. However, Aurobindo also objects that such an interpretation does not reflect an adequate account of reality, for there is no clear observation which affirms that such a relationship between moral good and evil and pleasure and pain exists at all. If we do not see such reward and punishment in this life alone, on what basis should we believe that this principle works better in rebirth?[54]

Yet, though rejecting the theory of retribution and reward, there is an important truth in the theory of karma, a truth that involves evolutionary energy, not ethics or morality as generally conceived. "As is his use of the energy, so was and will be the return of the universal energy to him now and hereafter. This is the fundamental meaning of Karma."[55] This evolutionary energy is found at work in many forms within the progressive unfolding. One suspects that had Aurobindo rewritten these sections of the work later, he would have discussed more forms of this energy; but in *The Problem of Rebirth* he speaks of energy of the physical being and nature, energy of the vital being and nature, energy of the mental being and nature, and energy of the spiritual being and nature. Each of these energies operates on its own principles and, thus, to the finite mind it should appear that the principles upon which karma acts vary, though when one has reached a higher consciousness he will see their integration in the whole.

> There is a rule of right in the world, but is the right of the truth of Nature and of the truth of the Spirit, and that is a vast and various rule and takes many forms that have to be understood and accepted before we can reach either its highest or its integral principle.[56]

As the individual seeks to progress in the line of evolution he is rewarded by progression, a personal development of consciousness, realization, understanding according to the appropriate principle of development inherent in the evolution at that stage. It is the complicated nature of this process that is misunderstood when one reduces karma to traditional theories of reward and punishment or to conventional ethical principles. Aurobindo summarized the movement of this energy:

> And at each stage she gives returns according to the development of the aim and consciousness of the being. At first there is the return of skill and effective intelligence—and her own need explains sufficiently why she gives the rewards of life not, as the ethical mind in us would have it, to the just, not chiefly to moral good, but to the skilful and to the strong, to will and force and intelligence—and then, more and more clearly disengaged, the return of enlightenment and the satisfaction of the mind and the soul in the conscious use and wise direction of its powers and capacities and, last of all, the one supreme return, the increase of the soul in light, the satisfaction of its perfection in knowledge, its birth into the highest consciousness and the pure fulfilment of its own innate imperative.[57]

The law of karma, then, has only a brief relationship to issues of justice, morality, ethics, generally conceived: "the maintenance of human standards of morality." These are temporary relative conceptions of the limited mind.[58] Though one could speak of the law as a new ethic,[59] Aurobindo has little desire to think in such terms. It is instead the becoming of the Divine, the law of evolution which Aurobindo calls *dharma*, the progressive movement of Reality in its multi-principled manner to its goal of *saccidānanda*. Cooperation and appropriate response to that movement bring its own reward, a growth in consciousness, while inappropriate responses which result from ignorance and egoism retard personal growth.[60]

However, as noted above, the process is inevitable and, though the human being may egoistically cling to his stage of the process and make it more difficult or painful, asserting what is often called freedom, this is not real freedom for Aurobindo but the ego boasting of freedom while all the time it is "the slave, toy and puppet of countless beings, powers, forces, influences in universal Nature."[61] This egoistic notion of free will ignores the facts of Nature at work. At this level, as he had argued earlier, the individual is not really free, though ego assertion desires a pseudo-freedom. This idea of freedom and the futile search for it, given the evolutionary fact of reality, must be abandoned in order to attain true freedom. "Our total being can rise out of subjection to [the] fact of present Nature only by an identification with a greater Truth and a greater Nature."[62] The individual must realize, in an integral view of reality, by supramental consciousness that he is essentially one with the Absolute and, therefore, really desires the very process he is egoistically fighting. By relinquishing the exclusive nature of the individual ego, the surface self, and identifying with the true self, one's desires become those of the Absolute and one is free then to do all that one desires. Aurobindo then, is not concerned with showing that somehow the individual is free except as he identifies with the evolutionary process. The very criticism that karma and rebirth destroys human freedom is wrongly put, an egoistic concern which is out of touch with the realities of the world.

Based, he believed, on his religious experiences, but not without the use of traditional vocabulary and concepts, Aurobindo traces the normal process of rebirth not merely as that of an immutable psychic entity born into a new physical body but including a new psychic personality for the soul which is reborn.[63] Though the process varies among individuals, based upon the variety of needs of each soul and the stage of its development, upon death the departed psychic being or soul in a subtle body may linger in the earth realm near the body or scene of death for a period.[64] It then enters the vital plane of reality for a time until the vital sheath dissolves, followed by entrance into the mental plane until the mental sheath, its last, dissolves. In these planes, traditionally thought of as heavens and hells, the soul goes through experiences which are the result of its earthly existence. Finally it retires to the psychic world, the world of the soul itself, where it assimilates the essence of its experiences, not the details (hence, the lack of memory of previous lives).[65] This process of assimilation forms the future psychic personality, thereby readying it for rebirth on earth. "There is an assimilation, a discarding and strengthening and rearrangement of the old characters and motives, a new ordering of the developments of the past and a selection for the purposes of the future without which the new start cannot be fruitful or carry forward the evolution."[66] Aurobindo's letters to his disciples discuss some other possibiliites, though this is the normal course.

Retrograde movements in this process may take place in order that the soul may work something out so as to progress more efficiently.[67] Yet the general movement is upward. Aurobindo refuses to deny dogmatically that the soul which has arrived at humanity can return to lower forms of life. It seems impossible, he says, but Nature's movement is too complex to be certain. To the question, why a succession of human rebirths is necessary, Aurobindo answers that it is required by the spiritual evolution because humanity itself must be developed into higher possibilities, some of which may be unknown at this time.

Since the whole of evolution is the Spirit's free becoming, experiencing freely the involution and evolution of the many possibilities of the process, it follows that the key to rebirth is education of the soul, the creating of greater consciousness in it. Nature's reactions are not reward and punishment, they are not reactions to good and evil as the human mind conceives of it.[68] Ethics is relative, not absolute as the process of evolution is. However, it also follows that the positive absolute process is not one from which to escape. *Saṃsāra* is becoming and to reject it is to turn away from the purpose of the Universal, not to fulfill it.[69] The goal is to participate in the becoming of the Absolute and in this Aurobindo's evolutionary interpretation has reversed traditional understandings of the relationship of *samsāra* and liberation or, as he would prefer, has integrated *saṃsāra* into an integral understanding. The process itself becomes crucial to the goal when understood as the becoming of the Absolute, as real as being.

RADHAKRISHNAN'S RELATIVE EVOLUTIONARY KARMA AND REBIRTH

Radhakrishnan's discussions of karma and rebirth are always dominated by the apologetic concern which began with his Master's thesis. His first published article in 1908 was entitled "Karma and Free Will"[70] and from that point on he continued to argue that karma and rebirth do not preclude the ethical life by either resulting in fatalism or destroying the significance of the world of *saṃsāra* as the place of ethics. Unlike Aurobindo, who removed karma and rebirth from the conventional realm of ethics, Radhakrishnan wishes to maintain a clear link between karma and rebirth and discussions of ethics. It mattered that karma and rebirth not conflict with the discipline of ethics as a part of philosophy, and this is not surprising. In his days at Madras Christian College, karma and rebirth were crucial issues of discussion. Radhakrishnan's mentor, A.G. Hogg, found these doctrines a controversial challenge to his own Christian stance.[71] His earliest response was published in the *Madras Christian College Magazine* in 1904-1905, immediately before Radhakrishnan arrived, and reprinted as *Karma and Redemption* with Professor Hogg's "Preface" dated July 13, 1909, the year after Radhakrishnan received his M.A.[72]

It was later that Radhakrishnan began to present a defense of the rationality of karma and rebirth itself, adding this to his continuing defense of its relationship to ethics. His most extended defense is found in *The Hindu View of Life* (1927), *An Idealist View of Life* (1932), and *The Brahma Sūtra* (1960).[73]

As Aurobindo had, Radhakrishnan affirmed that the true self (*ātman*) is one with Brahman, the Absolute and, therefore, unaffected by the process of karma and rebirth. Radhakrishnan's argument for rebirth is, also like Aurobindo's, based upon an evolutionary view of the universe and the consequent evolution of the soul. Karma denotes continuity with the past and the future according to order, law. "The human individual is a self-conscious, efficient portion of universal nature with his own uniqueness. . . .Human growth is an ordered one and its orderedness is indicated by saying that it is governed by the law of Karma."[74] This ordered continuity is thought of as progressive, growth, and upward movement. "Rebirth is change within a general structural progression."[75] There is no difference in kind then, between the growth of the world process and that of the human being, for they are a part of the same movement.[76] This connection of karma and rebirth with the evolution of the universe is, for Radhakrishnan as for Aurobindo, the decisive element in his argument for belief in karma and rebirth.

The doctrine of rebirth, he begins, is not unique to India. It ought to be seriously considered because it has a long and even influential history.[77] Objections to rebirth on the basis of the lack of memory of past births are without force. As yet there is no clear understanding of the work of memory, but even if there were, the doctrine does not teach that one will remember the facts of one's past lives but only that the past lives will have an effect upon the present.

> Though we may not have conscious memory there is a persistance of dispositions and tendencies. Though at death we may lose the memory of the detailed knowledge and the skill and the habits, still we start our next life in consequence of having possessed these with more efficient dispositions and a greater power to reacquire the detailed knowledge and insight.[78]

In fact, to retain a memory of the events could be a positive nuisance, for it would hinder our relationships with fellow human beings by bringing in memories of lower relationships in past lives.[79]

Yet the evolution of the self appeals more to Radhakrishnan as a sensible scientific argument for belief in rebirth. Science, he says, infers that if we see a certain stage of development in time there must have been a past to it. Likewise, Radhakrishnan argues that it is difficult to believe that "the rise of self with a definite nature is simply fortuitous."[80] Instead, the theory of previous lives which has molded the present explains the various natures with which people are born in a manner consistent with the asumptions of modern science. "In an ordered world, sudden embodiment of conscious life would be meaningless and inconsequential. It would be a violation of the rhythm of nature, an effect without cause, a fragmentary present without a past."[81] Thus, given that one accepts an element of the human being beyond the physical, Radhakrishnan argues that it is fair, just, and rationally pleasing to expect the self to emerge through rebirth as the world process emerges. Otherwise our fates are due to caprice and cruelty and all education and experience are superfluous. Rebirth is tied to evolution as a reasonable theory.

This means then, that the process of *saṃsāra* is neither meaningless nor futile. "It is obvious that rebirth is not an eternal recurrence leading nowhere but is a movement with a meaning. . . .It is a genuine growth into personality and character from the humblest beginnings in the sub-human world."[82] To view this life in negative terms—as merely an existence from which to escape, with no value for the individual—is to miss its importance as the place of self development. Renunciation is an incorrect response to *saṃsāra*. Instead, the person who understands, who grows with the process, needs to apply his spiritual knowledge to the process. Radhakrishnan reinterpreted renunciation as the renunciation of personal egoistic desires. Thus, those who have attained personal liberation, *mukti*, return to the world to work with the insight they have gained, universal consciousness, realization of oneness with the Absolute.

> We hear of many cases of liberated individuals who are engaged in the work of the world. They live as universal men with no private attachments or personal feelings. When the realised soul returns to the plane of conduct, his action will neither add to nor detract from the value of his realisation. Action itself will be of a different kind. It has no selfish motives behind it but is a manifestation of spiritual peace.[83]

However, though this evolutionary process is not the negative experience of traditional interpreters, it does not hold the final clue to the universe. *Saṃsāra*, even though more positively interpreted, will come to an end, for unlike Aurobindo's affirmation of a continuing becoming, Radhakrishnan believes the evolution will continue only as long as there are unrealized souls. "Till the end is achieved the temporal process has a meaning and a value as the stage of soul-formation and growth."[84] When all are liberated, world redemption (*sarva-mukti*) takes place and this less than real world-order ends, all returning to being, oneness. There may be other expressions, future forms through the creative freedom of the Absolute, but we have no knowledge of these.[85] At the point of *sarva-mukti* there will be nothing less than the real, no becoming but only the real in itself, the Absolute, being. *Saṃsāra* may not be an experience from which to escape, but it is less than complete, less than real nevertheless, and perfection is the removal of *saṃsāra*, not just for the individual but for all.

Radhakrishnan too wishes to remove from karma and rebirth the idea of hedonistic retribution, of reward and punishment in the physical realm. "The law of Karma is not to be confused with either a hedonistic or a juridical theory of rewards and punishments. The reward for virtue is not a life of pleasure nor is the punishment for sin pain."[86] In fact, love sometimes results in suffering and hatred may end in a kind of satisfaction.

Though Radhakrishnan also speaks of karma in terms of energy, and though the key to karma is found in the evolution of the soul, unlike Aurobindo, Radhakrishnan does not wish to sever the basic connection of karma and discussions of ethics. Radhakrishnan began his defence of karma in terms of its place in an ethical life and his discussions throughout his works are dominated by ethical issues. "Karma is not so much a principle of retribution as one of continuity. God produces good; evil, produces evil. Love increases our power of love, hatred our power of hatred."[87] His discussions are posed in ethical language, not just the language of energy and the return of Nature for appropriate action. This is clear when he speaks of karma as the embodiment of the will of God, the Absolute in relationship to the world.

> . . .the principle of Karma insisted on the primacy of the ethical and identified God with the rule of Law. All's law, yet all's God. Karma is not a mechanical principle but a spiritual necessity. It is the embodiment of the mind and will of God. God is its supervisor, *karmādhyakṣah*. Justice is an attribute of God.[88]

Thus, he continues his discussions of karma and rebirth in terms of ethics as he had from the beginning in his argument that karma does not preclude the ethical life, an argument against his Christian teachers and other critics who claimed that karma resulted in fatalism and therefore did not allow for the kind of ethics to which Christianity calls its followers.

However, to identify karma with the will of God is not to assume that somehow the karmic process may be overthrown by prayer or the work of a transcendent being. It is certain in its working. Though Radhakrishnan speaks of repentence and mercy, as Michael points out, for Radhakrishnan mercy is no different than justice, and by definition, karma deals justly.[89] "Guilt cannot be transferred. It must be atoned for through the sorrow entailed by self-conquest. God cannot be bought over and sin cannot be glossed over."[90] Yet ultimately the will of God is not something external to the individual. As an advaitin who believed that all is *Brahman* and especially the true self, *ātman*, Radhakrishnan affirms that: "The judge is not without but within."[91]

Since good action furthers the evolutionary process, moving the individual toward universal consciousness, this idea of progressive development mitigates traditional understandings of rebirth as an animal. Radhakrishnan ascribes the origins of these teachings to aboriginal tribes in India, not the Aryan invaders responsible for Vedic literature.[92] Though he hestiates to be dogmatic about the matter, he says return to animal births is not the normal process, but possibly should be understood as "a figure of speech for rebirth with animal qualities."[93] Thus, his understanding of *Vedānta Sūtras* III.1.24-27, which discuss this matter is that the connection of human rebirth with animals and plants is metaphorical, "and real rebirth is as human beings."[94]

Radhakrishnan attempts to move rationally to his understanding of the mechanism of rebirth, not declaring that this is an insight from religious experiences of his own. He says that since continuity of life requires continuity of organism, there must be a subtle body, *liṅga-śurīra*, which carries past tendencies forward. Accepting this traditional understanding, and pointing out that the forms of matter with which we are familiar are not necessarily the only forms, he describes the subtle body as another form of matter, transparent and invisible, which is the basis of consciousness and memory and "the form on which the physical body is moulded."[95] This mechanism, however, is difficult to know with any assurance.

Yet the issue which draws Radhakrishnan's regular attention is that karma is not fatalistic. In the past some Indians have taken it to be so; but besides providing continuity with the past, karma actually points to a variety of possibilities for the future. Radhakrishnan points out that no one is completely free in any case. "Free will in the sense of an undetermined, unrelated, uncaused factor in human action is not admitted, but such a will defies all analysis."[96] All human beings have a life context given to them. "The character, at any given point, is the condensation of our previous history. What we have been enters in the 'me' which is not active and choosing. The range of one's natural freedom of action is limited."[97] The future is not determined but conditioned by the past. Within these conditions the human being has choice as to what the future may be. In his earliest writings, Radhakrishnan describes this free choice as the exercise of reason, but soon he speaks more generally of the spiritual faculty or spirit within that can triumph over these forces.[98] As Michael points out, for Radhakrishnan the will is an aspect of the Self in action and "by freedom of the Will is meant actually the determination by the Self."[99] Thus, just as true religious experience is experience by the whole person for Radhakrishnan, so the freest decision is described as a decision of the whole self. "Self-determination means not determination by any fragment of the self's nature but by the whole of it. Unless the individual employs his whole nature, searches the different possibilities and selects one which commends itself to his whole self, the act is not really free."[100] The most well known image of the relationship of karma and rebirth to freedom in Radhakrishnan's writings is that of a card game:

> Life is like a game of bridge. We did not invent the game or design the cards. We did not frame the rules and we cannot control the dealing. The cards are dealt out to us, whether they be good or bad. To that extent, determinism rules. But we can play the game well or play it badly. A skilful player may have a poor hand and yet win the game. A bad player may have a good hand and yet make a mess of it. Our life is a mixture of necessity and freedom, chance and choice. By exercising our choice properly, we can control steadily all the elements and eliminate altogether the determinism of nature.[101]

Thus, character is self-created in the past and continually molded by decisions made in the present, but a possible choice for each individual, available within the constraints of the present life, is to press on to self-fulfillment.

In all of this Radhakrishnan presents a positive understanding of karma and rebirth, progressive, resulting in self-fulfillment. *Saṃsāra* is an opportunity for the soul, not a dreaded process from which to escape. He believes this understanding is not new but that the Upaniṣads taught it long ago. Thus, it is true Vedānta, as Radhakrishnan views it. "Samsāra is only a succession of spiritual opportunities. Life is a stage in spiritual perfection, a step in the passage to the infinite. It is the time for preparing the soul for eternity."[102] Though the process is not the goal, it is the means by which one will ultimately leave the process. Yet, when one has personally attained liberation, this does not mean the renunciation of the process but the application of liberation to advance all beings to *sarva-mukti*, the end of the becoming.

SUMMARY

Both Aurobindo and Radhakrishnan, responding to criticisms of karma and rebirth, attempt to defend the process as a positive evolution of the world process toward the revelation of the Absolute. Rebirth is a process of growth of consciousness toward that end. Aurobindo understands the evolution as absolute, as the becoming of *saccidānanda* which is no less than its being. Thus, *saṃsāra* is also absolute and the goal of the evolution is not to escape *saṃsāra* but to affirm it integrally. Karma and rebirth are, therefore, integral to the becoming, but traditional discussions of ethics are not. Ethics is relative to the stage of mind in the evolution and, being relative, is not related to the process as a key to its working. Karma and rebirth are the working of the evolutionary energy which takes multifarious forms depending upon the level on which one is moving. *Samsāra* is, therefore, real and as valuable as the Absolute itself.

Radhakrishnan, however, relegates *saṃsāra* to the relatively real level, whereas the Absolute is independently real. Karma and rebirth are a positive process by which the soul prepares for its ultimate goal which is the transcending of the evolution itself. Renunciation in order to seek one's own *mukti* is rejected however, for even the liberated one returns to work in the world for the good of others and, thus, ethics is a central theme in discussions of the evolutionary process. Radhakrishnan's view is not surprising, given his concern both early and throughout his life to show that Vedānta, Hinduism, is ethical in response to criticisms he experienced throughout his education, and from his continual reading and constant exposure to the culture that presented the attack. Though

Aurobindo was aware of such attacks, his withdrawal into the practice of Integral Yoga placed him at some distance from continual reenforcement of such criticisms. He was removed both from that culture and from concern for the authority of its mind, the level on which he placed ethical concerns.

NOTES

1. Studies of his evolutionary theories are found in most secondary works. For sustained presentations see Rama Shankar Srivastava, *Sri Aurobindo and the Theories of Evolution* (Varanasi: Chowkhamba Sanskrit Series, 1968); Beatrice Bruteau, *Worthy is the World: The Hindu Philosophy of Sri Aurobindo* (Rutherford, Vermont: Farleigh Dickenson University Press, 1971); Robert N. Minor, *Sri Aurobindo: The Perfect and the Good* (Columbia, Missouri: South Asia Books, 1978); and Robert A. Mc Dermott, "Sri Aurobindo: An Integrated Theory of Individual and Historical Transformation," *International Philosophical Quarterly* XII, No. 2 (June, 1972), 168-180.

2. For studies of the relationship of Aurobindo's experience to his thought see Robert N. Minor, "Sri Aurobindo and Experience: Yogic and Otherwise," *Religion in Modern India*, ed. Robert D. Baird (Columbia, Missouri: South Asia Books, 1981), pp. 277-304; J. Feys, *The Yogi and the Mystic: A Study in the Spirituality of Sri Aurobindo and Teilhard De Chardin* (Calcutta: Firma KLM Private, 1977); Robert A. McDermott, "The Experiential Basis of Sri Aurobindo's Integral Yoga," *Philosophy East and West* XXII, No. 1 (January, 1972), 15-23; and Minor, *Sri Aurobindo*, pp. 174-177.

3. Sri Aurobindo, *Birth Centenary Library* (Pondicherry: Sri Aurobindo Ashram, 1972), XXI, 599. Hereafter this set of Aurobindo's complete works will be abbreviated *BCL*.

4. For discussions of the levels of reality-consciousness in Aurobindo's thought see Minor, *Sri Aurobindo*, 104-115 and notes.

5. *BCL*, XVIII, 78. Cf. 357, 377.

6. Ibid., 142.

7. *BCL*, XIX, 636. Cf . XVIII, 322, 378.

8. *BCL*, XV, 396.

9. *BCL*, XVI, 43.

10. Robert N. Minor, "Sarvepalli Radhakrishnan and 'Hinduism' Defined and Defended," in Baird, pp. 305-338.

11. *International Journal of Ethics* XXIV, No. 3 (April, 1914), 436-437.

12. Ibid., 439.

13. Ibid., 439-440.

14. Ibid., 444.

15. Ibid., 445.

16. "The Ethics of the Bhagavadgita and Kant," *International Journal of Ethics* XXI, No. 4 (July, 1911), 466.

17. *Indian Philosophy* (London: Allen and Unwin, 1926), II, 583.

18. "The Religion of the Spirit and the World's Need: Fragments of a

Confession," in *The Philosophy of Sarvepalli Radhakrishnan*, ed. Paul Arthur Schilpp (New York: Tudor Publishing, 1952), 41. Cf. Radhakrishnan, *Eastern Religions and Western Thought*, 2nd ed. (London: Oxford University Press, 1940), p. 31; S. Radhakrishnan, *The Hindu View of Life* (1960 reprint. London: Allen and Unwin, 1927), 49.

19. For example see "Reply to Critics," in *The Philosophy of Sarvepalli Radhakrishnan*, 800-802; *An Idealist View of Life*, 2nd ed. (London: Allen and Unwin, 1937), 272; *Eastern Religions and Western Thought*, 27, 85-86; and other references in Minor, "Sarvepalli Radhakrishnan and 'Hinduism,' " 310.

20. "The Religion of the Spirit and the World's Need," 41.

21. Ibid., 27. Cf. "Evolution and its Implications," *The New Era* I (November, 1928), 111; *East and West in Religion* (London: Allen and Unwin, 1933), 124-125; *Eastern Religions and Western Thought*, 91-92.

22. *A Idealist View of Life*, 10. Note that he means something different by the term than Charles Hartshorne in his critique:, "Radhakrishnan on Mind, Matter, and God," in *The Philosophy of Sarvepali Radhakrishnan*, 315-137.

23. "The Vedantic Approach to Reality," *The Monist* XXVI, No. 2 (April, 1916), 225. Cf. *The Reign of Religion in Contemporary Philosophy* (London: Macmillan, 1920), 442-443; "The Religion of the Spirit and the World's Need," 27.

24. *An Idealist View of Life*, 268. Hartshorne finds Radhakrishnan's description of the relationship between the Absolute, God, and the world unclear (pp. 317-322), yet that is the affirmation of *māyā*. Clement C.J. Webb concludes that Radhakrishnan is an "absolutist" with an unclear use of language ("Theism and Absolutism in Radhakrishnan's Philosophy," *The Philosophy of Sarvepalli Radhakrishnan*, pp. 385-390). Radhakrishnan is clear, however, that the viewpoint of theism is subordinate to absolutism. See Robert N. Minor, "Sarvepalli Radhakrishnan and the Nature of 'Hindu' Tolerance," *The Journal of the American Academy of Religion* L, No. 2 (June, 1982), 275-290.

25. "The Religions of the Spirit and the World's Need," 41; *The Principal Upaniṣads* (London: Allen and Unwin, 1953), 60-72; *The Brahma Sūtra: The Philosophy of Spiritual Life* (London: Allen and Unwin, 1960), 143.

26. *Eastern Religions and Western Thought*, 92. Cf. *An Idealist View of Life*, 271-273.

27. "Progress and Spiritual Values," *Philosophy* XII, No. 47, (July, 1937), 261.

28. *An Idealist View of Life*, 268.

29. "The Religion of the Spirit and the World's Need," 42-43.

30. *An Idealist View of Life*, 268.

31. *BCL* XIV, 43-117.

32. William Archer, *India and the Future* (London: Hutchinson & Co., 1917), 64.

33. Ibid., 65.

34. Ibid., 67-68. Archer's final judgment of "Hinduism" is that it has "incomparably the lowest" place among the world's religions (p. 82).

35. *BCL* XIV, 73.

36. Ibid., 73. Cf. *BCL*. XVIII, 23; XVI, 151; XIII, 79n.

37. *BCL* XVI, 79-220.
38. *BCL* III, 380.
39. *BCL* XIX, 742-823.
40. *BCL* XVI, 80. Cf. *BCL* XIX, 819.
41. Ibid., 81.
42. Ibid., 83-84.
43. Ibid., 87.
44. Ibid., 97.
45. Ibid., 102.
46. Ibid., 106-107. Cf. *BCL* XIX, 826.
47. Ibid., 107.
48. *BCL* XIX, 761, 764; *BCL* XVI, 112, 123.
49. *BCL* XVI, 110-112.
50. Ibid., 112.
51. Ibid., 113.
52. Ibid., 162; *BCL* XVII, 33.
53. Ibid., 164. Cf. *BCL* XIX, 812.
54. Ibid., 165-167.
55. Ibid., 175. Cf. 126.
56. Ibid., 176. Cf. *BCL* XIX, 810; XVII, 34.
57. Ibid., 220.
58. *BCL* XX, 128, 191; *BCL* XVIII, 97, 625.
59. See Minor, *Sri Aurobindo*, 132-145. Note also Aurobindo's language in *BCL* XIX, 812.
60. *BCL* XVI, 212.
61. *BCL* XX, 53.
62. *BCL* XIX, 926. Cf. 925-926, XIII, 202-213.
63. *BCL* XVI, 95; *BCL* XXII, 453.
64. *BCL* XXII, 436-437.
65. Ibid., 433, 437, 458.
66. *BCL* XIX, 802. Cf. *BCL* XXII, 433, 437, 444.
67. *BCL* XXII, 434. Cf. *BCL* XIX, 762.
68. *BCL* XIX, 814.
69. *BCL* XXII, 443; XVI, 115. Cf. XXVI, 109.
70. *The Modern Review* (Calcutta) III (May, 1908), 424-428.
71. A.G. Hogg, *The Christian Message to the Hindu* (London: S.C.M., 1947), 10.
72. A.G. Hogg, *Karma and Redemption: An Essay Toward the Interpretation of Hinduism and the Re-statement of Christianity* (Madras: The Christian Literature Society, 1923). The story is still told by Radhakrishnan's close acquaintances in Madras that Radhakrishnan rose to his feet in a Madras Christian College philosophy class to deny the professor's (Hogg's?) charge that Hinduism has no basis for morality.
73. *The Hindu View of Life*, 50-56; *An Idealist View of Life*, 208-247; *The Brahma Sūtra*, 183-207.
74. *An Idealist View of Life*, 218.
75. Ibid., 230. Cf. 239.
76. Ibid., 211.

77. Ibid., 227; *The Brahma Sūtra*, 205-207.
78. *The Brahma Sūtra*, 200.
79. *An Idealist View of Life*, 238.
80. Ibid., 229.
81. *The Brahma Sūtra*, 190.
82. *An Idealist View of Life*, 239.
83. *The Brahma Sūtra*, 218. Cf. *Recovery of Faith* (Delhi: Hindu Pocket Books, 1967), 161-163: "The Religion of the Spirit and the World's Need," 65-66.
84. Ibid., 220. Cf. "The Religion and the Spirit and the World's Need," 45-47.
85. Ibid., 221.
86. *An Idealist View of Life*, 219.
87. Ibid., 218-219. Cf. *The Brahma Sūtra*, 194.
88. *The Hindu View of Life*, 53. Cf. "The Religion of the Spirit and the World's Need," 42.
89. Aloysius Michael, *Radhakrishnan on Hindu Moral Life and Action* (Delhi: Concept Publishing Co., 1978), 14.
90. *The Hindu View of Life*, 54.
91. *The Principal Upaniṣads*, 114. Cf. *The Hindu View of Life*, 53.
92. *Indian Philosophy* (London: Allen and Unwin, 1923), I, 251.
93. *An Idealist View of Life*, 232.
94. *The Brahma Sūtra*, 442.
95. *An Idealist View of Life*, 234. Cf. *The Brahma Sūtra*, 205.
96. *The Hindu View of Life*, 54. Cf. *The Brahma Sūtra*, 195; "Karma and Free Will," 426.
97. *An Idealist View of Life*, 221.
98. Cf. "Karma and Free Will," 426, with *The Hindu View of Life*, 54.
99. Michael, 17.
100. *An Idealist View of Life*, 220.
101. *The Bhagavadgītā* (London: Allen and Unwin, 1948), 49. For other versions see *An Idealist View of Life*, 221-222; *The Hindu View of Life*, 54.
102. *Indian Philosophy* I, 147.

CHAPTER THREE

Swami Vivekananda's Conception of Karma and Rebirth

GEORGE M. WILLIAMS

Swami Vivekananda has never been accused of being a systematic thinker. In fact, Agehananda Bharati has placed firmly on Vivekananda's shoulders the blame for creating the diction and style of the Hindu Renaissance. This diction and style enthrones sadhus over philosophers; English over Sanskrit; medieval Hindu pietism over "traditional, Sanskrit-based learning;" religious experience over philosophical insight; and syncretistic, "softline Vedānta" over the distinctive contributions of Indian philosophy.[1] This is clearly not a positive evaluation of Swami Vivekananda's contribution to Indian thought, but it does suggest that he deserves the title of Father of Modern, English-language Hinduism. Whether or not the tendencies which Bharati has pointed to are fatal to the "wonder that was Indian" (Basham) and continued glory of Indian philosophy may be indirectly inferred.

In attempting to account for Swami Vivekananda's sometimes confusing and seemingly contradictory manner of speaking about karma and rebirth, reformulating Vivekananda's teachings within familiar structures of Indian philosophy was an initial temptation. Yet some gentle surprises came by letting Vivekananda's conceptions speak in the contexts and frameworks which he set for them. After a search through a million words of extant primary materials certain patterns finally emerged.

A word must be said about the setting of Vivekananda's teachings. While the doctrines of karma and rebirth[2] are presupposed in his thought and occasionally addressed, there is never what one could characterize as any in-depth treatment. Most of the materials about karma and rebirth come from the Swami's talks before four different kinds of audiences:

(1) Westerners ignorant of basic Indian notions and often antagonistic to them even when explained; (2) Western disciples; (3) Indian audiences with widely divergent interests, with always one or two guru-baiters; and (4) Indian disciples. Most of the extant materials were notes by a disciple on his talks. Besides his personal correspondence, his essays and four books began as English talks recorded by a scribe, corrected by Vivekananda usually the next day, and often given Sanskrit terms and quotes from appropriate scriptures.

The wide religious, educational, and philosophical range of his audiences affected the formulation of his thought almost as much as a conception Vivekananda held about the tendencies of each individual. He believed that he needed to be all things to all people because a teacher must teach not only at the level and in the language of his audience but also according to the spiritual tendency of each individual in his audience. Vivekananda represented himself as articulating the discoveries of Śri Ramakrishna. These discoveries taught that: (1) persons have differing tendencies (*saṃ*skāras, pravṛttis) and these require different *yogas*; (2) a teacher must teach the correct yoga to each individual; (3) all paths (*yogas*) are one.

Some of the apparent inconsistencies in his teachings about karma and rebirth are caused by these multiple points of view and the varying conceptions about karma and rebirth these produce. Yet it is difficult to determine if Swami Vivekananda always knew which viewpoint he had switched to and why. An example of the range of his positions on karma includes the following : (1) that God is the sole doer (*bhakti yoga*); (2) that one is liberated by *jñāna* and bound by karma (*advaita, rāja yoga,* jñāña yoga); (3) that one's merit may be transferred to another (*niṣ*kāma *karma, karma yoga,* Buddhist *sādhana*); (4) that one gets only the results of one's own actions and there is no help except from one's own actions (just karma).

If one is aware that Swami Vivekananda changed his religious convictions dramatically during his lifetime (from a traditional Hindu child to a Brahmo Samaji, to a skeptic, to a devotee of Ramakrishna and Kālī, to an advaitin, to a yogi seeking initiation from Pavhari Baba, to a missionary of the Sanātana Dharma),[3] one might suspect that the differences in points of view were not within Swami Vivekananda's own mature teaching but a result of changes in patterns of belief. What is surprising is not that Vivekananda held these beliefs at earlier times in his life but that he taught each of these conceptions about karma during his so-called mature stage.

Thus the varying conceptions about karma and rebirth will involve Vivekananda's use of multiple points of view (the viewpoint of the religious tendency of the experiencer). Vivekananda's apparent inconsistencies were articulated by him in what he might call a twofold paradoxical loop:[4] (1) each religious tendency is true, separately or jointly, for those in that path or yoga; (2) all paths are one. Not only will Swami Vivekananda teach as though a particular point of view is the truth, but he will also teach that the viewpoints which have been taken as mutually inconsistent by certain earlier Indian philosophers are really in harmony. This set of claims leads to a presentation of his views which will attempt to show his notion of unity in diversity as it applies to karma and rebirth.

SPIRITUAL TENDENCIES AND KARMA

As has already been noted above, Vivekananda conceived of religious tendencies governing how and what one would be taught—even concerning karma and rebirth:

> Past lives have moulded our tendencies; give to the taught in accordance with his tendency. Intellectual, mystical, devotional, practical—make one the basis, but teach the others with it. Intellect must be balanced with love, the mystical nature with reason, while practice must form part of every method. Take every one where he stands and push him forward. Religious teaching must always be constructive, not destructive. Each tendency shows the life-work of the past, the line or radius lead to the centre. Never even attempt to disturb anyone's tendencies; to do that put back both teacher and taught. When you teach Jnana, you must become a Jnani and stand mentally exactly where the taught stands. Similarly in every other Yoga. Develop every faculty as if it were the only one possessed, this is the true secret of so-called harmonious development. That is, get extensity with intensity, but not at its expense. We are infinite. There is no limitation in us, we can be as intense as the most devoted Mohammedan and as broad as the most roaring atheist.[5]

What becomes interesting is observing when Vivekananda applied this heuristic approach. The taxonomy of four religious tendencies (*rāja yoga, jñāna yoga, bhakti yoga, karma yoga*) is reduced in actual usage to three, since *rāja yoga* and jñāna yoga are merged in his presentations. But his intention remained to encompass the variety of religious experience in their differing points of view. There were times when he taught within a single point of view—*bhakti*, for example. There were times when he would criticize *bhakti* and its modification of karma's causal laws with either *advaita* (*rāja yoga* and *jñāna yoga*) or straight, undiluted karmic doctrine. Each was seen by him as a path, a practice, a way of knowing, a set of teachings, an experience of the Absolute. Each would have its own view of karma and rebirth. And, though each would differ, all would be true.

BHAKTI-MODIFIED KARMA

During the period from 1881 to Ramakrishna's death in 1886, Narendranath Datta, the future Vivekananda, was led by his master to worship Kālī, and at least on one occasion, to affirm Ramakrishna as an *avatāra*. Yet this Ramakrishna *pūjā* and Kālī *pūjā* were precisely what Vivekananda came to condemn in his *gurubhais* (brother disciples), and he left them to their devotionalism in 1889 to search for the universal religion, the Sanātana Dharma. Later, when he taught from the point of view of *bhakti yoga*, he drew directly from the teachings of Ramakrishna. But some differences do occur, as will be noted.

The belief in, as well as the direct experience of God, who is capable of modifying the consequences of the worshipper's actions, allows for grace (*prasāda*), an unearned gift from God, and for God's power (*śakti*) to give help and grant prayerful requests. Since Ramakrishna experienced God the Mother as all-powerful, he taught that God is the sole doer. Ramakrishna used either gender to refer to God: "God is the Doer. He alone is doing everything. I am doing nothing. Man's suffering and worries spring only from his persistent thought that he is the doer." (*GRK* 142) Ramakrishna taught that God would cancel even the effects of *prārabdhakarma* of those following *bhakti yoga*. (*GRK* 250-251, 276, 951) "In the Kaliyuga the best way is *bhakti yoga*, the path of devotion—singing the praises of the Lord, and prayer. The path of devotion alone is the religion for this age." (*GRK* 143) Ramakrishna taught *bhakti* rather than rituals; (*GRK* 252, 611) Ramakrishna asserted that "A paramahamsa sees that it is God who gives us evil tendencies as well as good tendencies." (*GRK* 250)

In speeches, writings, and personal correspondence Vivekananda at times articulated a *bhakti*-modified karma doctrine. To an audience in Madras in 1897 Vivekananda spoke from a *bhakta* point of view, with the missionary spirit learned from Keshab Chundra Sen and the Brahmo Samaj, and augmented by a little "softline Vedānta."

> That I went to America was not my doing or your doing: but the God of India who is guiding her destiny sent me, and will send hundreds of such to all the nations of the world. No power on earth can resist it. This also has to be done. You must go out to preach your religion, preach it to every nation under the sun, preach it to every people. This the first thing to do. And after preaching spiritual knowledge, along with it will come that secular knowledge and every other knowledge that you want; but if you attempt to get the

secular knowledge without religion, I tell you plainly, vain is your attempt in India, it will never have a hold on the people. (*CW* III, 223)

Among Vivekananda's papers an outline to a book entitled *The Message of Divine Wisdom* was discovered. Vivekananda, who died at 39 years of age, only completed books which evolved out of English lectures. *The Message* began with a section on "Bondage", a second on the "Law", and the third on "The Absolute and the Attainment of Freedom." After setting forth sacred formulas describing *Brahman* as "Impersonal and the real Infinite," Vivekananda identified *Brahman* and *śakti* as Ramakrishna had done.

> Every existence from the highest to the lowest, all manifest according to their degree as energy (in the higher life), attraction (in the higher love), and struggle for equilibrium (in the higher happiness). This highest Energy-Love-Beauty is a person, an individual, the Infinite Mother of this universe—the God of gods—the Lord of lords, omni present yet separate from the universe—the Soul of souls, yet separate from every soul—the Mother of this universe, because She has produced it—its Ruler, because She guides it with the greatest love and in the long run brings everything back to Herself. Through Her command the sun and moon shine, the clouds rain, and death stalks upon the earth.
>
> She is the power of all causation. She energises every cause unmistakably to produce the effect. Her will is the only law, and as She cannot make a mistake, nature's law—Her will—can never be changed.
>
> She is the life of the Law of Karma or causation. She is the fructifier of every action. Under Her guidance we are manufacturing our lives through our deeds or Karma. (*CW* V, 433-34).

In his personal correspondence during two different controversies, Vivekananda relied upon God the Mother as the final cause of his sufferings. The first controversy involved his lack of credentials for being a delegate at the World Parliament of Religions in Chicago in 1893 and his manufacturing a dossier which did not stand careful scrutiny [6] He had claimed to be a Brahmin, a monk of the Śankarācārya Order, and a representative of Hinduism. Only by getting letters from the followers of Ramakrishna, whom he had left, and from Hindus in Madras could his claim be accepted that he was the only representative of all Hinduism coming from India to the World Parliament of Religions and thus void problems in truth with the other two claims. In a letter to a disciple in

Madras, in which his own gender shifts in reference to God occurred, he stated: "Good-bye, I have had enough of the Hindus. Now His will be done, I obey and bow down to my Karma." But not without a touch of resentment: "It was my foolishness—the forgetting for a moment that we Hindus have not yet become human beings, and giving up for a moment my self-reliance and relying upon the Hindus—that I came to grief. Every moment I expected something from India. . . .But it is the punishment for relying upon man and upon brutes, for our countrymen are not men as yet." (*CW* VIII, 312, 313)

An articulation made in personal crisis as he faced the possibility of being discredited over a seemingly minor twisting of the truth should not be confused with a theological teaching. But the use of a devotional point of view in its negative form, of God being solely responsible for what happens in the universe cannot be ignored. Vivekananda implied that the punishment was not deserved, which does raise that thorny issue of a God who acts and is all-powerful but not just. He had abandoned a similar belief which he held as a Brahmo Samaji, and he never tired of criticizing Christians whose God was all-powerful, but whose God could not be saved from being thought unjust. Only the doctrine of karma placed responsibility upon humans, where it belonged. But when Vivekananda's own actions brought him suffering or embarrassment, he seemed to shift blame from himself. He seemed to suggest that God the Mother both caused and was served by his lingering illness before his death. Two years before his death he wrote: "I can only say, every blow I had in this life, every pang, will only become joyful sacrifice if Mother becomes propitious to India once more." (*CW* VIII, 486) During an earlier illness he wrote to Swami Brahmananda:

> It may be either a physical or a mental disease. Now I have come to the conclusion that I am unfit for further work,. . .[editor's elision] I now understand that I have been very harsh to all of you. . . .Whatever has happened is now past—it is all the rush of past Karma. What is the good of my repentence? I do not believe in it. It is all Karma. Whatever of Mother's work was to be accomplished through me, She made me do, and has now flung me aside breaking down my body and mind. Her will be done! (*CW* VIII, 430)

ADVAITA-MODIFIED KARMA

While the *bhakta*'s goal is God's gift of a personal, transforming relationship with the Divine, there results a modification of the causal structure of karma. God's *prasāda* modifies the precise equation of getting exactly what you deserve, God's *śakti* energizes all activity and makes God ultimately responsible for every action in the universe, and God's *līlā* removes the causal structure of karma from human understanding and control. Likewise, the advaitin's goal to seek a realization of that which has been hidden by ignorance of *ātman-brahman* modifies karma—but in different ways. Vivekananda taught that transcendental insight (*aparokṣ*ānubhūti) shows the relation of actions and the soul to be illusory. In his version of *rāja yoga* and *jñāña yoga* (in which he did not distinguish between the intellectual and the mystical paths) Swami Vivekananda taught as an advaitin that knowledge of the Absolute liberates, but he would attempt to connect absolute knowledge and relative work, even as he did when speaking as a karma yogi.

A conversation at Belur Math in 1901 (which evidences considerable editing by the Ramakrishna Order) illustrates Vivekananda's tensions when he attempted to preserve a relative concern for others' welfare and an absolute perspective.

> Disciple: But, sir, according to Shankara, Karma is antagonistic to Jnana. He has variously refuted the intermingling of Jnana and Karma. So how can Karma be helpful to the manifestation of Jnana?
>
> Swamiji: Shankara after saying so has again described Karma as indirect help to the manifestation of Jnana and the means for the purification of the mind. But I do not contradict his conclusion that in transcendent knowledge there is no touch of any work whatsoever. So long as man is within the realm of the consciousness of action, agent, and the result of action, he is powerless to sit idle without doing some work. So, as work is thus ingrained in the very nature of man, why don't you go on doing such works as are helpful to the manifestation of the knowledge of the Atman? That all work is the effect of ignorance may be true from the absolute standpoint, but within the sphere of relative consciousness it has a great utility. When you will realise the Atman, the doing or non-doing of work will be within your control, and whatever you will do in that state will be good work, conducive to the well-being of Jivas and the world. With the manifestation of Brahman, even the breath you draw will be to the good of Jiva. Then you will no longer have to work by means of conscious planning. Do you understand?
>
> Disciple: Yes, it is a beautiful conclusion reconciling Karma and Jnana from the Vedantic standpoint. (*CW* VII, 221-222)

Curiously, Vivekananda's starting point for his advaita perspective on karma dealt with creation *ex nihilo*, a notion he fought in Christian theism. He argued hypothetically: "Admit that there was a time when there was no existence. Where was all this mass of matter? To create something new would be the introduction of so much more energy into the universe. This is impossible." Here he felt on the side of nineteenth century science and its steady state theory. He continued: "Old things can be re-created, but there can be no addition to the universe." (*CW* VII, 422) Since there could be no creation *ex nihilo*, he next treated that which has always existed—the Absolute, the Soul, the Self. In Vivekananda's monism their equivalence was not questioned.

> There is no change whatsoever in the soul—Infinite, Absolute, Eternal, Knowledge, Bliss, and Existence. Neither can there be birth or death for the soul. Dying, and being born, reincarnation, and going to heaven, cannot be for the soul. These are different appearances, different mirages, different dreams. (*CW* I, 421)

Vivekananda taught that the Soul/Self appeared to travel through various states of manifestation: "This soul is without birth and without death. It is not a compound or combination, but an independent individual, and as such it cannot be created or destroyed; it is only traveling through various states." (*CW* I, 260) In a puzzling attempt to relate the absolute soul to actions in an apparent world of mirages Vivekananda drew upon the image of two wheels, a pole, and an axe:

> This pure and perfect being, the soul, is one wheel, and this external hallucination of body and mind is the other wheel, joined together by the pole of work, of Karma. Knowledge is the axe which will sever the bond between the two, and the wheel of the soul will stop—stop thinking that it is coming and going, living and dying, stop thinking that it is nature and has wants and desires, and will find that it is perfect, desireless. But upon the other wheel, that of the body and mind, will be the momentum of past acts; so it will live for some time, until that momentum of past work is exhausted, until that momentum is worked away, and then the body and mind fall, and the soul becomes free. (*CW* II, 281)

Vivekananda's error as an advaitin that the "soul becomes free" involves failing to stay with a single point of view. Vivekananda taught in many other places that the soul is ever free and realization of that is freedom itself. But this error arises more from his desire to limit Advaita's devaluation of the relative than the contrary force of advaita modifying and totally relativizing that which cannot effect the soul. It has been noted elsewhere that Vivekananda's Practical Vedānta resides in Viṣiṣṭādvaita.[7]

When Vivekananda does not wish to burden advaita with ethics (as might be concluded from the preceding), he takes the absolute perspective, as in these remarks made in the year 1900 in Los Angeles:

> Whoever thinks that I am little makes a mistake, for the Self is all that exists. The sun exists because I declare it does, the world exists because I declare it does. Without me they cannot remain for I am Existence, Knowledge, and Bliss Absolute—ever happy, ever pure, ever beautiful. Behold the sun is the cause of our vision, but is not itself ever affected by any defect in the eyes of any one; even so I am. I am working through all organs, working through everything, but never does the good and evil of work attach to me. For me there is no law, nor Karma. I own the laws of Karma. I ever was and ever am. (*CW* II, 404)

But Vivekananda's image which best represented this point of view, at least to C.J. Jung who utilized it in his own "India: Land of Dreams," was evoked in a poem written in 1898 for Prabuddha Bharata:

> And tell the world—
>
> Awake, arise, and dream no more!
> This is the land of dreams, where Karma
> Weaves unthreaded garlands with our thoughts
> Of flowers sweet or noxious, and none
> Has root or stem, being born in naught, which
> The softest breath of Truth drives back to
> Primal nothingness. Be bold, and face
> The Truth! Be one with it! Let visions cease,
> Or, if you cannot, dream but truer dreams,
> Which are Eternal Love and Service Free.
>
> (*CW* IV, 388-389)

Vivekananda wrote a commentary on Patañjali's *Yoga Sūtras* as source material for his conception of the *rāja yogi*. He thus conceived that the *rāja yogi*, upon attaining perfection, would not be bound by his actions, "because he did not desire them. He just works on; he works to do good, and he does good, but does not care for the result, and it will not come to him." (*CW* I, 295) He added: "A man who wants to be a perfect Yogi must give up the sex idea. The soul has no sex; why should it degrade itself with sex ideas?" (*CW* I, 260) But when Vivekananda reached *Yoga Sūtra* IV 29, teaching that upon the attainment of *samādhi* "comes cessation of pain and works," Vivekananda commented: "When the cloud of virtue has come, then no more is there fear of falling, nothing can drag the Yogi down. No more will there be evils for him. No more pain." (*CW* I, 303) Vivekananda was not unaware that this passage presented the absolute viewpoint and separated realization and works. Here Vivekananda attempted to hold both perspectives and to avoid any real exogesis of the passage.

Vivekananda often spoke enthusiastically about man's divine nature. He taught others not to be too concerned about human frailty.

> I have committed many mistakes in my life; but mark you, I am sure of this that without every one of those mistakes I should not be what I am today, and so am quite satisfied to have made them. . . . So if we are Advaitists, we must think from this moment that our old self is dead and gone. The old Mr., Mrs., and Miss So-and-so are gone, they were mere superstitions, and what remains is the ever-pure, the ever-strong, the almightly, the all-knowing—that alone remains for us, and then all fear vanishes from us. Who can injure us, the omnipresent? All weakness has vanished from us, and our only work is to arouse this knowledge in our fellow beings. We see that they too are the same pure self, only they do not know it; we must teach them, we must help them to rouse up their infinite nature. (*CW* II, 358)

An example of Vivekananda not forcing himself to operate solely within *advaita*-modified karmic doctrines arose when he shifted back to the relative view to attack libertinism or non-ethical inaction. Yet even in the following critique he failed to maintain a single viewpoint.

> You may find many fools in this country at the present time, saying "I am not bound; I am God Himself; let me do anything I like." This is not right, although it is true that the soul is beyond laws, physical, mental, or moral. Within the law is bondage; beyond the law is freedom. It is also true that freedom is of the nature of the soul, it is its birthright. (*CW* II, 282)

Had Vivekananda remembered the scathing attacks of Shivanath Shastri, whom he followed in the Sadharan Brahmo Samaj for one year (1879/80) or his own letters to Pandit Mitra during 1888-1889, he might have addressed other issues.[8]

From Vivekananda's advaita viewpoint, karma resided in the realm of relative topics, in *māyā* and *avidyā*. No great effort was warranted by Vivekananda to develop systematically an understanding of its nature. That lack of interest by Vivekananda might just well arise from his subsuming *jñāna yoga*, the intellectual path and its analytical functioning, to *rāja yoga*. To make them indistinguishable vitiates the concern for intuition balanced by reason, which he taught, and provided him with a weak basis for philosophical inquiry.

Before turning to Vivekananda's articulation of a doctrine of karma that is not modified by actions superceding human action or processes relativizing actions of limited beings, his favored perspective, *karma yoga* will be examined.

KARMA YOGA: SERVING OTHERS

Vivekananda favored a conception of karma that promoted serving others. Unlike *bhakti-karma* which held that God could suspend karma's rules and change what one should reap or *advaita-karma* which denied that any consequence could affect the soul, Vivekananda's *karma yoga* taught another doctrine of karma which allowed (1) that desireless activity would not bring bad consequences to the doer; and (2) that activity for others could actually benefit them as receivers of the fruits of meritorious works. He lumped these two elements together into one doctrine which he found variously in the Buddha's teachings and in the *Gītā*. His version was taught in English with only a few Sanskrit terms suggesting its roots in the Indian tradition. *Niṣkāma-karma, seva, vairāgya* and *dāna* were the key terms which were utilized in teaching this perspective.

Vivekananda's *karma yoga* was a path for others. "Who cares whether there is a heaven or a hell, who cares if there is a soul or not, who cares if there is an unchangeable or not? Here is the world, and it is full of misery. Go out into it as Buddha did, and struggle to lessen it or die in the attempt." (*CW* II, 353) Despite the unfortunate phrasing, Vivekananda intended effective, unselfish service (*seva*) for others to lessen their sufferings: "This renunciation is the only positive power in the universe." (*CW* II, 354) He taught that "The true Nishkama Karmi (performer of work without desire) is neither to be like a brute, nor to be inert, nor heartless. He is not Tamasika but of pure Sattva. His heart is so full of love and sympathy that he can embrace the whole world with his love." (*CW* IV, 107) He found support for his notion that *karma yoga* is the spiritual practice of this age: "Says our Vyasa, 'In the Kali Yuga there is one Karma left. Sacrifices and tremendous Tapasyas are of no avail now. Of Karma one remains, and that is the Karma of giving.' And of these gifts, the gift of spirituality and spiritual knowledge is the highest; the next gift is the gift of secular knowledge; the next is the gift of life; and the fourth is the gift of good." (*CW* III, 222)

From the *Gītā* Vivekananda boldly restated how moral responsibility for one's actions may be diverted: "Good and evil will both have their results, will produce their Karma. Good action will entail upon us good effect; bad action, bad. But good and bad are both bondages of the soul. The solution reached in the Gītā in regard to this bondage-producing nature of work is that, if we do not attach ourselves to the work we do, it will not have any binding effect on our soul." (*CW* I, 53)

The discipline of the *karma yogi* intended the development of unselfich service to others. A letter in the early part of his mature period was typical of the advice he gave.

> Do you want to forgo even your own salvation for the good of the world? You are God, think of that. My advice to you is to live the life of a Brahmacharin, i.e. giving up all sexual enjoyments for a certain time live in the house of your father; this is the "Kutichaka" stage. Try to bring your wife to consent to your great sacrifice for the good of the world. And if you have burning faith and all-conquering love and almighty purity, I do not doubt that you will shortly succeed. Give yourself body and soul to the work of speaking the teaching of Shri Ramakrishna, for work (Karma) is the first stage. (*CW* VI, 280)

In a story about Pavhari Baba from whom Vivekananda had sought initiation in 1890, Vivekananda would place within that story key notions of service to others: "When asked on another occasion why he, a great Yogi, should perform Karma, such as pouring oblations into the sacrifical fire, and worshipping the image of Shri Raghunathji, which are practices only meant for beginners, the reply came: 'Why do you take for granted that everybody makes Karma for his own good? Cannot one perform Karma for others?' " (*CW* IV, 293)

What is notable about Vivekananda's attitude about rituals and service to help others was that it differed so completely from Ramakrishna's. Ramakrishna seemed to operate consistently within the *bhakti* perspective when he discouraged *saṃdhyā* and other practices. (*GRK* 611, 612. Cf. 142, 252) Ramakrishna had experienced God's grace directly and found that relationship primary; rituals and attempting to pass merit to others might even be viewed as questioning the sufficiency of God's grace. Ramakrishna scoffed at the idea of taking God's place: "You speak of doing good to the world. Is the world such a small thing? And who are you, pray, to do good to the world? First realize God, see Him by means of spiritual discipline. If He imparts power, then you can do good to others; otherwise not." (*GRK* 142)

That there may be two causal theories about karma's workings within Vivekananda's *karma yoga* teaching is evidenced in two ways. First, Vivekananda formulated *karma yoga* by calling upon his notion of the Buddha's teachings: care not for heaven or hell or even the unchangeable. This *bodhisattva* appeal works less well in a Hinduism that maintains a strong causal theory (you get only what you sow) and strong rebirth doctrine (you are reborn in accordance with your past deeds). If rebirth looms ahead, only a fool would not care—or someone who believes something else. That something else, the inner workings of another karma theory, would allow rebirth to be ignored. However, it might be stated,

Vivekananda invoked a doctrine of karma which modified its functioning. He taught that an attitude, *niṣkāma*, could disconnect the actor from direct responsibility for the results of actions taken.

The second way *karma yoga* works in Vivekananda's formulation requires a modification of simple or undiluted karma—but for something desired. In this form of karma one renounces (*vairāgya*) the fruit of one's own meritorious activity to give (*dāna*) it to needy and suffering persons. Serving others implies a merit transfer theory; somehow what is done will help alleviate the negative effects of another's karma—and possibly help one's own as a bonus. Vivekananda did not address this matter.

A difference between desireless karma and karma for others' benefit would be maintained on at least the ground of their dissimilar functioning. But for Vivekananda both are subsumed in *karma yoga*'s way of apprehending karma and rebirth.

JUST KARMA: YOU REAP WHAT YOU SOW

There remains an interesting set of conceptions about karma which is not connected to Vivekananda's theory of religious tendencies and their correlative paths or *yogas*. While I have entitled this section "Just Karma" to imply a causal theory of retribution and compensation for one's actions that functions justly and without modification, there were a few complaints by Vivekananda about undiluted karma. Vivekananda's complaints corresponded to experiences of fatalism and cynicism regarding karma in the Indian tradition. When one lost the courage to act, when one no longer believed that a positive result was possible by one's own actions, when one cried for help and sought changes in the rules of just effects, when one despaired or resentment took over, undiluted karma lost its power to ennoble and enrich life. Vivekananda spoke occasionally of the bondage of karma and rebirth: "Man is a slave of nature, and slave eternally he has got to remain. We call it Karma. Karma means law, and it applies everywhere. Everything is bound by Karma." (*CW* I, 450) He would even use karma as the reason for India's fate at the turn of the twentieth century: "The mass of Brahmin and Kshatriya tyranny has recoiled upon their own heads with compound interest; and a thousand years of slavery and degradation is what the inexorable law of Karma is visiting upon them." (*CW* IV, 328)

Although certain points of view exploit human ineffectiveness in combating karma's effects and posit ways of suspending its rule (at least in the spiritual realm), Vivekananda rather often evoked a doctrine of karma which placed total responsibility upon "man the doer." He taught: "Man is not bound by any other laws excepting those which he makes for himself. Our thoughts, our words and deeds are the threads of the net which we throw round ourselves, for good or for evil. Once we set in motion a certain power, we have to take the full consequences of it. This is the law of Karma." (*CW* II, 348) Vivekananda would appeal to the absolute level for the power to operate in the relative: "The Vedanta says that Infinity is our true nature; it will never vanish, it will abide for ever. But we are limiting ourselves by our Karma, which like a chain round our necks has dragged us into this limitation. Break that chain and be free. Trample law under your feet. There is no law in human nature, there is no destiny, no fate. How can there be law in infinity? Freedom is its watchword. Freedom is its nature, its birthright. Be free, and then have any number of personalities you like." (*CW* II, 323) Vivekananda taught that this infinite freedom and power needed nothing from anyone else: "Be free; hope for nothing from anyone. I am sure if you look back upon your lives you will find that you were always vainly trying to get help from others which never came. All the help that has come was from within yourselves. You only had the fruits of what you yourselves worked for, and yet you were strangely hoping all the time for help." (*CW* II, 324)

So strongly did Vivekananda believe in man's own freedom to act that he once criticized the oppressed. The following story was retold within the Ramakrishna Order:

> It was in Almora that a certain elderly man, with a face full of amiable weakness, came and put him a question about Karma. What were they to do, he asked, whose Karma it was to see the strong oppress the weak? The Swami turned on him in surprised indignation. "Why, thrash the strong, of course!" he said, "You forget your own part in this Karma; Yours is always the right to rebel!" (*CW* VIII, 262-263)

Besides this doctrine of revolution Vivekananda's expressions about undiluted karma inspire great expectations about human possibility. "If what we are now has been the result of our own past actions, it certainly follows that whatever we wish to be in the future can be produced by our present actions; so we have to know how to act." (*CW* I, 31) "It [future possibility] depends on the intensity of the desire." (*CW* VII, 97) "You have taken fate in your own hands. Your Karma has manufactured for you this body, and nobody did it for you." (*CW* III, 161)

Vivekananda extended individual karma to a notion of collective karma; but this notion changes simple karma (reaping what you sow) to a compounded karma (reaping what others sow as well).

> Karma is the eternal assertion of human freedom. If we can bring ourselves down by our Karma, surely it is in our power to raise ourselves by it. The masses, besides, have not brought themselves down altogether by their own Karma. So we should give them better environments to work in. I do not propose any leveling of castes. Caste is a very good thing. Caste is the plan we want to follow. What caste really is, not one in a million understands. There is no country in the world without caste. In India, from caste we reach to the point where there is no caste. Caste is based throughout on that principle. The plan in India is to make everybody a Brahmin, the Brahmin being the ideal of humanity. If you read the history of India you will find that attempts have always been made to raise the lower classes. Many are the classes that have been raised. Many more will follow till the whole will become Brahmin. That is the plan. We have only to raise them without bringing down anybody. (*CW* V, 213-214)

While there is a new element in this formulation—shared karma and karma's functioning are thereby made slightly more complex than when one's own action is the sole determinent of one's fate—Vivekananda seems to hold both simultaneously. He even extends the notion of a collective karma to a collective mission, India's "national ideals."

> But as a Hindu everything else must be subordinated to our own national ideals. Each man has a mission in life, which is the result of all his infinite past Karma. Each of you was born with a splendid heritage, which is the whole of the infinite past life of your glorious nation. Millions of your ancestors are watching, as it were, every action of yours, so be alert. And what is the mission with which every Hindu child is born? Have you not read the proud declaration of Manu regarding the Brahmin where he says that the birth of the Brahmin is "for the protection of the treasury of religion"? I should say that that is the mission not only of the Brahmin, but of every child, whether boy or girl, who is born in this blessed land (*CW* III, 152) . . .Let us all work hard, my brethren; this is no time for sleep. On our work depends the coming of the India of the future. She is there ready waiting. She is only sleeping. (*CW* III, 154)

If undiluted karma taught responsibility for creating a new future, it contained a corollary pertaining to bad karma. When utilizing this formulation of karma doctrine, Vivekananda admonished one to look for the subjective reason for a negative happening. On several occasions Vivekananda regarded his illnesses and the criticisms of one of his British disciples (Sturdy) as completely of his own making: "Mrs. Johnson. . .is of opinion, no spiritual person ought to be ill it also seems to her now that my smoking is sinful. . . .I am sure that the fault is mine and mine only for every wave of dislike or hatred that I get—it could not be otherwise and thank you and Mrs. Johnson for this calling me once more to the internal."[9] He accounted for his contracting diabetes a little less directly but finally as from his own karma: "In India the moment I landed they made me shave my head and wear 'Kaupin,' (loin cloth) with the result that I got diabetes, etc. Saradananda never gave up his underwear—this saved his life, with just a touch of rheumatism and much comment from our people. Of course, it is my Karma, and I am glad that it is so. For, though it smarts for the time, it is another great experience of life, which will be useful, either in this or in the next." (*CW* VIII, 471)

One last example contains most of the elements of undiluted karma—a world real enough to be concerned about it, actions having consequences and adhering to the actor even beyond death, actors only having responsibility for their own actions whether from past lives or not, and boundless freedom to change the future. This example does not perceive any disability which requires help—even for women:

> Are you the Lord God that you should rule every widow and every woman? Hands off! They will solve their own problems. O tyrants, attempting to think that you can do anything for any one! Hands off! The Divine will look after all. Who are you to assume that you know everything? How dare you think, O blasphemers, that you have the right over God? For don't you know that every soul is the Soul of God? Mind your own Karma; a load of Karma is there in you to work out. Your nation may put you upon a pedestal, your society may cheer you up to the skies, and fools may praise you: but He sleeps not, and retribution will be sure to follow, here or hereafter. (*CW* III, 246)

Such heroic resolve characterized Vivekananda's teaching on *karma yoga*. They taught self-exertion (*puruṣakāra*), the innate power to shape one's own destiny, and a disdain for crying to others, even to God, for help. But from this viewpoint one's own future and rebirth was all of one's own making.

VIVEKANANDA AND REBIRTH

I have chosen to summarize Vivekananda's teachings on rebirth in one section although you will now anticipate that, once linked with his different religious tendencies, certain formulations are to be expected. Possibly because of his concern about his audiences or even his own habits in formulation of his teachings, Vivekananda's ideas about rebirth shifted perspectives much more than usual. Once again Vivekananda lacked the consistency of Ramakrishna's *bhakti*. When asked: "Sir, is there such a thing as reincarnation? Shall we be born again?," Ramakrishna replied: "Ask God about it. Pray to Him sincerely. He will tell you everything." Then he added: "First of all realize God; then He Himself will let you know whatever you desire." (*GRK* 916) On another occasion Ramakrishna showed how little rebirth interested him: "Many people have spoken about reincarnation; therefore I cannot disbelieve it." (*GRK* 153)

Even though Vivekananda spoke at length several times about reincarnation or metempsychosis (he did not use the term "rebirth"), he did not develop the topic systematically, philosophically, theologically, or in accordance with his notion of multiple points of view in the four spiritual tendencies. When he spoke about this topic, it was in the context of his promotion of Hinduism or its defense. Accordingly, he shifted to whatever point of view was needed to gain maximum effect upon his audience. This evidences a missionary or hortative concern. Three classes of treatments were found: statements defending Hinduism as superior to Western religion; statements calling into question Western devotional religion; and statements commenting on Indian scriptures. If these statements followed the Swami's own guide for a teacher and focused upon the needs of the audience as dictated by the path which governed their spiritual instruction, the statements would have been set more carefully within a spiritual viewpoint.

Vedānta or Hinduism as Superior. Vivekananda argued that reincarnation or "metempsychosis is one of the most widely-accepted beliefs among the Eastern races, and one that they are ever ready to defend, at home or abroad." (*CW* VII, 422) He pointed out that great scholars like Professor Max Müller accepted it: "That Advaitism is the highest discovery in the domain of religion, the Professor has many times publicly admitted. That doctrine of reincarnation, which is a dread to the Christian who has identified the soul with the body, he firmly believes in because of his having found conclusive proof in his own personal experience." (*CW* IV, 412) Vivekananda's shifting from one viewpoint to another appears to have caused an error—an error which he would not make were it not for his missionary zeal. He has confused Advaita, Vedānta, and Hinduism in these remarks, and he does not present Advaita as teaching reincarnation of the soul elsewhere. But his trump card was discovered in Christianity itself; Vivekananda found that Jesus believed in reincarnation. ". . .Jesus himself directly asserted that John the Baptist was the Prophet Elias come back again. 'If ye will receive it, this is Elias, which was for to come.' Matt. XI, 14." (*CW* IV, 264)

Unlike Christianity with its doctrine of creation *ex nihilo*, Hinduism or Vedānta was scientific, Vivekananda claimed. "Reincarnation is the evolution of nature and the manifestation of the God within." (*CW* V, 281) The Hindu theory of transmigration of souls "is on the basis as the theory of conservation is to the scientist. This theory was first produced by a philosopher of my country. The ancient sages did not believe in a creation. A creation implies producing something out of nothing. That is impossible." (*CW* V, 313) Vivekananda further believed that reincarnation better accounted for inherited characteristics, another scientific issue. "Our experiences cannot be annihilated. Our actions (Karma) though apparently disappearing, remain still unperceived (Adrishta), and reappear again in this effect as tendencies (Pravrittis). Even little babies come with certain tendencies—fear of death, for example." (*CW* IV, 270)

While Christianity cannot defend God from being blamed for injustice and impartiality, reincarnation puts the blame where it belongs. "My own Karma is sufficient explanation of my present state." (*CW* VIII, 184; cf. V, 281, 316) Vivekananda taught that reincarnation points man to his true nature: his perfection, his divinity. (*CW* III, 479)

Missionary Statements. A sketchy account of an exchange between Swami Vivekananda and a woman demonstrated both his desire to convert her to another viewpoint and his shift from his usual perspective of serving others to one which challenges her beliefs. "Answering the remark of a disciple who felt that it would be better for her to come back to this life again and again and help the causes that were of interest to her instead of striving for personal salvation with a deep longing to get out of life, the Swami retorted quickly: 'That's because you cannot overcome the idea of progress. But things do not grow better. They remain as they are; and we grow better by the changes we make in them.' " (*CW* VIII, 262) Vivekananda has answered the same question differently elsewhere; only the person was different.

Another example of Vivekananda attempting to convert his audience to a different view of rebirth occurred in 1900 in Oakland. The sermon made headlines in two papers, *The Enquirer* and *The San Francisco Bulletin*. He had preached about "keeping out of Heaven." He countered a devotional Christian view with notions of "karma and reincarnation, the concepts of Hindu cosmology, the theory of cyclic evolution and involution, and the theory of Maya."[10] The shift to an advaita viewpoint produced maximum shock.

Commentator of Hindu Scriptures. Vivekananda's handling of passages from the *Yoga Sūtras*, the Upaniṣads, the *Gītā*, and the *Mahābhārata* yield nothing but the most basic descriptions or definitions about reincarnation. (*CW* II, 269-270; IV, 112-113, 270; VIII, 51)

It seems safe to conclude after surveying all references to reincarnation and metemphychosis in Vivekananda's extant teachings that rebirth was not a major notion in his thought. It functioned more as a weapon for his mission to preach the Sanātana Dharma than as an article of belief directly related to his own spiritual experience. This later point may seem strange in an academic analysis of Vivekananda's thought, but the claim that his teachings were based upon spiritual experience—his own or Ramakrishna's—was fundamental to his aproach.

A Karmic Postscript

At least on the doctrines of karma and rebirth, Vivekananda is more a preacher than a philosopher. His formulations do not knit loose threads into a single fabric. He does not fully apply his own theories, especially about spiritual tendencies and the harmonization of all viewpoints, or draw his insights together into a coherent whole. This survey of all his extant references to rebirth demonstrated that he did not explicate the doctrine of rebirth in each of the contexts in which he developed karma.

Even so, there is power in what Vivekananda taught and that may be just because he was a spiritual counselor, attempting to start with his listener's spiritual tendency and to teach what the listener needed to know. But from an independent viewpoint it is not clear that Vivekananda knew where he was in all his heuristic shiftings or where, in fact, the absolute perspective might be found when even the *advaita* perspective was linked to one relative type—the intuitive and its mystical religious tendency. Vivekananda's treatments of karma and rebirth are hopelessly lost in larger issues. These issues involved harmonization of all points of view, articulation of the *Sanātana Dharma* or eternal principles in which all spiritual teachings find their unity, and the interpretation of the absolute perspective in relative terms of each of the four spiritual paths. If Vivekananda became lost in his exposition of karma and rebirth according to each spiritual type or tendency, then he failed to show that one teacher could explicate four different experiences of karma and rebirth. If Vivekananda found one of the four tendencies, *advaita*—which he placed in the domain of *rāja yoga*—as the perspective of the absolute itself, then he failed to create a strange loop or paradox in which all four perspectives participate equally in the truth but are not equal to the absolute. If Vivekananda interpreted spiritual tendencies from a perspective independent of spiritual tendencies, then he failed to teach where that perspective might be. Since Vivekananda's teachings about karma and rebirth are set in philosophical concerns that he did not solve in his brief lifetime, to extricate them from their varying concerns and contexts seems impossible. Yet Vivekananda's treatment of karma and rebirth points to a spectrum of Indian experiences exceeding any single individual's capacity to comprehend karma and rebirth through personal experience and reflection.

Swami Vivekananda linked the absolute and the relative, but in the case of his teachings about karma and rebirth the promised harmony of all views seems to have remained a conundrum rather than the strange loop or paradox which suggests more than might be possible to comprehend.

NOTES

1. Agehananda Bharati, *Journal of Asian Studies* (February, 1970).

2. "Rebirth" was not a term that Swami Vivekananda used. He preferred terms like reincarnation, metempsychosis, and transmigration of the soul.

3. These changes have been discussed in earlier studies: George M. Williams, *Quest for Meaning of Svāmī Vivekānanda* (Chico: New Horizona Press, 1974), "Svāmī Vivekānanda: Archetypal Hero or Doubting Saint?" in *Religion in Modern India*, Robert Baird ed. (New Delhi: Manohar, 1981), and "Methodological Problems in Documenting Religious Change When Change Is Denied: Svāmī Vivekānanda's Early Years," in *Proceedings of the Indian History and Culture Society* (New Delhi, 1981). Methodological considerations which would also apply to this paper have been previously discussed in *Quest*, loc cit., pp. 1-9. See also, Robert D. Baird, *Category Formation and the History of Religions* (The Hague: Mouton, 1971), pp. 1-16.

4. "Paradoxical loop" is being used here in light of the discussion in Douglas R. Hofstadter's *Godel, Escher, Bach* (New York: Vantage Books, 1979) in which he distinguished between simple loops and strange or true paradoxical loops.

5. *The Complete Works of Swami Vivekananda* (Volumes 1-8. Six editions to date. Calcutta: Advaita Ashrama, 1964) VII, 98 (hereafter abbreviated *CW* followed by volume and page). *The Gospel of Sri Ramakrishna*, recorded by Mahendranath Gupta and translated from Bengali into English by Swami Nikhilananda (New York: Ramakrishna-Vivekananda Center, 1969), hereafter abbreviated as *GRK*.

6. For a more extensive treatment see Williams, "Svāmī Vivekānanda: Archetypal Hero or Doubting Saint?" in Baird, op. cit. and Marie L. Burke, *Swami Vivekananda in America: New Discoveries* (Calcutta: Advaita Ashrama, Second Revised Edition, 1966). Burke cites some of the times Vivekananda identified himself as a "Brāhmin monk." (pp. 69f.) She defends this as being "due to expediency" and thus "a careless but forgivable error." (p. 69)

7. Williams, op. cit. (1974), pp. 85-90.

8. Williams, in Baird, op. cit. (1981).

9. Marie Louise Burke, *Swami Vivekananda: His Second Visit to the West* (Calcutta: Advaita Ashrama, 1973), p. 78, 80.

10. Ibid., pp. 328-329.

CHAPTER FOUR

Karma, Rebirth and the Contemporary Guru

DAVID MILLER

THE GURU AND MERIT TRANSFER

I begin with a situational model. It was 4:30 a.m. at Desasvamedha Ghat in Benares, and as I stood watching the panorama of activity that accompanies each sunrise over the Gaṅgā, a young couple approached. The man, his face grief-stricken, carried a child over his left shoulder. The child was a boy whom I guessed to be no more than two years old. His skin was a deathly grey hue. His right arm hung lifelessly down his father's back, and the boy's head bounced uncontrollably on his father's shoulder. The boy's mother followed slightly behind her husband; her face was partly covered with the hood made from her sari. Her eyes revealed a deep sadness. As the couple and the child came nearer, the boy rolled his head in my direction and opened his jaundiced eyes.

Suddenly, a tall, handsome, aged *saṃnyāsin* moved gracefully through the crowd toward the couple who had stopped briefly on the upper steps of the *ghat*. As the *saṃnyāsin* came up to the couple and the child, he marked the boy's forehead with white ash. The *saṃnyāsin*'s lips moved silently as he administered the ashes, his words becoming lost in the clatter and noises that precede the dawn. He made a similar mark upon the father's forehead whose face took on a different, stronger expression—one of hope rather than sorrow. The woman immediately dropped to her knees and touched the *saṃnyāsin*'s feet with her hands. As she rose, the *saṃnyāsin* smeared white ash on her forehead as well. The *saṃnyāsin* moved away, disappearing into the masses of bathers, priests and hawkers who were preparing for the first rays of the sun. The couple stood very still for a few seconds, and then they moved down towards the sacred waters of the Gaṅgā. The spell of enchantment and mystery was broken by the clanging gongs and cymbals that announce the early morning *ārati* and the beginning of another day.

Now the question is, what had I observed? The child, no doubt, was dying from a liver infection that had caused his body to assume a greyish color and his eyes a jaundiced yellow. One might conclude that the parents had brought their child to die along the banks of the Gaṅgā, after a bath in the most sacred waters in India. Let me, however, go further and analyze this situation from the standpoint of karmic theory as understood by O'Flaherty and others in the excellent series of articles entitled *Karma and Rebirth in Classical Indian Traditions*.[1]

The child, because he was very young, could not have accrued evil or bad (adharmic) karma within his present lifetime. Therefore, his condition was the result of karmic residues that were the product of acts performed in a previous lifetime or lifetimes. This is called, as Potter notes, *prārabdhakarman*, and most writers whom I have read on the subject use the term.[2] No doubt the child's parents were aware of this understanding also. But they were not willing to accept the fatalism that is implied in this understanding of *prārabdhakarman*. They brought their dying son to the banks of the Gaṅgā in order that, by the ritualistic act of bathing, the *jīva* or soul of the boy would be born into a better condition in the next birth. Perhaps they also held the hope that the negative effect of the karmic residues could be reversed by the ritualistic bath. Bathing in the sacred waters of the Gaṅgā is efficacious in itself, as is well known and understood by all. In this case however, an additional element was present. A merit transfer would necessarily take place, as O'Flaherty has pointed out.[3] The parents by participating in the act of bathing and by (perhaps) employing a brahmin specialist to officiate would transfer some of their good karma to their son, thereby negating, or at least neutralizing, much of the effect of the *prārabdhakarman*. The *saṃnyāsin* confronts the couple, and the reversal of the *prārabdhakarman* is assured. The intervention of the *saṃnyāsin* might be understood by the couple as an act of divine grace, a common motif in Epic, Puranic and folk literature. God often appears, at times of distress and tragedy, before his devotees in the form of an old man, or a beggar, or again, a *saṃnyāsin*. The grace of God in his human form reverses the tragic situation. But this is not immediately the case here.

The *saṃnyāsin* was well known in Benares as Svami Maheśvarānanda Tīrtha, the head (*mahānta*) of the Sumeru Matha, which is held to be the fifth *maṭha*, or monastery founded by Śaṃkara.[4] Maheśvarānanda Tīrtha traces his spiritual lineage (*guruparamparā*) back through fifty-nine other *mahāntas* to Śaṃkara, who lived in Benares during his travels to the North. As head of the Sumeru Matha, Maheśvarānanda Tīrtha is the guru to thousands of disciples, ascetic and lay, who hold Maheśvarānanda to be a liberated being (*jīvanmukta*), one who has gained that intuitive awareness (*anubhava*) of the Oneness of reality that brings about release from karmic bondage.

Therefore, as Maheśvarānanda smeared the sacred ashes (*vibhūti*) upon the child's forehead and as he recited a Sanskrit *mantra*, he infused into the sick child his spiritual energy (*tejas*). A transfer of merit took place and the evil (adharmic) karma in the child was displaced by the good or meritorious (dharmic) karma of Maheśvarānanda. In the same manner. Maheśvarānanda infused his spiritual power into the child's father and mother effecting a further merit transfer. Having completed this compassionate act, Maheśvarānanda returned to the Sumeru Matha. Even if the boy were to die later that morning, his parents would know that their son's *jīva* would be reborn to a better, longer life, perhaps as their next son. The act of positive merit transfer carries with it a reinforcement of Hindu faith.

O'Flaherty uses a fluid analogy to describe the process of merit transfer;[5] I prefer Long's electrical circuit analogy, which is more expressive of the Sanskrit meaning of ascetic power (*tapas*) and of spiritual energy (*tejas*).[6] The spiritual current generated by the agent of transfer is grounded in the individual whom he/she touches. This current, like that used in electric shock therapy, can cleanse the individual and radically transform him or her.

One of the best examples of the infusion of spiritual energy by touching is the description given by Svami Vivekananda (Narendranath Datta) of his second meeting with Ramakrishna. I quote it at length in order to make my point:

> . . .I reached the garden somehow and went straight to Shri Ramakrishna's room. I found him sitting alone on the small bedstead. He was glad to see me and calling me affectionately to his side made me sit beside him on his bed. But the next moment I found him overcome with a sort of emotion. Muttering something to himself, with his eyes fixed on me, he slowly drew near me. I thought he might do something queer as on the previous occasion. But in the twinkling of an eye he placed his right foot on my body. The touch at once gave rise to a novel experience within me. With my eyes open I saw that the walls, and everything in the room, whirled rapidly and vanished into naught, and the whole universe together with my individuality was about to merge in an all-encompassing mysterious void! I was terribly frightened and thought that I was facing death, for the loss of individuality meant nothing short of that. Unable to control myself I cried out, "What is it that you are doing to me! I have my parents at home!" He laughed aloud at this and stroking my chest said, "all

> right, let it rest now" . . . All this happened in less time than it takes me to narrate it, but it revolutionized my mind.[7]

For Narendranath this was a conversion experience that radically changed his life, but it must have involved a merit transfer as well. Narendra came to Ramakrishna as a skeptical, British-educated modernist, born into the Kayastha caste and hence of lower caste than Ramakrishna. Through his touch Ramakrishna transformed Narendranath, in the spirit of *Chāndogya Upaniṣad* IV, 4, into a brahmin, in terms of philosophical outlook, values, and status.

The power of touch of a holy person is an archaic concept and is, perhaps, as old as the beginnings of religion. In Navaho curing rites the singer (medicine man) touches the diseased part of the patient's body; then he touches the dry painting, representing the Hero Twins (Navaho deities), on which the patient is sitting. He repeats this act several times until the holy or good power from the deities neutralizes the evil within the patient.[8] I could, of course, cite other examples, but the point that I am making is that the guru, at the folk level, is believed to be one who not only can reverse the effect of *prārabdhakarman* but who also functions as a healer, miracle worker and semi-divine personage possessing all of the marvellous *siddhis* (yogic powers) described in the Epic, Puranic and Yogic literature.

In the *Śaṅkara Digvijaya: The Traditional Life of Śrī Śaṅkarāchārya,* Śaṃkara, the principal exponent of the advaita system is said to be an incarnation of the god Śiva; or at least Śaṃkara's mother "become pregnant with a foetus that was charged with the spirit of the great God Śiva."[9] The *Śaṅkara Digvijaya* narrates one miraculous event after another in which Saṃkara reveals that he is of superhuman or divine origin in the tradition of other folk heroes, especially Kṛṣṇa in the Tenth Book of the *Bhāgavata Purāṇa*.

Śaṃkara, who took the vows of *saṃnyāsa* at age eight, was once sitting in meditation with his guru Govindapāda and other advaitic *saṃnyāsins* near the banks of the Narmada River. Indra, who was disturbed by the intensity of their meditation, caused the monsoon rains to flood the lands for five days, threatening all human and animal life. Śaṃkara uttered a powerful *mantra* and gathered all the flood waters into his *kamaṇḍalu* (water pot), humiliating Indra in typical Puranic fashion.[10]

Later in time, after he had defeated Maṇḍana Miśra the leading exponent of Pūrva Mīmāṃsā, Śaṃkara was challenged by Maṇḍana's wife, Ubhaya Bharati, to debate the art of sexual love. Although Śaṃkara had had no experience of sexual intercourse, he remained undaunted, accepted the challenge and all "in a twinkling of an eye," caused his *jīva* to enter the dead body of a king. As the king, miraculously returning from the dead, Śaṃkara engaged in sexual pleasures with women of the royal court. Then, causing his *jīva* to leave the body of the king, he returned once again to the debate and easily defeated Ubhaya Bharati.[11]

More relevant to the topic of this paper is the story of the learned brahmin Prabhākara, who brought his mute, idiot son before Śaṃkara. The son, who prostrated himself along with his father at Śaṃkara's feet, remained on the ground after his father had arisen. Śaṃkara bent down, lifted the boy to his feet and asked his name. The boy, who at the age of seven had never uttered a word, spoke in elegant terms about the advaitic doctrine of the *Ātman*. Śaṃkara "was surprised to see that this boy had knowledge of the *Ātman* even without the instruction of a teacher, and he blessed him, placing his hands on his head." Śaṃkara then asked permission of Prabhākara to allow the son to take *saṃ*nyāsa and to become his disciple. Prabhākara granted the request.[12]

In terms of karmic theory, the boy was working through his *prārabdhakarman* at the time he encountered Śaṃkara. That is, the son was a mute whom his father described as an idiot incapable of learning elementary education. His present situation was, therefore, the result of karma performed in a previous lifetime or lifetimes. Upon being touched by Śaṃkara, all *prārabdhakarman* was erased and the son spoke as a liberated being, *jīvanmukta*. Although the passage infers that the boy must have possessed "inborn intuitive knowledge," being "touched" by Śaṃkara certainly quickened a process that might have taken another lifetime to work its way through.

In the legends of Rāmānuja, Caitanya, and other founders of the principal vedantic *darśanas*, tales of miraculous events and merit transfers abound, but I shall return to the contemporary scene which is the focus of this paper.

A marvellous story is found in T.M.P. Mahadevan's life history of Ramana Maharshi.[13] In 1903, when Ramana was twenty-four (and already well known throughout Tamil Nadu), Ganapati Sastri, a learned Sanskrit scholar, came to him at Arunacala to gain intuitive insight into the nature of the ultimate reality that he knew from his study of vedantic texts, but that he had not experienced. Ganapati Sastri felt "the grace of the sage enveloping him," but he left Ramana without attaining the experience he had sought. About one year later, Ganapati underwent an eighteen-day meditation in a town (Tiruvorriyur) some distance from Arunacala. As Mahadevan tells the story:

> On the eighteenth day, while he was lying down wide awake, he saw the figure of Ramana come in and sit near him. This was an agreeable surprise. He tried to get up, but Ramana's hand on his head kept him down. Ganapati Sastri felt a strong current pass through his body. He regarded this as an initiation (*dīkṣa*) by touch administered to him by the Master.[14]

Twenty-five years later, Ganapati came before Ramana again and Ramana narrated the same story from his point of view, describing his experience of astral travel.

What happened to Ganapati Sastri was similar to what happened to Narendranath Datta (Svami Vivekananda) upon being touched by Ramakrishna. Ganapati underwent a conversion experience which he called "initiation by touch," but the "touching" must have involved not only an infusion of spiritual energy (*tejas*), but also a transfer of merit. This did not occur at their first meeting in which Ganapati received *darśana* (viewing) of Ramana. At the second (miraculous) meeting Ramana "touched" Ganapati and Ganapati was transformed. Unfortunately, Mahadevan tells us little more than the words quoted above. Not all of those who receive *darśana* of a liberated being participate in the merit transfer that can take place; it is only received by those few whom the guru chooses and into whom the guru infuses his spiritual power. Therefore touching, not viewing, is the cardinal act in the process of *darśana*.

I came to this conclusion at Hardwar in 1977 when I had the privilege of witnessing hundreds of disciples and others "take *darśana*" of Sri Anandamayi Ma, who is regarded by Khushwant Singh as "the most famous" of living saints in India.[15] Those seeking *darśana* of Anandamayi Ma were lined up along the hall on the ground floor. One devotee after another, carrying a garland of flowers or a basket of fruit, moved slowly up the stairs to the small room in which Anandamayi sat, flanked on both sides by her closest disciples. As the devotee approached Anandamayi, he/she bowed before her, touched the ground near her feet (some touched her feet), and presented the garland or the fruit to an attendant. The attendant would give the garland or the fruit back to the devotee, who then left the room. Rarely did Anandamayi Ma touch the garland or the fruit. But in a few cases she would receive the gift herself and place the garland around the neck of the devotee or again, hand back the fruit, lightly squeezing the devotee's hands as she did so. Her selection seemed to me to be totally arbitrary, but of course it was not. She carefully chose those whom she touched and into whom she infused spiritual power.

At Hardwar my wife and I heard a rumor that we had heard before in Delhi: earlier that year Sri Anandamayi Ma had given a *mālā* (sacred beads) to Mrs. Gandhi, who had lost the Prime Ministership to Desai. According to the rumor, Anandamayi Ma had told Mrs. Gandhi, "be patient, wait, and you will return to power in three years." Three years later (some say, on the exact day) Mrs. Gandhi returned to power, and she continued to wear the *mālā*.

To interpret Mrs. Gandhi's return to political power simply on the basis of merit transfer would be a gross oversimplification, but I personally know Indians who think in these terms. Their thinking runs thus: Mrs.

Gandhi had accrued evil (adharmic) karma for wrongs that she had committed during the Emergency; her son, Sanjay, had accrued even more evil karma. Being blessed by Sri Anandamayi Ma and having received the *mālā* from her helped neutralize some of the evil karma. Mrs. Gandhi, three years later, regained the Prime Ministership. The sudden death of her son and the sufferings that were then hers erased more evil karma. Mrs. Gandhi, therefore, has returned to political power in a purer (sattvic) state than she had been in before the Emergency. Whatever else might be said, her support among the masses, according to a well-known political scientist, has never been stronger.[16] In assessing Mrs. Gandhi's political life, the historian or political scientist might gain a deeper insight into her ever growing popularity by acknowledging the belief in merit transfer held by the masses.

Throughout this section I have used materials from the folk tradition or from what Potter (following Marriott) has called "the transactional tradition." Potter argues that:

> The textual evidence itself strongly suggests that there were from early on in India two traditions (at least) which had dissimilar futures— the transactional and the philosophical. For example, it is likely that the changing of the *trivarga* to a *caturvarga*—the adding of liberation (*mokṣa*) to the triad of *dharma, artha*, and *kāma*—represented some kind of attempt to synthesize the two traditions. Quite possibly the addition of the *saṃnyāsin* to the other three *āśramas* represents a similar attempt at synthesis.[17]

Problems arise, however, as soon as the investigator of Hindu traditions looks beyond the textual evidence and experiences India and Indians as a participant observer. From this viewpoint it seems as if philosophers delight in creating dichotomous abstractions which in the reality of lived experienced continually interact with each other, blending and blurring clear-cut distinctions.

In this paper I have identified the *saṃnyāsin* with the guru, although only a few of the total number of *saṃnyāsins* or *sādhus* (ascetics) have been held by Indian society to be gurus of important rank. But it is the guru, both as the ascetic and as the miracle-worker, who stands at the meeting point of the philosophical and transactional traditions. The guru, as the *saṃnyāsin* and living embodiment of his *saṃpradāya* (teaching tradition), traces his lineage (*guruparamparā*) back through a series of gurus to the *Acarya* or founder himself. The guru then, is the living interpreter of a particular philosophical tradition (*darśana*) and as such is regarded by his disciples to be a liberated being (*jīvanmukta*). At the same time the guru, as the miracle-worker, the healer, the one who is able to transfer merit by his spiritual and ascetic power (*tejus* and *tapas*), enters fully into the samsaric world and aids those who are entangled in karmic bondage.

The dichotomy of *nivṛtti* (withdrawal from worldly action) and *pravṛtti* (commitment to worldly action), underlined by Potter and Long,[18] is thus reconciled in the life of the guru who participates in both approaches. A disciple of Svami Śivānanda referred to this ability of the guru to hold both attitudes as "his double-sightedness," meaning that the guru, as a liberated being, sees at the same time both the multiplicity of the world and the ultimate oneness that negates all multiplicity. We who are unenlightened, he added, have difficulty in understanding how this could possibly be, but then that difficulty is part of our *avidyā*, our ignorance. Ultimately we must agree with Śaṃkara who, according to Ingalls,[19] held that *avidyā*, whatever its modality, was not a problem for the enlightened or liberated being, but rather it was a problem for the ignorant person who had asked the question in the first place.

KARMA, SAṂSĀRA AND THE CONTEMPORARY UNDERSTANDING OF THE PATH OF NIVṚTTI

I do not intend to venture into the field of philosophical analysis and critique. Rather, I shall return to the folk level of understanding, to the life histories of gurus in order to determine where the guru "fits" within the samsaric world of karmic bondage as defined in contemporary India. But first it might be helpful to restate the ideal of *saṃnyāsa* or *nivṛtti* as set forth in the *Manu Smṛti*.[20]

Prior to the state of *saṃnyāsa*, or total renunciation of worldly life and action, the "twice-born" male becomes a *vānaprastha* (forest hermit): "when a householder sees his (skin) wrinkled, and (his hair) white, and the sons of his sons" (VI, 2). That is, when the twice-born male reaches the latter years of his life and when his inheritance is assured by the birth of grandsons, then he may depart from his home and begin the first ascetic *āśrama*. The *Manu Smṛti* lists thirty negative and positive injunctions that describe and define the ascetic life of the *vānaprastha* (VI, 3-32).

After an unspecified period as a *vānaprastha*, the twice-born male reaches a state of spiritual purity (*sattva*) and ascetic power (*tapas*). He then abandons "all attachment to worldly objects" (VI, 34), takes the vows of total renunciation (*saṃnyāsa*), and wanders "alone, without any companion, in order to attain final liberation" (VI, 42). Upon gaining enlightenment, the *saṃnyāsin* neither desires to live nor desires to die, but waits "for (his appointed) time as a servant (waits) for the payment of his wages" (VI, 45). That is, the *saṃnyāsin* must wait for final release until his *prārabdhakarman* is burned-up and his death occurs as a natural process with the extinguishing of all karmic residues. The author of the *Manu Smṛti* devotes more than sixty stanzas to the description of the stage of *saṃnyāsin*. Potter provides us with an excellent summary of the vows of *saṃnyāsa* and relates the stage of *saṃnyāsin* to karmic theory:

> In Sanskrit parlance we find philosophers speaking of two approaches to things, the positive approach of action (*pravṛtti*) and the negative approach of withdrawal from action (*nivṛ*tti). The *saṃ*nyāsin is one who takes the latter approach. When a *saṃnyāsin* takes his vows he promises to adopt that kind of attitude. He does not promise to stop moving, speaking, eating, sleeping, and performing natural bodily functions. What he promises to do is to stop thinking transactionally, to "withdraw from the world" in the sense of losing interest in worldly transactions. On Śaṃkara's account, indeed, a *saṃnyāsin* is a *jīvan-mukta*, a liberated person; in him only *prārabdhakarman* is still impelling his body, but no actions, properly speaking, are taking place at all. He has gotten this way because he has realized that transactions and worldly affairs generally are merely projections of ignorance, that in fact nothing like that really happens.[21]

Ideally then, the *saṃnyāsin* is one who, in the latter portion of his life, renounces attachment to worldly objects and to worldly transactions and who adopts the negative approach of withdrawal from action (*nivṛtti*). As such, he wanders about as a solitary ascetic until he attains final liberation or *mokṣa*.

Although the wandering, solitary ascetic has remained the Hindu ideal throughout time, "the solitary ascetic" is only one type or category of ascetic (*sādhu*).[22] The numbers of ascetics who have lived in India at any given time are simply not known, but on the basis of recent statistics an educated guess would place the total number of ascetics at roughly .5 to 2 percent of the population of India, or on the basis of the 1970 census, somewhere between 3,250,000 and 13,000,000.[23] The most important gathering of ascetics is the Kumbha Mela, which takes place every twelve years at Allahabad. G.S. Ghurye says of the 1977 Kumbha Mela that it was "memorable. . .because it drew the largest ever number of people, over ten million, among whom figure European and other foreign sadhus."[24] If three-fourths of that crowd were ascetics, they would nearly equal the population of New York City.

But whatever the total population of ascetics might be, the monastics, although fewer in number than the solitary ascetics, have played a more important role in the development and maintenance of Hindu tradition. Of the monastics, only a relative few would be recognized by informed Hindus as gurus who have made a significant contribution to Indian culture. Śaṃkara provides the classic model of a wandering ascetic who became a monastic and India's most renowned guru. According to the *Śaṅkara Digvijaya*, Śaṃkara renounced the world at the age of eight, took *saṃnyāsa* under the guidance of Govindapāda, and thereafter in his wanderings about India he defeated all opponents in argument, including the Jains and the Buddhists. He is also credited with establishing four monasteries at the cardinal points of the Indian subcontinent, and thus he undercut the growth of the Buddhist Saṅgha as the strongest monastic institution in India. At the folk level Śaṃkara is seen as an incarnation of the god Śiva, who took human birth in order to check the growth of Buddhism and to restore Hindu tradition to its rightful place of dominance.

Śaṃkara therefore, is three incredible individuals in one person; he is the undisputed philosophical debator pictured in his commentaries upon the Upaniṣads, the *Brahmasūtra* and the *Bhagavad Gītā*; he is the folk hero of the *Śaṅkara Digvijaya* who performed merit transfers and miraculous feats; and he is the highly efficient institutional organizer who has been acclaimed by Indian historians and sociologists as the Founder of Hindu monasticism.

But whatever might be said of Śaṃkara, his life, according to the *Śaṅkara Digvijaya*, does not fit the ideal pattern of a *saṃnyāsin* as defined and described in the *Manu Smṛti*. He renounced worldly life at an extremely early age; he maintained transactions with worldly society by entering into debate with learned individuals representing various philosophical positions and by establishing monasteries that have social as well as religious functions. Although his ascetic life was one of constant travel, he did stay in urban areas for prolonged periods of time. In fact, if we were to look at the life histories of other gurus who are held by Indian society to be models of renunciation, we would encounter the following features.

1. In contradiction to the four āśrama theory, as recorded in the *Manu Smṛti*, most gurus took vows of renunciation at an early age. Many of those who joined the *saṃpradāya* or the monastic order associated with Śaṃkara and Advaita Vedānta philosophy took vows of *saṃnyāsa* without having participated in the other *āśramas*, especially the stage of *gṛhastha*, which involves marriage. Those who entered *saṃpradāyas* associated with Ramanuja, Caitanya or other theists often were married (as were Rāmānuja and Caitanya) before taking vows of renunciation. They therefore left their wives and families in adopting an asthetic way of life.

2. Hindu biographers (many of whom are disciples) often write life histories of gurus that identify the guru as an incarnation (*avatāra*) of Śiva, Viṣṇu or Kālī. Thus, in the re-telling of the story, the guru is not subject to karmic bondage, and as O'Flaherty has stated: "the doc-

trine of karma is a straw man. . .it is set up in order to be knocked down."[25] This generalization applies less to those gurus associated with the tradition of Śaṃkara who, because they are advaitins, hold ultimate reality to be nir-guṇa-Brahman and not Īśvara. Nevertheless, they also are depicted by their biographers as incarnations of God. Such was the case with Svami Sivananda who, during his lifetime, emphatically denied that he was an incarnation. In 1960, three years before Sivananda's death, one of his foremost disciples, Svami Venkatesananda, popularized his guru as an incarnation of Śiva in a monumental volume entitled *Gurudev Śivānanda*.

In order to establish these points, let me make a few notes about other contemporary gurus. Ramakrishna was twenty years old when he had his first vision of Kālī at Dakshineswar; at twenty-five he was instructed in Tantric *sādhanā* by the female ascetic Bhairavi; and at twenty-nine, under the guidance of Tota Puri, a Naga ascetic, Ramakrishna took the vows of *saṃnyāsa* and later realized *nirvikalpa samādhi.*[26] Ramakrishna however, had entered into a "token-marriage" with Saradamani Mukhopadyaya when he was twenty-three and she was five. Although Sarada came to live with Ramakrishna much later (when she was eighteen), they acted toward each other as brother and sister rather than husband and wife, and their marriage was never consummated. Mathur, the business manager at the Dakshineswar temple, was the first devotee to witness Ramakrishna as an incarnation, first as Kālī, then as Śiva. That was when Ramakrishna was twenty-four, and thereafter others "saw" Ramakrishna as Hanuman, Rāma and even Rādhā. On his deathbed, Ramakrishna's last words to Narendranath were: "He who once was born as Rama, and again as Krishna, is now living as Ramakrishna within this body—and not in your Vedantic sense."[27]

The story of Anandamayi Ma is similar in certain respects to the life history of Ramakrishna but since Anandamayi Ma is a woman, her life is seen from a unique perspective.[28] From her early childhood Anandamayi was prepared to become the ideal wife and mother. At thirteen years of age she was married to Ramani Mohan Cakravarti (later nicknamed Bholanath, an epithet of Śiva). According to Lipski, Ramani was "considerably older" than she. Anandamayi came to live with her husband when she was eighteen, but her marriage, like Ramakrishna's, was not consummated. In her nineteenth year a neighbor recognized Anandamayi as a divine embodiment of the Mother Goddess Kālī, and thereafter he referred to her as "Ma." During the next few years her husband witnessed Anandamayi in ecstatic seizures that he attributed to a divine presence within her. Lipski notes that: "During that period various Vibhuti (supernormal powers) manifested. She cured people from all sorts of diseases by merely touching them."[29] At the age of twenty-six,

Anandamayi "initiated herself" by enacting the role of a guru and of a *śiṣya* (disciple) simultaneously. A few months later she initiated her husband who became her first disciple. Within the next two years others began to recognize her as an incarnation of Kālī and her reputation and following grew. According to her biographers Anandamayi Ma has allowed many of her closest disciples to see her body transformed into that of Kālī.

Both Ramakrishna and Anandamayi Ma took vows of *saṃnyāsa* early in life; Ramakrishna was twenty-nine and Anandamayi Ma was twenty-six upon entering the path of renunciation of worldly life. Both attracted disciples who held their guru to be an incarnation of the Divine. Therefore, neither Ramakrishna nor Anandamayi Ma were entangled in karmic bondage, yet both gurus frequently entered into the samsaric world of everyday life in order to help their disciples reach a higher level of existence. In time their ascetic disciples established monastic orders with a monastery headquarters and several branches. Ramakrishna never left Dakshineswar but Anandamayi Ma travels constantly from one branch monastery to another. Neither Ramakrishna nor Anandamayi Ma conform to the ideal of the *saṃnyāsin* as pictured in classical Sanskrit literature, yet both gurus would be held by their contemporaries as models of renunciation *par excellence.*

Earlier in this paper I said that Ramakrishna performed merit transfers; in light of the present analysis this statement is not wholly accurate since the spiritual energy effecting the transfer was of divine, not human origin. Thus, Ramakrishna, Anandamayi Ma, and other gurus who are held to be incarnations, infuse those whom they choose to help with a divine spiritual power that operates independent of merit transfer. The guru, as the incarnation of the Divine, is, as Long argues, "another factor" among a variety of causal elements that determine human destiny and that contradict or at least complicate the doctrine of karma in its philosophical presentation.[30] But gods and goddesses in Hindu tradition never touch the earth, their feet always remain slightly above the dust and dirt of the samsaric world.

Nowhere in the biographical literature that describes the life of Ramana Maharshi have I found any attempt on the part of his biographers to identify him as an incarnation of the deity. This is, I am certain, because Ramana Maharshi remained committed to an Advaitan position that places Īśvara within the category of mere appearance. Ramana's interpretation of the doctrine of karma is also in accord with Advaita Vedānta (as summarized by Potter), although Ramana did perform merit transfers.

Characteristic of the other gurus whom I have mentioned, Ramana renounced worldly life at an early age. He was nearly seventeen when he left his mother in Madurai, renounced the world, and took up residence at Arunacala (Tiruvannamalai). Like Anandamayi Ma, Ramana took the vows of *samnyāsa* without the aid or instruction of a guru. According to Mahadevan, in response to a request from his mother to "break his silence" and to return home, Ramana wrote:

> In accordance with each person's *prārabdha* (karma in the past which is responsible for his or her present birth), the Almighty [sic] ordains all things always. What is not destined to happen will not occur regardless of any effort to bring it about; and what is so destined will not cease to happen regardless of the obstacles placed in its way. Since this is certain, it is good to keep quiet.

Mahadevan adds a commentary that nearly fits into an advaitin interpretation of the law of karma:

> But for the sage who has been liberated from all bonds, there is no will and there are no deeds. What others see in his actions are the results of *prārabdha*. Since he stays in and as the Self, what happens in his life does not affect him. This is what Ramana taught in the brief note that he wrote for his mother. That he had left Madurai and was now in Tiruvannamalai, was none of his doing; it was due to *prārabdha*.[31]

Ramana's understanding of the law of karma, of himself, and of his relationship to the samsāric world support Potter's generalizations about the *saṃnyāsin* and *prārabdhakarman* as stated above. In the early part of his ascetic career, from the age of seventeen until he was thirty-seven, Ramana followed the typical pattern of behavior for one who has taken the vows of *saṃnyāsa* and who follows the path of *nivṛtti*. Immediately upon accepting the vows of *saṃnyāsa*, Ramana took up residence in a secluded shrine beneath the 1000-pillar hall of the great temple at Tiruvannamalai. Mahedevan provides a vivid description of Ramana's austerities:

> In the little dark chamber to which the steps lead, there is a Śiva-linga behind which Ramana sat leaning against the wall. Since he rarely came out, he did not know when the sun set or rose, and the days rolled by uncounted. He was living in a timeless Reality. He did not even feel the bites of ants and other insects. The blood and pus that oozed out of his back and thighs stained the wall and the floor. . . .He would sit motionless as was his wont, rarely regaining outer consciousness. Sometimes he had to be forcibly fed, without his being conscious of what was happening. . . .The sage never spoke . . . .He sat on the floor for hours at a time without opening his eyes

> and without being aware of what was happening around him. . . . His hair became matted and his finger-nails grew long and curly. He was the picture of extreme asceticism.[32]

At the age of twenty-one Ramana moved out of the temple complex and up Arunacala hill to Virupakṣa Deva cave, where he lived until he was thirty-seven. Here he began serious study of vedantic texts and in 1903, at the age of twenty-four, he met Ganapati Śastri, whose story I narrated earlier in this paper. Ganapati Sastri was extremely impressed with Ramana's understanding of Advaita Vedānta and it was he who gave the title Maharshi to Ramana. From that time onwards Ramana's fame spread throughout India and the West. In 1916, at the age of thirty-seven, Ramana and his ever-growing "family" of disciples moved further up Arunacala hill and established the Ramanāśrama which remained his residence until his death in 1950. Ramana Maharshi was visited by thousands of people, great and small. Among those were: Rajendra Prasad, the first President of India; Dr. S. Radhakrishnan, the second President of India; authors Arthur Osborne, Paul Brunton and Somerset Maugham from the West; and numerous *pandits* and *sādhus*, among them Svami Sivananda. Everyday at exactly 2:00 p.m., Ramana came before his devotees for *darśana* and for a question and answer period. He "re-entered," as it were, the transactional world of religious and intellectual exchange with his disciples and friends. He also continued to perform merit transfers; the story of his mother's death is an excellent example of merit transfer.

In 1916, when Ramana was thirty-seven, his mother came to the *āśrama* in order to spend her last years with her son. Six years later, in the final hours before her death, Ramana placed his right hand on his mother's chest near her heart and his left on her head until "the soul was absorbed into the Infinite Spirit." Later, Ramana commented upon what had taken place during the ten hours that he had touched and massaged his mother's chest and head:

> Innate tendencies (*vasanas*) and the subtle memory of past experiences leading to future possibilities became very active. Scene after scene rolled before her in the subtle consciousness, the outer senses having already gone. The soul was passing through a series of experiences, thus avoiding the need for re-birth and so effecting union with Supreme spirit. The soul was at last disrobed of the subtle sheaths before it reached the final Destination, the Supreme Peace of Liberation from which there is no return to ignorance.[33]

Through his spiritual energy and power (*tejas* and *tapas*), transferred to his mother by his touch, Ramana had quickened the process of liberation (*mokṣa*) which would have taken future rebirths to accomplish. In that ten-hour period Ramana's spiritual powers had burned-up all of his mother *prārabdhakarman* and thus her soul was absorbed (*samādhi*) into Brahman, not to be reborn again. The body of his mother was buried rather than cremated as is the Hindu custom of disposal of one who has attained liberation.

Ramana remained a strict advaitin throughout his ascetic life. His interpretation of Advaita Vedānta had been given in his initial experience of the absolute reality of Brahman during his early period of austerities, and he never lost that vision, although it was enriched by later experiences. In the last year before his death in 1950, his comments on his condition (he had sarcoma) illustrate his world view and understanding of *prārabdhakarman*. In February 1949, doctors suggested amputating his left arm in order to limit the malignancy of the sarcoma. In response Ramana said:

> There is no need for alarm.
> The body is itself a disease.
> Let it have its natural end.
> Why mutilate it. Simple dressing
> of the affected area is enough. . . .
> It is for us to witness all that happens.

And again, in December 1949, after repeated unsuccessful attempts by various types of medical practitioners, Ramana replied:

> Have I ever asked for any treatment? It is you who want this and that for me, so it is you who must decide. If I were asked, I should always say, as I have said from the beginning, that no treatment is necessary. Let things take their course.

Sometime during his last days Ramana chided his disciples:

> They take this body for Bhagavan and attribute suffering to him. What a pity! They are despondent that Bhagavan is going to leave them and go away; where can he go, and how. . . .Do you know what Moksha (Liberation) is. . . .Getting rid of non-existent misery and attaining Bliss which is the only existence, that is the definition of Moksha.[34]

On April 14, 1950, Ramana Maharshi died.

According to many South Indians, Ramana is regarded as "the most saintly of modern Hindu ascetics," and most informed Hindus would cite Ramakrishna, Anandamayi Ma and Ramana as contemporary examples of those who have followed the path of renunciation or withdrawal from worldly action (*nivṛtti*). Yet these gurus, all of whom took vows of *saṃnyāsa* and all of whom are held by Hindu tradition to be liberated persons (*jīvanmukta*), continued to interact with individuals who were following the path of worldly action (*pravṛtti*). Often these gurus eased the situations of a few of those who were burdened with karmic residues by reducing or eliminating their *prārabdhakarman*. The question remains: were these involvements in transactional relationships "the last vestiges of. . .ignorance" as Potter claims,[35] or were these actions the ability of the enlightened guru to participate on two ontological levels, the Absolute and the relative levels, at the same time? I believe the second explanation to be true and, as I have argued earlier, the guru maintains a "double vision" that allows him/her to "see" in ways that are beyond our understanding, but that is confirmed by mystics of other religious traditions.

CONCLUSION: THE MODERN MYSTICAL VISION AND TRANSACTIONAL RELATIONSHIPS

All that remains is for me to describe what I have called "double-vision" or the new mystical vision that provides the philosophical basis (*darśana*) for the contemporary guru. Here, as before, I shall use material taken from life histories.

Perhaps one of the most significant events occurred in 1884, when Narendranath Datta (Svami Vivekananda) was twenty-one. While sitting among his devotees, Ramakrishna swooned into *samādhi* uttering, "compassion to all creations." After a few minutes Ramakrishna regained consciousness and muttered the following words: "No, it cannot be. It is not compassion for others, but rather service to man, recognizing him to be the veritable manifestation of God!" Hearing these words Narendranath thought:

> How beautifully has he reconciled the idea of Bhakti with the knowledge of the Vedanta. . . .The ordinary impression is that. . . Vedanta demands an utter ostracism of society and humanity and a rooting out of all tender sentiments such as love, devotion, compassion, etc. The aspirant thus goes astray in cherishing an uncompromising hatred towards the world. . . . Whatever may be the avocation of a man, let him understand and realize that it is God alone who has manifested Himself as the world and created beings. . . .Service to

> man, knowing him to be the manifestation of God, purifies the heart, and in no time, such an aspirant realizes himself as part and parcel of God, Existence-Knowledge-Bliss Absolute.[36]

Later in time, Svami Vivekananda and the other disciples of Ramakrishna established the Ramakrishna Mission which is attached to every branch *maṭha* (monastery) and which functions as the service arm of the organization. Service to man or rather to humanity became the cardinal goal for the *saṃpradāya* or teaching tradition that followed in the inspiration of Ramakrishna. Service to humanity is Svami Vivekananda's rendering of *karma yoga*, which is traditionally translated as: "the way of disciplined action;" "the way of unattached action;" or again "the way of dispassisonate action." Svami Vivekananda's interpretation of *karma yoga* therefore, reflects the synthesis implied in Ramakrishna's utterance, "compassion for all creatures" understood in the Vedāntic sense that God "has manifested Himself as the world and created beings." Since another paper in his section has presented a more detailed account of karma and rebirth in the thought of Svami Vivekananda, I shall turn to Svami Śivānanda, whom Bharati describes as Vivekananda's "latter day imitator."[37]

In 1923, at the age of thirty-six, Svami Sivananda took the vows of *saṃnyāsa*, and at Rishikesh a certain Paramahansa Visvananda Sarasvati initiated him into the Śaṃkara-Daśanāmi Saṃpradāya. Prior to that time he had been trained in medicine and had practised for ten years in Malaya. Therefore, even before entering monastic orders, Svami Sivananda had committed his life to the service of mankind centered in the philosophy of *karma yoga*, which Sivananda translates as "the discipline of selfless service." In his autobiography, published in 1958, Svami Sivananda notes of his Malayan experience:

> I spent all my energy and time relieving human suffering by serving the poor and the sick, day and night. . . .This kind of selfless service gave me purification of heart and mind and led me to the spiritual path. . . .I had a special gift from God for the miraculous cure effected in the patients and (they) acclaimed me as a very kind and sympathetic doctor.[38]

Like Ramana Maharshi, once Svami Śivānanda had renounced worldly life he underwent the severest of austerities, wandering about North India in the heat of the summer and bathing at 3:30 a.m. in the ice-cold waters of the Gaṅgā in the winter. Yet Śivānanda balanced the ascetic life of austerities with his commitment to "relieving human suffering by serving the poor and the sick." In 1924, he opened a small, free dispensary at Lakhmanjhula, across the Gangā from Rishikesh, and treated hundreds of wandering ascetics and pilgrims who passed through Rishikesh. In 1936, Sivananda and four disciples established the Sivananda (Ft008)śrama at Rishikesh, and Sivananda created a larger, better equipped dispensary, which by 1950 was enlarged to a two-story hospital and staffed with three full-time doctors.

In words similar in intent to those quoted from Vivekananda above, Sivananda exhorted his ascetic disciples to:

> put forth every effort at attaining ethical improvement to render yourselves perfect for the service of Man. See God in Man. Look upon Man as God. If your conception of God includes the idea that He is All-Pervading, then why can't you see Him in all creatures? What makes you hesitate in translating your belief into action? You will have to give up such notions that He is available only behind locked doors and closed eyes.[39]

In *Practice of Karma Yoga*, Sivananda makes his point stronger; in a section entitled "Sannyasins, wake up" he argues that

> The central teaching of the Gita is Self-realization *in* and *through* the world. . .to serve humanity, God in manifestation, and to think of God, while living in the world amidst various activities is far superior to a cave-life. Selfless work is Yoga. . . .Have the mind firmly rooted in the Self amidst all activities. Then you will become a true Karma Yogi.[40]

The new mystical vision (which elsewhere, following Bharati, I have characterized as the modern mystical vision) is a creative synthesis of absolutistic (Advaita Vedānta) and theistic (in the main, Viśiṣṭādvaita Vedānta) philosophical positions.[41] For gurus such as Vive-kananda and Sivananda, the modern mystical vision combines the oneness of Advaita with compassion for all creatures, the central teaching of the theistic systems, especially the system of Caitanya, who no doubt, was a major influence in Ramakrishna's thinking. Hence *karma yoga*, understood as "service to humanity" or "selfless service" becomes the principal approach to others who, as Ramana Maharshi noted on his deathbed, are trapped in a world of "non-existent misery" that is a mere appearance, a product of their ignorance (*avidyā*). The guru who practises austerities, who is a master of meditational techniques, and who has "seen through" the samsaric world to the one ultimate reality, engages in *karma yoga* to help others attain that mystical vision, or at least make a start toward that understanding. Through "double-vision" the modern guru enters into the world of transactional relationships while at the same time knowing that such relationships are illusory, non-existent from the higher level of absolute knowledge. This mystical insight, this "double-vision" is, therefore, a paradox, but only a paradox for those of us who remain in ignorance (*avidyā*). It is, after all, our problem; the enlightened guru transcends that paradox.

NOTES

1. Wendy Doniger O'Flaherty, ed., *Karma and Rebirth in Classical Indian Traditions* (Berkeley: University of California Press, 1980).

2. Karl H. Potter, "The Karma Theory and Its Interpretation in Some Indian Philosophical Systems," in Wendy Doniger O'Flahergy, ed. *Karma and Rebirth in Classical Indian Traditions*, p. 249.

3. O'Flaherty defines "merit transfer" as "the process by which one living creature willingly or accidentally gives to another a non-physical quality of his own, such as a virtue, credit for religious achievement, a talent, or a power—often in exchange for a negative quality given by the recipient." Wendy Doniger O'Flaherty, "Karma and Rebirth in the Vedas and Purāṇas" in O'Flaherty, ed., op. cit., p. 3.

Unfortunately, O'Flaherty's definition of merit transfer indicates an "exchange" back and forth from the transferer to the "living creature" and from the "living creature" to the transferer. Malalasekere, however, argues that in the case of Sinhalese Buddhism merit transfer "does not in the slightest degree mean that the 'transferer' is deprived of the merit he had originally acquired. . . ." G.P. Malalesekere, "Transference of Merit in Ceylonese Buddhism," *Philosophy East and West* 17, nos. 1-4 (January-October 1967), p. 86.

The cases I shall offer are similar to those used by Malalasekere in that the agent of transfer, the guru, is not deprived of merit, although on some occasions the guru will "take on" the sickness, disease or ailment of the person who is the object of the transfer. Thus, the guru "removes" the evil (adharmic) karma that is the cause of the infliction, but he/she quickly recovers without loss of good merit or dharma karma.

4. Surajit Sinha and Baidyanath Saraswati, *Asceticsof Kashi: An Anthropological Exploration* (Varanasi: N.K. Bose Memorial Foundation, 1978), p. 60.

5. O'Flaherty, "Karma and Rebirth in the Vedas and the Purāṇas" op. cit., p. 36.

6. J. Bruce Long, "The Concepts of Human Action and Rebirth in the *Mahābhārata*," O'Flaherty, ed., op. cit., p. 58. *Tapas*, from the verbal root *tap* "to give out heat" is variously translated as "warmth," "heat" or "fire." *Tejas*, from the verbal root *tij* "to sharpen" is translated as "top of a flame, or ray;" hence, "light," "fire" or "brilliance."

7. Swami Gambhirananda et al., *The Life of Swami Vivekananda*, (Calcutta:

Advaita Ashrama, 1960), p. 48.

8. Clyde Kluckhohn and Dorothea Leighton, *The Navahō* (Garden City: Doubleday & Company, 1962), pp. 213-221.

9. Swami Tapasyananda, trans., *Śaṅkara-Digvijaya: The Traditional Life of Śrī Śaṅkarāchārya by Madhava-Vidyaranya* (Madras: Sri Ramakrishna Math, 1980), p. 15. I treat the folk legends and the life history accounts that I cite in this paper as documents of the faith, and therefore, I am not interested in the historical accuracy or inaccuracy of the accounts. These accounts tell us what disciples or followers of a particular guru *believe* about their guru. The quest for the "historical Śaṃkara" is a complex task, if not an impossible one. See Karl H. Potter, "Śaṃkarācārya: The Myth and the Man," JAAR *Thematic Studies* XLVIII/3 and 4, pp. 111-125.

10. Tapasyananda, op. cit., pp. 51-53.

11. Ibid., pp. 110-124.

12. Ibid., pp. 140-142.

13. T.M.P. Mahadevan, *Ramana Maharshi, The Sage of Arunacala* (London: George Allen and Unwin, 1977), pp. 39-40.

14. Ibid., p. 40.

15. Khushwant Singh, *Gurus, Godmen and Good People* (Bombay: Orient Longman, 1975), p. xii. See also Lily Cohen-Miller, "Notes on the Life of Anandamayi Ma" (unpublished paper, presented at Harvard University, Center for the Study of World Religions, 1980).

16. Bashiruddin Ahmed, "The Prime Ministers of India" (unpublished paper, presented at YWCA, New Delhi, 1982).

17. Potter in O'Flaherty, op. cit., p. 266.

18. Ibid., p. 265. Long, op. cit., p. 41.

19. Daniel H.H. Ingalls, "Śaṃkara on the Question: Whose is Avidyā?" *Philosophy East and West* Vol. III, Number 1 (April 1953), pp. 64-67.

20. G. Buhler, trans., *The Laws of Manu* (Oxford: Clarendon Press, 1886), pp. 198-216.

21. Potter, op. cit., p. 265.

22. See G.S. Ghurye, *Indian Sadhus* (Bombay: Popular Prakashan, 1964). See also David M. Miller and Dorothy C. Wertz, *Hindu Monastic Life: The Monks and Monasteries of Bhubaneswar* (Montreal: McGill-Queen's University Press, 1976).

23. David Miller, "The Guru as the Centre of Sacredness," *Studies in Religion* 6/5 (Summer 1976-1977), p. 532.

24. G.S. Ghurye, "Foreword" in B.D. Tripathi, *Sadhus of India: The Sociological View* (Bombay: Popular Prakashan, 1978). p. vi.

25. O'Flaherty, "Karma and Rebirth in the Vedas and the Purāṇas," op. cit., p. 13.

26. Christopher Isherwood, *Ramakrishna and His Disciples* (New York: Simon and Schuster, 1965).

27. Ibid., p. 303.

28. Alexander Lipski, *Life and Teaching of Śrī Ānandamayī Mā* (Delhi: Motilal Banarsidass, 1977).

29. Ibid., p. 11.

30. Long, op. cit., p. 47.
31. Mahadevan, op. cit., pp. 34-35.
32. Ibid., pp. 24-27.
33. T.N. Venkataraman, *Sri Maharshi* (Tiruvannamalai: Sri Ramanasramam, 1973), p. 24.
34. Ibid., pp. 49-56.
35. Potter, op. cit., p. 265.
36. Gambhirananda, op. cit., pp. 107-108.
37. Svami Agehananda Bharati, "The Hindu Renaissance and Its Apologetic Patterns," *Journal of Asian Studies* 29/2 (1970). See also David Miller, "The Divine Life Society Movement" in Robert D. Baird, ed., *Religion in Modern India* (New Delhi: Manohar Publications 1981), pp. 81-112.
38. Swami Sivananda, *Autobiography of Swami Sivananda* (Rishikesh: The Divine Life Society Press, 1958), p. 11.
39. Sri Swami Chidananda, *Light Fountain* (Rishikesh: The Divine Life Society Press, 1972), p. 87.
40. Swami Sivananda, *Practice of Karma Yoga* (Rishikesh: The Divine Life Society Press, 1974), p. 241.
41. Bharati, op. cit. See also Miller in Baird, op. cit., pp. 106-110.

CHAPTER FIVE

Contemporary Conceptions of Karma and Rebirth Among North Indian Vaiṣṇavas

KLAUS K. KLOSTERMAIER

INTRODUCTION

When I set out, more than twenty years ago, to do an indepth study of modern Hinduism for a European Ph.D. thesis, I concentrated on Ram Mohan Roy's Brahmosamaj, Swami Dayananda Saraswati's Aryasamaj, Ramakrishna Paramahamsa and Vivekananda, Rabindranath Tagore and Mahatma Gandhi, Sri Aurobindo and Dr. S. Radhakrishnan, and similar movements and figures representing reform and renewal and addressing what I considered the crucial problems of India: poverty, casteism, superstitution, illiteracy, oppression of women, intra-religious strife, etc. Both my teachers and I thought that I had prepared myself well to plunge right into action in India.

To my great surprise I found what I had considered modern Hinduism restricted to relatively few centers and a tiny percentage of the population. Age-old Hindu devotionalism, largely unconcerned with what I had thought the life-and-death questions of India, was overwhelmingly alive. I found that reading the *Viṣṇupurānam*, the *Bhāgavatam*, the *Rāmacaritamanasa*, the *Bhaktamālā* and other such wholly un-modern literature helped me much more to understand contemporary Hinduism in Uttara Pradesa than did a study of the *Satyārthaprakaśā*, the *Gītāñjalī*, the *Life Divine* or *The Hindu View of Life*.

In many ways I found devotionalism not only more attractive but also more real than the so-called modern movements. On the surface it was even more different from the world from which I had come as compared to the Western-inspired reform movements. Its complexity proved astounding. Hindu devotionalism could not be called archaic without overlooking its manifest contemporaneity. It could not be described as emotional without denying its solid doctrinal background. It could not even be called devotional if that meant excluding rationality and discipline.

Hindu devotionalism has no normative system[1] but it has definite bases: the immortality of the soul, the eternity of God, the belief in a reward for good deeds and punishment for evil acts, the efficacy of rituals, the necessity of worship. It is strongly person oriented. The ultimate is the 'Supreme Person.' The effects of ritual are personal. The archetype of man's relation to the Absolute is the personal child-parent, or Lord-servant, or love-beloved, relationship. Devotionalism rejects *mokṣa-nirvāṇa*, it does not understand karma as an impersonal absolute law of nature, it continues to respect *bhūtas*, it maintains a fairly realistic idea of heaven, it insists on ritual as a means to provide saving grace and ignores or bypasses a great deal of nontheistic classical Mīmāṃsā, Sāṃkhya and Vedānta.

While *bhaktas* have always been conscious of the otherness of God they have always affirmed the reality of this world too. For devotionalism the world was never wholly false, wholly wicked or wholly contemptible. Neither as a whole nor in any of its parts could it ever be conceived as the absolute opposite to the Divine. In consequence also karma and rebirth never became the ultimate metaphysical horror which they are for the Advaitins. Sin (*pāpam*) and grace (*kṛpa*) are more important categories for the *bhakta* than karma and *jñāna*.[2] Devotion is the overriding concern of the *bhakta*, not rigorous consistency in systematic thought. God's own actions are seen as *līlā*, as unpredictable play—how should human logic ever grasp it? Devotionalism is prepared to accommodate a variety of philosophies as long as they safeguard the central concerns of *bhakti*.

A SUMMARY, ANALYSIS AND EVALUATION OF PARALOKA AURA PUNARJANMĀNKA

The Gitapress in Gorakhpur can be considered to be the most important publisher of Hindu devotional literature in Northern India. Its monthly *Kalyāṇa* (in Hindi) has a regular circulation of over 150,000 copies per month and contains contributions by well-known as well as by unknown authors, learned treatises as well as devotional poems and readers' reports of incidents in their own lives or those of their acquaintances which are designed to prove the truth of their religious beliefs. Every year one of the issues is a book-size special number usually of more than 500 pages, containing either abbreviated editions of classical Sanskrit texts with a Hindi paraphrase or collections of essays and other contributions on some central topic.[3]

The special number of Volume Forty-three (*saura māgha* 2025/January 1969) is entitled *The Beyond and Rebirth.* It contains 280 individual contributions (all in Hindi, with ample Sanskrit quotes), 80 illustrations (many in color) and comprises altogether over 700 pages.[4] As far as I know, it is the most comprehensive recent statement on the theme of karma and rebirth.

Apparently the volume is the fruit of years of systematic effort. The (then) living leaders of all major *saṃpradāyas* and a great number of well-known scholars contributed essays on all aspects of the topic. Each of the five ruling Śaṃkarācāryas is represented with a substantial statement, as is the ruling Śrī Nimbārka Ācārya, the ruling Venkaṭa Ācārya, the Rāmānuja Ācārya of Paṇḍharpur, and famous and authoritative Hindu leaders like M.S. Golwalkar. Gopināth Kavirāj, a legend among scholars already during his life-time, contributed no less than eight separate pieces—several of considerable length.[5] The volume also contains a number of unsigned contributions, summaries of classical texts, popular poetry, and editorials.[6]

While not all of the contributors could be called devotionalists, the thrust of the whole volume is clearly in that direction, as the cover pages and the editor's remarks show.[7] Its spread of topics is designed to demonstrate that the belief in karma and rebirth is not only an integral part of Hindu devotionalism, but an organic part of a world view, intrinsically meaningful and plausible.

Throughout, the devotionalists emphasize their understanding of devotionalism as Sanātana Dharma and quite often they state that belief in rebirth is *the* central article of faith in the Vedas, Upaniṣads, Smṛtis, Purāṇas, and Śāstras.[8] Thus a great many contributions overlap and certain classical texts are quoted over and over again.

To organize the presentation I shall summarize the contents of the volume under ten themes, delineating the central place of rebirth and karma in the whole of a devotionalist's outlook.[9]

1. Mṛtyu

One of the leading ecclesiastics, Anantaśrīvibhūṣita Ācārya Śrī Aniruddhācārya Venkaṭācāryajī Mahārāja Tarkaśiromaṇi offers in his *mṛtyu mīmāṃsa*, after some general thoughts about death as the medium of beyond and rebirth, etymologies of rebirth and an exegesis of references to death in some Brāhmaṇas. Vedic literature, he states, knows 101 deaths: sickness, sorrow, hunger, etc., are deaths against which there are remedies. There is no remedy against the one death remaining. After a survey of Smṛtis and Śāstras he concludes by enumerating a triad of *vivartas*, (*adhibhūta*, *adhyātma*, *adhidaivata*) and *rūpas* (*bhūtarūpa*, *prāṇa*rūpa, abhimānirūpa) of death. His intention is to give a Veda-based interpretation of the nature of death. This knowledge, he asserts, is of utmost importance to those who want to know about rebirth and the next world.[10]

Gopināth Kavirāj's second contribution to the volume deals with *mṛtyu-vivecana*. He clarifies first the difference between *mṛtyu* (death) and *dehatyāga* (shedding of body). Both death and rebirth depend on karma. Dealing with the distinction between *kalamṛtyu* (a death in good time) and *akāla* (untimely) or *upaccheda* (accidental) death and its relation to karma, he suggests that karma is not the only cause for the suffering of the *jīva*. Suffering is embedded in the very structure of creation.

He deals next with the importance of the last thought—a theme taken up by several authors. He suggests that mantras should be recited into the right ear of a dying person. In this context he recommends an *Antyakarmadīpaka* which contains suitable passages from the *Bhagavad-gītā*, the *Mahābhārata*, the *Bhāgavatam*, the *Rāmāyaṇa*, several Sahasranāmas, etc.[11]

Ṭhākura Śrī Sudarśana Siṇha provides a fairly complete summary of contemporary devotionalist beliefs in connection with death and dying. He begins by dealing with the importance of the last thought of a dying person. The context is the doctrine of *prārabdha*: humans alone are *karma-yoni* creatures, all others are *bhoga-yonis*. It is at the moment of death that all *prārabdha* is produced according to which a person enters a *bhoga-yoni*. When a man is about to abandon his body all the *prārabdha* is consumed because the body can no longer serve as a vehicle for *bhoga*. All karma produced by the *jīva* is then located only in his consciousness. From there, by way of the last thought, it is transmitted into the next birth, either in heaven, hell or on earth.

Next comes a discussion of the willful termination of one's life. Ending one's life in an act of self-sacrifice is meritorious (*puṇya*). Taking one's own life in a suicide is a great sin (*mahāpāpa*); it is a fleeing from one's *prārabdha*. To wish for one's own death can assume various forms: it could mean a free acceptance of death when it comes; or choosing one's time; or giving up one's body in accordance with śāstraic injunctions.[12]

Unusual births are considered next with reference to examples of Vaśiṣṭa and Agastya, followed by unusual deaths with reference to Kapila, Caitaṇya and Mīrābāi. In the question of untimely death also, this author asserts that "for a bhakta there cannot be an untimely death."[13]

Several authors stress the great privilege of birth in a human life and thus they encourage their readers to take steps to prolong their life and avoid what might shorten it. Dr. Tribhovanadāsa Danodaradāsa Setha says that longevity in good health is desirable because it enhances the chances to make use of the unique opportunities for good which a human life affords. He describes the daily regimen of the devout Hindu as designed to ensure health and long life and thus to achieve the presence of God. Specifically, there are six means to prolong life: *brahmācārya*, *prānayama*, the blessings of a *siddha*, recitation of OM, use of herbs and elixirs, moderation in eating.[14]

By way of complement Rajīndrakumāra Dhavana offers a list of six *doṣa* which shorten life and are to be avoided: excessive talking, lack of self-control, anger, worry about one's food, ill-will towards friends, excessive arrogance.[15]

2. PARALOKA

Dr. Nīrajākānta Chaudhari, M.A. LL.B. Ph.D., tries to prove the reality of the beyond by referring to visions of the soul outside the body experienced by himself in four instances which are recorded. He also insists that the messengers of Yama, Yama's world and Yama himself are real (*satya*). He goes into details concerning *pitṛyāṇa* and *devayāṇa* which are taken as descriptions of real paths to a real beyond. Knowledge of these *lokas* can apparently be found already in the *Ṛgveda*.[16]

The contribution of Mahātma Anantaśrīvibhūṣita Ṭhākura Śrī Sītārāmadāsa Omkarānanda Mahārāja is interesting from a literary standpoint. He entitled his essay *Pāgala kī Jholī* (A Fool's Bag): *Parama Pada* (Supreme Abode) in the subtitle. It is in the form of a dialogue between Pāgala (fool) and Haladhara (bearer of the Ploughshare, Balarāma). The fool brings up all the objections against the beyond that one can think of while Balarāma cites all the texts from the various holy books that describe the highest world. Quotes from the *Kauśītukī Upaniṣad*, some Vaiṣṇava Upaniṣads, the *Viṣṇupurāṇam*, and the *Bhāgavatam* are brought in to give a complete scriptural picture of Brahmaloka and Vaikuṇṭha. Apparently the author wishes *Bhāgavatam* 3, 15 to be understood as a real description of a real beyond, answering all the fool's questions and doubts.[17]

R.M. Chingale quotes ancient and modern Eastern and Western sources to prove the necessity of the beyond. Referring to an unidentified ancient Sanskrit *śloka* he enumerates the characteristics of persons returning to earth from heaven (charitable, sweet-spoken, devout, fulfilling their ritual duties) and from hell (miserly, ill-speaking, ill-mannered, associating with low people, angry, harsh-voiced) and concludes that these qualities in people, which can be observed, cannot be explained without assuming another world.[18]

A different approach is taken by Yugalasiṁha Khīcī in a contribution entitled "A Scientific View of the Spiritual World." He refers to discussions with American and British scientists in the course of which he develops a scientific understanding of traditional Indian teaching: while all gross bodies disintegrate eventually into molecules and atoms, the subtle body is permanent as the sub-atomic particles of proton, electron and neutron are permanent—an exact parallel to Kapila's *triguṇa* doctrine, which anticipated modern science.[19]

Several substantial contributions dwell on descriptions of Viṣṇu's place as the true *paraloka*. A great number of texts from Epics, Purāṇas, Samhitās and Bhakti-poets are brought together to give a detailed picture of the great beauty of Vaikuṇṭha and to offer advice on how to reach it.[20] Others deal with the supreme beyond under the names of Ayodhyā, Kailāsa, Devīdvīpa or also in a general manner.[21]

3. PUNARJANMA

As is to be expected, the contributions addressing themselves to the topic of rebirth are most numerous. Many authors attempt to prove that belief in rebirth in its present form had been part of the ancient Aryan Vedic heritage, shared by Buddhists and Jains in spite of their rejection of the Vedas and Brahmanism.[22]

Several authors wrestle with the question of how to prove rebirth. While Ācārya Vinoba asserts that it can be proved not only through the *śāstra* but also through experience and inference, ending with the statement that without rebirth life would be *nirasa* (flat, boring, uninteresting),[23] Pandita Devadatta Miśra establishes the case for one kind of proof only: *āptavacana*. *Āptavacana* depends on an *āptapuruṣa*, who is defined as a person free from attachment to the world, beyond affection and hatred. It is by those people that the scriptures have been written from which we have proof of rebirth. Also the stories of people who remember their own rebirths (which have appeared in *Kalyāṇa* on previous occasions) are to be accepted as proof.[24]

Two contributions by Gopināth Kavirāj offer some new perspectives. In the first essay he explains that beyond the three bodies accepted by Vedāntins (*sthūla-*, *sūkṣma-*, *kāraṇa-śarīra*) Vaiṣṇavas, Śaivas and Śāktas know of a *mahākāraṇadeha*. He identifies it with the spiritual body (*adhyātmika deha*) of St. Paul. This body can only be gained through God-knowledge or by an act of divine grace. All residents of Vaikuṇṭha possess such a body, and Viṣṇu's own body is of this nature.

The second essay, although restricting itself to teachings of the tantrik traditions (Vajrayāna, Baüls, Sahajīyas) and their *caricandra sādhana* (consisting of *ādicandra*, *nijacandra*, *unmattacandra*, *garalacandra*), links up with the concern expressed in the first essay. All these *kāyasiddhis*, i.e., disciplines to attain a birth from above, obtaining a spiritual body while still alive, reaching higher worlds, opening of the inner eye (which is not totally metaphorical!), constitute an aspect of rebirth not normally considered.[25] The point which the author wants to make, apparently to underscore the body-mind nature of the human person also in the context of attainment of the highest state, is that liberation and ultimate bliss are as much a matter of the elevation of the body as of the mind.

Ṭhākura Śrī Sudarśana Sinha offers a systematic discussion of the central topic *karma-yoni* and *bhoga-yoni*. He sets out to answer the question why only humans are *karma-yoni's*, given that other classes of beings like *devas, siddhas* and *rakṣasas* are much more powerful and more intelligent. First of all, only humans are *adhaḥśrota* whereas all other *jīvas* belong to *urdhvaśrotas* and *tiryak-śrotas*. The major argument, however, is that offspring are always born *asīkṣita* (untrained, unskilled, raw) and have to learn everything. Man, however, has an infinite capacity to learn. (The author maintains, not quite correctly, that animals do not have to learn anything but are born with all their skills.) Thus the condition of the human child is unique. It is characteristic for the *karma-yoni* that everything, for which there is a *prārabdha*, can actually be done.

By contrast the *devatas* and other *bhoga-yoni's* cannot produce karma in their own *lokas*. Bali, for example, had to come to earth to perform his *yajña*. The creator has destined the earth to be the only *karma-bhūmi* whereas all other *lokas* are *bhoga-bhūmis*. The earth is the proper *karmakṣetra*. *Devas* can do karma only after assuming a human form and appearing on earth: from their blessings or curses no *pāpa* or *puṇya* accrues. The *devas* can see Śiva and Viṣṇu when they assume human forms but they can neither attain to *bhakti* nor to *mukti* and cannot receive *saṃskāras*. Man is distinguished from all other beings through his *dharma-buddhi* (moral conscience). Thus one can proudly assert, "there is nothing higher than man" (*na hi mānuṣāt parataram hi kaścit*).[26]

Swami Asaṅgānanda from the Ramakrishna Mission extends the validity of *punarjanma-siddhānta* beyond the borders of India. After a brief comment on the Cārvāka position—the only one in India denying rebirth and beyond—he gives an exposition of the orthodox Hindu doctrine regarding rebirth, using references to the *Gītā* and the *Kathopaniṣad*. He also offers parallels from Western traditions, refers to Orphic texts, to Pythagoras, Plato, and Gnostics, the Manichaeans and Giordano Bruno. He also finds references to rebirth in the New Testament and quotes appropriate texts.[27]

The purpose of rebirth is the subject of Anilavaraṇa Rāya's contribution. With the help of quotes from the *Gītā*, several Upaniṣads and the *Ṛgveda* he explains that the purpose of rebirth consists in giving the soul a chance to mature and develop into its fullness, something which cannot be accomplished in one lifetime. He also informs us that after death a soul will not immediately reincarnate but will spend some time in the other world before returning to earth.[28]

The individual and social benefits of the belief in rebirth are detailed by Dr. R.C. Mahendra, who emphasizes that the belief in karma and rebirth encourages everyone to perform good deeds now so as to ensure a better future.[29]

Gaurīśaṅkara Dwivedi, in an article on psychology and rebirth, throws in a couple of English quotes in his attack on modern Western behaviourist psychology. In contrast to it, the understanding of psychology as science of the soul in Swami Vivekananda's sense would make it the basic science in the tradition of the *Yogavāsiṣṭa*, helpful to overcome the lower urges which bring about rebirth. This kind of psychology would be an instrument of liberation.[30]

Two contributions elaborate the position of the Rāmasnehīs by quoting from the *Bālabodha* on our topic. They deal extensively with the following eight reasons for rebirth:

(1) the Lord's command
(2) the exhaustion of one's *puṇya*
(3) the need to bear the consequences of a sin
(4) the need to enjoy the fruit of one's good deeds
(5) the need for a change
(6) the need to terminate a previous change
(7) an untimely death
(8) the completion of an incomplete *sādhana*[31]

Descriptions of stories of rebirths—partly from Purāṇas and Epics, partly from reports in newspapers, partly from the writers' own experiences eagerly collected over many years—occupy a prominent place in the volume. They are, in the writers' opinion, unfailing proof for the theory of rebirth. The international spread of the stories from more recent times also supports the argument that rebirth is a universal phenomenon.[32]

4. KĀLA

Since it is commonly asserted that the realm of rebirth coincides with the realm of time, it is not surprising to find some essays discussing the nature of time. A substantial contribution on the subject of *kālavijñāna* is offered by Jayarājī Vaśiṣṭa. It is worth reporting in some detail.

Under the heading *kalatattva* he compares and contrasts time and soul. Both are unborn, undying, immaterial, all-pervading, equal, permanent, unknowable, infinite, beginningless, and unprovable. They differ, however, insofar as *ātman* is self-luminous and illuminating everything else, all-powerful and of the nature of knowledge and experience. Time is a non-intelligent principle whereas the *ātman* is an intelligent principle and the former is proved through the latter: time is not ruling the soul.

Time is one of the aspects of the Lord's *līlā*, of which all except time are undergoing change. The events and circumstances are the measure of time but time does not have form or substance. Time is God's instrument in order to embody himself in many forms.

Under *kāla-vibhajana aura kāla-cakra* the author continues with his parallelism of *ātma* and *kāla*. As one *ātman* is divided into many *jīva-ātmans*, so also the one time is divided into many times from a *paramāṇu* to *mahākāla*. In Viṣṇu's realm, time is timeless.

Under the third and last subheading, *kālacakra se nivṛtti*, we are informed about ways to liberate the *jīva* from the circle of time. Liberation can take place through *jñāna* (the means is *buddhi*; the goal, *ātman*), *yoga* (the means is *manas*; the goal, *murdha jyoti*), *bhakti* (the means is *hṛdaya kā bhāva*; the goal, *bhagavad darśana*), and *niṣkāma karma* (the means is *niṣkāma*; the goal, *niṣkārmatā*). Each of these disciplines involves three steps:

(1) to see *ātma, jyoti, bhagavān, niṣkāmatā* in oneself
(2) to realize them in all beings
(3) to recognize the sameness of them in all

All these *tattvas* are beyond time and the practice of any of these disciplines leads to disentanglement from time.

In a series of steps extending from the cleansing of oneself to others, the *saccidānanda* form of reality appears. Thus time and the cycle of time are finally transformed into *saccidānanda*, the stopping of time for the whole world.[33]

5. KARMA

It may be in its understanding of the nature of karma that devotionalism differs most from other expressions of the Hindu tradition. The most comprehensive statement from the devotional standpoint comes again from Sudarśana Sinha. He begins his dissertation on karma with an example illustrating *karmabhoga* and *karmaprayaścitta*: two saints of Vrindaban are involved. *A* contemplates in his mind the *Kṛṣṇa līlā* with such intensity that he starts laughing aloud. At the same time *B*, who is lame, crawls out from the Yamunā after having taken his bath; *B* is deeply hurt, thinking that *A* is laughing at him and his misfortune. Although *A* had no evil intentions at all the law of karma works in such a way that he is no longer able to re-enter into the joy of *Kṛṣṇa līlā* which had amused him so much. Each karma has to be cooked depending on circumstances of time and place. *Prayaścittas* are helpful to cure the sickness of the mind, namely, sin.

Next the topic of the fruit of karma is dealt with. The author quotes the *bīja-vṛkṣa-nyāya* as the shortest formula to express its essence. He answers the question of why some bad people enjoy a good life while some good people have to suffer by pointing out that last year's work in the fields shows in this year's crop. The kind of life we live right now has been determined in our previous life and not by our current deeds. The author also subscribes to the belief that good deeds done in *tīrthas* bring more fruit than in other places and sins committed in these places bring more severe punishment with them. The same is true with regard to specific times—good deeds done on *ekādasī* are more fruitful than on other days. The fruit of karma also depends on one's status in life: a millionaire giving away a thousand rupees acquires less *puṇya* than a beggar giving away five paise.

The author exhorts his readers to have faith in the future fruit (of rituals performed) as a farmer needs faith in the next crop after having sown his seeds. Our responsibility is to learn how to perform our acts well. He does not accept excuses from people who say that they do not know how to perform *śrāddha, yajña, pūjā*, etc. Also, badly performed rituals bring no fruit. He reassures his readers that acts performed in the spirit of *niṣkāma*, out of pure devotion to the Lord, will never have any bad effects. Several acts can result in one fruit, and one and the same act can have several fruits. One may have to perform a variety of rituals to obtain one favour and a single ritual may be beneficial in many ways.

Another principle to be considered is that each act is counteracted (*pratikriyā*). The author quotes the Indian Golden Rule, *ātmānah pratikūlāni pareṣāṁ na samacaret*, and adds that not only deeds but also thoughts produce such a countereffect. Furthermore, there is a correspondence rule. Misuse of a certain organ is punished with a weakening of this organ, e.g., too much cinema viewing results in weak eyes. This correspondence rule also applies to rebirth: misuse of one's voice in this life will be punished by dumbness in the next; boasting of, and misusing one's physical strength will result in weakness and sickness in the next life; cunning and argumentativeness will show in madness. On the other hand, good use of one's faculties will result in a better rebirth.

The last major question addressed in this essay is how much of the fruit of karma is reaped here in this life and how much in the next? He asserts that it is not true that *all* fruit experienced in this life is the result of the karma of the previous life for some karma will come to fruition in the same life. The gross portion (*sthūla amśa*) of an act results in fruit in this same life. The transcendent fruit (*paralaukika phala*) is not consumed here. Most acts have both visible and invisible fruits. Some acts have only *adṛṣṭa phala*, others, like eating and drinking, have only *dṛṣṭa phala*. However, even these can be transformed into acts that also have *adṛṣṭa phala* by acts of remembrance that the Earth is God's spouse, by offering food to the deity, etc. *Śrāddha-tarpaṇa* has only *adṛṣṭa phala*. Actions like feeding a hungry person, performing *pūjā* in a temple, and doing *sūrya namaskāra* have mixed fruits. The author finally complains about increasing laxity and negligence in the performance of the rituals and admonishes his readers to exert themselves so as to generate for themselves and for others the fruits of good karma.[34]

Gopināth Kavirāj provides a thorough and systematic survey of the different categories of karma with special reference to *kliṣṭa* and *akliṣṭa* karma. There are four kinds of karma present at or before birth: *janaka karma, upaṣṭambhaka, utpīḍaka karma,* and *upaghūtaka karma*. Four more kinds of karma are added to or present after birth: *guru karma, asanna karma, acarita karma,* and *upacita karma*.

Of particular interest is the distinction between *kliṣṭa* and *akliṣṭa* karma. *Kliṣṭa* karma is the result of the activity of *avidyā, asmitā, rāga, dveśa* and *abhiniveṣa*. Their cooking (*vipāka*) takes place through *janma, āyu, bhoga* in a *karmāsaya. Akliṣṭa* karma consists of *śukla, kṛṣṇa, miśra* and *aśukla-akṛṣṇa*.[35]

The process of the cooking of karma (*karmavipāka*) is the subject of an essay by Śāntiprakāśa Atreya, M.S. Ph.D. The body is the *bhogāyatana,* necessary for the fruition of karma as well as the production of karma. The world is a network of karma. He repeats the fourfold distinctions of karma already mentioned above: *śukla* (*puṇya* or *dharma*), *kṛṣṇa* (*pāpa* or *adharma*), *śukla-kṛṣṇa* (mixture of *puṇya* and *pāpa*) and *aśukla-akṛṣṇa* (neither *puṇya* nor *pāpa*). The emphasis of the essay is on *śukla-karma,* which is largely defined in terms of altruistic behavior—not doing harm to anyone and doing good to all brings *puṇya. Kṛṣṇa* actions are those which are socially harmful. With ample reference to the *Gītā,* the *Yogavāsiṣṭha,* and the *Saṃnyāsa Gītā,* the author gives a full exposition of the process of the maturing of karma along traditional lines.[36]

A more modern and polemical approach is taken by Maṇḍana Miśra. He compares the Hindu conception of rebirth with modern evolutionism. Although superficially similar, the two are in fact very different. Darwin's intention was to explain the great variety of living beings through his theory of evolution. By his own admission, he failed to do so. In the opinion of the author, Hindu *karma vipāka* alone is capable of explaining the great variety of forms of life and providing a rational basis for the great difference of fates into which humans are born. The author also deals critically with the idea of a day of judgment and finds that it poses unsurmountable problems. He maintains that Hinduism, in contrast to other religions, keeps the doors to salvation open for all.[37]

Ṭhākura Śrī Sudarśaṇa Sinha devotes a detailed investigation to the notion of *prārabdha,* explaining how *prārabdha* and freedom of action (*karmasvatantrya*) can go together in view of the famous *Gītā* saying (2,47) *karmāṇi eva adhikāraste. . . .* He enumerates seven causes of change of *prārabdha*.

(1) An extraordinarily criminal or meritorious act. According to a *smṛti* text the effect lasts for 3 years, 3 months, 3 half months (*pakṣā*) and 3 days.

(2) A refusal (in this life) to enjoy the fruits of one's meritorious deeds.

(3) Making a gift of one's *puṇya-prārabdha* or of the *puṇya-karma* acquired during the present life to another person.

(4) By means of rituals instituted for that purpose (*savidhi anuṣṭhāna*).

(5) Transfering one's sins to a suitable person.

(6) Through the blessings of curses of *devatā*, *ṛṣi-munis*, ascetics, *siddha-bhaktas*, *satī*, *siddha-yogis*. Such actions, however, diminish or cancel out the *puṇya* of the agent.

(7) Through special intervention of *devas*, *siddhas*, *pītara*, *pretas*; etc.[38]

6. THE BHAKTA DOES NOT DESIRE MUKTI

One of the most striking differences between devotionalists and absolutists is their attitude towards *mukti*. Ācārya Śukaratna Upādhyāya points out the difference between *advaitins* and *bhaktas* which significantly changes their attitude towards karma and rebirth. He marshals numerous quotes from the *Bhāgavatam*, the *Caitaṇya Caritāmṛtam*, the *Bhaktirasāmṛtasindhu*, and the *Rāmacaritamanasa* to point out that the only interest of the devotionalist lies in being near to his Lord, wherever and in whatever form. Vedantic identity would make a meaningful relationship impossible, so it cannot be the *bhakta's* goal. Thus also karma and rebirth are relativized. They are part of God's *līlā*, and not a metaphysical evil. He ends by quoting from Rupagoswami's *Bhaktirasāmṛtasindhu*: "Those devotees who have found rest for their mind in the service of Kṛṣṇa's lotus-like feet will never desire *mokṣa*."[39]

Nevertheless, though the *bhakta* is content to walk with his God during his life and does not desire anything else, the hour of death remains crucial, and several contributors expand on the theme of the importance of uttering the names of God at the time of death. Kānta Śaraṇjī, a specialist on Tulasīdāsa, offers a string of beautiful quotes demonstrating the great power of Rāma's name to dissolve all sin and bring bliss to a dying person.[40] Yājñika Samrāṭ Paṇḍita Śrī Veṇirāmajī Śarmā Gauḍa Vedācārya uses the *Bhāgavatam* extensively to make the same point. His contribution is a good example of the devotionalist's reverent and respectful approach to life. All limbs are given by God and must therefore be used in the services of God. A mouth which is not praising God is useless.[41]

K.V. Bhakade, B.A. B.T., offers a study of the Mahratta Bhaktas (Jñāneśvar, Nāmdev, Eknāth, Tukarām). *Mukti* understood as becoming one with God, is *not* their aim. They want to be with God, see God, serve God forever. This kind of *bhakti*, they contend, goes beyond *mukti*; it is its own goal. The fruit of *bhakti* is *bhakti* itself. *Bhukti* is the fifth *puruṣārtha*, transcending *mokṣa*. For the devotee of God rebirth is the primary *sādhana* to enjoy the pleasure of *bhakti* age after age, and he employs this device time and again.[42]

7. Devotional Practices Designed To Reach The Other World

In spite of the heroic attitude by leading authorities, a great many *bhaktas* do consider rebirth less desirable than heaven and consequently look for means to make sure they will not have to come back to earth.

Śrī Rāmapyārijī Miśra, M.A. (Sanskrit and Hindi), Vyākaraṇācārya, Sahityaratna elaborates on Kṛṣṇa's words to Arjuna (*Gītā* 8, 16b), *Māmupetya tu kaunteya punarjanma na vidyate*, supporting his argument with numerous quotes from the *Bhāgavatam*, the *Śvetāśvatara Upaniṣad*, the *Praśna-* and *Kaṭha-Upaniṣads* to demonstrate that surrender to the Lord brings about cessation from rebirth.[43] Another Kṛṣṇa-word from the *Gītā* (4,9), declaring freedom from rebirth after death as a result of truly knowing Kṛṣṇa's own *janma-karma*, is used by Śrī Kṛṣṇa Prasāda Śarmā Dhīmire, Śāstrī, Kavyatīrtha, Bhāgavata.[44]

Bhāskara Rāmakṛṣṇamācārgyulu explains how the *arcā* of the Lord in the form of his image can be employed to gain freedom from rebirth. After some general remarks concerning the universality of rebirth and the difficulty of obtaining liberation without worship of Viṣṇu, he gives a detailed exposition of *Pancaratra* theology focusing on the *arcā-mūrtis* and the benefit derived from their worship. His major authority is the *Brahmāṇḍapurāṇam* from which he quotes extensively.[45]

An essay entitled "Sādhana to Obtain the Nectar of the Other World," whose author did not give permission to publish his name but who modestly allowed his contribution to be subtitled, "Greatly Important Advice by a Perfect Being Established in Brahmā Free from Pain," issues these commandments to *bhaktas*:

(1) Serve the cow and brahmins.

(2) Do not eat and drink in the house of a married woman, not even if she is your own daughter or niece.

(3) Do not marry your child outside the *gotra* of your own *jāti*.

(4) Do not speak contemptuously of temple, image, pipal-tree, cow, *sādhus*. Keep them always on your right side.

(5) Do not commit a sin near the holy rivers Ganges, Yamunā, Sarayū, Triveni, etc. Do not spit into them, do not wash yourself in them with soap or oil, do not evacuate into them. Take your bath in them with faith and devotion.

(6) Do not look with wicked eyes on another woman. Do not have any relations with another woman. For a *sādhu* even to look at the picture of a woman is sinful. For a *bhakta* to talk to another woman is sinful.

(7) Do not eat meat, fish, eggs and do not drink liquor. Give up onion and garlic, turnips, biscuits, ice, tea, Coca-Cola, *bidī*, and cigarettes.

(8) Do not watch films. Do not watch boys and girls dancing together. Do not watch theater performances which might increase your attachment to sense objects.

(9) Do not read dirty novels, slippery stories and atheistic books.

(10) Do not eat food prepared in a hotel or food prepared by cow-eaters or unchaste women. Eat only at home, carefully, etc.

(11) Do not eat sweetmeats.

(12) Do not eat a *paisa*'s worth of alms.

(13) Do not consort with enemies of *dharma*, cows or brahmans, atheists.

(14) Do not follow the customs of the *mlecchas*. Do not urinate while standing. Do not dress in western fashion.

(15) Never remove the *śikha* and the sacred thread. Always recite the names of Rāma and Kṛṣṇa.

(16) Do not cause trouble to any living creature.

(17) Do not dishonour mother, father, or guru.

(18) Do not disobey the *Śāstras*.[46]

Pandit Baladeva Upādhyāya, M.A. D.Litt., deals with a peculiar Vaiṣṇava belief expressed in a sentence whose origin I was not able to trace: *Rathastaṁ dṛṣṭvā punarjanma na vidyate*. He first gives a literal explanation. A person who sees Śrī Kṛṣṇa carried in the chariot at the public procession in Jaganāthpūrī does not have to undergo any further rebirth. Besides this material exegesis there is another spiritual one. With reference to *Kaṭhopaniṣad* 1,3,3 he explains the *ratha* as the body and the *vāmana* as the soul.[47]

Śrī Mādhava Goswāmi in an article, "Bliss Beyond and Vallabhācārya," makes the point that if a *bhakta* after *śaraṇāgati* commits a sin, he has to atone for it and suffer its fruit before becoming eligible to enter into the Lord's abode. According to him it is the widespread lack of faith in the world beyond which causes all the social unrest in our times.[48]

8. ŚRĀDDHA AND TARPAṆA

Throughout it has been emphasized that devotionalism as understood by the great majority of its adherents is not a sectarian movement or a particular theological school of Hinduism but mainstream Hindu religion. This becomes clear also in the contributions which deal with *śrāddha* and *tarpaṇa,* common Hindu practices with Vedic sanctions and Śāstric regulations.

Rājendrakumar Dhāraṇa interprets *śrāddha* as charity to be upheld in the face of the contemporary "me-alone" mentality. He collects his arguments for the need to perform *śrāddha* mainly from the *Viṣṇupurāṇam. Śrāddha* can help the deceased in a human rebirth, in an animal rebirth, and in heaven. The sun's rays act as vehicles for the transport of *puṇya.* The author uses the ingenious modern parallel of money sent through the postal money-order arrangements to benefit distant receivers. When *brahmins* are given food by way of *śrāddha,* the *pitṛs* take the subtle substance of it.[49]

Vallabhadāsa Binnani Vrajeśa deals with the mystery of *śrāddha-tarpaṇa.* After general remarks to the effect that the Hindu *sanātana dharma* is the best in the world, superior to all other religions, he endeavours to offer a scientific explanation of *śrāddha.* During *pitṛpakṣa* the moon is closest to the earth, the attraction is the greatest and therefore, the transmission is easiest. He distinguishes the materials which constitute the *piṇḍas* as hot and cold electricity. Under hot are listed oil and milk, under cold, rice and barley, and tulsi leaves contain both. While ordinary speaking produces cold electricity the recitation of Vedic texts produces hot electricity! This provides the vehicle for the transmission of *śrāddha.* Kuśagrass insulates the *piṇḍas* and hinders their electricity from entering into the earth. The transmission of the subtle substance of *Śrāddha* to the subtle bodies of the *pitṛs* is explained as an analogue to radio-transmission. Only the deceased have the capacity of being receivers, not the living. Television provides the analogue to explain the omniscience of the *pitṛs* who freely communicate throughout the ether.[50]

An unsigned half-page contribution emphasizes the absolute necessity of *śrāddha.* A modern note is brought into it by comparing the way in which the *puṇya* from *śrāddha* performed for someone already released returns to the giver in the same way in which a money-order returns to the sender if the addressee is no longer found at the address indicated.[51]

Ācārya Gadadhāra Rāmānujan Phalahari's contribution *Śrāddha in Gāyā* mentioned, together with recitation of *Gītā,* the use of Gaṇgā water and cow-service as the means to gain rebirth from an existence as *preta.* He draws on a number of experiences to document one by one the truth of the assertion.[52]

Several contributions are devoted to the theme of preparing for death, all of them designed to make sure that one would reach Viṣṇu's realm without being reborn, without having to lead a *preta*-existence, or having to undergo punishments in Yama's world.

9. YAMA AND HIS REALM

Many contributions deal with Yama and his realm, where those who have to atone for sins committed in a human life have to dwell. There are lengthy extracts from the *Nāradapurāṇa*,[53] the *Brahmapurāṇa*,[54] the *Skaṇḍapurāṇa*,[55] and the *Bhāgavatam*[56] which contain all the details of eschatology accepted by most Hindus: a description of Yama's messengers who come to fetch the soul of the dying sinner, the judgement by Yama, and the various tortures meted out to each category of sinner.[57] To reinforce the texts, the editor has added illustrations of a great number of devils lustily cutting up sinners, boiling them in oil, throwing them headlong into cesspits, piercing them with spikes, etc. The artist gives a modern touch to some of these scenes. In one particular hell, where sins are punished by sawing off the offenders' limbs, Yama's servants use what looks like electrically powered circular saws of huge dimensions. For the rest these modern Hindu drawings resemble in a great many details Christian medieval and equally horrible woodcuts of the punishments in hell.[58]

There is little which contemporary devotionalists could add to these descriptions. The few original contributions under this heading restrict themselves to a reaffirmation of the Puranic materials and eye-witness accounts of Yama and his realm. Bhakta Śrī Rāmaśaraṇadāsa describes an incident related to him by a person who bodily saw the messengers of Yama and was terribly frightened.[59] The same author offers in a separate contribution a number of cases of people who returned after having seen King Yama, that is, the accounts of people who had the experience of dying and came back to life again.[60] All cases are dated and the names of the persons are given. Not all of the witnesses are Hindus but the experiences described are the same. Some had been guided through Yama's realm and there they had met former acquaintances.

A number of articles deal with appearances of deceased persons. Exact descriptions of such occurrences are given, even dialogues with some of them are verbally recorded, and ways to establish communications with them are discussed.[61]

A related issue is the entering of a soul into other bodies, something defended by several writers possessing Western academic qualifications.[62] Religiously more relevant however is a half-page of advice on how to save oneself from hell and make one's way to heaven.[63] Combined with the basic Hindu moral exhortations are some typical Vaiṣṇava items of diet and worship. The essay also explains how to ensure the entrance of a good soul into the womb at the time of conception.[64]

10. PRETAYONI

One of the more frightening prospects for devotionalists is the possibility of being reborn in a *pretayoni*. Belief in spirits, the restless ghosts of deceased persons who for some reason or other are neither in heaven nor in hell, is fairly universal in India. Our volume contains a substantial number of contributions which recount incidents of such spirits who appeared to the living. Quite often the spirits appeal to perform certain rites on their behalf, in order to right some wrong which they had no time to do on earth, or otherwise to help them to better their lot.

An unsigned article enumerates the causes which lead to rebirth as a *preta*, and adds a number of means to bring liberation to them. Someone who entertained intense aversion to or hatred against another person, or intense attachment or possessiveness is born as a *preta*. Persons for whom the last rites were not performed or not properly performed are reborn as ghosts. Those who perform spirit-worship in this life, are given to *tāmasik sādhana*, consume *tāmasik* food and drinks, and follow *tāmasik* rules of life will be *pretas*. Drinkers of liquor, thieves, dacoits, murderers, adulterers, offenders against śāstric rules, and irreligious people are reborn as ghosts. People committing suicide will be *pretas*. A person causing the death of someone through another will also be reborn as a *preta*. Foremost among the means to save oneself from such a rebirth are the performance of *śrāddha*, the *Śrīmad Bhāgavad Saptāha*, the recitation of the *Viṣṇusahasranāma*, the *Gāyatrī*, *kīrtan* of the Holy Name, the repetition of the twelve-syllabled mantra (*Om namo bhāgavate vāsudevāya*), *śrāddha* in Gāyā or in other *tīrthas*.

People who lead a virtuous life, do good deeds, follow the injunctions of the *śāstras*, pay respect to father, mother and guru, care for the welfare of all living beings, and worship the Lord will not be reborn as *pretas*. This is one more reason to exhort the reader to repeat ceaselessly the name of the Lord and remember his name. A *bhakta* will never be a *preta*!

The writer reaffirms that *pretas* appear in reality and not just in the imagination of certain people. Mostly, however, they appear to immoral and unholy people. They do not come near those who regularly perform their ritual worship and lead a holy life. The appearance of the *pretas* is due to some unfulfiled *vāsanā*.

If one is troubled by a spirit or if a spirit has appeared, one should humbly ask him: Who are you, What do you want? If he answers, one should fulfill his proper wishes. Food, cloth, and water should be offered to the dead souls without their asking for it. Improper and sinful requests should be denied. In order to rid someone of an affliction caused by a *preta*, one should use the following device: One should perform continuous *kīrtan* of the name of the Lord in the room or house of a person who is afflicted by a *preta*. Water, blessed with the *Gāyatrī mantra* should be sprinkled everywhere in the house. A small quantity of the water should be given to the afflicted person to drink at dawn and dusk and sprinkled at the bed. The *Gāyatrī mantra* should be recited into his ear. A little of the blessed Gaṅgā water should be put on his forehead at the time of bath. He should be made to listen time and time again to the *Gītā* 11,36: "*sthāne hṛṣikeśa*. . . ." The verse should be inscribed on several plaques fixed to walls. The *yantra*, represented below, should be drawn with red chalk on birchbark, on a Tuesday, and with the above *Gītā* verse written underneath. During the burning of incense, it is to be put into a copper amulet and tied to the patient. Every day blessed Ganges water must be sprinkled over him and given him to drink.

24	31	2	7
6	3	28	27
30	25	8	1
4	5	26	29

There are many such *yantra-mantras* which are a safe means to get rid of oppression by spirits. But there are very few people who know them and nowadays they are found in only a few places.

The author mentions that there is also an Ayurvedic cure for spirit-affliction, making use of different kinds of incense. Some *devasthānas* specialize in these things but he warns that much cheating is going on in this area. He adds that also reciting the *Mahāmṛtyuñjaya*, the Śrī *Hanumāncalisā* and reading the *Bajarangabana* can banish *preta* afflictions. He concludes with an exhortation never to perform worship of *pretas*. One also should never try to obtain a favour from *pretas*. All this is *tāmasik*. As a result of it one forgoes the supreme goal and obtains an existence either as *preta* or in a hell.[65]

Two lengthy articles, one by Dr. Vāsudeva Kṛṣna Caturvedi, the other by Swami Jagahnāthācāri, deal with the *Śrī Bhāgavata Saptāha* as means to bring release from *preta*-rebirth. By way of general introduction, Dr. Caturvedi describes the rebirth in a *pretayoni* as one in which the *jīva* does not find any peace. *Pretajīvas* are always in pain, unsatisfied, full of fear and rage, desire, anger, and greed. They take up their abode in desolate places, in unclean and unholy locations like burial and cremation grounds. It is extremely difficult to find release from it. It is a *pāpayoni* and if it were not for the special grace of the Lord, *pretas* would have to live forever in this condition.

The power of the Lord is manifested in the words of the *Bhāgavatam*. Quoting extensively from the *Bhāgavatam Mahātmyam*, the example of Gokarṇa is cited. He liberated his brother Dhundhukara from a *preta* existence through a performance of the *Bhāgavata Saptāha*, revealed to him by Viṣṇu, after all the traditional means like pilgrimages, *japa*, etc., had failed.

The body of the article describes in great detail the way in which the *Bhāgavata Saptāha*, the foremost means to liberate someone from a *preta-yoni* (liberating from even the blackest sins) is to be performed. The week-long recitation is to begin at sunrise and go on until late afternoon with two hours rest permitted around noon. Ideally the performer should not eat any food at all during this time. If he has to eat, *ghī* and milk should be given. The performer has to be an initiated *Viṣṇubhakta*, he must observe *brahmācārya* during the week, sleep on the floor and observe a number of dietary restrictions. He must purify himself of feelings of lust, anger, and greed. Also, a great many restrictions apply to the audience; no woman in her menses, no *mleccha*, no person from a low caste, no uninitiated twice-born, no atheist or Brahmin-hater can be admitted. After completion, *prasād* is to be distributed, garlands are to be handed out and all should join in a festive *saṃkīrtan* (*karma ke śānti ke liye*). A single person should hold a *Gītā* reading on the next day, a householder should perform a *havan*, during which one *śloka* each from the 11th *skandha* of the *Bhāgavatam* should be recited while pouring honey, *ghī*, oil, etc.

The feeding of twelve Brahmins and the offering of a cow and/or gold should conclude the ceremony. If the performer is wealthy, he should have a throne made from three *tolas* of gold, place on it a beautifully written copy of the *Bhāgavatam*, wrapped in a beautiful cloth, pay homage to it and make a gift of it all to a Jitendra Ācārya. The *Bhāgavata Saptāha* is capable of freeing from the bonds of birth and death, cancelling all sins and fulfilling the four *puruṣārthas*. It unfailingly saves one from a *preta-yoni*.[66]

The volume concludes with a paraphrase of some sections of the *Brahmapurāṇa* under the title, "Who is Free from the Bondage of Karma and goes to Heaven?" providing a portrait of the ideal devotionalist. He is described as a follower of the true *dharma*, serene and without any doubt, helpful to everyone, kind, and clean. He is restrained in thought, word, and deed. He has acquired auspicious karma, has never injured a living being, extends his love to all. The lengthy list of virtues and merits does not contain anything that has not been mentioned before, but it again helps to underscore the idea that devotionalists to not consider themselves a sect, or members of an exclusive church, or as a group of people apart. They understand their devotionalism as true humanism, as the flowering of natural religiosity, as an expression of the *Sanātana Dharma*.[67]

CONCLUSION

While obviously not always in full agreement with each other on matters of systematization and classification, and while quite openly advocating a variety of practices to counteract the effects of sin, the number of basic common assumptions and the practical concord as regards ritual practices emerging from a survey of the contributions to *Paraloka Aura Punarjanma* is quite astonishing.

Devotionalism is built upon an implicit faith in the fairness of the world order: the present is the fruit of the past; it also is the preparation for the future.[68] Regardless of what has happened, the future has to be taken care of the same way in which a farmer, in spite of crop failures in the past, goes out in spring and does his work.

Far from inducing a careless or fatalistic attitude towards this life, the belief in rebirth implies that each person has to achieve as high a moral perfection as possible in order to avoid suffering in the next existence. This is certainly a powerful incentive to realize high ethical values. It also satisfies a sense of justice. Belief in rebirth actually suggests that human perfection is a question of a process of maturing as a whole.

The ease with which devotionalists use scientific and modern proofs for their beliefs does not, in my opinion, suggest that modern science supports their views. The two worlds do not really touch. We need not anticipate an Indian parallel to the recent Western conflict between religion and science. There are, to be sure, stridently anti-modern-science voices to be heard from the devotionalist camp (Swami Bhaktivedanta and his ISKCON as appearing in the *Back to Godhead* magazine on many occasions) and devotionalism with its supernatural realism is intrinsically opposed to the modern project in which man's reason alone is lord of a fairly abstract world. Devotionalism is seeking truth, not making it; it waits to be transformed by the Lord rather than attempting to transform the world. The primarily practical concern with 'crossing over safely' and 'earning God's grace' has been in the way of a construction of a complete scientific theology. Devotionalists contend that the philosophical categories used by theology are not large enough to comprise the essentials of their faith. To use a metaphor, Vedānta as a philosophy of the *jñānamārga* provides a skeleton, a structure to which, in a logical fashion, are added the various elements of the Way of Knowledge.

Devotionalism provides a receptable for *bhaktimārga*. While excluding certain positions and practices, it does not give a precise place to its positive content within the open space it provides. Its fairly loose organization, again in contrast to the centralized Advaita, the co-existence of a large number of important branches, sects, and movements is not accidental.

Devotionalism as ordinary religion offers a parallel to ordinary language philosophy or ordinary life sociology or history. It is made up of the accumulated practical religious experiences of many generations of ordinary people, a religion found necessary for daily life, in real life. This can be refined and made more or less sophisticated, but it cannot be replaced or argued out of existence. Its contradictions reflect the contradictions of real life. It is concerned with life in its fullness, its integrity, with all its dimensions, whether these are accessible to critical rationality or not. The primacy of life over thought is upheld without any apology.

Devotionalism easily absorbs cognate systems. It has no difficulty incorporating foreign-born saints and extra-Vedic scripture, but it instinctively rejects non-devotional positions, even if they come with a claim of being indigenous and Vedic.

At its core there is the acceptance of the Lordship of the Divine, the power, authority and salvific will of the Supreme. It is mediated by all human faculties, not only (and not even primarily) through the analytic/synthetic mind. It is the religion of those who have to care for a family, a house, a farm, a business, a temple.

As ordinary-life-religion it is cumulative and repetitive. Time and again the same kind of divine help is needed, time and again the Lord appears. Seen from this perspective the history of mankind becomes a *Heilsgeschichte*. In it salvation of man by God constitutes the most important objective individually as well as collectively.

Devotionalism is a religion both for his life and the next. Its wisdom is a wisdom for life here and hereafter. Its practice ensures well-being on earth and in heaven. It is the religion of the Lord and this world is the Lord's as well as the beyond.

NOTES

1. I am aware, of course, of the devotional systems of Rāmānuja, Madhva, Caitanya, etc. While I consider them certainly as important expressions of devotionalism I cannot consider any of them as normative. Devotionalism existed in genuine form long before these systems. It comprises many facets not considered in them and continues to express itself in new ways. While Ramanujists and Madhvites and Caitanyites, etc., have their controversies over certain specific points of Rāmānuja's, Madhva's or Caitanya's systems, they all agree on the bases which I tried to identify, and so do those devotionalists who have no affiliation with any of the major theological schools.

2. Caitanya Mahāprabhu's Śīksāṣṭakā (*Caitaṇya Caritāmṛtam* III, 20, 3-45) offers a description of the true Vaiṣṇava as one "who is humbler than a blade of grass, has more endurance than a tree, is free from self-conceit while honouring others, who wishes neither for wealth, lineage, beauty nor knowledge but is longing only for causeless love (*ahaituki bhakti*) in life after life." Only a devotee can generate devotion in another person.

Rūpagoswāmi in his *Bhaktirasāmṛtasindhu* takes care to exclude karma and *jñāna* from his definition of *bhakti*: anyābhilāṣitaśūṇyam jñānakarmādyanāvṛtam ānukūlyena kṛṣṇānuśīlanam bhaktiruttamā (I,1,11).

A famous hymn by Narsī Mehtā, much loved by Mahatma Gandhi (it is No. 102 in his *Ā śrama bhajanāvali*) also defines a Vaiṣṇava without any recourse to doctrine (in particular, without any reference to karma and rebirth).

vaiṣṇava jana to tene kahīye, je pīḍa parāī jāne re;
paraduḥkhe upakāra kare toye, mana abhimāna na īṇe re.
sakaḷa lokamāṁ sahune vaṅde, niṅdā na kare kenī re;
vāca kācha mana niścaḷa rākhe, dhana dhana jananī tenī re.
samadṛṣṭi ne tṛṣṇā tyāgī, parastrī jeṇe māta re;
jihvā thakī asatya no bole, paradhana nava jhāle hātha re.
moha māyā vyāpe nahi jene, dṛḍhavairāgya jenā manamāṁ re;
rāmanāmaśuṁ tīḷi lāgī, sakaḷa tīratha tenā tanamāṁ re.
vaṇalobhī ne kapaṭarahita che, kāma krodha nivāryā re;
bhaṇe narasaiṅyo tenuṁ darasana karatā, kuḷa ekotere tāryāṁ re.

3. Its English counterpart *Kalyāṇa Kalpatāru* (circulation unknown to me) is not an English version of the Hindi *Kalyāṇa* but a completely different journal, devoted, however, to the same objective. Its special numbers too are completely different from the Hindi special numbers.

4. The February issue (XLIII/2), a regular number of 58 pages, is labelled *Pariśiṣṭāṇka* (supplementary). It contains—besides some of the regular features of the magazine—another 13 articles on the theme of *Paraloka Aura Punarjanma*, some of them continuations of essays begun in the Special Number.

5. *Jīvanmukti, videhamukti, kaivalya aura pūrṇatva* (pp. 80-85); *Mṛtyu vivecana* (pp. 94-97); *Gati-vijñana Aura Samuccaya-rahasya* (pp. 97-98); *Deha-vivecana* (pp. 133-141); *Kāyasiddhike prakāra* (pp. 144-151); *Kāla-vivecana* (pp. 215-219); *Karma kā śreṇī vibhāga aura kliṣṭa-akliṣṭa karma* (pp. 237-242); *Śvetadvīpa-Mahāgoloka* (p. 386).

In the context of this conference only a brief summary of these very substantial scholarly papers can be given. I intend to provide a full translation of these and other papers somewhere else.

6. A contributor who signed as Su——(Ṭhākura Śrī Sudarśaṇa Sinha) seems to represent the official standpoint of Kalyāna. His four lengthy and systematic pieces (*Mṛtyu para kucha vicāra* [pp. 106-114]; *Karmayoni aura bhogayoni* [pp. 142-144]; *Karmasambandhi vicāru* [pp. 224-250]; *Prārabdha vicāra* [pp. 730-736]), summarize the most important doctrinal positions and, coming as they do after other contributors' opinions, correct them (without explicitly referring to them).

7. The front cover shows Viṣṇu surrounded by the cosmic egg inscribed with the names of the fifteen *lokas* (from *pātala* to *paramadhāma*). The inside cover carries the usual doxologies to all major deities, prominently the 28 syllable *Hare Kṛṣṇa* mantra and a couplet of Tulasidas a entitled *Jīvana ka phala*.

The frontispiece, a color print, illustrates in a series of vignettes the ways of sin punished in hells, and the ways of devotion rewarded by the vision of Viṣṇu. A second full-page color print facing the first page of the journal (after the index) again shows Viṣṇu standing inside a stylized lotus containing symbols of sun, moon and fire. It carries the caption, *Sūrya-candra-agni ko sūryatva candratva agnitva denevale bhagavan*, "The Lord who gives to sun, moon and fire their sun-ness, moon-ness and fire-ness." The first page, identifying the issue in the manner found in all regular issues, carries a short hymn in the three *ślokas* to *Sarvaprakāśaka jyotirmaya bhagavān* taking up the theme of the color picture. The following page carries the text of *Kaṭhopaniṣad* 1,2,20,23,24 and 1,3,7,8,9, with Hindi translation under the caption, *Janma maraṇa rūpa saṃsāra se chuṭṭakāra bhagavān ke paramapāda ko kauna prāptā hotā hai?*, *"Who will obtain* the supreme abode of the Lord who liberates from the world of birth and death?" On the opposite page, numbered *ga*, we find a lengthy poem in seven stanzas by Paṇḍita Rāmanārāyaṇadatta Śāstrī 'Rāma' Sahityācārya, entitled *Amṛtaloka* in praise of Rāma, Kṛṣṇa and Rādha.

8. "Rebirth is the foremost principle of *sanātana dharma*. Its truth is promulgated in Vedas, Śāstras, Upaniṣads, Smṛtis, Purāṇas, etc." This statement (p. 319) is echoed in many contributions.

9. As Yugalasinha Khācī, M.A., Bar-at-Law, Vidyāvāridhi says in his *Adhyātma loka kā vijñānātmaka āloka* (pp. 616-619) these four *siddhāntas* are at the root of Indian culture: *ātman, karmaphala, paraloka, punarjanma*.

10. Pp. 14-19.

11. Pp. 94-97.

12. Bhakta Śrīrāmaśaraṇadāsajī deals (pp. 534-536) with the topic *icchā mṛtyu* by way of examples and Paṇḍita Śrīmuni Devarājajī Vidyāvācaspati adds a short note (p. 536) on delaying death.

13. *Mṛtyu para kucha vicāra*, pp. 106-114.

14. *Ā yuṣkāla kā rahasya yā āyukī abhivṛddhi*, pp. 130-132.

15. *Ā yuko kāṭanevāle chaḥ doṣa*, pp. 121-123. The point of ill will is dealt with by Dr. Sampūrnānda Pāṇḍeya, M.A. Ph.D., pp. 747ff. *Śāpa aura varadānase āyu nāśa aura āyu vṛddhi.*

16. *Paraloka, punarjanma aura mokṣatattva*, pp. 180-188.

17. Pp. 38-48.

18. *Janma-mṛtyu, paraloka aura punarjanma kā svarūpa tathā rahasya*, pp. 200-206; 682-688.

19. See note 9.

20. Paṇḍita Oṃkāradatta Śāstrī, *Śrī bhagavān kā divyadhāma evam uskī prāpti* (pp. 375-376). Swāmi Śrīnirvikarānandajī Saraswati, *Parama dhāmakā varṇana* (pp. 376-378). Rāstrapatipuraskrita Dr. Śrīkṛiṣnadattajī Bhāradvāja, M.A. Ph.D., *Śrivaikuṇtadháma aura uskī prāpti* pp.379-385). *Śrīmahavīraprasādajī Śrīvastava Anuraga, Paramapāda athavā paramadhāma vijñāna* (pp. 640-651).

21. Mānasa-tattvānveṣī Paṇḍita Śrīrāmakumāradāsajī Rāmāyaṇī, *Saketa-divya ayodhyā* (pp. 388-395). Paṇḍita Śrīśivanāthajī Dube, *Nitya kailāsa* (pp. 395f) and *Divya devī-dvīpa* (pp. 396-398). Śrīrāmalālajī, *Paramadhāmakā cintana* (p. 398).

22. A substantial number of contributions deal with Jainism and Buddhism. Paṇḍita Śrīcainasukhadāsajī Nyāyatīrtha, *Jaina dharma kā karmavāda* (pp. 460-462). Śrīkailāśacandrajī Śāstrī, *Jaina dharma men ātma, punarjanma aura karma siddhānta* (pp. 463-465). Dr. Śrīrajanarāyaṇajī Pāṇḍeya, M.A. Ph.D., Sahityaratna, Sahityālaṃkāra, *Jaina mata men punarjanma tathā karma siddhānta* (pp. 466-469). Lāmā Anagarika Govinda, *Punarjanma* (pp. 485-488) Paṇḍita Śrīchedījī Sahityālaṃkāra, *Bauddha mata anusāra paraloka karma-phala-bhoga* (p. 489).

23. *Punarjanma: Anumāna, anubhava, śastrasiddhi* (pp. 68-70).

24. *Janmāntara rahasya* (pp. 173f).

25. Pp. 133-141 and 144-151.

26. Pp. 142-144.

27. Pp. 90-93.

28. Pp. 189-192.

29. Pp. 192-194.

30. Pp. 220-224.

31. Śrīsrīpuruṣottamadāsajī Śāstrī Mahārāja, Śrīkhedāpā Rāmasnehī Sampradāyācārya, *Rāmasnehī mata men jivātma kī ṣthiti evam gati* (pp. 450-454). Rāmasnehī Sampradāyācārya Pradnanapithadhisvara Siṅthala Śrīsrībhagavaddāsajī Śāstrī Mahārāja, *Punarjanma aura paraloka* (pp. 454f).

32. Paṇḍita Śrījanakīnāthajī Śarmā, *Purānoñ meñ varṇita punarjanma kī kucha kathaeñ* (pp. 489-504 and pp. 742-745) and the following contributions summarize classical stories of rebirths. Dr. Hemendranātha Banerji, *Punarjanma kī videśī ghaṭanāeñ* (pp. 539) reports a total of 25 cases of rebirth from countries outside India, including one from Canada. The same author adds six Indian examples under *Punarjanma kī ghaṭanāeñ* (pp. 554-559). More examples of proven rebirths are provided in Ācārya Śrībalarāmajī Śāstrī, M.A., Sahityaratna, *Punarjanma tathā mṛtyu evam punarjanma ke samayāntara kī kucha ghaṭanāeñ* (pp. 560-563). Five more examples are recounted by Śrī Ajaya Kūmara Bajaja (pp. 564-568). The strangest collection is doubtlessly offered by Prof. Hemendranātha Banerjī, *Aneka janmon kī smṛti*, (pp. 595-602), where individuals are quoted who remembered their previous births as dinosaurs, as slaves in Roman households, as medieval knights, etc. Some individual cases are recorded (pp. 589-592) where the sex had changed in rebirths, boys remembered having been girls in previous lives and vice versa.

33. Pp. 228-237. Plotinus *Enneads IV*, 4 offers a striking parallel to the discussion of the three steps for each of the disciplines.

34. *Karmasambandhī vicāra*, (pp. 244-250).

35. Pp. 237-242.

36. Pp. 251-254.

37. *Punarjanma, Kayāmuta aura mukti*, (pp. 242-243).

38. *Prārabdha vicāra*, (pp. 730-736).

39. *Bhagavatpremī mukti nahiñ cāhatā*, (pp. 256-264). The *Bhaktirasāmṛtasindhu* offers a few more arguments against *mokṣa* in the following *ślokas*. The author, however, does not make use of them. There is a passage in the *Imitatio Christi* which offers a striking parallel to this attitude: II, 59: Eligo potius tecum in terra peregrinari quam sine te coelum possidere. Ubi tu ibi coelum.

40. *Mṛtyu ke samaya bhagavan nāma kā mahatva*, (pp. 269-271).

41. Pp. 271-274.

42. *Bhagavadbhakti aura punarjanma*, (pp. 254-256).

43. Pp. 720-725.

44. *Śrī Kṛṣṇa ke janma karmakī tattvataḥ jānane se mukti*, (pp. 717-720).

45. Pp. 319-322.

46. P. 622.

47. P. 366.

48. P. 417ff.

49. *Śrāddha tattva praśnottarī*, (p. 346).

50. P. 347.

51. P. 639.

52. P. 521ff. According to an author (p. 585) the spirits of people who had been members of other religious communities ask for *Gāyapiṇḍa* to be released from their suffering.

53. P. 400ff.

54. Pp. 404-415.

55. P. 418f.

56. P. 419f.

57. Wendy Donigar O'Flaherty, "Karma and Rebirth in the Vedas and Puranas," in *Karma and Rebirth in Classical Indian Traditions*, has critically analyzed, from a current anthropological perspective, some of these Puranic materials. See especially p. 27ff.

58. P. 624ff.

59. P. 537.

60. Pp. 579-585.

61. Śrī Nirañjanadāṣajī Dhīra, *Mṛtātmaon ke dvāra-āveśadvārā aura prakaṭa hokara saṁvada denā*, (pp. 573-579).

62. Śrı Śyāmakāntajī Dvivedi Ananda, M.A. B. Ed., Vyākaranācārya *Parakāya praveśa-siddhānta, prakriyā evaṁ pramāna*, (pp. 524-527) provides exact descriptions with appropriate *yantras* for the purpose. Classical as well as modern examples are collected in Balarāma Śāstrī, *Punarjanma aura parakāyā praveśa* (pp. 527-530) with a contribution by Bhakta Śrīrāma Śaraṇadāsajī (pp. 530-536).

63. P. 893.

64. *Acchī santānakeliye kyā kare?* p. 497.

65. *Kalyāna meñ bhūta-preta-carcā kyõn? Pretayoni kabhī na mile isliye!* (pp. 586-588).

66. *Śrībhāgavata saptāhase pretayonikā kalyāṇa* (p. 422f).

67. *Śrībhāgavata saptāha se pretava mukti* (pp. 424-429).

68. Cf. pp. 624-632: *Hama apnā bhalā-burā svayaṁ hī harate hain.*

CHAPTER SIX

Critical Response

KARL H. POTTER

In the papers of Creel, Klostermaier, Miller, Minor and Williams our attention is drawn to a wide spectrum of contemporary Indian approaches to karma and rebirth. Karma and rebirth, as characterized by these writers, seem to me to have a common core as well as fringe areas about which differences of opinion appear to exist. Examples of these areas include such questions as: whether or not karma can be transferred; whether one can ever be completely free from karma and rebirth and so liberated, and if so, how; whether God does or does not manipulate the conditions under which the maturation of karmic residues takes place; whether karma can be cancelled by God's grace; how the workings of karma mesh with the patent facts of biological reproduction, ecology and psychology; and, how the karmic history of an individual fits into the overall history of the cosmos. Since there is a widespread range of differences about the details and implications of different thinkers' accounts of karma, it will be conducive to clearer thinking if, before plunging into a discussion of the papers, I try to indicate what the common core is.

I am going to dub this common core the "classical karma theory of India," the CKTI. The CKTI, as I see it, holds that certain fundamental features of one's present life—vis., the genus, species, and class into which one has been born, the length of life one is (likely) to live, and the type of affective experiences one is having—are conditioned by one's actions in a previous existence. I call the CKTI, thus understood, the "common core" because this much seems to be accepted by all classical Indian philosophers and scientists, be they Hindu, Buddhist, or Jain.

To what extent the CKTI was accepted by the Indian public, the man on the street (so to speak), is not clear. We have no evidence, to the best of my knowledge, of what the ordinary man in classical times in India thought about these things, so discussion of the question soon devolves into the kind of controversy stimulated by Marxist readings of Indian history, according to which all Indian literature is the work of an elite group exploiting masses who allegedly held materialist views far different from those promulgated by the elite. The Marxist may be correct. On the other hand, it may be that Klostermaier is right, that the common Indian has tended to be a "devotionalist" from time immemorial. Or it may be that, as many Indian writers would have us believe, the understanding of the Vedas continued in some manner to prevail in Indian thinking throughout history (though whether karma and rebirth can be accounted part of Vedic thought is doubtful, it seems to me). We just don't know. We are, by necessity, confined to speculating on the basis of the evidence that is available, and that evidence is by necessity literary, the product of the intelligentsia.

In Volume One of the Karma series, the volume edited by Wendy O'Flaherty and cited in several of the papers here under discussion, I chose to contrast "the philosophical theory of karma" (i.e., the CKTI) with "popular theories of karma," accepting that the latter are still karmic theories though they relax, for example, the strict requirement that the three types of karmic results identified in the CKTI (birth, length of life, and type of experience) can only be outcomes of one's own past actions and no one else's. I have since reconsidered this way of speaking, and believe it produces more confusion than clarity to allow notions such as "group karma," "transfer of karma," etc., to constitute variations on a common theme. I prefer now to view such "variations" as in fact departures from *the* theory of karma, the CKTI.

An alternative course would be to catalogue all the variations found in the literature and to develop on such a basis a catalogue or map of possible karma theories by permuting all such variations. I have tried this; it results in a vast number of possible karma theories, most of which are unlikely ever to have been held. Since *karman* and *saṃsāra* are terms which seem to me to have had wide currency over a long period of time with the common meaning I have specified, it seems the better part of wisdom to call that the karma theory, the CKTI, and to treat other theories as departures—whether major or minor—from it.

I do not take this line because I am a philosopher and the CKTI as I understand it is most notably expressed in the philosophical literature. If there were a single notion of karma different from the CKTI to be found in, say, the Epics or the Purāṇas, it would be possible to specify the CKTI as a philosophical theory of karma, as opposed to an Epic or a Puranic theory of karma. The papers in O'Flaherty's volume suggest a more complicated situation than that, however. And the more one learns about the philosophical literature the more impressive one finds the agreement over the features of the CKTI to be. They are found, after all, in understandings so widely divergent as idealism and realism, Buddhism and Mīmāṃsā, Advaita and Nyāya, Jainism and Yoga, medicine and grammar.

The five papers I am to discuss show, in their various ways, that it is the CKTI that is still in modern times understood as karma and rebirth by Indian writers, whether they are concerned to support, defend, attack or modify that theory. Creel notes that in the modern philosophical literature "there is a current of affirmation of karma and rebirth, with some modifications of, and certain exceptions to past views" (p. 2). His discussion shows that it is the CKTI that is affirmed. But perhaps that is what one would expect; Creel is reviewing the philosophical literature. Klostermaier, on the other hand, provides us with a welter of detail concerning the views of a group expounding a position which, on their own account, stems from a stance antithetical to the philosophical emphasis on liberation. Since it is the CKTI which is being explicitly defended, it would suggest that the CKTI was by no means an understanding restricted to philosophers.

Nevertheless, though there seems to me to have been and still to be general agreement that karma and rebirth have their primary meaning in the context of the CKTI, the business of most of the papers I am reviewing can be summarily stated as the demonstration of how modern Indian philosophical and religious thinkers and leaders qualify, reinterpret, and deviate from the CKTI. This is so despite the efforts of several of the authors of these papers to convince us that the writers they are studying provide "responses given in defense and definition of karma and rebirth." I shall revert at the end of these comments to the significance of the fact that a great many contemporary Indians who hold views at odds with the letter or the law of the CKTI still feel it important to couch their thought in its terminology. First, let me review the various sorts of qualifications, reinterpretations and deviations to which our attention is called in the five papers.

Vivekananda, Aurobindo and Radhakrishnan, studied by Minor and Williams, propose theses—about "evolution" and what not—which allow them to propound theories which seem to overlap with the CKTI when stated vaguely but turn out to contradict it when spelled out in detail. One may admit that there is nothing in general unIndian about the four theses Minor formulates on pp. 15-16—that the world is evolving toward a desirable spiritual end and that our correct way of living is to participate actively in this evolutionary progress. Likewise, construed in a general way the three statements on p. 16 about karma and *saṃsāra*—that karma and rebirth provide positive opportunities, are not fatalistic, and constitute as rational, even scientific, an explanation of experience as any—are not at odds with the CKTI. But the conclusions that Vivekananda, Aurobindo and Radhakrishnan draw from these premises are antithetical to the CKTI in several specific ways.

First, in a passage Minor quotes on p. 25, Aurobindo downplays the the individual's control over his own destiny and replaces it with evolutionary guidance. This is accomplished by misinterpreting the CKTI so that it appears to involve universal determinism of actions. Thus Aurobindo writes, "The whole of causality may be defined as previous action leading to subsequent actions, *karma* and *karmaphala*. . . ." This clearly implies that *karmaphala*, the "fruits" of action, the maturations of karmic residues, are to be understood as including subsequent actions, so that our actions are determined by previous actions. But if Aurobindo thought this actually was the message of the CKTI he was mistaken. There are many affirmations, in unmistakably clear language in the texts, of the ability of human agents to initiate actions designed to counter the conditioning factors produced by their past actions. Furthermore, the CKTI limits the *karmaphala* to birth, length of life, and type of experience; actions are missing from that list. Aurobindo attempts to head off the fatalistic conclusion which most will draw from this action-determinism by assuring us that the Absolute, the true Self, is not caught up in the process of karma and rebirth, though how that helps is not made clear by Minor nor, I suspect, by Aurobindo. Of this, more later.

A second point: Minor reports that Aurobindo holds that the "true reward" for good actions is not "reward," and presumably the "true reward" for bad actions is not "punishment;" rather, that the true reward is "spiritual growth." Vivekananda suggests similar things. But when one recalls the specific outcome of karma according to the CKTI—viz., birth, length of life, and type of experience—it is clear that Aurobindo is not defending the CKTI but replacing it with a different view. The "rebirth" that follows from spiritual experiences and evolutionary theory is not the rebirth as higher or lower beings or classes, which is what the CKTI refers to. The description of the soul's progress after death in Aurobindo (Minor, p. 30), although it places that progress within a scheme which verbally resembles the CKTI's—with talk of "subtle body," heavens and hells, sheaths, etc.—has to do with a very different progression essentially oriented toward the "fruitful carrying foward of the evolution." Indeed, Aurobindo, we are told, was disinclined to allow that the soul could retrogress, a possibility which is very clearly an essential part of the CKTI regardless of the apologetics of a good many modern Hindu writers. Radhakrishnan is particularly outrageous on this score, as Minor's paper reports (p. 34). Actually, it seems likely that the CKTI flourished in classical times mainly within a view about history precisely opposite to that of evolutionism, a view in which the world is constantly running down in cycles, being revived, and running down again.

The various authors whose views Creel summarizes are also in their several ways participants in the undermining of the karma theory—or perhaps the theory has, in their minds, already become *passé*. I suggest that group karma is antithetical to the CKTI, and that the notion that "karma. . .is not limited to individuals" is even more so. If the CKTI had assumed or implied that one's environment "is. . .a joint project of the karma of countless men who interact with one another," as Pratima Bowes is quoted as saying, it is hard to suppose it would have won much adherence, since it would have been a view with hopelessly irrational implications. The mistake she makes is to suppose that the environment, according to the CKTI, is in any way affected by one's own karma or anyone else's karma. When the question of the source of environmental happenings was considered by those expounding the CKTI, it was either taken to be "the nature of things" or (by the relevant sort of theist) "God's will." On this point, it seems to me, Daya Krishna (as reported by Creel, p. 6) is perfectly correct: "'Not only do one's own actions have consequences on oneself but, if the world is to be a moral world, nothing else could.' "

David Miller's paper provides some fascinating materials for a study of the way in which a guru or *saṃnyāsin*, through his or her personal life, manages to resolve the dichotomy between *pravṛtti* and *nivṛtti*. There is one important feature of the modern understanding of how the guru functions which flies in the face of the CKTI, however, and that is the doctrine that the guru can transfer karma from himself to another or from another to himself. I find this notion of karma transfer foreign to the CKTI, though it is hinted at in Puranic passages, as Wendy O'Flaherty shows. Insofar as the resolution to the *pravṛtti/nivṛtti* tension by the guru depends on the possibility of such transfers, it represents, to my understanding, a departure from the CKTI and an avoidance of the traditional tension rather than a resolution of it. But, though I think such a notion of karmic transfer is sometimes assumed, none of Miller's own examples necessitate such an assumption, even though his account of those examples involves it.

Karmic transfer is not the same thing as merit transfer, at least if we understand merit transfer as Wendy O'Flaherty does in a definition quoted by Miller (his footnote 3). She writes that merit transfer is

> the process by which one living creature willingly or accidentally gives to another a non-physical quality of his own, such as a virtue, credit for religious achievement, a talent, or a power—often in exchange for a negative quality given by the recipient.

This definition makes no specific mention of, nor does it necessarily have anything to do with, transfer of karma. For merit transfer, so defined, to occur, neither one's actions nor their results are transferred. No doubt good things, or bad ones, may be transferred, but that doesn't affect karma theory unless one assumes that every happening is the result of someone's karma, and even then it has to be shown that somebody's satisfaction (*sukha*) or frustration (*duḥkha*) is due to someone else's acts in the karmic way. The mere fact that *A* causes *B* to experience satisfaction or frustration does not prove karmic transfer.

Here are some situations, possibly instantiated in some of the cases mentioned in these papers, which are not instances of karmic transfer, though they may be of merit transfer.

1. *A* does a good act. *B* experiences satisfaction as a result. This is not karmic transfer. It is consistent with the CKTI that one person's action can occasion pleasure or pain in another.

2. *A* does a good act, and says to *B*, "I bequeath you the results of this act." *B* subsequently experiences satisfaction. This is not necessarily karmic. Perhaps *A* experiences satisfaction too. Perhaps *A*'s doing or saying brings it about that *B* experiences the results of *B*'s karma. Perhaps *A* is talking through his hat.

3. *A* does something which results in *B*'s speeding up the maturation of his (her) karmic residues. It is consistent with the CKTI that one can experience one's karmic results at different speeds.

4. *A* infuses spiritual energy into *B* so that good karma displaces bad karma in *B*—i.e., so that the residues of *B*'s good acts displace the residues of *B*'s bad acts, leading to a better birth in the next life. This is not karmic transfer. *A*'s karma remains *A*'s and *B*'s *B*'s.

5. *A* does something which results in *B*'s karma being erased, so that *B* is no longer saddled with the necessity of "working off" or living out the fruits of that karma. This is not karmic transfer; nothing is transferred.

None of these are cases of karmic transfer, though some of them involve merit transfer. For example, Williams writes, (p. 53) "Serving others implies a merit transfer theory; somehow what is done will help alleviate the negative effects of another's karma—and possibly help one's own as a bonus." He thinks this means that "Vivekananda's formulation requires a modification of simple or undiluted karma." It need not be construed that way. Service is perfectly consistent with the CKTI if it is understood along the lines of any of the above five types of situation.

Miller considers a number of situations which allegedly involve merit transfer and thus, he thinks, possibly the qualification or abandonment of features of the CKTI. Some of these, such as Narendranath's conversion experience with Ramakrishna or Ramana Maharshi's treatment of his mother, may be called merit transfer but need not be thought of as involving karmic transfer. For example, Ramana Maharshi's touching his mother and activizing her *vāsanās*, so that "scene after scene rolled before her," is a recent instance of a commonly believed ability of yogins to speed up the experiencing of their's or others' karmic fruits. After all, it is *her* karma, not her son's, that she sees in her vision. One suspects that Narendra's vision is to be thought of in the same way, though the description is more vague—we don't know precisely what he saw. Likewise, Śaṃkara's taking the body of the king in order to have amorous experiences need not be construed as karmic transfer unless the suggestion is that it is the dead king's karma, not Śaṃkara's, which is responsible for those experiences.

In two of Miller's cases I suspect the description Miller provides may go beyond what is necessary to explain what is going on. When Śaṃkara enlightened Prabhākara he surely did not erase all Prabhākara's *prārabdhakarman*; if he had, Prabhākara would have died, since one's *prārabdhakarman* is precisely what provides the karmic support for a given embodiment in that particular lifetime. Rather, Śaṃkara must have erased Prabhākara's *sañcitakarman*, the karma that was not being worked out in this lifetime and which, if it had not been erased, would have led to countless further rebirths for Prabhākara. A *jīvanmukta* is one whose *sañcitakarman* is erased or "burnt up," who will not have any further or *āgamī karman*, but who is still working off his *prārabdhakarman*. There is nothing contradictory to the CKTI in this set of assumptions about the process of liberation.

As for the case Miller himself witnessed, in which Maheśvarānanda Tīrtha blessed the sick child, one may doubt that, as Miller writes, "a transfer of merit took place, and the evil (adharmic) karma in the child was displaced by the good or meritorious (dharmic) karma of Maheśvarānanda" (p. 63). If Maheśvarānanda was, as his disciples believed, a *jīvanmukta*, then as was pointed out above, he would have had no stored-up karma to give to the child or the parents. And he could hardly give away his *prārabdhakarman*, which is all he had left! The trouble here, I think, is that the term "karma" means action as well as the stored-up residues laid down by actions. What Maheśvarānanda did, or at any rate what his parents hoped he had done, was to infuse into the child the power to act in dharmic ways for whatever time the child had left in this life. Then, as Miller writes, "even if the boy were to die later that morning, his parents would know that their son's *jīva* would be reborn to a better. . .life" (p. 63).

Thus merit transfer does not necessarily imply karmic transfer, and so does not overtly challenge the CKTI. The CKTI is consistent with philsoophical accounts of liberation, and the notions about the guru or *saṃnyāsin* which Miller finds prevalent in India today are largely understandable through and consistent with those accounts. However, I am not at all clear that the same can be said about the understanding of karma found among those Klostermaier calls "devotionalists."

Klostermaier defines "devotionalism" as follows:

> Hindu devotionalism has no normative system but it has definite bases: the immortality of the soul, the eternity of God, the belief in a reward for good deeds and punishment for evil acts, the efficacy of rituals, the necessity of worship. It is strongly person oriented. (p. 84)

He suggests, and I cannot disagree, that devotionalists in this sense have been around in India forever. He gives us a thoroughly detailed account of what a body of contemporary writers, whom he characterizes as largely comprising devotionalists, have to say about karma and rebirth. This material is extremely valuable for a correct understanding of contemporary thinking about those topics, and we are much indebted to Klostermaier for making a summary of these points available to non-Hindi readers. What is not entirely clear to me, is to what extent these views on karma and rebirth reflect views that can be associated with "devotionalism," not in Klostermaier's sense, but in the sense of those who carry forward the heritage of the *bhakti* period.

In Volume Three of the series of karma of which the O'Flaherty volume is the first, specialists on medieval Indian sectarian devotional movements attempt to address those sects' attitudes toward and beliefs about karma and rebirth. What they find is that there takes place what A.K. Ramanujan (an editor of the volume) calls a "*bhakti* reversal." Examples of what is reversed in this *bhakti* reversal include the turning on its head of caste hierarchy, so that the lowest castes become the highest, and the reversal of traditional male dominance. Both reversals are sure to lessen commitment to the implications of the CKTI concerning birth in the following ways: the questioning and reversal of the value of merit (*puṇya*) over demerit (*pāpa*), as well as the postulation of new heavens, bring into question the traditional connection between good actions and the affective (satisfying or frustrating) nature of the maturations of those actions; the notion of God's grace replacing that of individual discipline as the means to salvation, and the idea that unintended good deeds (e.g., speaking God's name by accident) can be efficacious in helping toward higher spiritual ends, undermine the strictly mechanical workings of karma and *saṃsāra* as viewed in the CKTI. None of these features in and of itself contradicts what the CKTI says, yet the entire body of such views, so the writers in Volume Three agree, tends to subvert the CKTI.

The medieval sectarian writers who announce the *bhakti* reversal are all devotionalists in Klostermaier's sense, and they utilize the language of the CKTI in setting forth their thought. Yet the upshot of their revolutionary views is to bring into question much of what the CKTI was thought to be good for by those who expounded it in classical times. The karma theory functioned then to support commitment to traditional values, to encourage morality and discourage immoral acts, perhaps to support a class hierarchy and the supremacy of some life-forms over others, as well as to provide the background for the ideal of liberation which is taught in the philosophical literature as the highest aim of man. The *bhakti* reversal revolted against traditional values, reveled in amorality if not immorality, subverted class hierarchies and notions of preferable forms of life, and jettisoned the ideal of liberation in favor of an ideal of servitude to God. As a result, their continued use of the language of karma and rebirth, though appearing to constitute a remarkable monument to the staying power of a tradition that had lost its usefulness, enabled others to use that same karmic terminology to say things which were more and more contrary to the letter as well as the spirit of the CKTI while still appearing to speak its language. I believe it is the outcome of this tendency which explains how modern writers, of the sort reported on in the papers under discussion, can continue to affirm their belief in karma and rebirth but mean things entirely different from what the CKTI meant by those terms.

Klostermaier's account pictures devotionalists as those who accept the CKTI but do not accept certain other doctrines classically associated with it, such as the doctrine of liberation as the fourth and highest aim of man. He emphasizes the amount of basic common assumptions and the practical concord among devotionalists, as expressed in *Paraloka Aura Punarjanmāṅka*, as "quite astonishing." I think this may be somewhat over stated. I suspect that the Śaṃkarācāryas who contributed may not be enthused about the notion that the *bhakta* does not seek *mukti*. And I also suspect that those devotionalists who retain the fervor of the *bhakti* reversal may not be enthused over the bland acceptance of moral preaching which is indulged in by many writers in the book. What *is* quite astonishing, however, is that the language of karma and rebirth maintains itself in spite of the abandonment of much that traditionally made it useful.

Let me try to indicate what I believe is the reason for the continued adoption of the language of the CKTI at a time when it has less and less relevance for the kinds of concerns it served in classical times. A way of getting at it is to start with what Creel calls the contrast between "the exclusive and the associational views of causality in karma, the former being the 'absolutistic' one where karma is the exclusive cause of happenings, and the latter holding that our karma is associated with other forces which combine to form our present state" (p. 4). I have complained about a too literal reading of the former view: karma is not the exclusive cause of happenings for the CKTI. Nevertheless, it is not merely one among many causal conditions either. The famous Radhakrishnan simile of the card game, quoted by both Creel and Minor, is too ambiguous on the crucial point here. The crucial question is, how *much* of us is due to our karma, and thus, to what *extent* do we control our destiny? That "there is always a choice" is comforting, but only if that choice is conditioned by enough of our own doings.

In the terms of the card game analogy, what *is* "our hand" that is "dealt to us"? It seems to me that the CKTI would not have held any particular attraction for those whom it did attract were it not that they viewed karmic conditioning to be on the one hand strictly confined to certain features, but on the other hand a conditioning which to a great extent permeates our understanding of what we are. It is this latter aspect which modern writers (including Indian writers) regularly fail to comprehend. Karma is not a peculiar thesis to be appended to what appears to a Westerner to be the natural account of what man is made of. Rather, for those who believe in it, karma lies at the very heart of what a man is. It is for this reason, given the conviction that what a man is is on balance frustrating, that the ideal of liberation from *saṃsāra* became a dominant view of human striving. So it is not in fact the contrast between the exclusive and associational views which is critical in understanding the CKTI, it is rather the gauging of the *extent* to which one's previous actions condition what one is now. If karma were everything or nothing to us, no one would be interested in it.

What makes the CKTI fascinating is that it purports to constitute an account of human nature. In India, you are (or were) literally what you do, and that includes not only "you are what you eat," but also "you are what you think" and "you are what you say," since thinking and speaking are kinds of action. The nature of my inclination to respond in human, rather than, say, feline ways to stimuli is held to be a matter of my former actions as a human being. When I am reborn as a cat I will respond as a cat does since I was a cat before and have feline dispositions at the ready. In Jainism one finds a vast and complex theory of the stuff of which a person is made and which is called *karman*. That karma is what we are, is given *a priori* for all Indians, whether Hindus, Buddhists, of Jains. Everything which makes me the animal that I am is, as long as certain circumstances prevail, a matter of my karma. The possibility that those circumstances may not prevail, that one may through meditation, a fortunate choice of guru, hard work, sudden insight, or even God's grace come to understand and take an attitude of nonattachment must be held open at least to those on a sufficiently high rung of the great chain of being. But this does not mean that those on the higher rungs are any less creatures of their own actions; rather, it means that they have learned, whether intellectually or intuitively, what the circumstance is under which the karmic law continues to operate, and thus can through this understanding avoid further karmic conditioning. Karma is what Indians have in their bones, and that is why karma talk continues to be in fashion even when aspirations change, foreign ideas ("science") become persuasive, social distinctions collapse, and other changes take place.

If this has not been as well appreciated as it should have been, it may to some degree be because those writing about Indian thought, people such as Aurobindo, Radhakrishnan, and many others expounding the glories of Indian philosophy to an audience in Western languages, tend to indulge in a way of speaking which seems to me to invite confusion. That way of speaking involves language about "the Self" and its "higher" point of view, from which it will be seen that karma and human nature in general is illusory. Advaitins even in classical times indulged in this sort of language, but I do not for a moment believe they took it literally in the way many modern writers do. It is not that the Advaitin supposes that man's karmic conditioning is really no problem because it is unreal and that emancipation comes merely from a sudden enlightenment about Brahman. Śaṃkara, I believe, anticipated the possibility of this facile reading of Advaita thought, and kept insisting that the world exists and that that is a serious problem for us. As Advaita developed, his strictures were sometimes forgotten, the result being that Advaita, originally requiring rigorous discipline toward an essentially lonely emancipation, was more and more easily co-opted by devotionalists, proponents of Western sages, mystics and occultists. Radhakrishnan is not unaware of this (as Minor shows, p. 21) but he is not really an Advaitin. Aurobindo, when he says that the fact that "the true Self is not caught up in [karma and rebirth]" is what makes the CKTI non-fatalistic (Minor, p. 25) seems to be appealing to Advaita precedents, but he is, I suggest, guilty of breeding—and perhaps himself being taken in by—the kind of confusion to which I am alluding. Karma is definitely not "a convenient fiction" (to borrow Eliot Deutsch's phrase, though he meant something else by it), even for Advaitins.

Where are we then, in understanding karma? I conclude with the thought that much more needs to be done to assess accurately the details of indigenous Indian assumptions about human nature, of just how—in nitty-gritty terms—the deceased person gets into its next body, of what is included, and what not, under the terms "birth," "length of life," and "type of experience," of what is an action and what is not, and so forth. Standard scholarly accounts of Indian philosophy fail to discuss these details, and thus unwittingly contribute to the notion that karma is an aberration of the sort that occultist writers present it as being. The CKTI was not a myth or a metaphor for classical Indians, and it still holds sway in the very "bones," as I said, of Indians of modern times, despite its being overlaid with other notions of different origins. It will take some doing to unearth the earthy aspects of that view which lies behind the CKTI, but it is a task worthy of the attention of scholars.

II

The Buddhist Context

CHAPTER SEVEN

Post-Classical Developments In The Concepts of Karma and Rebirth in Theravāda Buddhism

BRUCE MATTHEWS

This paper aims to assess some of the developments in the concepts of karma (*kamma*) and rebirth (*punabbhava* or *upapāta*) in Theravāda Buddhism[1] since the end of that tradition's classical period. Ñāṇamoli[2] and others argue that the classical age ended about the 4th century A.D. It included the canonical period, which saw the establishment of the Tipiṭaka over a period of three or four centuries, and the setting down of the *Milindapañha* just before the beginning of the Christian era. Between the first and fifth centuries, however, a pronounced decline in religious interpretation persisted until Buddhaghosa, ca. 400. With Buddhaghosa the great age of commentaries commenced, inspiring a host of profound exegetical work. It was also the beginning of post-classical development in the Theravāda. If one takes Ñāṇamoli's chronology one step further, the commentarial period is, in its turn, slowly sapped of its initiative until it finally expires with the Coḷa invasions of Lanka in about 1000.[3] Only when a Buddhist polity is restored there by Parākramabāhu I (1153-1168) does the 'modern' era in Theravāda history begin. The Buddhist revival in Lanka had an interesting an important influence in Southeast Asia, notably in Tambralinga (Malaya), Sukhodaya (Siam), and Pagan (Burma), indicating the transmission of a homogenous *dhamma* to several great centres of civilization.[4] The outcome of this was a shared doctrinal understanding and religious worldview over a large social and geographical arc that has more or less persisted up until the present.

To come to grips with the subject matter in an orderly way, I propose an analysis from four perspectives. First, because the classical understanding of karma and rebirth obviously has a bearing on later speculation, it is necessary to set down the canonical interpretation, however briefly. In fact, as I shall go on to point out, this initial teaching was undoubtedly elaborated on by future savants, but it was not radically changed in the process. Gombrich is correct when he observes that even amongst the villagers of up-country Sri Lanka today there is a surprising orthodoxy in matters of doctrine. Other things (viz., merit-making and spirit cults) may have long been incorporated,[5] but the *dhamma* is essentially perceived in its wholeness.[6] It is important, then, to articulate this basic canonical model on which to build further analyses. Secondly, I propose to examine the interpretation of karma in one medieval work of significance, the *Abhidhammattha Saṅgaha* of Anuruddha (c. 900). It can be argued that the *Saṅgaha* is the most outstanding, late, post-classical Theravāda distillation of doctrine. Certainly it is still widely used in the Theravāda world, particularly in Burma. Thirdly, I want to review the contributions to the study of karma and rebirth by several contemporary Buddhists in Sri Lanka. Here one sees interesting attempts to explicate the nuances of karma and rebirth by comparisons with Western psychology and philosophy. This is a sign of the vigour of Theravāda Buddhist thought as it strives to meet the challenges of a modern worldview and new ideological pressures. Fourth and finally, it is desirable to note that these doctrinal issues are expressed at the village level, where they are interpreted and applied in practical everyday life. This is not the place to elaborate fully such a complex theme, but karma and rebirth are more than dry philosophical concepts. They enter fully into the religious consciousness of Theravāda devotees in a far-reaching manner.

THE CANONICAL TEACHING

In turning to the Pāli canon, much reference to karma and its causal implications can be found in both the Sutta and Abhidhamma Piṭakas, although the record is admittedly haphazard.[7] There is no single major systematic exposition on this subject, and an account has to be put together from the dozens of places where karma is mentioned in the texts.[8] This lack of a cohesive presentation has led some to maintain that the doctrine was incidental to the main perspective of early Buddhist soteriology. This is an important point that warrants discussion.[9] If Bellah and others are correct, Buddhism was (and is) not a 'world-accepting' religion.[10] Its basic aim is to flee the world as if it were a burning house, as if life itself is "a mass of glowing embers" (*rūpaṃ kukkulaṃ* S.3.177).[11] In this situation of withdrawal, the Indian concept of karma would be too social, too concerned with acts and deeds to be of much soteriological use. By this analysis the entire objective was to escape from the clutches of karma, to head for the other shore of *nibbāna*.[12]

There is a case for this interpretation, but it has to be balanced by an evolving theodicy found in the Canon, one that definitely involves karma in the soteriological process. Although pursuit of good karma was never in the final analysis sufficient for salvation (*A*.5.262),[13] awareness of its function and potential was pertinent to living the holy life conducive to perfection and better rebirth (*M*.1.390). Consistent with the Buddha's understanding that each individual responds according to the spiritual level of development (*upāya*), the doctrine of karma was seen as crucial for the average person's religious vocation. The wise may know better, reaching out for the *nibbāna* state which transcends such an apparently worldly device as karma. But for many, strong social needs and limited metaphysical comprehension engendered an emphasis on how to cope with life's crises here and now, to direct answers to the problems of pain, injustice, and death. The doctrine of karma met these exigencies so acceptably that in time it became an important soteriological aim in its own right.[14] *Nibbāna* was not necessarily a pessimistic goal, but for the ordinary villager it was not as meaningful as continued rebirth, governed by karma, in superior states of worldly or heavenly existence.[15]

This was consistent with the place karma already had in the Indian world-view. Canonical Buddhism rearranged the symbolic pattern of that view, however, by introducing an anti-substance or *anatta* (no-self) doctrine, thereby radically changing the definition of karma. Karma still had an eschatological function[16] in that it was involved as an agency of rebirth (*S*.2.82), but early Buddhism denied that any personality or substance carried over the energy of karma into new life. What was reborn was not an entity (*M*.1.256), but an evolving consciousness (*saṃvattanika* or the *viññaṇa sotam*, stream of consciousness, *D*.3.105), whose quality had been conditioned by karma. Furthermore, karma was understood to be more than just acts and deeds in any one life.[17] It was above all the volition (*cetanā*, *M*.3.207) that stood behind those deeds. This was the most significant change the Buddha made to the concept of karma. He gave it a moral, even providential force not seen before, indicating that there was a creative and saving possibility in every situation.[18] In this sense, as C.A.F. Rhys Davids has rightly observed, Buddhism was "a gospel of hopeful wayfaring from Good to Better. . . a pilgrim's progress, not so much with a load of sin to be discarded, as with an evergrowing force of *artha*—the good, the needed, the better."[19]

This volitional aspect of karma also prevented the theory from becoming fatalistic. As *M*.3.203 indicates, karma provoked (*saṃvattanika*) tendencies or conditions (*kammapaṭisaraṇā*)[20] rather than consequences as such. There was a definite modification of Hindu determinism, an openness to free will (*attakāra*) and individual initiative (*ārambhadhātu*, *A*.3.338). If anything could be said to be predetermined, it was the physical environment (*utupariṇāma*) that can give rise, or not give rise, to opportunity.[21] Canonical Buddhism recognized apart from karma, other forces that affect causality. These included biological laws (*bīja-niyāma*), accident (*adhiccasamuppanna*) and attack (*visama parihara*). It would be incorrect to assume that *dukkha* (pain) or *sukha* (pleasure) were the product only of one's karma or actions (*sayaṃkatam*).[22]

Generally speaking, however, karma was expected to produce results either here or in another rebirth consistent with the law of cause and effect (*paccaya*). Repentance or merit-making was not considered effective for the expiation of bad karma (although there is evidence that later Theravāda Buddhism allowed for it).[23] At best a sense of shame (*hiri*) leading to avoidance of further transgression (*ottappa*) might come from an unwholesome karmic experience. More conventionally, one was to expect the fruits (*phala*) of karma to follow in the undetermined future according to an operation not fully comprehendable (*acinteyya*, *A*.2.80) except to a Buddha. The Sutta Pitaka does not explain the procedure in any detail, but in one key text (*A*.1.223), karma's involvement with consciousness (*viññāṇa*) and craving (*taṇhā*) was seen to be necessary in order to set the process in motion.[24] In this passage, craving has a dynamic role as the ingredient of moisture which nourishes the seed of consciousness. Under certain conditions, it is presumed that the seed will ripen and produce more seed in a continual process of regeneration. The analogy of karma as the field or soil necessary for consciousness to grow in represents both past and present intentions. In another, quite different passage (*S*.2.82), consciousness was said to be conditioned by the merit and demerit of acts. Such acts, whether speech, thought, or behavior, were also said to make up karma, which in turn affects rebirth.[25]

It could be argued that karma's association with rebirth came to overshadow its straightforward conative role as a guideline on how to manage the will here and now.[26] There was much interest in an explanation of the inequalities and injustices (*hīnappaṇītatā*) of life, of the differences between low and exalted being (*M*.3.202ff). Some Sutta passages gave quite extraordinary accounts of various kinds of rebirth in order to illustrate this as, for instance, the vision seen by Moggallāna at Gijjhakūta Mountain (*S*.2.254). The bizarre physical forms flying through space (a skeleton, a lump of flesh, a man bristling with knives, another with an enlarged scrotum, a monk with robes, and bowl on fire) are all explained as the results of residual karma.

The point to be made here is that in early Buddhism, karma's involvement in rebirth was acknowledged as an empirical truth, but not in an overtly mechanistic way. Karma only conditions differences between individuals; it gives direction to rebirth and does not determine such a thing as caste (*vaṇṇa*). The distinguishing factor of righteousness (*dhamma*) is more important than caste in any given life (*Sn*.650).[27] That this depends on moral volition is everywhere recognized in the Sutta. Nonetheless, how all of this was linked to the rebirth process (*gati*) increasingly dominated future speculation on karma.

THE ABHIDHAMMA

Not unexpectedly, the later Abhidhamma Piṭaka greatly elaborated on this aspect of Sutta doctrine, particularly in the *Dhammasaṅgaṇi* and the *Paṭṭhāna*.[28] Both Buddhaghosa[29] and Anuruddha in turn codified much of the Abhidhamma, but, given its strategic importance in later Theravāda doctrine, a few observations should be made on what additional theories were advanced here that influenced the understanding of karma.[30] First the Abhidhamma was (and is) often described by the Theravāda as the ultimate teaching (*paramattha-desanā*),[31] indicating that its concern was less concrete and more philosophical. Certainly there is still a resistance on the part of many contemporary Theravadins to make allowance for reductive simplification of the Abhidhamma, particularly in Western psychological or metaphysical language. Accordingly, a clear, succinct analysis of karma based on the Abhidhamma is not available. What it teaches needs to be wrestled with and meditated upon.[32]

Second, the Abhidhamma scholiasts (viz., the Abhidhammikas) laid down lists of constituent mental and material elements, possibly to assist in meditation as well as to protect the unity of the *dharnma*. One of these was a detailed description of karmic production (*uppanna, Dhs*. 1035, 1416). The emphasis here was on karma as a continuum, a process interpenetrating and spanning past, present, and future occasions.[33] In such a way they understood that past karmic energy (*kammavega*), apart from its potential to mature in a later rebirth, could also be transmitted to a present state of consciousness. Despite the fact that the past evaluating experience (*anubhavitvā*) had gone, it still maintains present significance (*bhūtāpagatuppanna*). The *Paṭṭhana* put it another way in its celebrated exposition of causality (*paccaya*) as foundation. The traditional twelve spokes (*nidāna*) of the *paṭiccasamuppāda* (*S*.2.10) were doubled to give twenty-four aspects of conditionality that defined what can happen in any one particular cause-effect relation. In summary, it showed how every mental state is related to the succeeding one in at least four different ways: by proximity (*anantara*) in time and place; by contiguity (*samanantara*) as in touching; by absence (*n'atthi*); and by abeyance (*avigata*) or a state of waiting or expectation. Simply stated, this meant that each inspired thought process renders service (*upakāra*) to the next mental state, passing on the totality of its energy (*passayā sati*). Karma was involved as both accumulated volition and result. Nevertheless all the factors were based on a precedent so-called root condition (*hetu-paccaya*) made up of moral and immoral roots (*kusala-akusala-mūlā*) which might be considered as being below the threshold of consciousness.

This leads to the third and final point, the development in Abhidhamma of a doctrine loosely associated with the Western idea of the unconscious, expressed by the term *bhavaṅga* (*Ath.*72). *Bhavaṅga* does not occur in the Sutta Piṭaka,[34] but its appearance in both the *Dhammasaṅgaṇi* and the *Paṭṭhāna* assured that it received much post-classical attention in the Theravāda. Its involvement with karma is at once apparent. Although there is disagreement about how *bhavaṅga* should be interpreted,[35] two meanings are possible. Some conceive it to be an 'unconscious continuum,'[36] others as something not necessarily unconscious but as a transmitting factor in rebirth.[37] Both these interpretations are plausible and both involve the action of karma. Either way, *bhavaṅga* assumed a kind of ultimate reality (*paramattha*). It can be argued that in the post-Buddhaghosa period of the Theravāda, *bhavaṅga* may have assumed the connotation of residue or substance as part of its own peculiar characteristic (*svabhāva*).[38] That this was an issue by the time of Anuruddha is quite likely, as he gives much attention to the question of karmic transfer in rebirth. It is recognized that Buddhism from the fifth to the tenth centuries was experiencing both internal and external challenges. The steady rise of Mahāyāna doctrine, with its other-worldly but tangible sense of paradise and future life, might well have obliged the Theravāda to counteract any aberration of the central doctrine of momentariness. Pressures from other religions, notably Vedantic Hinduism, might have intensified perplexity about how karma and rebirth could operate without some ongoing entity, such as *bhavaṅga*, to provide the necessary link. These questions receive careful analysis in Anuruddha's remarkable medieval compendium of philosophy, the *Abhidhammattha Saṅgaha*.[39] I regard this work as a major watershed of post-classical Theravāda doctrine, providing as it does a medieval reformulation of traditional doctrinal interpretations. It, therefore, met the changing climate of opinion in the Buddhist philosophical world, forthrightly reaffirming the central notions of the *dhamma* in a new and interesting way.

THE ABHIDHAMMATTHA SAṄGAHA

In this work, karma is discussed in each of the nine chapters, but particularly in the fifth, where its relationship with rebirth is fully worked out. In order to lead up to this, however, in 4.3.1 the *Saṅgaha* first places karma in the context of consciousness, for the initial aim was to discover how consciousness works as a process of seventeen discrete moments (*sattarasa cittakkhaṇāni*). Consciousness (synonymously referred to as *citta, mana, viññāṇa, nāma*) was said to involve the entire range of thought processes. This begins with consciousness as a blank screen, disengaged from the stimulative world. As the essentially passive state of *bhavaṅga*,[40] it is still part of the flow or continuum of being. This is interrupted when objects appear, activating the senses and various faculties of perception (eye, ear, nose, tongue, touch). The object so received (*sampaṭicchana*) is then examined (*santīraṇa*) and held on to (*votthapana*, established). There follows the crucial conative action of discriminative judgement or will (*javana*, literally impulse),[41] which in turn results in moral and immoral action. This combination of will and action constitutes karma. If the object is judged rightly (*yoniso manaskāra*) the karma becomes moral; if wrongly, it becomes immoral. The process is concluded by the so-called registering consciousness (*tadālambana* or *tadārammaṇa citta*), a discrimination that has no equivalent in Western psychology.

Rebirth and karma are exhaustively reviewed in the Paṭisandhicatukkam (On the Fourfold Rebirth) and Kammacatukka (On the Fourfold Karma) of Book Five. The key passage is 5.3.7. There karma is analyzed from four perspectives, each pertinent to rebirth. First, the four functions of karma are outlined as reproductive (*janaka*), supportive (*upatthambaka*), obstructive (*upapīḷaka*) and destructive (*upaghāta*). Second, the effects of karma are set down as weighty (*garuka*), near or proximate (*āsanna*), habitual (*āciṇṇa*) and residual, or yet to be worked out (*kaṭattā*, held in reserve). Third, karma is discussed with respect to the time in which it takes effect as experienced in this life (*diṭṭhadhamma*), the next life (*upapajja*), and some future life beyond that (*aparāpariya*) or as karma which no longer has any force (*ahosi*). Fourth, the places where karma might work out its effects are detailed, notably as moral and immoral karma in the world of pleasures (*kāmaloka*), or moral karma only in the world of form (*rūpaloka*) or without form (arūpaloka).

Of all these terms, the most relevant for the purpose of this paper is *janaka-kamma* or reproductive karma. It directly initiates on-going consciousness in this life, but includes rebirth consciousness (*paṭisandhi*) at the moment of death. The *Saṅgaha* is typical of post-classical Theravāda in its fascination with what transpires in the final moments of life. In 5.5.11, death is described as the decease of psychic life (*jīvitindriya*), heat (*usmā*) and consciousness (*viññāṇa*) of one individual in a particular existence. But whether death is timely (*kālamaraṇa*) or untimely (*akālamaraṇa*),[42] the past efficient action of karma continues to be reproductive, engendering conception in a new life. If timely or natural, the dying person is said to experience terminal (but still reproductive) thought consciousness (*maraṇāsanna-juvana-citta*), which is affected by one of three thought objects: recent karma (either as volition and deed just performed, or as something that has been habitual); a symbolic memory of one great act, good or bad (*kamma-nimitta*); or by some indication or anticipation of the place of rebirth (*gati-nimitta*). This experience is registered (*tadālambana*) by the final death-consciousness (*cuti-citta*).

Death-consciousness may be the last thought, but the preceding last karmic or conative action (*maraṅasanna-citta*) is more important.[43] It is this that has the power to enter into the appropriate matrix as rebirth consciousness (*paṭisandhi-viññāṇa*), carrying with it all the surplus karma of the previous existence. There, the "individual moral nucleus," as Nash calls it,[44] combines with sperm and ovum cells to create both the mental and material constituencies.[45] The rebirth consciousness, carrying with it reproductive karma, takes as its object the *bhavaṅga* (the unconscious continuum) of the new life, thus perpetuating the process indefinitely. As the *Saṅgaha* 5.5.15 puts it:

> So, to those who have thus grasped rebirth (*gahitapatisandhikānaṃ*), immediately after the cessation of the rebirth consciousness (*paṭisandhinirodhānantaratoppabhuti*) another consciousness. . .flows on. . . uninterruptedly like a stream until the arising of death consciousness (*cuticittuppāda*). Being an essential factor of life, this other consciousness is known as *bhavaṅga*. At the end. . .it arises as death-consciousness and is dissolved (*nirujjhati*). Thereafter the rebirth consciousness and others revolve and go forth in succession (*yathākkammaṃ* eva parivattantā pavattanti) like a chariot wheel (*rathacakkam*).

Consistent with Theravāda doctrine, there is held to be no intermediate state (*antarā-bhava*) between death and rebirth.[46] Karma continues on its course at once, according to the natural law of cause and effect. Whether any thing of substance passes from life to life is not clearly stated. It is true that later post-classical Theravāda embraced a largely dualist view of material and mental phenomena (*Saṅgaha* 5.4.7) along with a complex atomic theory (*paramāṇu*). We have seen how some scholars have assumed that such a substantialist position must have significance in the rebirth process, that the *bhavaṅga* in particular was an *ātmavāda* (self or soul) in disguise.[47] From the evidence of the *Saṅgaha*, however, I cannot be convinced that the same *bhavaṅga*, or anything else that had momentary existence, ontologically continues on in other lives. It is a new *bhavaṅga* that arises spontaneously from the various factors precipitating rebirth. The old one, as 5.5.15 notes, perishes (*nirujjhati*). I concede that there is room here for debate, but suggest that the Theravāda Abhidhammikas, both past and current, have always been able to link their understanding of the *Saṅgaha* with the Abhidhamma Piṭaka and, whenever conceivably possible, with the Nikāyas themselves. They remain very much within the Pāli Canonical doctrine of absolute momentariness.

By way of summary, up to this point I have set down some classical and post-classical reflections on karma and rebirth. It can be argued that significant embellishment on these doctrines began with the Abhidhamma Piṭaka, which devotees attribute to the Buddha but to which form critics give a later date. The introduction of such technical terms as *bhavaṅga, javana, cuti-citta* and *tadālambana,* most of which do not occur in the Sutta Piṭaka, gave rich exegetical resources to post-classical Theravāda Buddhist thinkers. Far-reaching psychological and soteriological conclusions were ventured. Veritable blue-prints of the mind were drawn up, marking out obstacles and hazards. Karma in particular was linked to the all-important conative dimension of the *dhamma* more emphatically than was the case in the early Buddhist texts. Rebirth was painstakingly dissected as process and phenomenon, but not with the same empirical emphasis with which earlier Buddhism invested it.[48] For karma was part of the higher truth which, in the long run, must be intuitively embraced in order to comprehend it; must be accepted with an element of faith or spiritual confidence (*saddhā*). Was understanding karma and rebirth just a matter of scientific investigation? This attitude, I have found, is rarely ventured by the monks versed in Abhidhamma. But curiously enough, it is vigorously promulgated by some modern lay Buddhist scholars, to whom we now turn.

MODERN THERAVĀDA INTERPRETATIONS OF KARMA AND REBIRTH

Much work has recently been done by several Theravāda scholars on karma and rebirth. Some of the most interesting studies are by lay thinkers responding to the challenges of explaining Buddhism to the modern world by demonstrating the experimental availability and objective facticity of such concepts. This essentially nomothetic approach argues that karma and its corollaries are grounded in general laws. The chief spokesman for this position is the late K.N. Jayatilleke, one of the most important Theravāda expositors of our time. Jayatilleke has written extensively on the subject of karma. It is important to note that he depends mostly on the evidence of the Sutta Piṭaka, with its strong emphasis on the empirical. In his seminal *Early Buddhist Theory of Knowledge* (1963), Jayatilleke carefuly unfolds how early Buddhism develops an epistemology based not on rational explanation but on the discernment of the senses (*saññā, A.*4.103) and inductive inference (*anvaye ñāṇam, S.*2.58). The latter is "the inferential knowledge that a causal sequence or concomitance observed to hold good in a number of present instances would have taken place in the past and will take place in the future."[49] All other ways of knowing thus have serious weaknesses. But both perception and inductive inference also make allowance for extra-sensory perception (*atikkanta-mānusaka*), something not necessarily accepted in the West as part of seeing things as they really are (*yathābhūtam*). Thus seeing in the paranormal sense may be expressed in several ways,[50] affording an independent validation of karma and rebirth. And, as Jayatilleke notes, "prominent among the doctrines derived as inductive inference on the basis of the data of extra-sensory perception is karma as taught in the Pāli Canonical texts."[51] Traditionally, such paranormal or higher knowledge is open only to those whose minds are cleared of impurities (*upakkilesa*).

Many Theravadins argue that there is essentially nothing metaphysical or otherworldly about this. Jayatilleke and others[52] go to great lengths to justify the scientific warrantability of paranormal knowledge. This becomes paradoxical when they bring forward as evidence a number of somewhat contentious cases, such as that of Bridey Murphy (1953) or Edgar Cayce (1960), individuals whom Westerners do not normally associate with the high meditational standards of awareness (*abhiññā*) and virtue reflected in the canonical description (viz., *D*.1.81). The evidence for rebirth is further related to research conducted in the West by scholars such as J.M. Yerkes, J. Eccles, I. Stevenson and M.V. Kline.[53] That an eminent Theravadin like Jayatilleke makes such an effort to guarantee the reality of karma and rebirth through these means shows how anxious he is to have proof in the scientific mode for Buddhist doctrines that others would prefer to leave as partial spiritual mysteries. Western students of Buddhism have long debated the adequacy of approaching Theravāda soteriology from a scientific viewpoint, some arguing that reason of a discursive type cannot reveal the intrinsic heart of the *dhamma*.[54] But the main point here is that to some informed Theravadins at least, there is nothing ultimate (*paramattha*) about karma and rebirth at all. For them, these concerns remain elementary facts of life, as they maintain they were thought to be for the Buddha.

Others prefer a more metaphysical approach, arguing that empirical evidence is not relevant. As Wendy O'Flaherty points out, despite "scars and patches," the karmic theory "survives healthily in the face of all the facts."[55] This is as true for Theravāda Buddhism as it is for any other paradigmatic approach to karma offered by the rich and complex Indian religious tradition. Zan Aung puts it another way when he maintains the West should not be expected to "swallow all that is said" about karma and related doctrines. For concepts like karma that are beyond quantitative verification, the "nearest approach to proof" is to show its "likelihood," a task "for each scientific generation to declare." But even this is largely questionable for something that has in the long run to be accepted on faith.[56]

Karma may not be one of the traditional inexpressibles (*avyākatā*, *M*.1.426), but its classical status as one of the four unthinkables (*acinteyyāni*, *A*.2.80) gives it a recognized degree of impenetrability, especially when it comes to the question of how karmic transfer takes place in rebirth. This essentially spiritual understanding of the nature of karma is consistent with the Abhidhamma position, and is widely accepted in the Theravāda world today.

Such an approach is a reflection of a more ideographic outlook towards the law of karma, not requiring verification by hard experiment, yet acknowledging that karmic events cannot be either precisely replicated or predicted. This interpretation would reject the assertion that the Buddhist doctrine of karma is mechanical and based only on retribution, as some eminent interpreters of Buddhism have averred.[57] It would seek rather to express karma in existential terms, as a description of the basic human condition. There are some contemporary Theravadins versed in modern Western philosophical and psychological theory who have written cogently about this. They reach out to such thinkers as Bergson, Whitehead, Nietzche, Heidegger and Freud, to explicate what they take to be the central focus of karmic doctrine. A good example is the *bhikkhu* Ñānajīvako, who feels it quite appropriate to mingle the Buddha with Heidegger. Seeing that the latter also deals with problems of human reality and temporality from a non-mechanistic perspective, Ñānajīvako senses that when Heidegger refers to man's thrownness, it is none other than his "karmically determined situation." But the situation can be taken in hand and altered for the better. So Ñānajīvako writes:

> Here conscience discloses itself as the awakening call which alone can liberate us from our lost condition and thrownness in *avijjā* (ignorance), or metaphysical nescience. Only in giving heed to the awakening call does Dasein understand itself with regard to its 'potentiality-for-being' in man's mindfulness, and resoluteness to take over his thrownness—right under the eyes of Death—that entity which Dasein is itself, and to take it over wholly, as his karmic load.[58]

This interesting account of karma through the language of a Western philosophical position points to a willingness on the part of some Theravāda Buddhist thinkers to go beyond traditional doctrinal postures and arguments in order to best express the metaphysical dimension of the *dhamma*. Ñānajīvako's work may be criticized for certain overgeneralizations, but the spirit of his endeavour is welcome for two reasons. First, it opens up some of the richness of Buddhist philosophical thought to Western readers. Second, and more important, it encourages Buddhist philosophical reflection at a time when dogmatism and tradition tends to stifle creative work of this nature.

The same can be said for the perceptive work in Theravāda Buddhist psychology, in particular by M.W.P. de Silva.[59] Recognizing that in the popular mind karma is associated with a judicial concept of reward and punishment, de Silva seeks to reassert what he takes to be the crucial heart of karmic doctrine in what he calls the craftsmanship model. De Silva's training in Western psychology has enabled him to express his case lucidly and persuasively. He does not force a Western schema on the Theravāda world-view, but identifies features in that world-view which might not be readily apparent to one familiar only with the "judicial" notion. In essence de Silva argues that karma is a dispositional concept, an expression of character. All actions reflect character, but behind the actions are the deep roots (*mūlas*), and latent dispositions (*anusayas*) which feed proclivity and habit. Development of good karma means coming to grips with the self in a motivational sense, with the soteriological aim of building up good character "rather than the possible material effects it may bring in this or some other life." So de Silva can conclude that "any attempt to isolate the doctrine of karma from the Buddhist concept of the springs of action, their motivational roots and the dynamic dispositional traits, is to turn a blind eye to a very rich facet of Buddhism, its psychology and the concept of human nature."[60]

De Silva's emphasis on the importance of seeing why individuals act as they do rather than why certain events transpire, gives karma an immediate psychological significance. Others have recognized this, of course, notably Ledi Sayadaw, who spoke of karma as a "refuge" (*saraṇa*) which can "save" by giving "support" and "protection."[61] He was referring to present karma (*sahajātakamma*) rather than past or asynchronous karma (*nānākkhaṇikakamma*), and especially to its volitional dimension.[62] But really de Silva is saying the same thing, albeit from a comparative perspective. While not necessarily a metaphysical interpretation of karma, it does have an existential or human quality to it that sets it apart from the judicial model so frequently appealed to.

Up to this point we have seen how in post-classical Theravāda, karma and rebirth were regarded as aspects of a higher truth, whose mysterious workings were not always self-evident. More recent scholarship has seen vigorous discussion on this point, with both empirical and metaphysical interpretations being argued. There is no clear-cut division between lay and monastic opinion on the matter, although in general the *saṅgha* supports a more metaphysical approach. This may be partly because of their reliance on Abhidhamma and medieval commentaries. However, I have found that most lay students of Theravāda tend to rely almost exclusively on the Sutta Piṭaka, which in turn supports a somewhat more empirical perspective.

KARMA AND REBIRTH IN THE LITTLE TRADITION

Students of Buddhism visiting Theravāda lands cannot help but be struck by the contrast between the formal *dhamma* of the sermon and text book, and the complex spiritual world of practical everyday religion. Wherever the Theravāda took root it adapted itself to the socio-religious environment, absorbing aspects of archaic beliefs always held with respect and veneration. The situation today is basically unchanged; many Theravāda Buddhists still order their lives through beliefs and rituals which have a pre-Buddhist etiology. In particular, the strong allegiance to the efficacy of merit-making and spirit worship would appear to compromise the Buddhist doctrines of improving karma and working out one's own salvation without the encumbrance of theistic beliefs and folk superstitions. And yet, curiously, the latent conflict is much less than meets the eye. Why is this so?

In turning first to the phenomenon of merit-making (*pinkama* in Sinhalese, *kutho* in Burmese, *bun* in Thai), Michael Ames is surely correct when he notes that it functions as a "pedagogical device" used to "express or explain more abstract principles and to evaluate concrete actions in terms of those principles."[63] The principles include karma, of course, and its improvement through formal, ritualized actions such as building a *cetiya*, partaking in the raising of a *hti* to the top of a *stūpa*, gilding a Buddha icon, or even feeding a monk.[64] Buddhism acknowledges the desire of devotees to merit-making, if only because it must involve positive volition (*cetanā*) to be effacacious. There is no suggestion that a ritual deed performed without noble intention can, by some mysterious process, render improved karma.

Merit-making may also seem to be inordinately selfish in a religion which is fundamentally based on reducing self-emphasis. For this reason, a long tradition of shared karma from meritorious action has developed. The karma of the one who engages in the actual merit ritual overflows so that others might benefit as well. By acknowledging the meritorious deed, the sharers produce their own positive *cetanā* (will), thus in a sense generating their own good karma. It is of interest to note, however, that strictly speaking, only merit can be shared in this way, but not demerit. In this context merit-making theoretically cannot be used to expiate past unwholesome karma, or spread such karma to others in order to lessen a personal burden. This at least is the orthodox position of the *saṅgha* today as I perceive it, with certain exceptions in Burma. Merit-making is still widely practised by all classes of Theravāda society in

Burma and Thailand,[65] although in Sri Lanka it is only commonly apparent at the village level.[66] Merit-making is thus an interesting example of the way an abstract philosophical principle such as karma can in fact gain collateral support from indigenous and possibly even pre-Buddhist religious belief.

Equally unique is the presence of spirit worship in a religion which doctrinally rejects the significance of otherworldly powers.[67] The spirits (*yakā* in Sinhalese, *nat* in Burmese, *phī* in Thai) are widely propitiated by all social classes throughout the Theravāda world. They present the most visible survival of archaic theology, particularly in the exquisite little spirit houses that adorn the entrances to dwellings and premises in Thailand; in their graphic representations on many Burmese temples; and in the colourful *tovil* masks of Sri Lankan spirit ceremony. Yet nowhere is it suggested that they are a stumbling block to appreciation of the *dhamma*. As gods or demons, the spirits are in no way absolute. They remain a means of assisting in the explanation of doctrine, and are not an item of doctrine as such. As Ames points out, invocation of the spirits and even the ancillary use of magic are not ends in themselves. They are means towards spiritual development.[68] The spirits can do this by giving confidence, by overcoming inward fears, or by urging the devotee on in pursuit of the wholesome life. If they in turn come to symbolize retribution or reward, it is not because they have power to interfere with karma. The spirits can do harm only if there has been bad karma accumulated in the past. Thus they operate within the law of karma, and become in effect agents of karma by helping to dispense the appropriate karmic justice as it comes due.

The point to note is the continued power of the doctrine of karma in folk culture and village-level Buddhism. We are not talking of something devoid of *praxis*, for even if both karma and rebirth may be in question to some at a theoretical level, their emotional and religious reality at a practical level can hardly be challenged.

In conclusion, karma and rebirth are not incidental to post-classical Theravāda doctrine. They remain very much a preoccupation of both the Great and Little Traditions. As a "total religious system,"[69] the Theravāda is both doctrinally and culturally in a state of evolution, like most other great living faiths. This means that periodic reinterpretations of key philosophical concepts and issues are both expected and welcome. In this sense, the doctrine of karma inevitably will take on added nuances as the Theravāda world meets new cosmological, technical and ideological changes. In fact, the doctrine of karma might turn out to be one of the most powerful political and economic incentives the history of religion has known, bringing forward the ability of each individual to direct the course of his future and that of humankind. This would be a far cry indeed from the mechanistic wheel of fortune associated by so many in the past with the Theravāda concepts of karma and rebirth.

NOTES

1. Theravāda was historically one of nine Sthaviravāda or Hīnayāna (Śrāvakayāna) schools, the two most important other schools being the Sarvāstivāda and Sautrāntika. Today, Theravāda conventionally refers to the various chapters or Theriya Nikāyas in Buddhist South and Southeast Asia. Differences in doctrine are outweighed by a common veneration of the Pāli Canon and its commentarial tradition. It should also be noted that this paper will use the traditional Sanskrit spelling for karma. The Pāli *kamma* is used only in textual quotations.

2. Bhikkhu Ñānamoli, trans., *The Path of Purification* (Colombo: A. Senage, 1964), p. IX.

3. See S. Pathamanathan, *The Kingdom of Jaffna* (Colombo: A.M. Rajendram, 1978), p. 3. This marks the end of the long and distinguished Anuradhapura Period in Sri Lanka. For a good account of this era, see W. Rahula, *History of Buddhism in Ceylon* (Colombo: M.D. Gunasena, 1956), pp. 78f, and C.W. Nichols and S. Paranavitana, *A Concise History of Ceylon* (Colombo: Ceylon University Press, 1961), Chap. 9.

4. On the spread of the Sinhalese Theravāda tradition in Siam, see T.O. Ling, *Buddhism, Imperialism and War* (London: George Allen & Unwin, 1979), pp. 11f, S.J. Tambian, *World Conqueror and World Renouncer* (London: Cambridge University Press, 1967), pp. 80f, and G. Coedes, *The Indianized States of Southeast Asia* (Honolulu: University of Hawaii Press, 1968), pp. 134f. For the impact of Sinhalese Theravāda Buddhism on Burma, see E. Sarkisyanz, *Buddhist Backgrounds to the Burmese Revolution* (The Hague: Martinus Nijhoff, 1965), p. 6. Sarkisyanz points out that Theravāda Buddhism may have been flourishing among the Mons since the fifth century, probably with origins in Pallava India.

5. See M. Ames, "Magical-animism and Buddhism: A Structural Analysis of the Sinhalese Religious System." *JAS*, Vol. 23 (1964), p. 41.

6. R.F. Gombrich, *Precept and Practise: Traditional Buddhism in the Highlands of Ceylon* (Oxford: Clarendon Press, 1971), p. 48. Paul Wirz, on the other hand, maintains that only a few villagers really comprehend the true Buddhist doctrine. See *Exorcism and the Art of Healing in Ceylon* (Leiden: E.J. Brill, 1954), p. 235.

7. See R.F. Gombrich, "Buddhist Karma and Social Control," *Comparative Studies in Society and History*, Vol. 17, No. 2 (April, 1975), p. 214.

8. Even the *Cuḷa-* and *Mahākammavibhaṅgasuttas* (M.3.203,207) offer only limited speculation on the function of karma.

9. Cf. R.F. Gombrich, op. cit., (1975), p. 216.

10. R.N. Bellah, "The Origin and Development of Religion," Lessa, W.A. *et al*, *Reader in Comparative Religion* (New York: Harper, Row, 1972), p. 38.

11. This was particularly so with the Gokulika ("Cinder") school, who interpreted S.3.177 and similar passages (viz., the *Ādittapariyāya Sutta* of the *Mahāvagga* in the Vinaya and S.4.19) "as if they meant that there is no happiness whatever of any kind in the world, but only unrelieved unhappiness." See A.K. Warder, *Indian Buddhism* (Delhi: Motilal Banarsidass, 1970), p. 242.

12. See A.T. Kirsch, "The Thai Buddhist Quest for Merit" in J. McAllister, (ed.) *Southeast Asia: The Politics of National Integration.* (N.Y.: Random House, 1973), p. 188.

13. In A.5.262, it is the destruction of the factor of karma (*kammanidāna-samkhayo*) that leads to *nibbāna*. But only in this sense can karma be considered peripheral to the basic doctrine of salvation. The danger of karma and rebirth replacing *nibbāna* as the symbolic goal of the *dhamma* amongst some Buddhists has doubtless always been a possibility. So Burma's great King Mindon (1853-78) was said to give the repeated instruction: "whatsoever meritorious deeds you do, long only for the absence of rolling on, not for rolling on." Pannasami, the *Sāsanavamsa* 6.151, as from E. Sarkisyanz, op. cit., (1965) p. 67.

14. M. Spiro, R.F. Gombrich and others therefore distinguish between nibbanic and kammic Buddhism, cf. R.F. Gombrich, op. cit., (1975) p. 213f.

15. Much has been written on whether *nibbāna* is a negative concept, cf. G.R. Welbon, *The Buddhist Nirvāṇa and Its Western Interpreters* (Chicago: University of Chicago Press, 1968), pp. 67f. In this regard, I agree with R.H.L. Slater when he writes "Nirvāṇa, in its religious context, may not be a simple, straightforward affirmation, but it is not denial. No religion could so persist if it merely brought man's elemental aspirations to a sharp cliff and threw them over," *Paradox and Nirvāṇa,* (Chicago, 1951), p. 9. Nevertheless, *nibbāna* is seldom held out to be obtainable for all but an exceptional few. In his study of contemporary Burmese Buddhism, M. Nash brings this to focus when he notes that mention of *nibbāna* (*neikban*) as a possibility only elicits smiles from villagers who perceive it as a remote likelihood. See *The Golden Road to Maturity,* (Chicago, University of Chicago Press, 1965), p. 107.

16. I use 'eschatological' guardedly to accommodate those events Buddhists associate with death and rebirth, following G. Obeyesekere, "The Rebirth Eschatology and Its Transformation: A Contribution to the Sociology of Early Buddhism" in W. O'Flaherty, ed., *Karma and Rebirth in Classical Indian Traditions* (Berkeley, University of California Press, 1980), p. 138.

17. Viz., bodily, verbal, or mental deeds (*kāya-vacī-manokamma*) defined as skillful or morally good (*kusala*), bad (*akusala*), or neutral (*avyākata*), M.3.205.

18. This definition of providence is offered by Paul Tillich, "The Meaning of Providence" in *The Shaking of the Foundations* (New York: Pelican Books, 1962), p. 111. Cf. also B. Hebblewaite, *Evil, Suffering and Religion* (London: Sheldon Press, 1976), p. 90.

19. C.A.F. Rhys Davids, *Sakya*, p. 104, as quoted from R.H.L. Slater, op. cit., (1931) p. 24.

20. *Saṃvattanika* literally means conducive to. *Paṭisarana* indicates refuge, but I.B. Horner prefers a sense of giving support to. See *Middle Length Sayings* (London: Pali Text Society, 1959) vol. 3, pp. 59, 249.

21. See the *Cakkavattisīhanādu Sutta* (*D*.3.63), where unstable social and economic conditions are said to be conducive to crime. This *Sutta* emphasizes that the five moralities (*pañcasīla*) are not only spiritually important, but socially and politically significant as the appropriate framework for domestic policy. See P. Dissanayake, *Political Thoughts of the Buddha* (Colombo: Department of Cultural Affairs, 1977), p. 101.

22. See. K.N. Jayatilleke, *Survival and Karma* (Kandy: Buddhist Publication Society, 1969), pp. 26f. Ames points out that in contemporary village Buddhism in Lanka, five laws are recognized as governing different aspects of the world. One is ethical (*kamma*) and thereby part of Buddhism. The others which are not the concern of the religion, include atmospheric, biological, physical, and curiously, psychological (*citta*) laws. The latter, it would seem to me, would be a part of the *dhamma*. Cf. M. Ames, op. cit., (1964) p. 38.

23. In his review of karma in the *Abhidharmakośa* (a fifth century Sautrāntika work, but highly regarded by the Theravāda as well), J.P. McDermott notes that the ethical potential of an act could be counteracted by repentance. See "Karma and Rebirth in Early Buddhism" in W. O'Flaherty, ed., op. cit., (1980) p. 188. Likewise, Nash points out that in modern Burmese Theravāda, unwholesome karma accumulated because of occupation can be expiated through sacrificial giving or merit-making. See op. cit., (1965) p. 158).

24. Kammaṃ khettaṃ viññāṇaṃ bījaṃ taṇhā sineho. Avijjānivaranāṇaṃ sattānam taṇhāsaṃyojanānaṃ hīnāya dhātuyā viññāṇaṃ patiṭṭhitam. (Karma is the field, consciousness the seed, craving the moisture. Of beings that are hindered by ignorance, fettered by craving, consciousness gets support in inferior conditions.) *A*.1.223.

25. Kammadāyādā sattā ti vadāmi. (I say beings are heirs to karma [action].) *M*.1.390.

26. See B. Matthews "Notes on the Concept of the Will in Early Buddhism," *The Sri Lanka Journal of the Humanities*, Vol. 1. No. 2, Dec. 1975. pp. 152f.

27. Sutta Piṭaka passages on caste are numerous (viz., *D*.1.87, 3.80; *A*.1.62). T.W. Rhys Davids' introduction to the *Ambattha Sutta, Dialogues of the Buddha*. (London: Pāli Text Society, 1965), Vol. 1., pp. 96f lists the relevant texts and provides a good background to the subject. In contemporary Theravāda, however, where caste is a social factor (Sri Lanka), its relationship with karma is admitted, contrary to Canonical instruction. See B. Ryan, *Caste in Modern Ceylon* (New Jersey: Rutger's University Press, 1956), p. 37.

28. See *Buddhist Psychological Ethics*, (Pali Text Society, 1974), reprint of C.A.F. Rhys Davids' *A Buddhist Manual of Psychological Ethics— the Dhammasaṅgaṇi* (London: P.T.S., 1923); and *Conditional Relations* (Vol. 1 of the *Paṭṭhāna*, trans. U. Nārada, London, 1969). Traditionally there are seven books in this *Piṭaka*, although the Burmese add the *Peṭakopadesa* and *Nettipakaraṇa* for a total of nine.

29. Viz., *The Expositor* or *Atthasālinī, Buddhaghosa's commentary to the Dhammasaṅgaṇi*, Vols. 1 and 2, trans. Pe Maung Tin, (London: P.T.S., 1921 and 1958).

30. Thus Warder writes that the "Abhidharma. . .is the glory of the Sthaviravāda school," op. cit., (1970) p. 299. Many devotees still find obvious refreshment and stimulation in reflecting on its teachings. Nonetheless, one wonders

how much relevance it has for villagers or even the average village monk, a point Nash raises with reference to present day upper Burma, op. cit., (1965) p. 107.

31. Bhikkhu Nārada, *A Manual of Abhidhamma—the Abhidhammattha saṅgaha* (Kandy: B.P.S., 1975), p. 1. The conviction that the Abhidhamma is the domain of the Buddhas (*Buddha-visaya*), conceived in the Buddha's mind right after the Enlightenment during the week of the house of gems (*ratana-ghara-sattāha*) and later preached to the gods, has strengthened its reputation for being the ultimate (*paramattha*) teaching.

32. Interview with U Thattila Sayadaw, Rangoon, July 1981. So also Ñanaponika notes that despite its somewhat formidable didactic structure, the Abhidhamma is meant "for inquiring and searching spirits who are not satisfied by monotonously and uncritically repeating ready-made (abhidhamma) terms." Furthermore, the Piṭaka should be open to hermeneutical study so that it "does not cease to become a living and growing organism." *Abhidhamma Studies* (based on the *Dhammasaṅgaṇi* and *Aṭṭhasālinī* (Kandy: B.P.S., 1965), p. ii.

33. This Abhidhamma interest in the three times dimensions is reflected in the often ornate (and frequently incomprehensible) charts appended to studies of causality. Even the relatively uncomplicated *paṭiccasamuppāda*, so important in Sutta Piṭaka, is divided up into three time sectors by later Abhidhamma thinkers, viz., Nārada, op. cit., (1975), p. 358, something not indicated in the Sutta itself. This device is first explicitly set down by Buddhaghosa in the *Sumaṅgalāvilasinī*, in its exegesis of *D*.2.55. It should be emphasized, however, that unlike the Sarvastivadins, who taught that everything exists, including past, present and future, the Theravadins accepted the ontological existence only of the immediate or static moment.

34. There is one contested passage (*A*.2.79). The Pāli Text Society manuscript edited by Morris (1955) renders *bhavagga* (best state of existence) for *bhavaṅga* here, but others, notably Jayatilleke and Sarachchandra prefer the reading *bhavaṅga*. See K.N. Jayatilleke, "Some Problems of Translation and Interpretation," University of Ceylon Review (1949), Vol. 7, p. 216, and E.R. Sarachchandra, *The Buddhist Psychology of Perception* (Colombo, University of Ceylon Press, 1958), p. 491. The latter in particular argues that *bhavaṅga*, although suggesting on the one hand a state of deep sleep or trance, is on the other hand implying that it is what survives in rebirth. It is interesting that Buddhaghosa's commentary on the passage rejects the reading *bhavaṅga* as misleading, and insists on *bhavagga* as the correct noun in this text. See *The Catukkhanipata-vaṇṇanā on the Apaṇṇakavagga of the Anguttara Nikāya*, edited by H. Kopp (London: P.T.S., 1936), p. 107. It is appropriate to conclude that the Anguttara reading *bhavaṅga* is not accurate, and that although *bhavaṅga* does appear in the Abhidhamma Piṭaka, it is not until the post-classical era that it receives much attention.

35. See M.W.P. de Silva, *Buddhist and Freudian Psychology* (Colombo, Lake House, 1973), p. 51.

36. See Bhikkhu Ñanatiloka, *Buddhist Dictionary: A Manual of Buddhist Terms and Doctrines* (Colombo: Frewin and Co., 1956), p. 29.

37. See Shwe Zan Aung, (trans.), *Compendium of Philosophy* (London, P.T.S., 1963), pp. 2f. D.J. Kalupahana gives a good review of Theravāda responses to

the *bhavaṅga* concept. See *Buddhist Philosophy* (Honolulu: University of Hawaii Press, 1976), p. 102.

38. Ibid., p. 99.

39. The *Saṅgaha* covers the same range of topics as the much earlier *Visuddhimagga*, but set down in *mātikā* (list of topics) style, there is less amplitude on points of doctrine. With this in mind, perhaps, Mrs. Rhys Davids could write "the little work will reward only those who can patiently soak the mind in the peculiar method of treatment." *Compendium of Philosophy*, op. cit., p. xix. It is dated between the ninth and eleventh centuries, and is attributed to Anuruddha of Kañcipura. I have chosen to examine it rather than the works of Buddhaghosa both because of its later date and because of its popularity in the monastic tradition of the Theravāda.

40. *Bhavaṅga* is given further expansion in commentaries on the *Saṅgaha*. So Nārada, op. cit., (1975), p. 34, indicates that it involves three stages: past (*atīta*), present (*calana*, quivering, unsteady) and interrupted (*upaccheda*), all activated in one sequence according to the law of cause and effect, and all bearing result (*vipāka*) that affects the ongoing thought process.

41. *Javana* is a complex psychological concept which indicates both a psychological and ethical stage in the thought process. Its effects are cumulative, that is, they become karma that they may operate in future rebirths. Later commentary argues that *javana* takes place over seven so-called thought moments, the point being that according to which thought moment *javana* is strongest, it can result in karma operating in this life (*diṭṭhadhammavedaniyu-kamma*) or in successive lives (*aparāpariyavedaniya-kamma*), ibid., p. 169. Commenting on this term, Rhys Davids remarks, "it suffices to remember that it is the mental aspect or parallel of that moment in nerve-process when central function is about to become. . .activity. Teachers in Ceylon associate it with the word 'dynamic.' And its dominant interest for European psychologists is the fusion of intellect and will. . . ." *Compendium of Philosophy*, op. cit., p. 249.

42. Most Theravadins believe that untimely or accidental death occurs only because of past powerful karmic forces, which can cut off the life term before it has had a chance to run its course. This kind of karma is identified as *upacchedaka* (breaking off). In recent conversations with the Sayadaws U Thattila and U Narada (Rangoon, July, 1982), this traditional teaching was unequivocably emphasized. Although there are evidently some controversial monks in Burma (i.e., U Okkhata) who have recently challenged this interpretation, the Theravāda *saṅgha* everywhere generally accepts the above established position reiterated at the Sixth World Buddhist Council in 1958.

43. Notes V.F. Gunaratna, "the *cuti citta*. . .perhaps no active function which can give rise to any result. Although it is the last thought in the dying process it is an unconscious thought. It merely registers the awareness of death." See *Rebirth Explained* (Kandy: P.T.S., 1971), p. 47.

44. M. Nash, op. cit., (1965), p. 106.

45. This is consistent with the canonical teaching that three things are necessary for conception (*okkanti*): coitus, the mother's right season and the appearance of the *gandhabba* or karmic being, cf. M.1.266. The *Saṅgaha* goes on to show (6.5.1.f) how karma is involved in the production of nine material qualities as the vitality (*jīvita*) that stands behind and is indistinct (*avinibbhoga*)

from the form (*rupa*). Other material production evolves accordingly from mind (*citta*), in the proper time (*utu*) and from food (*ahara*).

46. Cf. J.P. McDermott, op. cit., (1980), p. 170. Occasionally a Theravada scholar does refer to a brief intermediate stage between birth and death (see O.H. Wijesekere, "Vedic Gandharva and Pāli Gandhabba," *University of Ceylon Review*, Vol. 3, No. 1, 1945), but never in an elaborate sense, as, for example, in the Vajrayana (cf. Sidpa Bardo, Book Two, *Bardo Thodol*).

47. See D.J. Kalupahana, op. cit., (1976), p. 102.

48. A.K. Warder, Op. Cit., (1970), p. 300.

49. K.N. Jayatilleke, *Early Buddhist Theory of Knowledge* (London: George Allen & Unwin, 1963), p. 442.

50. Viz., the six kinds of higher knowledge (*chaḷabhiññā*, *D*.I.77f): psychokinetic activity; clairaudience; telepathic knowledge; antenatal recognition; knowledge of the decease and survival of beings; knowledge of the destruction of defiling impulses.

51. K.N. Jayatilleke, op. cit., (1963), p. 460.

52. See F. Story (Anagārika Sugatānanda), "Rebirth, Karma and Modern Science," in *Rebirth as Doctrine and Experience* (Kandy: P.T.S., 1975), pp. 46f., and E.C. Baptist, op. cit., (1969), p. 4.

53. See K.N. Jayatilleke, op. cit., (1963), p. 459, and in *Survival and Rebirth*, op. cit., (1969), pp. 10f.

54. See A.B. Keith, *Buddhist Philosophy in India and Ceylon* (4th ed., Varanasi: Chowkhomba Sanskrit Series, 1963), p. 33; C.A. Moore, "Buddhism and Science: Both Sides," in *Buddhism and Culture*, S. Yamaguchi (ed.), (Kyoto: Nakana Press, 1960), p. 103; E. Conze, *Buddhist Meditation* (London: George Allen & Unwin, 1959), p. 24.

55. W. O'Flaherty, (ed.), *Karma and Rebirth in Classical Indian Traditions*, op. cit., p. xxii.

56. Shwe Zan Aung (trans.), *Compendium of Philosophy*, op. cit., p. 284.

57. See L. de la Vallée Poussin, *Encyclopedia of Religion and Ethics*, (Edinburgh: Charles Scribner's & Sons, 1915), Vol. 7, p. 676.

58. Bhikkhu Ñānajīvako, *et al. Kamma and Its Fruits* (Kandy: P.T.S., 1975), p. 47.

59. See M.W.P. de Silva, *Buddhist and Freudian Psychology*, op. cit., *An Introduction to Buddhist Psychology* (London: Macmillan Press, 1979). Mention should also be made of the contribution to this area of Theravāda studies by the late Rune Johansson, notably *The Psychology of Nirvana* (London: George Allen & Unwin, 1969) and *The Dynamic Psychology of Early Buddhism*, (Oxford: Curzon Press, 1979).

60. M.W.P. de Silva, *Value Orientations and Nation Building* (Colombo: Lake House, 1976), p. 13.

61. Karma as one of the Four Refuges appears in *J*.6.102 and the later *Miln*. 65. See Ledi Sayadaw, *The Manuals of Buddhism*, *Maggana Dīpanī*, (Rangoon: Dept. of Religious Affairs, 1981), p. 228.

62. Ibid., *The Patthānudesa Dīpanī*, p. 51.

63. Michael Ames, (1964), p. 21. The subject of merit (*puñña*) receives much attention in the Pāli Canon, including the odd reference to merit-making

(*puññakiryā*, S.1.87). But it can be argued that the ritualization of merit-making as *dāna*, etc., comes somewhat later, as it is not carefully rehearsed in the Canon. A better translation of *puñña*, at least in its classical sense, would be 'virtue' or some such synonym.

64. Manning Nash outlines seven "levels of giving" associated with merit-making in modern Burma (see *The Golden Road to Maturity*, op. cit., p. 116). A slightly different list is appropriate to Thailand. See S.J. Tambian, *Buddhism and the Spirit Cults in North-east Thailand* (London: Cambridge University Press, 1970), p. 146.

65. Examples of the high profile merit-making still has in Burma and Thailand can be seen in the actions of political figures in public life. Thus, the King of Thailand and members of both his court and government are frequently involved in occasions of merit-making. Even the totalitarian chairman of the Burma Socialist Programme Party, U Ne Win, recently commissioned a *zedi* in Mandalay to house sacred relics gifted from Nepal. This contributed directly to his lustre as protector of the *dhamma* and generator of good karma. See John Wiant, "The Political Symbolism of Taw-Hlan-Ye-Khit" in *Military Rule in Burma Since 1962*, F.K. Lehman (ed.) (Singapore: Institute for S.E. Asian Studies, 1981), pp. 62f.

66. Michael Ames, op. cit., (1964), p. 40.

67. Good accounts of how a spirit mythology was incorporated into the earliest Buddha *dhamma* are found in Trevor Ling, *Buddhism and the Mythology of Evil* (London: George Allen & Unwin, 1962), pp. 75f; E.R. Sarchchandra, *The Folk Drama of Ceylon* (Colombo, Dept. of Cultural Affairs, 1966), pp. 9f; and M.M.J. Marasinghe, *Gods in Early Buddhism* (Vidyalankara, University of Sri Lanka Press, 1974), pp. 233f.

68. Michael Ames, op. cit., (1964), p. 36.

69. Ibid., p. 46.

CHAPTER EIGHT

The Chinese Understanding and Assimilation of Karma Doctrine

YÜN-HUA JAN

The introduction of the karma doctrine from the Indian to the Chinese culture was not an isolated incident, but a component of Buddhism in general. Before the spread of Buddhism, there were ideas of retribution in the indigenous traditions, but the concept of rebirth was quite foreign to the Chinese. As time went on, Chinese understanding of the doctrine became clearer as the result of the increase in the translations of Buddhist texts, and more knowledge of the subject was gained by direct contacts with Indian and Central Asian monks, who visited and settled in China. Consequently, the doctrine of karma and rebirth was assimilated into the Chinese culture. It merged with the ancient Chinese idea of retribution and became an intrinsic component of the Chinese tradition.

This paper will attempt to enquire into the process of Chinese understanding and assimilation of the karma doctrine through selected samples. The first segment of this paper will outline the basic Chinese ideas of retribution prior to the spread of Buddhism. The samples in this segment are all derived from ancient Chinese texts up to the Han period. The second segment of the paper deals with Hui-yüan's (慧遠 : 334-417) understanding of karma and rebirth. He has been selected as one Chinese representative of this period principally because he played a crucial role in the history of Chinese Buddhism, especially in the understanding of karma, and also because there is some misunderstanding of his thought in one of the early studies on this eminent Chinese Buddhist scholar.[1] The third segment of the paper will be on Tsung-mi (宗密 : 780-841), one of the most scholastic and systematic Buddhist thinkers in Chinese history. Samples from his writings indicate advance in knowledge of the doctrine and creative interpretation and adoption of it into the Chinese religious system.[2] The last segment of this study is an enquiry into the three collections of short stories published by Feng Meng-lung (馮夢龍:1574-1666). Feng was selected as a sample simply because of the high quality and scope of the 120 stories collected or written and published by this outstanding, late medieval writer. The socio-historical significance of Feng's short stories have been well summarized by Liu Wu-chi:

> The 120 stories in Feng Meng-lung's collection cover practically every phase of Chinese life. Their range includes: quasi-historical tales of kings and generals, faithful friends and filial sons; romantic yarns of strange lands and peoples; supernatural stories of marvels and prodigies, spirits and ghosts, Buddhist monks and Taoist immortals; realistic stories of scandals in the monastic establishment; daring exploits of brigands and thieves; murders, lawsuits, and court trials; domestic tragedies and bloody revenges; social comedies and family reunions.[3]

As all these stories are consistently presented with realism as an accent, samples from these collections may be taken as portraits of Chinese life during the period. No wonder then, that some historians in recent decades have used this source fully in their studies of Chinese thought and society of that time. C.T. Hsia's work is one of the well-known examples.[4]

I

From the ancient past until the introduction of Buddhism, Chinese ideas of retribution can be summarized as follows: (1) "Life and death are the decree of Heaven (*ming*); wealth and honor depend on Heaven."[5] (2) Heavenly decrees are influenced by one's morality or virtue. This point could be illustrated by the well-known passage from the *Book of Historical Documents*, that "The Way of Heaven is to bless the good and to punish the bad."[6] (3) Retribution from Heaven may take effect by cutting short one's life or causing one to die unnaturally, or by affecting one's family, especially one's descendants.[7] The present discussion will not examine early ideas in detail. A quotation from two Han dynasty works serve the purpose for this paper. One of the passages is from the *Po-hu T'ung* attributed to Pan Ku (班固:32-92 A.D.), the famous historian of Han China. It has been stated in Chapter XXXI, that the span of life has been destined by the Heaven, and there are three kinds of destinies, namely, Old-Age Destiny, Accident Destiny and Merit Destiny. The last one, Merit Destiny (*sui-ming*) "is the destiny as a consequence of one's behaviour."[8] This Confucian idea considers correct principles or virtues as the heavenly will. Any contravention of these principles is regarded as an act of despising Heaven, "so that on that account Heaven cuts off his life."[9] To some extent this passage is an illustration of an earlier and more authoritative passage from the *Doctrine of the Mean*, which says, "He who possesses great virtue will certainly attain to a corresponding position, to corresponding wealth, to corresponding fame, and to corresponding long life."[10]

The ancient Chinese belief in moral order and its connection with retribution created some difficulties when this theory was adopted as an explanation of life, because in many historical examples there were virtuous men who, though excellent in their moral standing, suffered in their lives. Ssu-ma Ch'ien, 司馬遷, the grand historian, saw the problem and sighed when he commented on the biography of Po I and Shu Ch'i.

> Someone said, 'It is the way of Heaven to show no favouritism. It is forever on the side of the good man.'[11] Are not persons such as Po I and Shu Ch'i to be called as 'good men'? They have accumulated benevolence and regulated their actions as such, but still died in starvation! Moreover, out of seventy disciples, Confucius only recommended Yen Yüan as the one who loved learning; though he never disliked a simple meal, (he) yet died prematurely. (As these are cases) what is Heaven's reward to the men who have practiced good?[12]

In order to explain this difficulty, some Han scholars like Pan Ku and Wang Ch'ung (王充 :27-194) put forward the theory of *tsao-ming* or Accident Destiny, trying to explain that in spite of good deeds, one might still have to face depraved encounters in life. These include unruly kings, natural calamities as well as extraordinary events.[13] Even if one took for granted that this explanation was satisfactory, the ineffectiveness of morality as a determining factor in retribution still remains unsolved.

It was within the aforementioned religious context that the Buddhist theory of karma and rebirth was introduced into China. Years after the spread of Buddhism over the land, the Chinese gradually understood what this doctrine was, and how radically it differed from the ancient Chinese idea. The Chinese astonishment at this concept was clearly expressed in the statement, "The Buddhists say that after a man dies he will be reborn. I do not believe in the truth of these words. . . ."[14] This astonishment is understandable, because according to their tradition retribution only affects one's own life or his posterity. The theory of rebirth, therefore, seemed very strange. Although the Taoist philosophy contained hints of life and death as an ongoing drama, it never explicitly discussed the possibility of rebirth. In the Taoist religion, apart from the cultivation of immortality so that life may extend beyond death, there is a passage referring to the possibility of "being born again" (*fu-sheng*),[15] as found in a Tun-huang manuscript in Sir A. Stein's collection #6825. But this text was compiled long after the introduction of Buddhism.

II

The Chinese understanding of the karma doctrine passed through different stages. The early Chinese Buddhists had clarified two points of the doctrine. First, karmic effects do not extend to the relatives of wrong doers. Hsi Ch'ao (郗超 :ca. 331-373) quoted from the *Ni-huan ching*, which declares that "when the father has done wrong, the son will not suffer in this place; if the son has done wrong, the father will not suffer either."[16] Hsi comments on the passage by saying that karma is such that "the one who does good automatically reaps happiness, and he who does wrong automatically undergoes its baleful results.[17] Second, it was not until Hui-yüan (慧遠 :334-417) that the Chinese understanding of karma and rebirth became more systematic. After reading the newly translated Buddhist scriptures of the time, Hui-yüan writes,

> The sutra says that there are three types of karmic response: (1) in this life; (2) in the next life; (3) in one of the following lives. They are explained as follows: Good deeds are rewarded and bad deeds are punished.[18]

As far as the three types of retribution are concerned, the above quoted statement from Hui-yüan's writing clearly indicates that the author's understanding of karmic effect is quite accurate. However, there are doubts about Hui-yüan's concept of karma, which require some clarification.

According to Liebenthal, the concept of karma in Indian Buddhism is "that at the beginning of all evil there is Error, *avidyā*, which narrows our vision and causes the split into individual things. It initiated the sequence of cause and result. . . ."[19] Liebenthal considers that in contrast with the Buddhists, the Taoist teaching regarding one's body is the cause of sufferings. The body, Liebenthal claims, "represents an individual interest, selfishness, partiality, and a definite position in the Whole and a destiny (*so*) is the consequence, for any thing short of the Whole is transient."[20] This understanding leads him to believe that in the Taoist scheme, "our end is predestined by the peculiarity of our beginning."[21] He thus claims,

> That is Karma, certainly not the Indian Buddhist Karma but that of Hui-yüan. For the Buddhist knows no Order of Things, no Fate,

even no individual predestined course or line. Each act, each reaction, each deed, draws its corresponding result. . . .[22]

Following this statement, Liebenthal has contrasted the position of Buddhism and the viewpoint he believes to be that of Hui-yüan. Liebenthal concludes:

> The Chinese has always been less afraid of himself, less moralistic than the Indian: more afraid of the accident than of the stick, more trustful of Nature than of a personal representative of the Law. Hui-yüan was, it is well understood, more of a heathen than, e.g., Kumārajīva, his Indian contemporary; he was less obedient, less orthodox than the following generation of Buddhists.[23]

The statement made by Liebenthal touches upon a number of problems, and some of these problems are involved with basic principles, which he did not elaborate. For example, when he mentions Indian Buddhism, he never clearly defined what it meant, or what the text was, or what school or phase of Indian Buddhism it represented. As he himself was not an expert of Indian Buddhist thought, one should not insist on these points, but as he was one of few scholars who had translated Chinese Buddhist texts and still has some influence in the field, one has to deal with his presentation of Hui-yüan's understanding of karma and rebirth. Unless this is done, it may imply that the Chinese did not understand the doctrine during the time of Hui-yüan. This is so because Hui-yüan was the outstanding writer among a few Chinese who contributed to the topic.

When one enquires into the evidence presented by Liebenthal on Hui-yüan, it seems that his conclusion on the subject is based on the misreading of Hui-yüan's works, which involves misunderstanding of the texts and misreading of some words from common sense into Neo-Taoist technical terms. Consequently he has read a lot of related Taoist systems into his translation and interpretation which might not be the intention of the original writings. As a result of this misreading, misunderstanding, and misrepresentation, Hui-yüan has been misunderstood by most of the English readers as a Taoist rather than a Buddhist. Let us read a few passages on karma and rebirth from Hui-yüan's text so that the new reading will explain Hui-yüan's understanding of karma.

> Ignorance (*avidyā*) is the abyss of illusionment (*moha-jāla*; desires (*rāga*) is the house of bondages. When these two principles (*li*, i.e., *avidyā* and *rāga*) wander jointly, they create invisible (*ming*) and subtle (*shen*) functions (*yung*): good or bad, worrisome or misery

> are all moved by them. One's feelings and thoughts would cling to external objects because ignorance has clouded his brilliance; the four great elements (*mahā bhūtas*) coagulated into a body because of the influx of desires into one's nature. When the body is coagulated one is wrapped up (=separated from others), and when feeling clings to objects, good and bad deeds have a master (=actor). When self and others are separated, one becomes selfish about his body (=existence), thus his existence may never perish. When good and bad deeds are connected with the actor, the actor would attach himself to life, and so life may well never end. Henceforth one rests comfortably and with great dreams.[24]

If one compares this rendering with the translation by Liebenthal, some of his difficulties become obvious. He has translated the same passage as follows:

> Illusion (*avidyā*) spreads its net of errors, greed builds its house of suffering; in the trails of these two, shen manifests itself (in life); good and bad luck and disappointments are merely the phases (or its trail). Illusion narrows the vision (of Shen) and causes his thought to focus on external things; greed makes it stray and causes the elements to coagulate to bodies. When a body coagulates, this creates a split between oneself and the rest; when thoughts are focussed on (external) things, the condition to discern between good and bad is fulfilled. When a split shows between oneself and the rest, then the body is cherished and more difficult to get rid of; when it is possible to discern between good and bad, then interest in life is created and (less easily) it is left behind. Then we sweetly sleep the Great Dream.[25]

Although there are some problems in the passage, these problems are common to language interpretation. The basic teaching of Buddhism is clear—that ignorance and greed or desires are the sources for man's being caught in bondage. From these two sources the longing for existence materializes, and *saṃsāra* becomes an on-going drama of sufferings. This passage and the previously quoted passage seem no different from the Abhidharmic doctrine on karma and rebirth. If this is the case, one may ask what the reason for Liebenthal's interpretation is? For an answer to this question, one must examine the evidence presented in his paper.

Let us begin with some key terms that he has pointed out. First, Liebenthal sees that there is a concept of the Whole in Taoism. This probably means the Tao, which he has translated as "universal fate."[26] It is true that the Tao is conceived by the Lao Tzu as universal, but it is not identical with fate. And more importantly, in what sense did Hui-yüan use the term? In an examination of Hui-yüan's original text, there is no support for Liebenthal's reading. As far as the essay itself is concerned, the author has used the term *tao* in two senses, namely as a proper noun, which usually reads as "the way," and in the sense of *tao-li* which usually means "reason." This reading of the Chinese text has been correctly translated by Makita Tairyo in his study of the *Hung-ming chi.*[27] The passage, "All that is induced by cause and conditions, all that appears in the change (of our life), is not Tao (universal fate), from which it comes?", as read by Liebenthal, should actually read, "Are not those which are produced by cause and conditions, and transformed through change due to their ways?" There is no sense of so-called universal fate, nor that "the 64 Hexagrams have a definite position in the Changes, the *i*," as Liebenthal has read it into the context himself.

Another term Liebenthal objects to as a non-Buddhist concept is *shu* which he spells wrongly as *so* and translates as "accounts" in the translation, and as "destiny" in his analysis.[28] There is no doubt *shu* could be a technical term when it is used in fortune-telling, yet it can also be understood in the sense of sequence non-technically. In the context of Hui-yüan's essays, it may be retranslated as follows:

> When evil deeds are accumulated, it will cause heavenly disaster;
> and when crimes are committed, hellish punishment will take place.
> This is an inevitable sequence, which is beyond any doubt.[29]

One may find some difficulty in the usage of the term like heavenly in Buddhist systems, yet the moral thrust of Hui-yüan's understanding of karma still remains. As far as Liebenthal's objection to *shu* as destiny is concerned, it seems groundless.

The third objectionable term Liebenthal has mentioned is what he terms as "the order of things." The original Chinese word for the term is *li*. This word in the sense of a noun usually denotes line, grain, regulation, principle, reason.[30] It is in the sense of line, grain, or structural signs in stone or wood, that it might be understood as the order or structure of things. The Taoist and the Legalist both used the word in that sense. However, the word also has its common usage in the sense of reason or principle without any technical or special connotation, and this second usage is the case in Hui-yüan. This term has twice appeared in the passage. (1) "*erh-li chu-yu, ming wei shen-yung* 二理俱遊，冥為神用" means, "when these two principles wander jointly, they created invisible and subtle functions."[31] Liebenthal, however, has translated it as, "In the trails of these two, Shen manifests itself (in life)."[32] Here he did not translate the words *li* or *ming*. (2) "*hui-chih yu pen, tse li tzu ming tui* 會之有本，則理自冥對" has been rendered by Liebenthal as, "All (we see) take place is rooted (in the past), it is the result of an *unknown Order of Things*."[33] But the original passage means, "When one understands that all happenings have their origins, then the reason (of these happenings) automatically matches to its invisible (origin)."[34] The happenings refer to the item mentioned in the preceding paragraph, namely, "when evil deeds are accumulated, it will cause heavenly disaster; and when crimes are committed, hellish punishment will take place."[35] The reference to happenings is also confirmed by the subsequent passage when it states. "The mind takes good and bad deeds as the cause, retribution takes crime and virtue as the outcome (and their relation is like) form and its shadow, sound and its echo." In both these instances, no problem of order of things has been found. And, consequently, how could Hui-yüan have been criticized as non-Buddhistic in his understanding of karma?

The remaining two problematic terms are nature and *shen*. As far as the usage of nature is concerned, it occurs approximately four times in the essays. Of these usages, the words *tzu-jan* stand three times as an adjective or noun, which Liebenthal has correctly rendered as "natural" or "nature."[36] But in another instance, he has translated it as "nature," and connected it to a term "order in nature," in his critical analysis of Hui-yüan.[37] However, if one checks the original text, one would find that the Chinese term which Liebenthal has translated as nature is *pi-jan*. The passage reads "*tz'u-nai pi-jan chih shu, wu-so- yun-i i*, 此乃必然之數 無所容疑矣 ,"[38] which means, "This is an inevitable sequence, which is beyond any doubt." *Pi-jan* is an adjective which stands for inevitable, and no sense of nature is contained in the original passage. The word *shen* appears at least seven times in the original text.[39] It denotes the meaning of mysterious or subtle when it is an adjective such as *shen-yung* 神用 (subtle functions) or *shen-tse* 神宅 (spiritual house); it means god or spirit as a noun, such as *shen-chi chu-tse* 神之居宅 (the dwelling-house of the spirit) or *shen-hsing* 神形 (spirit-body). Liebenthal has translated the phrase *ming-wei shen-yung* 冥為神明 (they create invisible and subtle functions) as "*shen* manifests itself (in life),"[40] *shen-chih chu-tse* as "the soul which dwells in the House," and *shen-hsing* as "body and soul." His reading of *shen*, an adjective, as a noun is a mistake. His translation of *shen* as soul is understandable, although it is really a problem. The Buddhist theory of karma denies *ātman* in its Indian context, but it has difficulty when it discusses the entity which carries causal strength into its effect. This difficulty had already created the controversy of *pudgalavāda* in the Indian context, and remains a problem in China. However, the Chinese did not translate *ātman* as *shen*. If the word soul is understood in the sense of *ātman*, *shen* cannot be the Chinese equivalent for it. *Shen* stands for spirit probably in the sense of the "immaterial element of a human being," as one of the definitions in the *Oxford Dictionary of English Etymology* puts it. If one reads the word *shen* in that sense, the term *shen-hsing* is very close to the Buddhist term of *nāma-rūpa*. However, the Chinese use different words in their definition of immaterial aspects of life, viz., *shen* for spirit, *hun-po* for soul, and *wo* for *ātman* in the sense of Self. All these words are related, but not necessarily identical.

The foregoing discussion has pointed out some of Liebenthal's inaccurate translations of Hui-yüan's essays on karma. If these mistranslations are true, then Liebenthal's contrast of the Chinese and Indian concepts of karma become largely groundless. The conclusion that should rather be drawn is that the Chinese understanding of the Buddhist concept of karma was accurate in Hui-yüan's work. In fact, T'ang Yung-t'ung already pointed out decades ago, that though Hui-yüan used some Neo-Taoist terms in his exposition of Buddhist doctrines, his usage was a means of making his contemporaries understand Buddhism. T'ang has no doubt that Hui-yüan's standpoint was Buddhist.[41] To explain a foreign idea to another culture in a native language has always had its limitations. One has to understand Hui-yüan in that light as well, although reading something else into his work is a different matter.

III

With the advance of time, especially with the new translations of Indian Buddhist scriptures into the Chinese language, the Chinese understanding of karma improved greatly. Because of the voluminous amount of literature, it is impossible to survey all Chinese Buddhist works on this topic. But one may choose one of the representatives and examine how the writer understood and adopted the doctrine into his own system. This portion of the paper will focus on Tsung-mi, a ninth century Buddhist thinker. He is chosen first because he is one of the few systematic thinkers, and second, because this author has been doing research on Tsung-mi for some time.[42]

By the time of Tsung-mi, the Chinese understood that karma was not a doctrine exclusive to Buddhism; it was also found in other Indian religions. Tsung-mi listed the 'Doctrine concerning Man and gods' as sharing the karma doctrine with Hīnayāna and Mahāyāna Buddhism. Although the teaching of karma is accepted by these doctrines, the Chinese thinker was also aware of the fact that this concept works for different purposes in each of these doctrines. He states that the "Doctrine of cause and effect of Man and gods preaches the retribution of good and bad karmas, to make people aware that the effect never differs from its cause."[43] In other words, "karma is the basis of one's existence."[44] This understanding of cause and effect would make man fearful about a rebirth into the hellish realm. Thus men would strive for good deeds in order that they may be reborn into the worlds of man and heavenly beings, or even into the realm of forms or the formless.[45] Good deeds can be achieved through alms-giving, moral life, and meditation. As far as this doctrine is concerned, the concept of karma plays a very crucial role in man's rebirth and it cannot be done away with completely. Only bad karmas should be rejected. One must cultivate good karma if one wishes to improve his existence. From a Buddhist viewpoint, Tsung-mi considers that this teaching of karma is not perfect because it does not give a satisfactory answer to the question "who creates the karma and who receives the consequences?"[46] This is a problem for Buddhists because they do not accept the existence of a permanent Self.

The Hīnayāna teaching of karma is understood by Tsung-mi as follows:

> That since the beginningless beginning, because of the power of causes and conditions, both physical matter and the thinking mind arise and perish continuously. . . .Body and mind, united temporarily, give this appearance of being a single and constant thing; the ignorant man. . .believing it to be the self.[47]

Greed, hate, and delusion will develop once one recognizes this as the self; they stimulate the mind, and karmas are created by thinking, speech, and action. "Once karmas are formed, there is no way to escape them."[48] These karmas will determine one's future existence, and cause one to remain in *saṃsāra*. Once one is reborn in one of the five transmigratory states, he will repeat the influence of the three poisons; thus "he creates new karma and bears its fruits. His form of existence repeats the cycle of birth, old age, sickness, and death. . . ."[49]

Although the Hinayanist's understanding of karma as the determining factor in one's existence is similar to the 'Doctrine concerning Man and gods', the solutions and outcome of the two teachings are quite different. For the 'Doctrine concerning Man and gods', karmas are the exclusive cause for one's future existence, and consequently, to accumulate good karmas is the only way that one's existence can be improved. To the Hinayanist, the accumulation of good karmas is merely a preliminary step, which is one of the measures that could improve one's power of understanding. Once one realizes that his body and mind are produced by cause and conditions, which is without self-nature, one is free from the hindrance of attachment, hate, and delusions. Thereafter, one may obtain the fruits of a stream winner (*srotāpatti*) and even achieve arhathood. From a Buddhist point of view, the religious goal of the other Indian religions is to remain in a good realm of existence. For the Buddhist, the final goal is to get out of the realm of existence, to move from the *saṃsāra* to *nirvāṇa*.

As far as the concept of man is concerned, Tsung-mi has identified himself with the position taken by the school of Dharma Nature (*fa-hsing/dharmatā*).[50] This means that he believes that all sentient beings possess the absolute Mind on the one hand, yet accept the concept of karma and its effects, on the other. In his view, karma is responsible for man being trapped in *saṃsāra* when his conduct is conditioned by false thought and the absolute Mind is hindered by ignorance. Tsung-mi explained the process of the Mind from its original to the conditioned states in ten stages. Under this scheme the seventh stage is the notion of Self, the eighth is the poisons of attachment, anger, and delusion, the ninth is mental calculation, and the tenth is karma. The last three items in the scheme are relevant to our discussion and are worthy of full quotation.

> 8. Taking the four great elements (*mahābhūtas*) as one's body, one attaches himself to the good states such as sensual pleasure to nourish him; and hates the bad states such as fear and hurt. Depending on those feelings he makes mental calculations.
>
> 9. Good and bad karma are created.
>
> 10. Once karmas are created, one cannot escape from its consequences. This is like a sound which corresponds with its echo.[51]

Like other Buddhists, Tsung-mi also held that man is capable of making karmas; yet at the same time, man is also capable of overcoming the karmic effect if he follows the Buddhist path. However, when the discussion of the path arises, Tsung-mi prefers Mahāyāna over Hīnayāna. To the Hinayanists it is the Eightfold Path that is the way; to the Mahayanist, it is the Perfections (*pāramitā*) that are important. Based on a statement from the *Awakening of Faith* attributed to Aśvaghosa, "There are five ways of practice which will enable a man to perfect his faith,"[52] Tsung-mi listed the five practices as the way to overcome karmic effects. The five practices are the perfections of giving (*dāna*); morality (*śīla*); patience (kṣānti); vigor (*vīrya*); concentration and wisdom (*dhyāna-prajñā*). Tsung-mi considered the last two items, namely concentration and wisdom, as one, partly because the *Awakening of Faith* mentioned it in that manner, and partly due to the statement by Hui-neng (d. 713), "Never under any circumstances say mistakenly that meditation and wisdom are different; they are a unity, not two things."[53]

There is another difference between the position taken by Tsung-mi and that of the Hinayanist regarding the nature of karma. According to Tsung-mi, karma belongs to the category of *dharmas* related to birth and death (*utpādanirodha*), which is unrelated to suchness (*bhūtatathatā*).[54] This is to say that from a higher viewpoint, karma possesses no self-nature, hence it is empty. This is, of course, not a denial of karma as a conditioning force for one's existence, Tsung-mi was asked, "If attachment and anger are empty, and they are called as the Mind-without any state (*wu i-chieh-hsin*), why then is it still necessary for corresponding remedies?" He answered as follows:

> Though atachment and anger are empty, yet they are capable of creating karma. Karmas are also empty, yet they are capable of producing sufferings. Sufferings are empty too, yet they are unbearable to experience. . . .Although karmas are considered as empty, yet when the empty karmas are accumulated, one would know the pains of burning and boiling when one is punished in the hells. The sufferings are empty, but they are still painful. If a person claims, let sufferings be as they are (because they are empty), can he let others burn him with fire. . . .If one looks at the scholars who are learning the Tao in our times, they are even unable to stand a single word of criticism against them. How could they be expected to let others burn or chop them?[55]

From this it is clear that the Chinese Buddhist thinker has a dialectical view on karma: at a practical level, karma is one of the *dharmas* which are related to the law of birth and death; from a higher viewpoint, it is empty, without self-nature and can be removed by the practice of perfections. For practical purposes, one has to deal with karma as the ground for religious cultivation. At the same time, one must be aware of the fact that karma, like many other *dharmas*, is empty.

Though karmas are ultimately empty, they are capable of producing sufferings. The logical solution would be that if sufferings are to be negated, one must begin with the dissolution of karma. Karma is formed by the influence of the three poisons—attachment, anger, and delusion—so the work must begin from there. The three poisons are there because of misconceptions of Self, objective world, etc., misconceptions come from false thought, and false thought is ultimately rooted in ignorance (*avidyā*). Tsung-mi has his own system of salvation which this author has dealt with in other places.[56] However, in another piece of Tsung-mi's writings, he has more to say on karma and rebirth. In a letter Tsung-mi wrote to Wen Tsao (温 造 :766-835), a Minister of Personnel (*Li-pu shang-shu*) in the T'ang government, he clearly outlined his views on karma and rebirth. In his view, a gradual cultivation—from the aspiration for englightenment to the attainment of Buddhahood—should involve the three masteries: the mastery of rebirth, of change, and of the ultimate.

The mastery of rebirth is described as follows:

> When a false thought arises, one should never follow it; one will then not be tied down to the karmic effect at the moment of death.

> Though there is an intermediate state (*chung-yu* or *antarūbhava*) between death and reincarnation, yet one is free to choose his future direction: wish to be reincarnated in heaven or in the world according to one's will.[57]

On this point, there seems no difference between the mastery of rebirth and that of the other Indian religion, the 'Doctrine concerning Man and gods', as has been discussed previously. It has been said that to a Buddhist this is merely the initial stage; the Buddhist scheme of salvation goes far beyond. So the mastery of change is described as follows:

> If the thought of love and hatred are eliminated, one will no longer be subject to the dispensation (*bhāgya*) in regard to the forms of his incarnation. He could change his duration of life from short to long, and his forms from coarse to the finest.[58]

Once this stage is attached, one is set for the last stage of mastery, namely, the mastery of the ultimate, Tsung-mi says,

> Be like trickling water, it (subtle karmic residues) disappears peacefully at the end. Only the great wisdom from the perfect enlightenment shines alone. One now would be able to manifest himself into thousands of forms in response to situations and needs, to save all the sentient beings who have linked themselves with the One. One is now called Buddha, the Englightened.[59]

Like most Buddhists, Tsung-mi never considered Mahāyāna Buddhism as an academic subject, but a practical way of religious life. Once the doctrine of karma has been analysed, practical advice been given, a practitioner is in a position to begin his religious life at once—here and now. So Tsung-mi composed an eight-line hymn on this topic.

To do what is meaningful,
And this is the awakening Mind.

To do what is meaningless,
And this is the wild and confused mind.

Wild and confused one follows passionate thought,
Thus pulled by karmas when death approaches.

Awake and do not follow passions,
And karmic effects are transformable at the moment of death.[60]

IV

The Buddhist influence on Chinese short stories and novels is a prominent feature in literary history. And indeed, a study on the topic has indicated that the concept of retribution has played a role in the Buddhist influence.[61] This influence of karma doctrine on Chinese literature is once more confirmed by the present study of the tales collected or written by Feng Meng-lung. As Feng's collection comprises 120 short stories in 2,153 pages, printed in small Chinese characters, any detailed study on the subject would require an independent monograph. The present enquiry will limit itself to the characterization of this influence. The three collections of Feng are entitled, *Yü-shih ming-yen* (Tales to illuminate the World), *Ching-shih t'ung-yen* (Tales to warn the World) and *Hsing-shih heng-yen* (Tales to rouse the World). They are known as the *San-yen* collections.[62] A preliminary study of these collections by Feng Meng-lung shows that there are a few features on the understanding of the karma doctrine as presented in the collections. Some of these features are clearly Buddhist and some are a mixture of Buddhist and pre-Buddhist Chinese ideas of retribution.

Among the Buddhist ideas of karma, the most repeated theme is the identity of cause and effect, that the effect may take place in a future rebirth, and that the actor will face the consequences of his or her own action.

We have seen in the previous discussion that the two Buddhist thinkers have agreed that the action and its effect or deed and retribution are always identical. This is described by Hui-yüan as follows: "When a form or a sound becomes distinct, then its shadow or echo will follow naturally" (*hsing-sheng chi-chu, tse ying-hsiang tzu-chang*).[63] In the words of Tsung-mi, "Once karmas are created, one cannot escape from their consequences. This is like a sound which corresponds with its echo."[64] The idea of the identity of deed and retribution is echoed again and again in the *San-yen* collections. In the well-known story "The Pearl-sewn shirt," the author says that "retribution does not fail to come."[65] The story describes a young and inexperienced wife of a merchant who was seduced by another travelling salesman, the Big Ch'en, when her husband was away from home. When her husband found out about the affair, she was divorced. As time went on, misfortune befell the travelling salesman, and his wife in turn became the wife of the merchant. When the merchant became aware that his newly married second wife was no one else but the former wife of the man who had seduced his first wife, he hold her the story.

> This pearl-sewn shirt was an heirloom in my family. Your husband seduced my wife and was given this shirt as a love-token. I met him

> in Soochow, and the sight of the shirt gave me my first inkling of the affair. On my return, I put aside my wife, Madam Wang. But who could have seen that your husband would die on his travels? Then, when I decided to marry again, I learned only that you were the widow of a trader named Ch'en of Hweichow—how was I to know that this was none other than Ch'en Shang? *Surely this is retribution piled upon retribution.*[66]

Through this story the author reminds his readers, "Men's hearts may be blinded, but the way of Heaven is unchanging. Let me not defile the womenfolk of others, and other men will not defile my wife."[67] Elsewhere in the same story, the author again states that "Good and ill and retribution are scrupulously apportioned."[68]

This identical nature of a deed and its effect is also emphasized in the Chinese proverb, "Sow hemp and you will reap hemp; plant beans and you will reap beans."[69] Other versions of this proverb, "Sow melons and you will reap melons, plant beans and you will reap beans," are also found in the other two collections of *San-yen*.[70] Of course, the doctrine of retribution in popular literature is not necessarily always restricted to theological dogmas; popular writers often give their own emphasis to certain points in their creative writings or rewritings. In the story "The Pearl-sewn shirt," the author says that the effect of karmic deeds is not only identical, but sometimes one has even to pay interest on one's deeds:

> The ways of providence are clear and ineluctable; Who reaped the advantage from the exchange of wives? Clearly, *a debt must be repaid with interest*: This love-match of three lifetimes was only withheld for a time.[71]

In another collection, "Tales to rouse the World," the author again says,

> Many evil thoughts turned into good ones;
> Many good thoughts turned into evil ones.
> I urge you, Sir, to practice good ones,
> And never to have any evil action.[72]

This concept of transformability of karmic effects is of course a Buddhist idea. We may recall Tsung-mi's advice to Wen Tsao, that "karmic effects are transformable at the moment of death."[73] The difference lies in the fact that the transformation of karmic effects in the popular writing has been speeded up in this lifetime.

As we have seen in part II of this paper, one of the distinctive features of the Buddhist doctrine, in comparison with the ancient Chinese idea of retribution, is that in the former, the retributive effects could be carried over to many lives, and are not necessarily limited to the present life. This doctrine is also clearly reflected in the *San-yen* collection. The story, "Yüan-san repaid his romantic debt at a Buddhist Nunnery,"[74] is a good illustration of this aspect of the doctrine. Here the story tells of Yüan-san, a handsome young man who met and fell in love with Miss Ch'en Yu-lan during the night of the Lantern Festival. Thereafter, the young man became love-sick. He bribed a nun who arranged a room for the two lovers at the nunnery. They met secretly but the young man died tragically in their first encounter because of sexual excitement as well as his sickness. The girl became pregnant as a result of the romance. She gave birth to a baby boy and remained loyal to her lover. When the baby was three years old, the girl visited her lover's tomb and offered a sacrifice to the deceased. In the same night, she saw the late lover in a dream. His spirit told her that in the previous life she had been a famous courtesan of Yangchou and he had been a young man from another city. They fell in love when he went to Yangchou and he had promised her that they would be married within a year's time. However, he could not fulfill his promise as he lacked courage to ask his father for permission to marry a courtesan. The courtesan waited for a year and died sorrowfully since she felt she had been abandoned. However, the effect inherited from their previous relation still remained unexhausted. This was the reason why they had fallen in love at first sight. When they met at the nunnery, the spirit explained, "I thought you came to collect the previous debt, and I died suddenly to pay the debt which caused you to die in our previous existence."[75]

Another story with the same tune is "Ch'en K'e-ch'ang passed away at the Tuan-yang festival." Here the story is about a Buddhist monk called K'e-ch'ang who, through his poetic talent, gained the favour of a prince, the lord of Hangchou. Later he was accused of having an affair with a singing girl in the prince's household. The monk made no attempt to explain or protest the accusation. He was banished by beatings and was disrobed. Finally, the singing girl told the truth—she had after all had no affair with the monk, but with another man who was the manager of the prince's household. She claimed she had involved the monk in the affair since she thought the monk was a favourite of the prince, so that she and the monk might not be punished. When the prince became aware of the mistake, he recalled the monk for an apology. However, it was too late, for the monk had just passed away. He had composed a hymn before his death and told people that the hymn might be reported to the prince should the latter ask for him. The first part of the hymn reads as follows:

Born and ordained in the double fifth,
Accused and died on the fifth of the fifth month.
I owe her something in the past,
I protected her without a protest.[76]

Similar stories on this theme are also found in other places of these collections.

It may be recalled that the lack of a rebirth doctrine in pre-Buddhist China had limited the Chinese idea of retribution to one's present lifetime. Consequently, if any retributive effect took place beyond the doer's life span, it would be left to his descendants to face. It is only in the Buddhist doctrine that the doer must face the consequences of his own deeds, either in the present or in his future life. The Buddhist doctrine is called *Tzu-yeh tzu-te* 自業自得 "Every man receives the reward of the deeds he has created by himself." This doctrine is also known as *Tzu-tso tsu-shou* 自作自受, "One suffers the consequences of one's own action.[77]

There are various stories in the three collections which have repeated this theme. The author often reminds his readers with poetic judgment, "Retribution has no self-purpose. One did it and has to receive the consequence."[78] The judgment may be in the form of exhortation, like "People are exhorted to practice what is good; one will receive what one did!"[79] or, "All fortune and misfortune, one receives what one has created!"[80] Unlike some of the monastic texts, the short stories put those judgments not merely as simple exhortations, but as comments on, or conclusions to the story. Some of these stories are not fictitious, but well-known court cases in China. It is these actual events, rather than empty words of exhortation which make the literary judgement more influential to the Chinese mind. Take the case of "The Canary Murders" as an illustration. Attachment to a beautiful canary resulted in the murder of its first owner, and subsequently in its second owner receiving capital punishment wrongly. The wrongdoers had murdered the first owner of the bird in order to make money by selling the bird. And the two stupid sons murdered their father in order to receive a reward for supposedly returning the head of the first owner. All were punished by execution. They paid for the crimes they had committed themselves.[81] The story, "The reunion of younger Sung with the old hat" is another example. The story is of a couple whose surname was Sung. The family owned some land and was doing very well. The only disappointment was that they did not have any children, and both of them were already in their forties. When they went to a temple for a pilgrimage, the husband encountered an old and dying monk who had travelled to that place from Shensi, a faraway province. The monk died without leaving any money or relatives. Mr. Sung gave away whatever money he had in his pocket and even pawned his garments in order to buy a good coffin and bury the monk. He had a dream the same night in which the deceased monk came and told Sung that according to his original destiny, Mr. Sung should have to die on that day, without leaving a child. However, because of the good deed he had done in looking after the deceased monk, the Supreme God extended his age for another six years as a reward. As he had looked after the old monk in the moment of the latter's death, the monk would reincarnate into the house as Sung's boy.[82]

The aforementioned two stories clearly illustrate that the deed and the retribution are identical, and that it is the doer who receives the retribution or reward for his deed. The retribution can happen in one's lifetime, or it may affect one's future existence. The story, "Esquire Kuei confessed when he had no place to go," tells how karmic deeds carry their effects beyond the present life.[83] The Esquire Kuei had lost his property in a business deal and had nothing to depend on for a living. Purely by chance he met a childhood acquaintance who paid off his debts and gave accommodation to Kuei and his family. Kuei vowed that if he did not repay the kindness in this life, he would be prepared to reincarnate as a dog or horse to show his gratitude to his host. He also engaged his baby daughter to a baby son of the benefactor. However, he became rich when he discovered some money hidden in the house where he was accommodated and secretly took it for himself. Years later fortunes changed and the other family became poor. Mr Kuei refused to help them when he was asked. The matter became even more ugly when he cancelled the engagement of his daughter to the boy. Fortunately, in a critical moment, the other family discovered more money hidden in their old house. Their son married another girl. As Kuei became rich he wished to become an official. He went to the capital and offered a bribe to obtain a rank, but failed and lost his money. In a state of confusion, Kuei found, in a dream, that his two sons had now become dogs in the house of his benefactor. On returning to his home, he found that his two sons had actually been killed. He went to the other house and begged the son of his late benefactor to have his daughter as a concubine. Although he confessed and gave his daughter to the other family and he redeemed himself from the destiny of a dog, yet the money and property, as well as his family were all gone. He was saved, but his wife and two sons all suffered in their rebirths as dogs.

The pattern of retribution as presented in the collection of the *San-yen* may create an impression that the Buddhist doctrine of karma was the only source of influence on Chinese short stories. There is no doubt that the Buddhist doctrine played an important role in that direction. But at the same time, not only does the pre-Buddhist Chinese idea of retribution also exist in these collections, but the author has even gone so far as to combine the Buddhist and non-Buddhist ideas of retribution. In the story, "The pearl-sewn shirt," the karmic effect is of losing a wife to another man because he has defiled the latter's wife first. This karmic effect has also been reviewed by the author as the way of Heaven, which predominated in the ancient Chinese idea of retribution. The author writes that "Men's hearts may be blinded, but the way of Heaven is unchanging. Let me not defile the womenfolk of others, and other men will not defile my wife."[84] Another verse from the same story states that "The ways of providence are clear and ineluctable: Who reaped the advantage from the exchange of wives? Clearly, a debt must be repaid with interest. . . ."[85] In another place in the book, the author says, "Worldly affairs overturn like rolling wheels, fortune or misfortune of this moment are not necessarily real ones. Retributions are explicit if you look for a while. The way of Heaven never fails to reward men of good action."[86] In Chapter 3 of the same collection, a man confessed that "one should never do anything against one's conscience. There are men in the world who know what is wrong and there are spirits in Hades who charge wrongdoers. . . ."[87] This presentation of men and spirits as moral watch dogs is, of course, a well-known position held by Moists in ancient Chinese philosophy.[88] Similar expressions are also repeated in the "Canary Murders." There one reads, "Take no illegal goods; commit no illegal acts. Here above the law will catch you, Down below the demons pursue you."[89] Or again, "Heaven, clear and profound, is not to be deceived. Before the design appears to you it is already known. Do nothing of which you need feel ashamed: who, throughout time, has been allowed to escape?"[90] "Store up good deeds and you will meet with good. Store up evil and you will meet with evil. If you think about it carefully, things usually turn out right."[91] Or, "The evil-doer fears the wrath of Heaven and Earth, the swindler dreads discovery by gods and demons."[92]

Similar to the belief in the Way of Heaven and the watch dog of spirit in Hades, the idea that retribution would effect one's descendants, is also retained and blended with the Buddhist doctrine of karma and rebirth. The story, "Monk Ming-yüeh ordains Miss Liu Ts'ui," is a good example of this effect. The story relates that when a Ch'an monk failed to attend the reception of a newly arrived official, the official was enraged and designed a scheme. A young and lustful prostitute was hired, sent, and successfully seduced the monk. The official used this as an excuse to disrobe the monk. Shocked and ashamed, the monk died. Before he passed away, the monk wrote a verse and instructed the attendant to give it to the official in case the latter asked for him. The verse read as follows: "You sent Red Lotus and destroyed my morality. I debted Red Lotus for the night. My merit has been damaged by your action. More ugliness will befall your family."[93] The deceased monk reincarnated as the daughter of the official, and grew up with beautiful features. Some years later, the official died and his surviving daughter became a prostitute. The author of the story commented, "This is solely because the official, Liu, failed to practice and accumulate good deeds in secret, and so lost his daughter." This is the retribution of an action, and the principle of Heaven is clearly seen from this. The future readers of this story should be very careful in this regard. Here is a poem to prove the point.

A clever plot will hurt its plotter,
Love to take but actually give away advantage.
Do not boast that you are luckily unscathed,
Your descendants would certainly be humiliated.[94]

Here in this story the break of morality caused the monk to be reborn in a lower existence as a prostitute. This illustrates the Buddhist view: a good karma creates a good effect, and the doer himself faces the consequences. However, in the case of the official, the retribution took effect on his daughter. This follows the pre-Buddhist idea of retribution of ancient China. The combination of these two is called the "principle of Heaven," and is a good example to show how the Buddhist concept of karma and rebirth has been assimilated into Chinese culture and become a component of it, side by side with the ancient idea of retribution.

V

To recapitulate: long before the spread of Buddhism into China, the Chinese had their own ideas of retribution, which had a moral quality. The effect of the deed would take effect on the doer or his family. The early Chinese Buddhist clearly understood that the nature and degree of karmic effect were identical with the deed; that it is the doer himself, not his relatives, who will face and receive the retribution; and the doctrine of rebirth is introduced so that the unexhausted effect of karma may be carried into the future existence of the doer. In the heyday of Chinese Buddhism, some Buddhist thinkers had a more accurate and clear perception of the Buddhist teachings of karma. Apart from a better understanding of its position in the Indian context, the Chinese thinkers now understood various aspects of the doctrine and were able to adopt it into their own system of soteriology. With the advance of time, the doctrine of karma and rebirth not only took a firm root in Chinese Buddhism, but even went out from the monastic communities into Chinese society at large. This preliminary study of the *San-yen* collections has demonstrated how the Buddhist doctrine penetrated into the Chinese mind, how it was understood by the Chinese at the grass roots, and how the Buddhist doctrine has syncretized with the ancient Chinese concept of retribution in which Heaven played an important role. It was through this pattern that Buddhism was understood and assimilated by the Chinese and became an intrinsic component of Chinese culture. This pattern of process may have a large significance beyond its Buddhist context, as it indicates the Chinese way in absorption and appropriation of foreign ideas.

NOTES

1. For the life of Hui-yüan, see E. Zurcher, *The Buddhist Conquest of China* (Leiden, 1959), 204 ff.; for his understanding of karma doctrine see W. Liebenthal, "Shih Hui-yüan's Buddhism as Set Forth in his Writings," *JAOS* vol. 70/4 (1950), *243-259. For Liebenthal's misreadings of Hui-yüan, see part II of this essay below.*

2. *For the life of Tsung-mi, see Yün-hua Jan, "Tsung-mi and his Analysis of Ch'an Buddhism," TP* 58 (1972), 1-54; and Shigeo Kamata, *Shumitsu kyogaku no shisoshi teki kenkyo* (Tokyo, 1975).

3. For Feng Meng-lung's life, works and its significance, see W.I. Idema, *Chinese Vernacular Fiction* (Leiden, 1974), 30-56. The quotation here is from Liu's *An Introduction to Chinese Literature* (Bloomington, 1966), 216-17.

4. Hsia, "Society and Self in the Chinese Short Stories," reprinted in his *The Classic Chinese Novel* (New York, 1968), 299-321.

5. From W.T. Chan's translation, *Analects* 2:5 in his *A Source Book in Chinese Philosophy* (Princeton, 1963), 39.

6. From the translation of J. Legge, *Book of Historical Document, Chinese Classics*, vol. 3 (Hong Kong, 1960 reprint), 186.

7. Yang Lien-sheng, "The Concept of 'Pao' as a Basis for Social Relation in China," in *Chinese Thought and Institutions*, ed. J. Fairbank (Chicago, 1957), 291-309; Yü Ying-shih, "Life and Immortality in the Mind of Han China," *HJAS* 25 (1964-65), 80-122, esp. 111-113; A.P. Cohen, "Avenging Ghosts and Moral Judgement in Ancient Chinese Historiography: Three Examples from Shih-chi," in *Legend, Lore, and Religion in China*, (San Francisco, 1979), 97-108.

8. From *Po-hu T'ung, the Comprehensive Discussions in the White Tiger Hall* II (Leiden, 1952), 572.

9. Ibid.

10. From W.T. Chan, op. cit., 102.

11. From the translation by D.C. Lau, *Lao Tzu Tao Te Ching* (Penguin Books, 1963), 141.

12. Translated from *Shih-chi*, ch. 61, Chung-hua shu-chu new and punctuated ed. (Hong Kong, 1969), 2124-25.

13. *Po-hu T'ung*, op. cit., and Lun Heng., *Philosophical Essays of Wang Ch'ung*, transl. by A. Forke (New York 1962, reprint of the 2nd ed.), Vol. 1, 313.

14. From *Mou Tzu li-huo lun* transl. by de Bary, et. al., in *Buddhist Tradition* (New York, 1969), 134.

15. Tsung-i Jao, ed., *Lao Tzu Hsiang-erh chu chiao-ch'ien* 老子想尔註校箋 (Hong Kong, 1956), 46.

16. The quotation is from *Pan-ni-huan ching* Ch. 1, *Taishō shinshū daizōkyō* 大正新脩大蔵経 Vol. 1, 1816, hereafter referred to as *T*. I am grateful to Professor Makita Tairyo and the Research Institute for Humanistic Studies, Kyoto University, for providing me with the copy of *Gumyōshū kenkyū* 弘明集研究 (Kyoto, 1975), which includes the most recent and scholarly work on the *Hung-ming chi*.

17. From *Feng-fa Yao* transl. by E. Zurcher, op. cit., 169.

18. From Liebenthal, op. cit., *JAOS* 70, 255-256.

19. Ibid., 255.

20. Ibid.

21. Ibid.

22. Ibid.

23. Ibid.

24. Translated from Hui-yüan's "Ming Pao-ying lun," selected and punctuated in *Chung-kuo fo-chiao ssu-hsiang tzu-liao hsüan-pien*, ed. Shih Chun, *et. al.* (Beijing, 1981), 90. I am grateful to Professor Ren Jiyu for providing me with a copy of this book for my reference.

25. Liebenthal, op. cit., 254.

26. Ibid.

27. *Gumyōshū kenkyū*, Vol. II, 310-322.

28. Liebenthal, op. cit., 254-255.

29. From "Ming Pao-ying lun", op. cit., 90.

30. See Wang Li 王力, *Ku Han-yü ch'ang-yung tz'u-tien* 古漢語常用辞典 (Hong Kong, 1978), 212f.

31. See Note no. 24.

32. Liebenthal, op. cit., 254.

33. Ibid.

34. "Ming Pao-ying lun", op. cit., 90.

35. Ibid.

36. Liebenthal, op. cit., 253-254.

37. Ibid., 254.

38. "Ming Pao-ying lun", op. cit., 90.

39. Ibid.

40. Liebenthal, op. cit., 254.

41. *Han Wei Liang-chin Nan-pei-ch'ao fo-chiao-shih* 漢魏両晋南北朝佛教史 (Beijing, 1955), I, 360. For a critical review on Hui-yüan's understanding of *karma* and *shen*, see Kajiyama 梶山雄 — "Eon no ho'o setsu to shinfemetsu ron 慧遠の報応説と神不滅論," in E. Kimura, ed. *Eon no kenkyū kenkyū-hen* 慧遠の研究 —研究篇 (Kyoto, 1962), 91-120, esp. 118f.

42. See Jan's papers in the *Philosophy East and West*, Vol. 30 (1980), 495-504; 31 (1981), 467-77; *Journal of Chinese Philosophy*, Vol. 4 (1977), 287-302; 7 (1980), 301-318, etc.

43. Transl. from *Ch'an Yüan chu'ch'uan-chi tu-hsü* 禅源諸詮集都序 bilingual ed., by S. Kamata, *Zen no goroku* 禅の語録 No. 9 (Tokyo, 1971) 103. Hereafter, this is referred to as *CYC*.

44. From de Bary, *Buddhist Tradition*, op. cit., p. 185.

45. Ibid.

46. Ibid., 185-6.
47. *CYC*, 104.
48. Ibid.
49. de Bary, op. cit., 187.
50. The full name of this school given by Tsung-mi is "Esoteric Teaching Revealing that the True Mind itself is the Nature." See Jan, "A Ninth-Century Chinese Classification of Indian Mahayana," in *Studies in Pali and Buddhism*, ed. by A.K. Narain, (New Delhi, 1979), 171-182, esp. 177 ff.
51. Transl. from *CYC*, 217-218.
52. From Y.S. Hakeda, *The Awakening of Faith* (New York, 1967), 93.
53. From P.B. Yampolsky, *The Platform Sutra of the Sixth Patriarch* (New York, 1967), 135.
54. *CYC*, 104.
55. Ibid., 248.
56. Jan, "The Chinese Buddhist Wheel of Existence and Deliverance," in *Studies in Indian Philosophy*, ed. by D. Malvania, *et. al.* (Ahmedabad, 1981), 165-180, esp. 166 ff.
57. Translated from *Ching-te ch'uan-teng lu* 景德傳灯錄 T. Vol. 51, 308a. About the origin of this piece of work, see Jan, "Tsung-mi chu *Tao-su ch'ou-ta wen-chi* ti yen-chiu" (A Study of the Questions and Answers between Master Tsung-mi and the laymen), *Hwakang Buddhist Journal* (Taipei) Vol. 4 (1980), 132-166, esp. 142-144, and 159-163.
58. Ibid.
59. Ibid.
60. Ibid.
61. Liu Tsun-yan, *Buddhist and Taoist Influence on Chinese Novels*, Vol. I (Wiesbaden, 1962), 160, 171.
62. See J.L. Bishop, *The Colloquial Short Story in China, A Study of the San-Yen Collection* (Cambridge, Mass., 1965). The first collection, *Yü-shih ming-yen or Ku-chin hsiao-shuo* 古今小說 has a selected English transl. by C. Brich, *Stories from a Ming Collection* (New York, 1958).
63. "Ming Pao-ying lun," op. cit., 90. Liebenthal has wrongly translated this as ". . .yet (we have to bear the consequences of former deeds) in accordance with the law of the mirror and the echo." Ibid., 254b.
64. *CYC*, 218.
65. From C. Birch, op. cit., p. 45.
66. Ibid., 90.
67. Ibid., 45.
68. Ibid., 96.
69. Transl. from *Yü-shih ming-yen* 喻世明言 (Hong Kong, Chung-hua shu-chu rep. 1965), 530. Hereafter it is referred to as *MY*.
70. *Ching-shih t'ung-yen* 警世通言 (Hong Kong, Chung-hua shu-chu rep. 1965), 312. Hereafter, it is referred to as *TY*. *Hsing-shih heng-yen* 醒世恒言 (Beijing, Zuojia chubanshe, 1956), 359. Hereafter, it is referred to as *HY*. These as well as many other similar sayings are found in C.H. Plopper, *Chinese Religion seen through the Proverb* (New York, rep. 1969), 282 ff.
71. From C. Birch, op. cit., 91. The underlining is mine.
72. Transl. from *HY*, 361.

73. See note 60.
74. See *MY*, 80 ff.
75. Ibid., 93.
76. See *TY*, 80 ff. The hymn translated here is from 86.
77. *A Dictionary of Chinese Buddhist Terms* (London, 1937), 518; also *Zengaku Daijiten* 禅学大辞典 (Tokyo, 1976), 427d and 428c.
78. *MY*, 503.
79. *TY*, 312.
80. *HY*, 359.
81. See Birch, op. cit., 151 ff., esp. 168 ff.
82. *TY*, 211-2.
83. Ibid., 377-397.
84. Birch, op. cit., 45.
85. Ibid., 91.
86. *MY*, 38.
87. Ibid., 77.
88. See B. Watson;, trans, *Mo Tzu: Basic Writings* (New York, 1963), 94-109.
89. Birch, op. cit., 163.
90. Ibid., 171.
91. Ibid.
92. Ibid., 158.
93. *MY*, 432.
94. Ibid., 435.

CHAPTER NINE

Tsong-Kha-Pa's Concept of Karma

LOBSANG DARGYAY

In order to understand Tsong-kha-pa's own concept of karma we have to put it into the context of the general development of this term as rooted in Indian Buddhism.

VASUBANDHU'S KARMA DOCTRINE

Vasubandhu, one of the greatest Buddhist philosophers, dedicated a whole chapter of his *Abhidharmakośa* to the discussion of karma. The first verse therein puts forward the central theme of karma philosophy in Buddhism: The world's variety is caused by act which is volition (*cetanā*) and its product (*cetanākṛtam*).[1] In his own commentary on the *Abhidharmakośa,* Vasubandhu explains that the crucial question of what causes the world to be as it is, caused him to talk about the world's variety right at the beginning of the chapter on karma. With this explicit statement he refutes any view which might claim that the world's variety is produced by an individual being, be it a cultural hero, a primordial giant, or a Creater God. No person, he says, has ever caused the world's variety; rather, the sentient beings' acts gave rise to the multitude of phenomena.

In the second part of that verse, Vasubandhu defines the term act (*karman*). With reference to the *sūtras* he differentiates between two aspects of an act. The first aspect of every act is volition; it may be understood as the will, the intention, that causes every physical act. Therefore, the texts speak of the mental act or spiritual act which precedes the actual physical act. The second aspect of an act is the act itself resulting from the preceding volition. The act itself may be performed by means of the body or the voice as the body's instrument. The texts speak of the second aspect as the bodily or vocal act.

In Buddhist philosophy the term "karma" was never understood as the mere physical act, but as a term identifying the complex process of being active, of planning and intending an act, and the result caused by this activity. As the Buddhists always upheld that any volition will have an impact on the future development of the individual, every act had to leave a trace on the individual. The process of acting separates into three basic phases:

1. the will, that is, the mental act;
2. the act itself, that is, the bodily or vocal act;
3. the imprint or trace left behind after volition and act have come to an end.

When this understanding of karma is correlated to the Buddhist doctrine of universal impermanence and No-Self, a serious problem arises as to where this trace is stored and what the trace left is. The problem is aggravated when the trace remains latent over a long period, perhaps over a period of many existences. The crucial problem presented to all schools of Buddhist philosophy was where the trace is stored and how it can remain in the ever-changing stream of phenomena which build up the individual and what the nature of this trace is. Nāgārjuna formulated this query brilliantly in this *MMK* (XVII.6):

> If (the act) lasted till the time of ripening,
> (the act) would be eternal.
> If (the act) were terminated,
> how could the terminated produce a fruit?[2]

In the *Akutobhayā*,[3] concerning the problem of how the result of karma can become manifest when the act as such disappears at the very moment when it is finished, long before the result materializes, it is concluded that both ways are impossible. Nevertheless, Buddhist philosophers continued in the pursuit of answering the question.

THE ANSWERS OF THE VARIOUS SCHOOLS OF BUDDHIST PHILOSOPHY

This section discussing the karma concepts created by the various schools of Buddhist philosophy is based on the information found in Tibetan Buddhist works. If one would include the analysis of non-Tibetan material, slightly different results might be expected.[4]

One group of the Vaibhāṣika claim that whenever an act has passed, this act gives birth to something that continues (*avipraṇāśa, chud mi za ba*). That which continues is called a thing (*rdzas*); it is a co-conditioned phenomenon (*'dus byas*) yet neither physical nor mental. This continuing phenomenon, the act's trace, exists as an independent fact. It is placed into the category of *ldan min 'du byed*, that is, into a category of fourteen composed phenomena which are not associated with body or awareness. The entirety of co-conditioned phenomena is divided into three categories: 1. physical factors; 2. mental factors (awareness); 3. neither mental nor physical factors, i.e., *Idan min 'du byed*. Although this category, which is called in Sanskrit *viprayuktasaṃ*skārāḥ,[5] is detached from awareness and body, it forms part of the aggregate of *saṃskāra*, composed factors, which are twofold in the Vaibhāṣika system. One part of it is mental, the other one neither mental nor physical. For this reason it will be rather difficult to find an English term covering these two aspects of *saṃskāra skandha* in Vaibhāṣika philosophy. One possibility might be "mental and neither-mental-nor-physical formations."

Another group of the Vaibhāṣika claim that the act brings forth a gain (*thob pa*, Skr. *prāpti*) which in turn produces the fruit.[6] This gain is thought to be a thing (*rdzas*) which is almost a material thing. These Vaibhāṣika illustrate their concept of gain in the following way: when a person takes monastic vows, he gains something that he has never possessed before. It is almost a substance which he gained after he took the vows. In a similar way the act leaves behind a gain or substance-like phenomenon. In general however, these Vaibhāṣika pursue the same route as the first group of the Vaibhāṣika.[7]

The Sautrāntika, the second philosophical school of later Hīnayāna, sees the finished act to result in a tendency (*vāsanā, bag chags*) which, however, asks for a support, a thing on which the tendency is engrained. The Sautrāntika call the support *rnam par shes pa'i rgyun* which might be translated as the stream of awareness. This term points out that awareness as part of the five aggregates (*skandha*) consists of numberless momentary entities which originate in an uninterrupted succession, even bridging the gap of dying. The tendency is stored in the stream of awareness until it results in the karmic fruit.

By creating this karma theory the Sautrāntika paved the way for the Cittamātra and the Svātantrika branch of Mādhyamika and their individual concepts of karma. All these schools agreed upon the tendency as that which remains after the act is finished; however, they developed individual concepts of that which supports the tendency.

The Cittamātra School claims that the act leaves a tendency (*bag chags*) behind. Unlike the Sautrāntika, this school sees the tendency stored in an awareness distinct from the general awareness. This resulted in creating the concept of *ālayavijñāna*. The prominent feature of the *ālayavijñāna* is that, although it is impermanent and mental, it continues without interruption, similar to a stream of thought. This storage-awareness (*ālayavijñāna*) is defined as an awareness, independent from the six senses and in itself neither good nor evil. It stores or supports the tendencies which come forth after the act is finished. However, some texts do not distinguish carefully between the *ālayavijñāna* functioning as a support for the karmic tendencies and other seeds (*rnam smin gyi kun gzhi*) and the stored or supported tendencies and seeds themselves (*sa bon gyi kun gzhi*).

The Svātantrika branch of the Mādhyamika School favors the concept of tendencies, and sees them, as do the Sautrāntika, as being supported by a stream of awareness (*rnam par shes pa'i rgyun*), which is a continuously ongoing process.[8]

The Prāsaṅgika branch of the Mādhyamika School refuted every concept of a support for storing the information left behind after the act is finished. The Prāsaṅgika philosophers assume that the completed act results in a potential (*nus pa*) which will substantiate whenever the situation is ripe. This potential is not a thing, and therefore does not need any kind of support. The concepts of universal impermanence and voidness added within the Prāsaṅgika tradition a new dimension to the discussion about karma. Candrakīrti[9] explains that the act does not originate as an inherently real phenomenon, therefore it cannot perish as a real phenomenon. For this reason, the act, though virtually passed, may still produce a fruit.

TSONG-KHA-PA'S VIEW OF KARMA

In India, the Prāsaṅgikas' various viewpoints of karma were never organized into a coherent and convincing system. Tsong-kha-pa, the famous Buddhist master of fourteenth century Tibet, felt this need very much. In order to clarify the Prāsaṅgikas' position on karma, Tsong-kha-pa discussed the subject in a detailed manner in some of his works: *rTsa shes ṭik chen*, ed. Gelek, pp. 218-223, and 353-369; *dGongs pa rab gsal*, ed. Gelek, pp. 283-285; *Drang nges legs bshad snying po*, ed. Gelek, p. 640. For his discussion of the Prāsaṅgikas' concept of karma, he uses sources as follows: *Prasannapadā* chapter 7, *Yuktiṣaṣṭhikā-vṛtti*, *Daśabhūmika-sūtra*.

The word *zhig pa* is a keyword to understanding Tsong-kha-pa's theory of karma. In the course of his investigation he points out that *zhig pa* equals the word *'jig pa*, which occurs in the Tibetan translation of Candrakīrti's works. According to Sarat Chandra Das' *Tibetan English Dictionary*,[10] both words belong to the same verbal root: *'jig pa*, to destroy, to abolish; *zhig pa* is the past form of this root. In the line of Tsong-kha-pa's logical reasoning, the explicit meaning of the present form of the verb and its past derivation diminishes and becomes insignificant.

When presenting his view of the Mādhyamika philosophy, Tsong-kha-pa discusses the verse (*MMK* XVII.6) where Nāgārjuna points out that the act is neither passed away nor lasting. Tsong-kha-pa summarizes the individual solutions to the query proposed by the various schools of Buddhist philosophy. Most of his statements follow the general line of these schools described in the previous section.

However, when Tsong-kha-pa elaborates the Prāsaṅgikas' karma theory, he presents an original interpretation of their classical position. He agrees with the fact that when the mental and physical acts have disappeared the act in total has passed, but he attributes a new quality to the passed act, that is, to be a substance or thing (*rdzas* or *dngos po*, Skr. *vastu*). According to Tsong-kha-pa, the passed act itself develops a virtual, though latent activity, which justifies the step of labelling this phenomenon a substance. So the passed act is understood by Tsong-kha-pa as something that continues after the act itself is accomplished; I shall call it the "after-act" (*las zhig pa*). The definition of the technical term after-act is no longer restricted to the meaning that the act has stopped existing in the present, but adopts a positive meaning in its own right. The after-act is an always present potential which produces the fruit whenever the entire situation allows for it. Tsong-kha-pa uses the term after-act to bridge the gap between the passed and finished act and its future result, namely, the karmic fruit. One might question whether this term is adequate because its literal meaning, act's cessation, points in a direction other than the one intended by Tsong-kha-pa; but as a traditional thinker he had to watch the limits of his own tradition. After this brief summary of Tsong-kha-pa's karma theory, I shall substantiate my statements through some passages selected from his works.

Tsong-kha-pa based his entire discussion of act and fruit on a single quotation from the *Prasannapadā*, where the question is raised whether a decaying thing can be a real object, thing, or substance (*dngos po*, Skr. *vastu*), when it is said that the decaying of a thing is without cause. In order to understand the argument, we should remind ourselves that all existential phenomena (*chos thams cad*, Skr. *sarvadharmāḥ*) are divided into two categories.

1. Those which are *dngos po*, thing or substance, which are impermanent and caused; they in turn are able to act as a cause and produce a karmic fruit.

2. Those which are no-thing, no-substance (*dngos po med pa*, Skr. *avastu*); they are permanent and do not partake in the causal situation.

In other words, a fact which is said to be without cause can never produce a result or fruit and cannot be labelled a thing or substance (*dngos po*). Here I have to admit that translating *dngos po* as thing or substance is only provisional and far from adequate. In the context of this paper, the term *dngos po* also means something that is imperceptible, virtually past but still potent, and that will become active in the future.

Let me now return to the *Prasannapadā*, where within the chapter 7, Enquiry into Co-conditioned Things, we find a short paragraph dealing with things decaying and their momentariness:

> Some may assert that decaying is without cause and say therefore, that co-conditions (*'dus byas*) are momentary. In such a case, "decaying" (*'jig pa*) because of being causeless like a flower in the sky, becomes nonexistent. However, how then can the momentariness of substances and the decaylessness of things be established? For this reason such views are entirely erroneous.[11]

In his *TSNS*, Tsong-kha-pa comments upon this paragraph as follows:

> There are some who claim that (the process of) decaying (*'jig pa*) is uncaused and state that (1) (the process of) decaying, which (they understand) as not lasting for an additional phase after the phase of accomplishment, is produced by the same cause as the substance, and that there is no need for a subsequent cause other than that, and (2) the "cessation" (*zhig pa*) (occurring) during the second phase is not a substance, because there is absolutely no cause.
>
> For this reason those who assert that "cessation" is without cause, cannot establish the co-conditions, because substances do not decay by momentariness.[12]

Behind this sentence there is Tsong-kha-pa's intention to demonstrate the opponents' inconsistent ways of thinking, when they claim that the process of decaying (*'jig pa*) is caused, and the finished process of decaying, in Tsong-kha-pa's wording, cessation (*zhig pa*), is uncaused. According to his logic, the opponents should say that the process of decaying and that which comes after the act's termination are either caused or uncaused. Although this paragraph is not related to any discussion on karma, it enticed Tsong-kha-pa to a new concept of karma. When he interprets Candrakīrti's *Madhyamakāvatāra* he correlates the theory of act as explained above with the karma doctrine:

> When during a dream a beautiful woman is perceived clearly as an object, then—after being awake—a strong passion will arise in the

> fool's (heart), although its object has vanished and does not exist anymore.
>
> In a similar way the act, although not existing inherently anymore, does produce the act's fruit. This means that the "cessation of act" (*las zhig pa*) produces the act's fruit.[13]

The first sentence paraphrases *Madhyamakāvatāra* (TTP. chapter VI, V.40) where the discussion on karma dominates. The last sentence renders the core of Tsong-kha-pa's concept of karma. This could be outlined as follows:

1. After the act itself has passed and is finished, a phenomenon called *las zhig pa* arises, which might be literally translated as cessation of act, but which is more adequately described as after-act.
2. The after-act is a *dngos po*, a thing or substance, participating in causality.
3. The after-act produces the karmic fruit or result.

For Tsong-kha-pa the karmic process manifests itself in the following sequence: volition—act—after-act—fruit.

Imitating a well established Buddhist habit, and following his model, the *Prasannapadā*, Tsong-kha-pa wants to demonstrate that his theory of karma—that is, the act results in a substance called the after-act, which in turn produces the karmic fruit—is not only verified by means of logical reasoning but also by the testimony of the Buddhist scripture. Having the seventh chapter of the *Prasannapadā*[14] in mind, Tsong-kha-pa states:

> When (the Buddha) states that birth is the cause for old age and death and that the characteristics (i.e., *skye ba* origin, *gnas pa* duration, *'jig pa* decaying) of the co-conditioned are included in the aggregate of formations (*saṃskāraskandha*), does that not show that the Teacher has explained that decaying (*'jig pa*) is connected with cause?

Then Tsong-kha-pa elaborates his individual ideas:

> Because it is said that "death" means the living being's "cessation" (*zhig pa*) generated by the cause "birth" it is testified that "cessation" is produced by cause.[15]

In this paragraph, Tsong-kha-pa makes it very clear that he thinks *zhig pa* and *'jig pa* to be identical, and therefore he argues that whatever criteria are applied with regard to one of them must also qualify the other term. For Tsong-kha-pa, the entire karmic process occurs within the realm of causality and reality; this concept however leads him to attribute the quality of substance or thingness to the after-act.

GO-RAMS-PA'S REFUTATION OF THE KARMA THEORY DEVELOPED BY TSONG-KHA-PA

Go-rams-pa, a well-known fifteenth century philosopher and follower of the Sa-skya tradition, criticized Tsong-kha-pa's philosophy severely. In his commentary on the *Madhyamakāvatāra*,[16] Go-rams-pa refutes Tsong-kha-pa's interpretation of that text in total, but in particular he attacks Tsong-kha-pa's concept of karma.[17] The main points of his criticism are as follows:

1. The concept of the after-act as a substance or thing is part of the Vaiśeṣika philosophy and therefore outside of Buddhist thought; further, the Vaiśeṣika system was rejected by Dharmakīrti.
2. Nobody before Tsong-kha-pa had ever established such a concept of karma and claimed it as part of the Mādhyamika tradition. Thus Tsong-kha-pa's pretense to reflect in his karma concept Candrakīrti's genuine intention is rejected by Go-rams-pa.

Also in his *lTa ba'i shan byed*,[18] he rejects Tsong-kha-pa's karma theory. Se-ra rJe-btsun-pa Chos-kyi-rgyal-mtshan (1469-1546), a prominent figure among the early dGe-lugs-pa philosophers, criticized Go-rams-pa for his attacks on Tsong-kha-pa and defended the latter's theory of karma as being authentically Buddhist in character.[19]

NOTES

Abbreviations

MMK	*Mūlamadhyamakakārikā*
TSNS	rTsa shes ṭik chen or dBu ma rtsa ba'i tshig le'ur byed pa shesrab ces bya ba rnam bshad rigs pa'i rgya mtsho.
GR	dGongs pa rab gsal or bsTan bcos chen po dbu ma la 'jug pa'i rnam bshad dgongs pa rab gsal.
DL	Drang nges legs bshad snying po or Drang ba dang nges pa'i don rnam par phye ba'i bstan bcos legs bshad snying po.
IASWR	The Institute for Advanced Studies of World Religions

1. Vasubandhu, *Abhidharmakośa*, The Tibetan Tripiṭaka (Peking edition, No. 5590-5597 Suzuki Research Foundation, Tokyo, 1962) Chapter IV, v. 1, cf. Louis de La Vallee Poussin, trans. *L'Abhidharmakośa de Vasubandhu*.

(Melanges Chinois et Bouddhiques, vol. XVI. Brussels, Institut Belge Des Hautes Etudes Chinoises, 1971) vol. 3, pp. 1f.

2. Nāgārjuna, *Mūlamadhyamakakārikā sDe dge Tibetan Tripitaka bstan ḥgyur* preserved at the Faculty of Letters, University of Tokyo, (dBu-ma) 1 (Tokyo 1977) Chapter XVII, v. 6, Max Walleser, trans. *Die Mittlere Lehre des Nāgārjuna* (Heidelberg, 1911) p. 91. cf. F.J. Streng, *Emptiness* (New York, 1967) p. 201.

3. *Mūlamadhyamakavṛtty-Akutobhayā sDe dge Tibetan Tripiṭaka* (Tokyo, 1977) pp. 32, 4.5.

4. For more information see A. Bareau. *Les Sectes Bouddhiques du Petit Vehicule*, (Paris, 1955).

5. L. de La Vallee Poussin, *L'Abhidharmakośa* (Brussels, 1971) vol. I, p. 178.

6. *Prāpti* connected with karma is already mentioned by Indian philosophers. See Candrakīrti's *Madhyamakāvatārabhāṣya* (print. Sehore, Bhopal M.P., 1968) p. 101.

7. Cf. *Abhidharmakośa*, Chapter II, v. 36.

8. See *Yid dang kun gzhi'i dka' gnas rnam par bshad pa mkhas pa'i 'jug ngogs* by Gung thang dkon mchog bstan pa'i sgron me, *the collected works of Guṅ thaṅ dkon mchog bstan pa'i sgron me*, Vol. 2. Reproduced by N. Gelek Demo, (New Delhi, 1972) pp. 341, 4.

9. *Madhyamakāvatāra, Cone Tanjur*, IASWR Vol. 23, ('A) ff. 203a, 2f.

10. Das, Sarat Chandra. *Tibetan-English Dictionary* (1902; rpt. Alipore, West-Bengal: West Bengal Government Press, 1960) p. 457.

11. The Tibetan Text:

> gang zhig 'jig pa rgyu med pa nyid du khas blangs nas 'dus byas rnams skad cig ma nyid du smra ba de'i ltar na nam mkha'i me tog ltar rgyu med pas 'jig pa med pa'i phyir dngos po rnams skad cig ma nyid dang/ 'jig pa dang bral ba rnams 'dus byas nyid du'ang 'grub par ga la 'gyur/ de'i phyir de thams cad mi 'grig pa nyid du 'gyur ro/

Prasannapadā, ed. by Jacques May (Paris, 1959) p. 367, Tibetan Edition, (Sehore, Bhopal, M.P.: Tibetan Publishing House 1968) pp. 145f. Cf. *Cone Tanjur*, vol. 23, ('AO) ff. 58b, 5.

12. The Tibetan Text:

> de la 'jig pa rgyu med du smra ba rnams ni rang grub pa'i dus las dus gnyis par mi sdod pa'i 'jig pa ni dngos po de'i rgyu nyid las skye bas rgyu de las gzhan phyi byung gi rgyu med par 'dod la/ skad cig gnyis par zhig pa ni dngos med yin pas rgyu gtan med du smra'o/ de'i phyir zhig pa rgyu med du smra ba la dngos po rnams skad cig gis 'jig pa med pas 'dus byas su mi 'grub pa dang. . . .

TSNS the collected works (gsuṅ bum) of Rje Tsoṅ-kha-pa bLo-bzaṅ grags-pa ed. N. Gelek Demo, (New Delhi, 1975) pp. 218.5ff.

13. The Tibetan Text:

> rmi lam na bud med bzang mo dmigs pa'i yul dag mthong nas ni/ de nas gnyid sad kyang ste sad pa'i tshe na yang skye bo blun po la da lta 'gags shing med pa la dmigs nas chags pa drag po skye bar 'gyur ba de bzhin du rang bzhin gyis yod pa min pa'i las 'gags pa las kyang ni/ las kyi 'bras bu 'byung ba yod pa yin no/ zhes las zhig pa las 'bras bu byung bar bstan no/

dGongs-pa-rab-gsal ed. N. Gelek Demo, (N.D.) pp. 288, 6-289, 1 cf. *Madhyamakāvatāra, Cone Tanjur,* IASWR, vol. 23 ('A) ff. 203a, 3ff.

14. *Prasannapadā*, Tib. ed. (Sehore, Bhopal, M.P. 1968) pp. 146f. Cf. *Cone Tanjur*, Vol. 23, ('A) f. 58b, 6.

15. The Tibetan Text:

> skye ba'i rkyen gyis rga shi zhes pa dang/ 'dus byas kyi mtshan nyid rnams 'du byed kyi phung po'i nang du 'du bar gsungs pa na/ ston pas 'jig pa rgyu bcas su gsal bar gsungs pa ma hin nam zhes pa yin te/ shi ba ni sems can de zhig pa yin la de skye ba'i rkyen gyis skye bar gsungs pas zhig pa rgyus bskyed par grub po/

TSNS ed. N. Gelek Demo , (New Delhi, 1975) pp. 219, 2-3.

16. Go-rams-pa, *dBu ma la 'jug pa'i dkyus kyi sa bcad pa dang pzhung so so'i dka' ba'i gnas la dpyad pa Lta-ba-ngan-sel The Complete Works of the Great Masters of the Sa-skya Sect of Tibetan Buddhism,* Vol. 13. (Tokyo: Toyo Bunko, 1969) pp. 24, 3, 1-84, 3, 6.

17. Go-rams-pa, *Lta-ba-ngan-sel* pp. 52, 3-55, 1.

18. Go-rams-pa, *Lta ba'i shan 'byed theg mchog gnad kyi zla zer The Complete Works of the Great Masters of the Sa-skya Sect of Tibetan Buddhism,* vol. 13. (Tokyo: Toyo Bunko, 1969) pp. 10, 1.1-10, 2, 5.

19. See Se-ra rJe-btsun-pa and bDe-legs nyi-ma, *Lta-ngan-mun-sel A Refutation of Erroneous Views regarding the Nature of the Void Expounded by Gser-Mdog Paṇ-chen Shakya-Mchog-Ldan and Go-bo Rab-'byams-pa Bsod-nams senge* (New Delhi, 1969) pp. 264-274.

CHAPTER TEN

Merit-Making and Ritual Aspects In The Religious Life of Zanskar (West Tibet)

EVA K. DARGYAY

INTRODUCTION

Through good one attains good;
From evil originates misery
Thus the result of good and evil
Karma has been pointed out[1]

This verse renders roughly what the Buddhist lay person thinks when talking of karma. To perform good deeds and to avoid evil ones is the basic rule of lay ethics in Buddhism. However, to comply with all major aspects of Buddhist ethics is almost impossible for laymen; for example, not to kill is a command hardly ever realized by a peasant. Even if he tries hard to avoid killing any living beings, he still destroys insects when he tills the soil. Another central command of Buddhism is to limit, decrease, and finally, to avoid every attachment to life. Nevertheless, a layman will devote most of his will and creativity to enlarging his and his family's property, fame, and prosperity. Marriage, love, and care for one's children and other relatives are cornerstones of every society. To become disenchanted with the romance and warmth of family life would end one's role as a lay person but, on the other hand, such an attempt is much favored by all Buddhist traditions. This situation entices many Western scholars to see Buddhism as primarily an ascetic, elitist, and monastic movement.[2] The question arises, how could the Buddhist laity accommodate its needs to Buddhist ethics?

Whenever a Tibetan Buddhist layman is asked about his central Buddhist concern, the answer is invariably, "*dge ba bsag pa*," to accumulate merit, a potential to facilitate the process of gaining liberation, namely, *Nirvāṇa*.[3] In a classical viewpoint this would come about through the practice of ethics (*tshul khrims*), the cultivation of meditation (*sgom pa*), and the development of wisdom (*shes rab*), ways which are beyond a lay person's reach, at least in general.

This dilemma—the command to accumulate merit on one side and the inability to practice Buddhist ethics on the other—is resolved by supplying opportunities exlusively devoted to the task of enabling the laity to accumulate merit.

Some of the merit-making activities are to be performed by the individual; others are carried out collectively. Only the latter category will be the subject of the present paper.[4] Most of the collectively performed merit-making activities become manifest in rituals which are embedded in festivals. For the present purpose I shall present material colected by me in Zanskar, a remote valley in South Ladakh, in the Western Himalayas.[5] The first case which I shall describe is a festival in which all lay people of this area participate and which is celebrated on the sacred premises of an ancient Buddhist temple. The second case is the final part of the funeral rituals conducted mainly at the local cremation ground. The third case to be discussed is somewhat different from the first two. It concerns the production of decorative manuscripts which are copies of famous Buddhist texts. Such a performance gave rise to a celebration which became almost like a festival.

1. THE NAROPA FESTIVAL AT SANI

The focal point for this event is the opening of the Naropa shrine situated within the sacred premises of Sani in the central part of the Zanskar valley.[6] Local traditions report that the Indian mystic Naropa, who lived during the tenth century, meditated at this place for a while. Today the sacred area consists of the main temple called Sani Mkhar (castle of Sani), a smaller temple devoted to Padmasambhava (probably eighteenth century), and the Naropa shrine which received its present form in the eighteenth century. The sacred buildings are located within a territory of distinct numinous character. In the symbolic language of Tantric Buddhism, the sacred place of Sani is said to be one of the eight cremation grounds which are considered favorable places for practicing Tantric meditation. Sacred trees, a spring with clear, fresh water, a lake, birds, and spirits—everything participates in this sacred cosmos in miniature. The shrine houses a gilded bronze statue of Naropa, supposedly one foot high. During the year the door to the small shrine remains closed and is opened only once in the summer.

I shall not dwell here upon the Naropa festival in all its historical, religious, and social complexity but rather limit the discussion to those aspects relevant to the general theme of merit-making.

When I participated in the Naropa Festival in 1979, sTag-sna Rin-po-che initiated the holy day with a series of three *dbang bskur* (rTa-mgrim, Phyag-na-rdo-rje, and Khyung). In the late afternoon the entrance to the shrine was opened by a monk from the Sani monastery. This happened in an informal way. The monk got the key and opened the padlock. Then he covered his mouth with a piece of white cloth in order to prevent the sacred image from being polluted by his breath. Assisted by another monk, he pulled a trunk out from the dark shrine room and placed it in front of the entrance. They placed the Naropa statue, which is enclosed in a small glass shrine, on the trunk and removed a white scarf from the front side of the casket.

Following these activities the lay people stepped forward one by one and bowed in front of the statue so that their foreheads touched the base of the statue. They put one or two rupees into a small box as a donation to the monastery. The long line of lay people moved slowly since they all took their time to worship the sacred image. At the same time other lay people paraded in their best outfits while they circumambulated the main temple. Although circumambulation is a merit-making performance, people had a good time chatting and exchanging all the news of the various villages. Almost at sunset young men and girls carried large bouquets of wild flowers, which they had picked from mountain slopes, and placed them in front of the Naropa statue while other laymen were beating drums and blowing trumpets. At sunset the people came together in the courtyard of the temple and spent the night singing, dancing, and drinking the locally brewed beer.

The monks participated in the religious activities only by bringing out the sacred statue, which must not be touched by lay people. Otherwise, only lay people participated in the festival. The presence of so many young lads and girls coming from various distant villages of the Sanskar valley added an atmosphere of love and romance to the religious festival. Circumambulation of the temple offered a good opportunity for the young men to meet informally with girls from places other than their own villages.

The religious significance of the Naropa Festival, as explained to me by various native participants, is to enable the laity to accumulate merit. This may be attained in two ways. First, the youth of the Sanskar valley donate wild flowers from the mountains to the sacred image of Naropa. This act provides the merit of donating, the first and basic virtue of the six perfections (*pāramitā*). Second, circumambulation of the sacred premises focuses the devotee's mind on the Buddha, *Dharma*, and *Saṅgha*. It is the act of taking refuge, the prime requirement for entering the path to liberation. On the other hand, taking refuge means to gain protection and security. Sgam-po-pa quotes from the *Mahāparinirvāṇasūtra*: He who takes refuge in the Three Jewels will gain fearlessness.[7] The Zanskari always feel endangered by all the demons, ghosts, and gods which animate mountains, rocks, water springs, and the earth. Therefore, to gain protection is much appreciated, and circumambulation of the temple provides an easy opportunity for gaining that. The act of circumambulating is a physical act performed by means of one's body (*lus*); therefore the mind (*sems*) and the voice (*ngag*), the two other instruments for merit-making, are idle. So for a Zanskari there is no inconsistency in circumambulating the temple to accumulate merit and amusing himself by chatting with young women.

The fact that, at least theoretically, the entire population of the village participates in the Naropa *darśan*, that is, to visualize the sacred image and the meaning it stands for, ensures that the whole community accumulates good karma, thus guaranteeing a bright future.

2. THE DGE-TSHA RITUAL

The *dGe-tsha* ritual is the final part of the funeral rites which, in three parts, lasts for at least a year. The blessing of the body and its cremation constitute the first part of the entire funeral. On New Year's Eve, the deceased's relatives proceed to the cremation grounds where they call the deceased by name and offer a meal to him. The third and final part is the *dGe-tsha* (Strengthening of the Virtue-Roots) which is celebrated in early summer on the 21st and 22nd day of the fourth month of the Tibetan lunar calendar.[8] The main purpose of the *dGe-tsha* ritual is to give permanent rest to whatever has remained after the body's cremation. The ritual is never performed on behalf of an individual, but always for the community of those who have died since the *dGe-tsha* ceremony was performed the previous summer. The ritual is set up in close interaction between the laity and the monastic community of each single village in the valley. The ceremony culminates in dedicating the merit derived from chanting and feeding the monks, to those who died during the last year.

The *dGe-tsha* ritual performed at Karcha in 1979 lasted for two days. The first day was reserved mainly for the monks' activities at the cremation grounds; the second day the monks chanted in their temple and the laity celebrated a feast. The monks who performed the *dGe-tsha* in Karcha belonged to the Karcha Byams-pa-gling monastery,[9] while the lay people who participated in the ritual were inhabitants of Karcha village. The geographical setting clearly reflected the interaction and cooperation of monastery and village. The monastery, its numerous splendid white buildings nestling on the steep rocky face of a high nameless mountain, hovered above the village whose farmhouses were spread out at the edge of the agricultural area, and along the banks of a small yet treacherous torrent. The village was earthbound and provided the commodities for earthly life, while the monastery was the link to the suprahuman world, the intermediary with the world of the mountain gods and the ghosts riding on clouds through the sky.

Let us now watch the *dGe-tsha* ritual as it was performed. Twenty minutes north of the village of Karcha I arrived at the cremation grounds—a mountain slope covered entirely with rocks of all sizes. In a small depression, sheltered from the gusty winds, the monks of the Karcha monastery assesmbled, seated in four lines facing each other. At the upper end was a kind of throne, built from natural stones. It was the seat for the bLa-ma, the head of this monastery. The morning hours were spent chanting various texts and prayers: a prayer in honor of the lineage ofthe bKra-shis-lhun-po monastery (*bkra shis lhun po bla brgyud*); a hymn in praise of Nāgārjuna as the lucid teacher of the doctrine of interdependence (*rten 'brel bstod pa*); a prayer to ensure a long life for the Dalai Lama (*zhabs brten gsol 'debs*). After that, the lay people donated their offerings to the *Saṅgha*, the monastic community. In this particular case, three farmers from Karcha provided buttered and salted tea with homemade bread for each monk, as well as giving them each a rupee. The lay donors were well dressed and received special attention from all who participated in the ceremony. White scarves wrapped around their necks indicated their rank.

Following these preliminary performances was the commencement of the essential part of the *dGe-tsha*—the *rus chog* or bone ritual. Only the elder monks stayed with their abbot, the bLa-ma, when he started to chant the text pertaining to the bone ritual. An old layman brought forward, on a slab of natural stone, some bones—remnants from the cremations which had occurred during the last year. Before the *dGe-tsha* ritual began, he had searched the cremation grounds for bones.

The man placed the bone fragments on a small table in front of the acting bLa-ma who blessed them by pouring water and scattering barley kernels over them. Next the old layman brought a ball of clay on which the mantra NRI, symbolizing the deceased's mind, was written by the abbot. Again he blessed the clay ball. Meanwhile, the old layman pounded the bone fragments on a flat stone laden with auspicious powder made from white stones, which had been placed on it before the pounding began. Then he blended the bonemeal with the damp clay, which he shaped into eight miniature *mchod rten*. A senior monk inserted a blade of grass into each *mchod rten*, which were then called *tsha tsha*.

When they dried they were placed into a full sized *mchod rten* where the *tsha tsha* will stay permanently.

At the end of the bone ritual, the younger monks prepared a soup for supper; the required ingredients were provided by the lay people of the village. Gradually more and more lay people came to the cremation grounds. Women carried large vessels filled with *chang*, the locally brewed beer, and baskets of bread. A huge copper vessel (approximately five feet in diameter) was slowly filled with beer.

Meanwhile, senior members of the lay community wrote the names of the recently deceased on a stone tablet. The abbot read each name aloud and dedicated the merit acquired through the *dGe-tsha* ritual to all the deceased to enable them to gain a good rebirth and finally, *Nirvāṇa*. Tea and bread was offered to the monks while the lay people had a good time drinking beer, albeit in absolute silence. In the early morning of the next day they returned to their homes singing noisily, for they had become drunk during the night. The monks ended the first day of *dGe-tsha* with a tantric ritual (*gaṇa-cakra pūja*) which reflected, on a more spiritual level, the elated condition of the laity.

During the second day of the *dGe-tsha*, the cremation grounds remained in solitude. In the temple the monks chanted endless rituals in order to secure the transference of merit to the benefit of the deceased. No one outside the monastic community was permitted to join or watch them.

At sunset, lay people met at the shores of the creek separating the village into two halves. Near a wall of natural stones the people sat down to drink beer. Men and women stayed in separate groups. A few women danced, each by herself; with slow movements they turned around, singing in very low voices. Boys and girls chased one another and shouted *joolay*, "hi," to everybody. With the next morning, *dGe-tsha* had come to an end.

When we analyze the *dGe-tsha* ritual we may distinguish between archaic and supposedly pre-Buddhist elements on the one hand, and Buddhist elements imported mostly from India during the Middle Ages, on the other. Let me first discuss those elements which I think are archaic and perhaps pre-Buddhist. The *rus chog* part of the whole ritual is actually a collective deposit of the bones of the recently deceased. The chronicle and annals of the Yar-lung Dynasty report that the funeral for the members of the royal family was performed in four steps.[10] Early Chinese sources tell of collective burials as a common habit among Tibetan tribes living at the Sino-Tibetan border.[11] The other element which betrays a pre-Buddhist character is the drinking of beer by all lay people and the ecstatic, yet solemn, mood of the congregation. It might be a survival of an ancient drinking ritual where living and dead joined in a performance which could secure the fertility of men and livestock.

With the introduction of Buddhism, the well-being of the deceased members of the community could only be ensured through the merit-making activity of that part of the community still on this earth. Thus the *dGe-tsha* ritual integrates the needs of archaic rural people with the ethical demands of Mahāyāna Buddhism.

3. Other Merit-Making Deeds On Behalf Of The Dead

From time to time families have chosen to complete exceptional deeds for the benefit of their deceased members. In Zanskar this usually took the form of installment of sacred images and the production of magnificently illustrated manuscripts, copies of famous Buddhist *sūtras*. To each manuscript an appendix was attached which "declared the sovereignty" (*chab brjod*), a brief chronicle giving the history of Zanskar as part of the sacred Tibetan cosmos and the story of the family ordering the manuscript to be made as a merit-making act. In this case the agent was not the village community but the individual family who provided everything for the benefit of the dead family members. However the dedication of merit was not limited to the family's dead but was also extended to the dead of the local royal family and finally to all dead. I will give a sample of such a donor chronicle attached to the *mDo mDzang blun*, a manuscript ordered by king Khri-dpal-lde of bZang-lha.[12]

The donor chronicle starts with praise of the Three Jewels, the deeds of Buddha Śākyamuni, further glorifying Maitreya, Mañjuśrī, Avalokiteśvara and Vajrapāṇi. The spread of the Buddha Doctrine manifest in the various sacred texts was celebrated together with its main promoters, in particular, the promoters of Buddhism in Tibet. Next the text gave the origin of the Royal House of bZang lha rooted in the Indian Ikṣvaku family, and mentioned briefly the spread of Buddhism in Tibet. That was followed by its main objective, i.e., describing Zanskar as part of a numinous cosmos and its inhabitants as blessed by the Buddha Doctrine.

> Among the four continents, Jambudvipa is the best one. The external (physical) world rests upon a *svāstika* of air, and the internal world, (living beings), have departed from the Gods of Clear Light. Under a sky resembling lapis lazuli and on the narrow petals of a lotus, between sky and earth, which are like (the halves of) a charm box, there is Jambudvīpa's Jambu tree, the King of Trees, south of the best mountain. At the world's navel, there is the Indian city of Vajrāsaṇa. From there, after crossing the Nine Black Mountains, there is Mt. Ti-se, the king of glaciers. At its West side, the river Sindhu flows down. To its left, there is Zangs-dkar, the country born from luck, the land of religion. In the centre of the earth (*sa*, the valley Zanskar) is the palace (*kho rang* for *pho brang*) of bZang-la which

is located in front of a mountain said to be an auspicious place resembling a Garuda with his wings wide spread and baring his teeth and claws. This is the homeland of scholars educated in the five disciplines.

On the roof of the imperishable palace, there is the mighty Dharmarāja Khri-dpal-lde, whose power never shrinks—like a Garuda's wings.

sKyid-lde-nyi-ma-mgon[13] who directed his horse toward mNga'-ris descended from the lineage of gNya'-khri-btsan-po of the Ŝakya family and he came to Tibet due to the strength of the Tibetans' merit.

Within this dynasty the Three lDe of sTod (appeared) as well as the Three mGon, but in particular the great king gShegs-lde who came to Zang-'kar (sic).[14] There his son Seng-ge-lde established his kingdom.[15] Since then the golden wheel of the dynasty never came to a stop nor was the yoke of his (gShegs-lde?) law ever overturned.

The treasure vase of prosperity (*longs spyod gter gyi bum*) never lost its miraculous power.

With regard to his enemies abroad he (Khri-dpal-lde) is wrathful like a meteorite of space iron, while with his beloved relatives he is soft like a Chinese silk cloth (*rgyal mo dar*).

With respect to religious and secular affairs, he protects his subjects like (his own) sons.

At a time when his helmet is high, under your (sic) gracious rule, the drum (announcing) your fame resounds in the sky and the flag of your reputation unfolds over the mountain peaks.

The pious queen and donor Ga-dun,[16] being of a goddess' character, attractive and gentle, an embodiment of Tara, she worships the bLamas and the Three Jewels.

She is very friendly with the royal parents (her parents-in-law?) and the friends. She lives in harmony with the princess, ministers, and magnates. She silences the mighty ones. She advises her entourage, servants, and sons.

Such was realized due to previously (accumulated) merit. In order to let the previous deceased attain to the path of liberation and in order to purge the defilements of the living ones, a statue of Buddha, the teacher, was established as a support of his visible personality (*sku*); the Sūtra *mDzangs-blun* was copied as a support of his word (*gsungs*); and a golden Stupa was constructed as a support of his mind (*thugs*).

In realizing that worldly wealth is without any essence, they donated all their belongings to the religion—what a joy! By means of their pure attitude the best prince No-no Mam-mkha'-dpal-lde[17] and the best princess Nor-bu-dpal-'dzom may both gain authority over a wealth similar to the treasure of sky. May the realm of their might expand like a lake in summer. May their lives be firmly grounded like the Lord of Mountains (Meru).

The purpose of this particular donation (the erection of a Buddha statue, the copying of the *mDzangs blun,* and the construction of a small scale *stūpa*) is threefold: to let the previous deceased attain to the path of liberation; to purge the defilements of the living ones; and to ensure the future prosperity and power of one's own dynasty.

The chronicle ends with a list of names of more than thirty people who all cooperated in performing this merit-producing donation. This fact firmly supports the view that the entire community, noblemen as well as peasants, worked together in a merit-making performance crucial for the future prosperity of the entire population.

When a family of the sTag-lung-pa clan in the village Ri-rnam decided to copy the *Prajñāpāramitāsūtra* as a part of a large donation, they as donors made their intention quite clear:[18]

The deceased (ancestors) had gained the leisure of a human body by acquiring merit. Endowed with the fate of an inspiring karma they understood the Noble *Dharma*.

The faithful donor Nam-mkha'-rgya-mtsho and his daughter (? or: wife, Tib. *bud med*) who has rejected the five faults and (enjoyed) a healthy body, and the venerable donor bKra-shis-dpal-'dzom had the entire *Yum-chen-pu-khri,*[19] as a support of (Buddha's) Word, written on a paper dark blue like the *dharmadhātu* in order to establish firmly the life of the venerable bLa-ma to strengthen those who cling to the *Dharma* firmly. (The first words of the) *Sher-phyin yum, rgya skad du* ("in the language of India") were written in a decorative manner embellished with seven jewels. The art (of this piece of calligraphy) is blooming like a lotus. The (script on the) cloth label (of this manuscript) was made of gold dust and silver. In order to perform this virtuous deed the following persons assisted the donors: 'A-pa Nam-mkha' -dpal-mgon, No-bo Rab-phyung-nam-mkha' -bkra-shis, Nam-mkha' -bsam-grub, and bLo-bzang-dpal-mgon; further the best sons: Nam-mkha'-phun-tshogs, rGya-mtsho-don-grub, bLo-bzang-don-grub, and Na-ma Nam-mkha'-chos-'dzom; further the daughters: Nam-mkha'-dpal 'dzom,bSod-nams-chab (?)-'dzom and. . . (name erased), and Nag-sug. May they all perform pious deeds like father and mother have done. The donor bKra-shis-dpal-'dzom prepared an exquisite and tasty meal which pleased the invited monks.

May all people, the donors and whoever had joined them realize the *Prajñāpāramitā* completely and join the Buddhas and their disciples. Sarva Maṅgalam.

The monuments of previous merit-making acts, and in particular the brilliantly illustrated and well designed manuscripts, contribute to the prestige and reputation even of the present members of that family. The performance of such a prominent donation highlights the social and religious concern of the entire community. Although one particular family provided the majority of the donation, all other members of the village community contributed minor assets, e.g., beer, food, money, paper, or ink. Even today the inhabitants of a village boast of the number of precious manuscripts kept in their homes.

The act of donating was always perceived as the focal point of lay religious life, as an extraordinary effort to ensure the well-being of the entirety of one's community, dead as well as living members.

NOTES

1. *Dran pa nyer bzhag chung ba* 36a, in sGam-po-pa, the Jewel Ornament of Liberation, tr. by H.V. Guenther, p. 82.

2. E.J. Thomas, *The History of Buddhist Thought* (London: Routledge & Kegan Paul, 2nd ed. 1951), 11ff; Sherry B. Ortner, *Sherpas Through Their Rituals* (London: Cambridge University Press, 1978), 33.

3. E.K. Dargyay, *Tibetan Village Communities—Structure and Change.* (Warminster: Aris & Phillips, forthcoming, 1982).

4. Individually performed merit-making acts were examined by Sherry B. Ortner in this study of Sherpa rituals, *Sherpas Through Their Rituals.* (London: Cambridge University Press, 1978).

5. The data presented here were collected during two expeditions to Zanskar in 1978 and 1979. The field trips were part of the Ladakh Project sponsored by the Institute of Indian and Iranian Studies, University of Munich, and financed by the German foundation Volkswagenwerk (Stiftung Volkswagenwerk, Hannover). Cf. E.K. Dargyay & L. Dargyay. Vorlaufiger Bericht uber zwei Forschungsreisen nach Zanskar (West-Tibet). *Zentralasiatische Studien* Vol. 14, pt. 2. (Wiesbaden: Otto Harrassowitz, 1981), 85-114.

6. According to local chronicles, Sani is the most ancient sacred site in Zanskar, perhaps dating back to the time of the Kushāna emperor Kanishka. For more information vd. David L. Snellgrove & Tadeusz Skorupski, *The Cultural Heritage of Ladakh*, 2nd vol. (New Delhi: Vikas Publishing House, 1980), 57f; Eva K. Dargyay & Ulrich Gruber, *Ladakh—Innenansicht eines Landes.* (Dusseldorf: Eugen Diederichs Verlag, 1980), 157ff.

7. Sgam-po-pa, Jewel Ornament, p. 100.

8. Funeral rites which were performed in sequential steps over a period of a few years were well documented for the Royal Dynasty of Tibet, seventh to ninth century. See Erik Haarh, *The Yar lung Dynasty.* (Copenhagen: G.E.C. Gad's Forlag, 1969), 357ff.

9. For more information vd. D.L. Snellgrove & T. Skorupski, *Ladakh*, vol. 2, 44-48.

10. Cf. E. Haarh, *Yar lung*, 360.

11. Cf. E. Haarh, *Yar lung*, 348, where he quotes from the Chinese source Wen-hsien t'ung-k'ao.

12. *Chab brjod* no.:79-33/10-17 (unpublished document). King Khri-dpal-lde is briefly mentioned in the Genealogy of bZang-lha, ed. by A.H. Francke, *Antiquities of Indian Tibet*. Archaeological Survey of Indian, New Imperial Series, vol. L. 1926 reprint. (New Delhi: S. Chand, 1972), 164.

13. King sKyid-lde-nyi-ma-mgon is said to be the prince of the Royal Tibetan Dynasty who went to the West, namely, mNga'ris, and founded there a Tibetan principality. He is one of the prominent ancestors of the later Ladakhi and Zanskari Dynasties.

14. The sentence reports the actual beginning of the Tibetan rule over Ladakh and Zanskar. The Three mGon from sTod, the Upper Land, are three kings who all had the word *mgon* as the last syllable in their personal names. These kings are: dPal-gyi-lde Rig-pa-mgon, bKra-shis-mgon, lDe-gtsug-mgon. For more information vd. L. Petech, *The Kingdom of Ladakh c. 950-1842 A.D.*, Serie Orientale Roma vol. LI. (Rome: Istituto Italiano per il Medio ed Estremo Oriente, 1977), 17. gShegs-lde, a native from Gu-ge, was the first ruler of Zanskar. In the Zanskar Chronicle his name is Sakya-thub-pa. See A.H. Francke, *Indian Tibet*, vol. 2, 156.

15. Seng-ge-lde is apparently identical with Seng-ge-ldor who is reported by the Zanskar Chronicle to be gShegs-lde's son. See A.H. Francke, *Indian Tibet*, vol. 2, 157.

16. Ga-dun is for Khatun, the Mongolian word for queen.

17. In the Genealogy of bZang-lha, ed. and tr. by A.H. Francke, *Indian Tibet*, vol. 2, 163f, king Nam-mkha'-dpal-lde is said to be Khri-dpal-lde's uncle. However I would see our source as more reliable because it was composed at that time, while the bZang-lha Genealogy was written in the early twentieth century.

18. The descendents of this family are still living in a small village called Ri-rnam, situated at the banks of the Zanskar river, several miles north of Karcha. *Chab brjod* no. 79-32/19-21 (unpublished document).

19. This is the *Prajñāpāramitā* version in Hundred-Thousand Slokas and the one in Twenty-Thousand Slokas.

CHAPTER ELEVEN

Shinran's View of Karma

LESLIE S. KAWAMURA

The emergence of the Kamakura period (1185-1335) in Japanese history not only opened an era of warfare and social chaos, but it also marked the beginning of a transformation in Japanese Buddhism from its earlier monastic orientation to a religion involving the masses. Although it cannot be doubted that in the earlier Heian (794-1185), Nara (710-784), and Late Yamato (533-710) periods, Buddhism had its contact with the common man and had influenced the etiquette and aesthetic values of the ordinary citizens through its magnificant and beautiful Buddha statues and its *Sūtra*-chanting that was believed to have magical effects,[1] it was not until Hōnen (法 然 :1133-1212), Shinran (親 鸞 :1173-1262), and Nichiren (日 蓮 :1222-1282) came upon the scene that there evolved indigenous forms of Japanese Buddhism which responded to the spiritual dilemma facing the ordinary person. Recognizing "that all religious efforts that appeal to the individual's self-interest in order to gain salvation, only reinforce the egoism which Buddhism declares is the source of suffering and from which we must be rescued,"[2] it was Shinran who "came to realize that the Vows of Amida Buddha provided the way out of the spiritual dilemma. . .and that salvation in every aspect is derived from Amida's compassionate intention."[3] This was Shinran's understanding of *Tariki* (他 力), which is the practice of the *Nembutsu* (念 佛 :*buddhānusmṛti*) not as a calculated means for salvation, but as Amida Buddha's Vow-Power manifested in human beings as a sign of salvation already firmly established. Thus, every instance of the *Nembutsu*, that is, every recitation of Amida Buddha's name, was for Shinran an expression of joy and gratitude for the past karma (*pūrva-karma*) that projected him into his present human situation. By tracing the historical development of karma, an attempt will be made in this paper to show how Shinran arrived at his appreciation of *pūrva-karma* or past karma (宿業:*shukugō*) as the past cause (宿縁:*shukuen*) for joy and gratitude.

The dynamics of karma goes back to the very beginning of religious thought in India and it plays an important role in the history of Buddhist thought. But the concept of karma has never been a static or single phenomenon, for not only has karma meant different things to different religious and philosophical systems, but it has also been interpreted differently within a single system like Buddhism.

According to Y. Tamura, in contrast to terms like *caryā* (action) that has a religious sense, the term karma referred to actions of the everyday kind, and these actions were good actions (*puṇya-karma*) or bad actions (*pāpa-karma*). Thus, in the period of Indian thought prior to the Buddhist period, the term *brahma-caryā* was used in the Vedic period to signify austere religious practices done by Brahmins who through those practices would be born into heaven where they gained eternal life (*amṛta*). Later, during the period of the Brāhmaṇas and the early Upaniṣads, the burden of life was more heavily felt by the common mortal and thus they sought heaven by accumulating the merits of good actions (*puṇya-karma*). Even if they managed to get to heaven, these common mortals could be reborn once again to this world. During this period, those who through *brahma-caryā* attained eternal life in heaven were considered to be practitioners of the Path of the Gods (*deva-yāna*), whereas those who entered heaven for shorter periods were practitioners of the Path of the Fathers (*pitṛ-yāna*). With the introduction of the possibility of falling into the depths of hell if one did bad deeds (*pāpa-karma*, we have the complete formation of the early rebirth theory in Indian thought. Buddhism inherited the whole gamut of extra-terrestrial life, re-incarnation, and rebirth, but with modification.[4]

First of all, although the Buddhists rejected the idea of *varṇa* and thereby rejected the idea that social status was determined by birth, they did continue the idea that karma determined what one was. Hence, we read in *Sutta-Nipāta 3.9.57*:

> na jaccā brāhmaṇo hoti na jaccā hoti abrāhmaṇo kammanā brāhmaṇo hoti kammanā hoti abrāhmaṇo.[5]
> One does not become a Brahmin by birth, nor does one become a non-Brahmin by birth. One becomes a Brahmin by (one's) action; one becomes a non-Brahmin by (one's) action.

Secondly, although they adopted the idea of *amṛta* and rebirth as an *upāya* (appropriate teaching device) for the common believer, in the final analysis, they claimed *nirvāṇa*, which transcends both birth and death, as their goal. Thus, for example, *Dhammapada IX.11* states:

> gabbam eke upapajjanti nirayaṃ pāpakammino saggaṃ sugatino yanti parinibbanti anāsavā.[6]
> Some are reborn in a womb; those who do evil, in hell. The righteous go to Heaven. Those without emotional afflictions attain *nirvāṇa*.

The adoption of *amṛta* and rebirth as appropriate teaching devices (*upāya*) was not without problems for the Buddhists. If, as the above quoted verse from the *Dhammapada* states, one can be reborn in a womb, or in hell, or in Heaven, then how were the Buddhists to defend their claim that there was nothing permanent underlying existence? In other words, if the Buddhists were going to claim *anātman* or *nairātmya* (non-substantiality), then what is it that undergoes rebirth? The Buddhists responded to this problem by re-interpreting karma in accordance with the idea of *nirvāṇa* as absolute freedom from emotional afflictions (*anāsavā*). Thus, the focus of karma was oriented more towards answering how it was that man found himself saddled with the pains and frustrations of life (*duḥkha*) or found himself blessed with happiness (*sukha*). This meant that karma was understood more in the sense of a psychological phenomenon rather than as a law governing substantial existence. Consequently, karma was re-interpreted in terms of understanding how the world and worldly affairs become subjugated by the mind. Thus we read in *Dhammapada I.1* and *I.2*:

> manopubbaṅgama dhammā manoseṭṭhā manomayā manasā ce paduṭṭhena bhāsati vā karoti vātato naṁ dukkham anveti cakkaṃ va vahato padam.[7]
> All beings are led by thought, are controled by thought, are made up by thought. If one speaks or acts with malevolent thought, then frustration follows one, just as the wheel, a foot of a drawer (an ox).
> manopubbaṅgamā dhammā manoseṭṭha manomayā manasā ce pasannena bhāsati vā karoti vā tato naṃ dukkham anveti chāyā va anapāyinī.[8]
> All beings are led by thought, are controlled by thought, are made up by thought. If one speaks or acts with benevolent thought, then happiness follows one, just as a shadow does not leave.

Although these passages are written as if they were directives for the future, they imply how the present moment of frustration or happiness came about, because a moment of frustration or happiness which has not yet occurred is nothing but a fiction. For frustration or happiness to constitute reality in Buddhism, a moment of existence must be frustrating or happy and because those various kinds of existences result from karma, which is none other than verbal and bodily actions produced from mental drive or attitude, the Buddhist understanding of karma is psychologically oriented. Consequently, Vasubandhu sums up the Buddhist view on karma with the following words:

> karmajaṃ lokavaicritryaṃ cetanā tatkṛtaṃ ca tat / cetanā mānasaṃ karma tajje vākkāyakarmaṇī //[9]
> The various kinds of life are produced by *karma* which is *cetanā* and what has been produced by it. *Cetanā* refers to mental drive. 'What has ben produced by it' refer to verbal and bodily acts.

Since karma and *cetanā* are synonymous, the idea that karma is a mental drive means that man cannot escape from his human situation of being karmically bound until all karmic drive has ceased.[10] Furthermore, because as a mental drive, *cetanā* can arouse the potential for verbal and bodily acts, which are, so long as they become operative within man's conscious moments, experienced as pleasant or painful, the human situation—i.e., the karmic situation—is one in which there constantly occurs a discriminatory calculation between gain and loss, the wholesome and the unwholesome, kind words and abusive words, and praise and blame. These eight are referred to as the eight worldly concerns because worldly people abide in them, enjoy them, and do not go beyond them.[11] Thus, if man's verbal and bodily actions are directed and driven by a mind intent on gaining the wholesome by using kind words to praise, then those verbal and bodily actions colored by the intention to gain something would on that account be emotionally afflicted, and hence, would not enable man to attain *nirvāṇa*. The reason for this is that such mental, verbal, and bodily actions would merely reinforce egoism which Buddhism declares as a source of suffering. Such was the spiritual dilemma in which Shinran found himself after twenty years of intense meditative practices as a monk on the Path of the Sages (聖道門 :*shōdōmon*).

Try as he might to rid himself of emotional afflictions in order to be freed from the bondages of karma and thus gain enlightenment, Shinran gained no assurance of enlightenment through such self-motivated, religious practices. In fact, the more diligently he applied himself to meditative practices, the more ego-bound he found himself. This led him to leave Mt. Hiei,[12] the center of Buddhist learning of the time.

Going into the city of Kyōto, Shinran entered a period of meditation at Rokkakudō temple. After some one hundred days of seclusion, he was inspired to visit Hōnen. Hōnen had already experienced and in his own way resolved the spiritual dilemma which confronted Shinran.

During Hōnen's time, there came into vogue a strong trend to interpret life's situations in terms of the principles that are necessarily associated with existence and change.

Of the four *yukti* (principles) listed in the *Śrāvakabhūmi* section of Asanga's encyclopedia *Yogācārabhūmi*,[13] Hōnen was attracted most strongly by the fourth one, *dharmatā-yukti*, or *hōni* (法爾) in Japanese, and he interpreted the working of Amida Buddha's Vow-Power in the light of this fourth principle of existence and change. This fourth principle refers to the nature of things and might be best translated as natural law. Hōnen states:

> Hōni-dōri to yu koto ari. Honō wa sora ni nobori, mizu wa kudari sama ni nagaru. Kashi no naka ni suki mono ari. Amaki mono ari. Korera wa mina hōni-dōri nari. Amida hotoke no Hongan wa, Myōgō mote zaiaku no shujō wo michi-bikan to chikai tama-tareba, tada ikkō ni nembutsu dani mo moseba, hotoke no raigō wa hōni-dōri nite sonawaru beki nari.[14]
>
> There is a phenomenon called 'natural law'. Heat rises; water flows downward. In pastry there is something attractive; there is something sweet. All of this is owing to the principle of natural law. The Vow of Amida Buddha promises to lead emotionally afflicted sentient beings to enlightenment; therefore, if one recites the *Nembutsu* to the exclusion of all other practices, then Buddha will appear before one according to the principle of natural law.

Hōnen understood himself to be one of the emotionally afflicted sentient beings and believed that so long as sentient beings were bound to past karma (*shukugō*, they were all equal, no one being better off than another. He understood his present state of existence as an effect of previous evil actions and also as the cause for negative effects to come in the future. This he understood to be the nature of things. Hence, Hōnen's view on past karma and past cause (*shukuen*) was negative; it was the basis for his total resignation to Amida Buddha and for his understanding the Pure Land of Bliss to be separate from and beyond human existence. For him, human existence was something to be negated, and therefore his interest lay not in improving his lot but in renouncing the world. The reason for this feeling can be found in the turn of events constituting the historical situation of his time.

Hōnen observed and physically experienced the declining power of the Imperial Government and the decadence into which the nobility was falling. He interpreted this event as characterizing the *mappō*, i.e., the last of the three periods of *Dharma* survival.[15] As he died before the Shōgunate government could instigate the social and cultural improvements after the Shōkyū War of 1221, he lived with feelings of despondency and hopelessness regarding human existence. Because of these feelings, he turned to the practice of the *Nembutsu* as the only means for salvation and believed firmly that in accordance with the principle of natural law, the good merits accumulated through reciting the Buddha's name would bring happiness to him in the Pure Land of Amida Buddha.

It was through Hōnen's guidance that Shinran came to know of the power of Buddha's Fundamental Vow (*pūrva-praṇidhānâdhiṣṭhāna*)[16] as the only means for salvation. This meant that there was no need to be knowledgeable about sacred texts, nor was any formal religious practice necessary, because the Power of the Vow was absolute. Simply by believing in the power of Amida's Vow to save, salvation was assured. Hence Shinran states:

> Nyakufu shōja no Chikai yue, Shingyō makotoni toki itari. Ichinen Kyōki suru hito wa, Ōjō kanarazu sadamari nu. Owing to his Vow "If (they) are not born. . .," The time for awakening Serene Faith has ripened. For him in whom 'One Thought of Joy' arises, Birth will certainly be determined.

However, for some *Nembutsu* practitioners, this seemed too simple a method and they felt that Shinran was keeping something secret from them or that Shinran had some mysterious or esoteric power. Thus they travelled to Kyōto from afar to inquire about this. Upon being questioned about his, Shinran assured them that he was hiding nothing and that he certainly had no mysterious or esoteric power that gave him the knowledge of how one might enter the Land of Bliss. Having assured them in that way, he went on to say:

> Shinran ni okite wa, tada Nembutsu shite Mida ni tasuke rare mairasu beshi, to yoki hito no ōse o kōmuri te, shinzuru hoka ni, betsu no shisai naki nari. Nembutsu wa makotoni Jōdo ni umaruru tane nite ya hamberan, mata jigoku ni otsu beki gō nite ya hamberu ran, sojite motte zonchi se zaru nari. Tatoi Hōnen Shōnin ni sukasare mairase te, Nembutsu shite jigoku ni ochi tari tomo, sarani kōkai su bekara zu sōrō. Sono yue wa, jiyo no gyō mo hagemi te, Butsu ni naru bekari keru mi ga, Nembutsu o moshi te jigoku nimo ochi te sorawa ba, koso, sukasare tatematsuri te, to yū kōkai mo sōrawa me. Izure no gyō mo oyobi gataki mi nare ba, totemo jigoku wa ichijō sumika zo kashi.[18]
>
> As for me, Shinran, there is nothing left but to receive and believe the teaching of the Venerable Master (Hōnen)—that merely by uttering the *Nembutsu*, we are saved by Amida. I am entirely ignorant as to

whether the *Nembutsu* is truly the cause for Birth in the Pure Land or as to whether it is the karma that will cause me to fall into Hell. Even if I should have been deceived by the Venerable Hōnen and should fall into Hell by uttering the *Nembutsu,* I will have no regrets. The reason is that, if I were one who could become a Buddha by performing some other practice and were to fall into Hell by uttering the *Nembutsu,* I would feel regret and say that I was deceived. But, because I am not capable of accomplishing any practice whatsoever, Hell would be my natural abode!

From the passage above, we gain an insight into the difference between Shinran's view on *Nembutsu* practice and Hōnen's view. Although for his teacher, Hōnen, the *Nembutsu* was the right and only cause for Birth in the Land of Bliss, for Shinran, the recitation of the *Nembutsu* gave no assurance of Birth in the Land of Bliss, because for him salvation, in every aspect, was derived from the Vow-Power. To say that salvation derives from the Vow-Power is to say that one has reached one's utter incapacity to attain enlightenment after having tried diligently to attain it through every possible channel. Hell became Shinran's natural abode because, given his human situation of being karmically bound and emotionally afflicted, there was no possibility for liberation and release. In short, no religious practice—not even the recitation of the *Nembutsu*— could give assurance for Birth in the Land of Bliss, because salvation was not determined by self-motivated, self-righteous, good or evil actions done for the sake of gaining it. Thus Shinran states:

Zennin nao motte Ōjō o togu, iwanya akunin o ya! Shikaru o, yo no hito tsuneni iwaku, "Akunin nao Ōjō su, ikani iwan'ya zennin o ya." Kono jō, ittan sono iware aru ni nitare domo, Hongan Tariki no ishi ni somuke ri. . . .Bonnō gusoku no warera wa, izure no gyo nite mo shōji o hanaruru koto aru bekara zaru o awaremi tamai te, Gan o okoshi tamō hon'i, akunin jōbutsu no tame nare ba, Tariki o tanomi tatematsuru akunin, mottomo Ōjō no shōin nari. Yotti, "Zennin dani koso Ōjō sure, mashite akunin wa" to ōse sorai ki.[19]

Even a good person is born in the Pure Land, all the more so an evil person! However, people in the world usually say, "Even an evil person is born in the Pure Land, all the more so a good person." However, although this view may seem reasonable at first sight, it is contrary to the purport of the Original Vow, *Tariki.* . . . The true intention behind (Amida's) Vow was to have evil persons gain birth in the Land of Bliss and it was established out of compassion for emotionally afflicted people like us who are incapable of setting ourselves free from the bondages of *saṃsāra*; therefore, the evil person who relies on *Tariki* is even more the one having a cause for birth in the Land of Bliss. Hence, I say, "Even a good person is born in the Pure Land, all the more so an evil person!"

Here Shinran completely reverses the normal course of moralistic thinking and totally upsets all presuppositions regarding the need for a distinction between good and evil. Consequently, many religious 'after-life seekers' have misunderstood Shinran's words. Some, paying lip service to the Vow-Power, thought that however inconceivable the working of the Vow-Power may be, it is the good who, after all, get saved. The bad are destined for hell. Others, thinking that the purport of the Vow is the intention of saving those who commit evil, purposely go out to do evil acts so as to support their karmic cause to be born in the Land of Bliss. These actions result from the belief that some kind of religious practice, however small, must be done in order to gain salvation. Shinran denies this, because the Original Vow of Amida encompasses all beings—good or evil, young or old—even those who would be so arrogant as to turn people away from religion because they believe that there are some people who are beyond salvation.

Shinran's denial of the belief that some kind of religious practice, however small, must be done to gain salvation stems from his understanding that the human calculations of good or evil are essentially emotionally afflicted and consequently more conducive to supporting karmically bound samsaric existence rather than to supporting the liberated nirvanic existence. Furthermore, even though humans may calculate that salvation is attainable through good acts, for Shinran such was not the case. For him, any good action or any evil action arose owing to past karma; hence, one could not will to abstain from doing evil nor to do good, if the conditions that supported the fruition of past karma were not present. This point is clearly stated in the following dialogue between Shinran and Yuien:

Mata aru toki, "Yuien-bō wa waga yū koto oba shinzuru ka?" to ōse no sōraishi aida, "San sōrō," to mōshi sōrai shika ba, "Saraba iwan koto tagau majiki ka?" to kasanete ōse no sōraishi aida, tsutsushinde ryōjō mōshi te sōrai shika ba, "Tatoeba hito sennin koroshi ten ya, shikaraba Ōjō wa ichijō su beshi", to ōse sōraishi toki, "Ōse nite wa sōrae domo, ichinin mo kono mi no kiryō nite wa koroshi tsu beshi tomo oboe zu sōrō", to mōshi te sōrai shika ba, "Satewa ikani Shinran ga yū koto o tagau majiki towa yū zo?" to. "Kore nite shiru beshi. Namigogo mo kokoro ni makase taru koto nara ba, Ōjō no tame ni sennin korose to iwan ni, sunawachi korosu beshi. Shikare domo, ichinin nite mo kanai nu beki gōen naki ni yori te gaise zaru nari.

Waga kokoro no yoku te korosa nu niwa ara zu. Mata gaise ji to omou tomo, hyakunin sennin o korosu koto mo aru beshi."[20]

Once Shinran asked Yuien-bō, "Would you believe whatever I say?" When he replied that he would, Shinran asked again, "Are you certain you will not disobey me?" Because Yuien replied that he was, Shinran continued, "Then, go and kill a thousand men, so that your birth will be assured."

Yuien replied, "With all due respect to your request, I cannot kill even one person."

Then came the retort, "Why did you say that you would not disobey what I, Shinran, request." And then Shinran continued to explain. "By this we know that if we could act as we pleased, we would kill a thousand men, if we were told to kill in order to reborn in the Pure Land. But because we lack the karmic conditions to kill even a single man, we will not injury anyone. We fail to kill, not because we have good thoughts! Even if you do not think of injuring anyone, we may kill a hundred or a thousand men.

Within the Buddhist context, the supporting conditions for karmic activities are the emotional afflictions. Hence, although samsaric existence is the manifestation of past karma's work, karma could not draw out another samsaric existence without the emotional afflictions as its supporting conditions. This fact has been brought to our attention by earlier Mahayanistic thinkers such as Sthiramati (510-570) who had this to say about it:

> saṃsārasya hi karma kleśāś ca kāraṇaṃ tayoś ca kleśāḥ pradhānaṃ. tathā hi kleśâdhipatyatvāt karma punarbhavakṣepa-samarthaṃ bhavati; nânyathā.[21]
>
> Truly, the causes for *saṃsāra* are karma and the emotional afflictions and among these two, emotional afflictions are primary. Therefore, karma is able to draw out another (samsaric) existence owing to the power of the emotional afflictions; not otherwise.

Thus, so long as man finds himself caught up in the bind of emotional afflictions he will be unable to release himself from his karmic existence. Consequently, Shinran saw himself as being incapable of overcoming the force of emotional afflictions and accordingly incapable of attaining liberation by removing emotional afflictions.

For twenty long years Shinran applied himself diligently to understanding how emotional afflictions support the function of karma, how emotional afflictions are to be removed, and how samsaric existence could be stopped by removing the emotional afflictions and, intellectually speaking, we can even say that he gained deep and vast knowledge concerning those topics. But he failed. He failed because inspite of his intellectual grasp of the teachings, he could not gain enlightenment. His failure reflected the existential dilemma of having to remove, somehow, the emotional afflictions without being emotionally afflicted in the process. However reasonable, logical, and feasible the possibility of removing emotional afflictions may have sounded, for Shinran it was an existentially impossible task. However, the failure itself did not end in failure, for through his efforts to overcome emotional afflictions, Shinran experienced the strong binding force of his attachment to life, his desire to remain in the human world, and the pathetic state of a totally exhausted practitioner who, try as he might to accomplish enlightenment through meditative practices, was constantly distracted by the pains and agony of disease, an accident, or untimely death of friends, all of which resurrected emotional afflictions which he might have succeeded in quieting. There was nothing left for Shinran except to accept his karmic existence, which he realized was the very foundation for Amida's Vow to save. He states:

> Mida no gokō shiyui no Gan o yoku-yoku anzure ba, hitoeni Shinran ichinin ga tame nari keri! Sareba, sokubaku no gō o mochi keru mi nite ari keru o, tasuken to oboshi-meshi tachi keru Hongan no katejikenasa yo![22]
>
> When I carefully consider the Vow which Amida brought forth after five kalpas contemplation, I find that it was for me Shinran, alone! Oh how wonderful is the Fundamental Vow of Amida who resolved to save such a person as I, who is totally karmic bound.

To sum up then, for Shinran, human existence afforded the opportunity to come into contact with the *Nembutsu* teaching. The *Nembutsu* teaching, which was Amida Buddha's Vow-Power manifested in human beings as a sign of salvation already firmly established, manifested to Shinran the depth of his evil passions and the strength of karmic binding. As it was the Vow-Power, not karma, that established his salvation, the recitation of the *Nembutsu* became a manifestation of joy and gratitude. Karma, for Shinran, as it was for all Buddhists before him, was a causality principle directed towards understanding how the present was derived from past karma. The focus on karma as the key to understanding the present human existential dilemma is probably Shinran's greatest contribution to the history of Buddhist studies.

NOTES

1. Hajime Nakamura, *Nihon Shūkyō no Kindai-sei* (Modernism in Japanese Religion) (Tokyo: Shunjū-sha, 1971 third reprint. First edition 1959), p. 215.

2. Alfred Bloom, *Tannisho: A Resource for Modern Living* (Honolulu: The Buddhist Study Center, 1981), p. 47.

3. Ibid.

4. Yoshiro Tamura, "Nihon ni okeru gō no jinen no shisō" (The Concept of the Naturalness of Karma in Japan) in Shōzen Kumoi (ed.), *Gō Shisō Kenkyū* (Studies in Karma Thought. Kyoto: Heirakuji Shoten, 1979), p. 641. I am very much indebted to Y. Tamura's paper in the writing of this paper. The anthology edited by S. Kumoi contains a mine of information on karma in all of its aspects from Indic through to Japanese thought. Appended to this valuable book is a most comprehensive bibliography on papers, articles, and books written on karma in Japanese and in all modern European languages.

5. Lord Chalmers, *Buddha's Teachings*, Volume 37, C.L. Lanman ed., *Harvard Oriental Series* (Cambridge: Harvard University Press, 1932), p. 154.

6. S. Radhakrishnan, *The Dhammapada* (London: Oxford University Press, 1954, second impression. First published 1950), p. 100.

7. Ibid., p. 58.

8. Ibid., p. 59.

9. Louis de la Vallée Poussin, *L'Abhidharmakośa de Vasubandhu*, Volume XVI of *Mélanges Chinois et Bouddhiques* (Bruxelles: Institute Belge des Hautes Études Chinoises, 1971), Tome VI, p. 13.

10. H.V. Guenther, *Philosophy and Psychology in the Abhidharma* (Lucknow: Buddha Vihara, 1957), p. 62. Reprinted by Sambala, Berkeley, 1974; Paperback, 1976.

11. Leslie S. Kawamura, *Golden Zephyr* (Emeryville: Dharma Publishing, 1975), p. 29.

12. The distinction that can be made between the earlier Heian and the Kamakura periods as far as Japanese Buddhism is concerned, is this: the Heian period reflected a focus on the monks or monastic type of Buddhism whereas the Kamakura period reflected a focus on the lay believer—not to the exclusion of the monastic society, however. Shinran was perhaps the first to bring Buddhism truly to the level of the ordinary person by giving up celibacy and by marrying Eshin. Through this marriage, Shinran showed that salvation through the Vow-Power was beyond external forms of etiquette and ethics and beyond human calculation. Salvation had nothing to do with whether one was a layman or a monk.

13. Alex Wayman. *Analysis of the Śrāvakabhūmi Manuscript* (Berkeley: University of California Press, 1961), pp. 78-79: *katamabhiś catasrabhir yad utāpekṣāyuktyā kāryakāraṇayuktya upapattisādhanayuktyā dharmatāyuktyā.* See also, S. Levi, *Mahāyāna-sūtrālaṃkāra* (Paris: 1907; Shanghai reprint 1940), p. 168 and Nathmal Tatia, *Abhidharmasamuccaya Bhāṣyam* (Patna: Kashi Prasad Jayaswal Research Institute, 1976), pp. 99 and 125. The last mentioned text gives a detailed explanation of each one of the four.

14. Yoshiro Tamura, op. cit., p. 660.

15. For *mappō*, see H. Inagaki, "The Bodhisattva Doctrine as Conceived and

Developed by the Founders of the New Sects in the Heian and Kamakura Periods," in Leslie S. Kawamura, ed., *The Bodhisattva Doctrine in Buddhism*, SR Supplements (Waterloo: Wilfrid Laurier University Press, 1981), pp. 167-170.

16. The Sanskrit term was taken from H. Inagaki, *Index to the Larger Sukhāvatīvyūha* (Kyoto: Nagata Bunshodo, 1978), p. 29.

17. *Jōdo Wasan*, Ryukoku Translation Series, Volume IV. Translated and Annotated by R. Fujimoto, H. Inagaki, and L.S. Kawamura (Kyoto: Tsuchiyama Printing Co. Ltd., 1965), p. 54.

18. *Tannishō*, Ryukoku Translation Series, Volume II. Translated and Annotated by R. Fujiwara (Kyoto: Tsuchiyama Printing Co. Ltd., 1962), pp. 19-20.

19. Ibid., pp. 22-23.

20. Ibid., pp. 49-50.

21. Sylvian Levi, *Vijñaptimātratāsiddhi, Deux Traités de Vasubandhu Viṃśatikā et Triṃśikā* (Paris: 1925. Shanghai reprint 1940), p. 38, lines 14-15.

22. *Tannishō*, op. cit., p. 79.

CHAPTER TWELVE

Critical Response

LAMBERT SCHMITHAUSEN

Among the papers this response is concerned with, two are dedicated to Tibetan Buddhism. Lobsang Dargyay's paper deals with a crucial theoretical problem of the Buddhist karma theory—the connection between the past deed and its fruition at a much later time in the framework of an antisubstantialist ontology—in the philosophy of Tsong-kha-pa (1357-1419). Eva Dargyay's paper, on the other hand, focuses on the practical concern of Buddhist lay people who want to make good for their shortcomings in Buddhist morality, necessitated by family life and professional obligations. In contrast with this, Bruce Matthews tries to give a comprehensive survey of the whole development of the doctrine of karma and rebirth in Theravāda Buddhism from the canonical works through the period of the Pāli commentaries, treatises and manuals written in Ceylon up to contemporary Buddhist thinkers and today's Buddhism on the village level. Yün-hua Jan presents three important stages in the development of the doctrine of karma and rebirth in China through an exhaustive treatment of typical examples. Leslie Kawamura's paper focuses on one special case of Japanese concern with karma, namely, the role and evaluation of karma in Shinran, against the background of Hōnen and Indian canonical Buddhism.

In the following comments on these papers, I shall discuss some of the important aspects of the doctrine of karma and rebirth found in one or several of the papers. I shall make use mainly of material from the classical period in order to facilitate understanding and contrastive evaluation of the later achievements, an endeavour also felt necessary in most of the papers, but to my mind needing a few supplements and sometimes corrections.

I

The topic of rebirth is treated more or less incidentally in all the papers except Matthews', who describes in detail the psychological process taking place at the time of death and rebirth according to Anuruddha. Unfortunately, Matthews' presentation of the material is not always correct[1] and mixes Anuruddha's own statements with materials from the notes of Nārada Thera[2] whose edition has been used. According to Matthews, the *Abhidhammatthasaṅgaha* provides "a medieval reformulation of traditional doctrinal interpretations . . . reaffirming the central notions of the *dhamma* in a new and interesting way" (p. 128). But it seems to me that there is not much difference in doctrine between Anuruddha's presentation and that of Buddhaghosa. At any rate, Matthews does not prove his thesis by way of concretely contrasting pertinent statements of both authors.

Of primary importance in the context of the process of death and rebirth in later Theravāda is the subliminal *bhavaṅgaviññāṇa,* which against Matthews, is not yet mentioned in the *Dhammasaṅgaṇi.* In contrast to the *ālayavijñāna* of the Yogācāras, the *bhavaṅgaviññāṇa* is not strictly continuous but only a kind of hiatus-bridger coming up as soon as ordinary, supraliminal perceptions and cognitions cease,[3] for example, in states of unconsciousness, between different cognitive processes, and especially at the moment of death and rebirth (*cuti* and *paṭisandhi,* the corresponding states of mind being altogether of the same type as,[4] or nothing but special functions of,[5] the *bhavaṅgaviññāṇa*). Like the *ālayavijñna,* the *bhavaṅgaviññāṇa,* too, has always the same object during one lifetime, but the object of the *bhavaṅgaviññāṇa* is much more specific, or limited: it is identical with the object of the last supraliminal cognitive process before death (see p. 206).

The dominant influence of karma on rebirth seems to be taken for granted by traditional Buddhist systems both in and outside India as well as by today's popular forms of Buddhism. Yet, the papers indicate, in post-classical developments, certain tendencies to restrict this relation.

One such case is Pure Land Buddhism as represented by Hōnen and Shinran in Kawamura's paper. In this tradition, karmically conditioned rebirth in worldly states is contrasted with rebirth in Amida's paradise, Sukhāvatī, a rebirth which is effected by Amida's Vow-power, not by the force of one's own karma, which means that the mechanistic-impersonalist causality of karma is superseded by a religiosity based on personal relationship to a gracious divine being.

A totally different case of deemphasizing the relation between karma and rebirth, obviously under the influence of Western standards of value, is M.W.P. deSilva's attempt to understand karma primarily as a dispositional concept, "an expression of character" (Matthews, p. 134), and "development of good karma" as aiming at "building up a good character rather than the possible material effects it may bring in this or some other life" (ibid.). DeSilva deliberately brings karma close to the roots (*mūla*) or dispositions (*anusaya*). This bears on the complicated problem of the relation between karma, that is, good and bad intentions (*cetanā*) or intentional acts, and wholesome or unwholesome emotional affections and mental attitudes, especially the unwholesome ones which are often called defilements (*kilesa, kleśa*). Although the relation is sometimes quite close if we disregard bodily and verbal acts, both categories—karma and defilements or (evil) dispositions—are usually carefully distinguished in the texts of most Buddhist schools, especially in the Vaibhāṣika and Yogācāra works, but unambiguous passages can also be found in Theravāda treatises.[6] Yet I admit that in special contexts there are problems of delimitation[7] and that especially in later Theravāda there may be a tendency towards effacing this distinction. But these problems have to be left to further systematic inquiry.

II

Not only do certain later developments deviate from what may be called the classical Buddhist doctrine of karma, in early Buddhism, too, the classical importance of karma with regard to rebirth cannot be presupposed throughout without question. Otherwise than in Jainism where the influx of karma into the soul is the decisive cause of rebirth and suffering, according to the well-known canonical explanation of one of the most famous formulas of early Buddhism, namely, the four Noble Truths[8] (*ārya-satya*), suffering, invariably involved in rebirth, is conditioned by craving (*tṛṣṇā*),[9] with no mention of karma. In a similar way, numerous other canonical texts, including passages in old verse collections like *Suttanipāta* (945, 740f) or *Dhammapada* (212-216), declare or presupose craving, desire (*kāma*), etc., to be the root of misery.[10] Such passages seem to disclose a view according to which karma had no essential, if any, function with regard to rebirth. Later on, it is true, at least in the Vaibhāṣika system, craving is declared to be responsible for the fact *that* one is reborn, whereas karma is said to determine *where* and *how* one is reborn,[11] but only if the presence of craving makes it certain that there is any rebirth at all. Thus, the canonical passages mentioning only craving could be interpreted as merely mentioning the cause of rebirth as such, not its specific form which may not have been a matter of much concern to ascetics striving for liberation. But wouldn't it also be possible that such passages were formulated under the more or less conscious presupposition that craving was the cause, or at least the decisive determinant, of both the fact and the specific form of rebirth,[12] karma being, at best, regarded as a subordinate intermediate element entirely determined by craving.[13]

In this connection, sporadic passages expressing or implying the idea that it is one's wish, thought, meditation, or resolve,[14] especially the one produced at the moment of death,[15] that determines where and how one is reborn may deserve special attention. It becomes clear, however, from these passages that this view, though originally quite distinct,[16] is, at least in the older canonical texts,[17] essentially linked up with a spiritual element, e.g. in such a way that its success is said or indicated to presuppose moral or other spiritual qualities[18] or that the last thought of a dying man is qualified as a morally bad one.[19] Thus, this view could easily be combined with the karma theory[20] which as Matthews suggests, may have belonged, in early Buddhist spirituality, primarily to a more popular level and Jaina influence apart, may have gained momentum and undergone elaboration especially in the context of the instruction of lay followers who were not so much interested in altogether escaping rebirth as in ameliorating their samsaric destiny, and at the same time were involved in active daily life and were expected to support the *saṅgha*.

Starting from craving as the main factor of rebirth may also have contributed to the typically Buddhist interpretation of karma as volition or intention (*cetanā*) or, at best, activity induced by intention. In this form, karma is much closer to craving or wishful thought or resolve, than in Jainism where it also includes automatic, unintentional bodily acts.

Matthews' paper shows how the notion of the special importance, for rebirth, of the last idea of the dying person has skillfully been combined with the karma doctrine in later Theravāda dogmatics:[21] the last cognitive process of the dying person (*maraṇāsanna-vīthi*, cp. n. 1) has, as its content, either a former karmic act (the one that is going to determine one's rebirth[22]) or some characteristic object or ideational image connected with that act (*kammanimitta*),[23] or some (visible) characteristic feature of the destiny one is going to (*gatinimitta*).[24]

In view of L. Kawamura's paper, attention may be drawn to the fact that the last thought or utterance at the time of death is especially emphasized in Japanese Pure Land Buddhism, most followers of the Jōdo school maintaining that thinking of Amida, or uttering the *Nembutsu*, is decisive for rebirth in the Pure Land.[25] For some of them, even one single *Nembutsu*, uttered at the moment of death, is sufficient.[26]

III

The non-occurrence of karma as responsible for rebirth in certain key passages is perhaps an additional argument for the suggestion made by Matthews, referring to a paper by Gombrich, that the karma doctrine may have been incidental to early Buddhist soteriology. Actually, karma is not mentioned in the explanation of the third Noble Truth either, which only says that the cessation of suffering is due to the cessation of craving (*tṛṣṇā*); and there are quite a number of canonical passages according to which liberation is attained by getting rid of craving, desire, etc.[27] In other passages, ignorance is added as another important factor to be eliminated, and insight is usually the decisive means for eradicating both ignorance and craving.[28]

U. Schneider, on the other hand, has maintained the view that the pith of the Buddha's doctrine was that actions (*karman*), both good and bad, cause bondage, and that liberation is brought about by non-action. His thesis is, however, based on one single passage which moreover is not unambiguous as far as the crucial second part (liberation by non-action) is concerned.[30] Such a view would, in fact, be quite close to the Jainas' position who, in accordance with their view that bondage is due to the influx of karma, regard non-action—more precisely, non-accumulating of new karma by avoidance of all karmic activity—as a decisive means of salvation. This, however, has to be supplemented by counter-activity consisting in artificial consumption, by means of austerity (*tapas*), of the karma already accumulated.

This Jaina theory is expressly rejected in the canon.[31] But there are also a few passages documenting attempts to assimilate it to the Buddhist view.[32] An especially interesting case of introducing the concept of karma into the Buddhist theory of liberation is *Majjhimanikāya* No. 57,[33] a passage also referred to by Matthews. This Sutta not only makes black (bad), white (good) and mixed karma responsible for rebirth, but also establishes neither black nor white karma as a kind of counter-karma conducive to the destruction of ordinary, retributive karma. This counter-karma, however, is conceived in a very Buddhist way, namely, as the intention (*cetanā*) to abandon the various kinds of retributive karma. It seems to me that this theory is not so much a kind of *ad hominem* theory as Matthews suggests, but rather an attempt at developing a specifically Buddhist doctrine of bondage and liberation centering on the concept of karma.

Also in the context of karma and liberation, the special connection of karma with a more popular level of Buddhism seems to be indicated by the fact that there are, in late and post-canonical laymen-oriented or more edificatory texts, passages according to which even liberating insight and *Nirvāṇa* are attainable through good karma or merit (*puṇya*).[34]

In Japanese Pure Land Buddhism as described in Kawamura's paper, personal action—be it moral behaviour or spiritual practice—is as useless for attaining rebirth in Sukhāvatī, which is, de facto, salvation, as is non-action. Good actions may even be more obstructive to salvation than bad actions. Salvation is altogether due to the power or influence of Amida's Vow (*praṇidhāna*). Yet, in Hōnen a last remnant of the salvific significance of personal activity is left when he still seems to consider the recitation of the *Nembutsu* a kind of meritorious act causing rebirth in the Pure Land of Amida. In Shinran, this last residue of salvific activity of one's own is thoroughly effaced. For him, even in the case of the *Nembutsu* there is no certainty that it actually leads to birth in the Pure Land, and its recitation is for him not a salvific act but merely a manifestation of joy and gratitude towards Amida whose Vow-power has already established salvation, without requiring any active contribution on the part of the individual to be saved.

IV

A crucial problem, touched upon in both Kawamura's and Matthew's papers, is the question of determinism and freedom.

Kawamura, if I understand him correctly, seems to understand the early Buddhist doctrine of karma as primarily an explanation of "how . . . '*present*' frustration or happiness came about," although the passage he adduces (*Dhp* I. 1-2) has, as he himself admits, the form of a directive for the future. I understand the verses as one of the many canonical passages in which the karma doctrine is referred to in order to stimulate effort for avoiding bad actions and practising good ones. It seems that Kawamura's interpretation of the canonical Buddhist doctrine of karma is somewhat influenced by the situation in Hōnen and Shinran, where the karma doctrine seems to have completely lost its creative aspect related to the future but only serves to explain the present situation which is essentially understood as a negative one. In Shinran, this interpretation of karma has led to a thoroughly determinist formulation when he even says that any *good or evil action* in this life arises owing to past karma.

Matthews, on the other hand, emphasizes that in early Buddhism, and also later Theravāda, the karma doctrine does not mean determinism, that "there was a definite modification of Hindu determinism." What Matthews wants to say is probably correct, but the sweeping expression "Hindu determinism" is at least misleading. To be sure, there is a strong deterministic current in Hinduism. But usually even in Hinduism karma is not only the determining heritage of one's past acts, but also, and sometimes primarily, free choice activity by means of which one is able to mold one's own future.[35] In most cases, karma is ambivalent, involving both determination and freedom, fate and effort, though the emphasis may vary.

The latter holds good also for early Buddhism, though there is, no doubt, a tendency to emphasize the effort or freedom aspect,[36] and, as I said before, even when indulging in the result or determination aspect, the texts may primarily aim at stimulating listeners to practise good and avoid evil acts. Yet, even a passage with a determinist flavor seems to be available, for how else could we understand the statement of *Majjhimanikāya* No. 129 (III 169f) that a foolish living being after having been reborn in an evil state of existence (hell, etc.) is unlikely to be reborn as a human being because *in such evil states of existence there is no moral but only immoral conduct* and thus no acquisition of merit, and that even if such a being happens to be reborn as a human being it will be reborn in a low and poor family and (again) *perform evil acts* of body, speech, and mind.[37] Such a view, however, seems to be quite rare in the canon and, though this is not explicitly stated, the main intention of this text, too, may be to stimulate listeners not to be foolish but wise.

Majjhimanikāya No. 129 is also proof for the fact that, against Matthews, caste, too, occurs among the factors determined by karma, for the text says that the evil-doer, if perchance reborn as a human being, is reborn in a low caste (as a Caṇḍāla, etc.: *M* III 169), whereas the person who has accumulated good karma is, after his return from heaven, reborn as a Kṣatriya or Brahmin, etc. (*M* III 177). The denial of relevance of caste in the context of spirituality and the ethical re-evaluation of notions like Brahmin[38] does not mean that caste was not recognized as a matter of fact in lay society.

Although karma is adduced to explain the inequality of human beings with regard to social status, wealth, life-span, external appearance, suffering and even intelligence (cp. Matthews, referring to *M* III 202), there are also passages which show that such factors need not be produced by karma without exception: pleasant, painful, and neutral feelings can also result from (the trouble of) any of the body-elements, or all of them (*sānnipātika*), from unseasonable weather (*utupariṇāmaja*),[39] from indulging (?) in what is unwholesome (*visamaparihāraja*),[40] or from violence (*opakkamika*)[41] It would be interesting and probably also illuminative to follow the development of this doctrine not only in Theravāda[42] but also in other Buddhist schools but this would exceed the limits of this response. In any case, in Buddhism, an increasing importance of karma as a device for explaining heteronomous events or realities is shown by the fact that some schools, for example, the Vaibhāṣikas and the Yogācāras, consider even the manifoldness (*vaicitrya*)[43] or the cyclical arising[44] and disappearance[45] of the external world to be influenced by the common (*sādhāraṇa*) karma of living beings.[46]

A special dimension of possible conflict or interaction of different types of causality touched upon by Matthews but needing more penetrating and comprehensive investigation is the problem of the relation of karma to popular beliefs in the efficacy of spirits and of ceremonies to influence them. A nice example of compromise is mentioned by D. Snellgrove: For the Tibetan Bon-pos. "fertile-fields and good harvests. . . , although some half (of such effects) is ordained by previous actions (viz., karmic effect), the other half comes from the powerful 'lords of the soil'. . . ."[47]

V

Another problem to be touched upon is the idea of *transference* of karma. The notion of transition or transference of karma to other persons, both voluntary and involuntary, and both of merit and demerit, is frequently met with in Hinduism[48] though distinctions will have to be made in view of the different currents and levels of this extremely complex religion. Involuntary acquisition (of bad) or loss of (good) karma and transfer of demerit against the will of the transferee clearly show the survival of magical substantialism. On the other hand, any possibility of transition or transfer of merit or demerit is, according to P.S. Jaini,[49] consistently denied in *Jainism* in accordance with the strictly individualist structure which seems to be an original feature of ethicization in terms of karma and rebirth, at least in the ascetic tradition. Similarly, the early Buddhist texts frequently stress individual responsibility.[50] Yet there are, even in the four Nikāyas, a couple of probably comparatively late[51] passages that have been adduced[52] in evidence of the practice and notion of karma transfer in the form of a *voluntary* transference of *merit* either to divine beings (local deities or the World Guardians) or to deceased parents or relatives.[53]

The only explicit passage known to me is *Aṅguttaranikāya* IV 63ff,[54] where a lay-woman at the request of the World-Guardian Vessavaṇa serves monks with food and assigns (*ādis-*) this gift or the reward for it (*dakkhiṇā*) to him by saying that the merit (*puñña*) of her donation should conduce to Vessavaṇa's happiness (*sukhāya hotu*).

Another passage adduced as evincing merit transfer to divine beings is *Dīghanikāya* II 88 (from the *Mahāparinibbānasutta*)[55] declaring that when settling down at a place one should feed virtuous men (namely, the Buddha or monks) and assign (*ādis-*) the reward (for one's gift) (*dakkhiṇā*) to the local deities. It should, however, be borne in mind that this passage can be taken as proof of merit transference only if it could be demonstrated that, in the expression *dakkhiṇaṃ ādis-*, *dakkhiṇā* invariably and from the very beginning has the meaning of "reward (for one's gift)",[56] as it unambiguously does at *M* III 255[57] and as would be, in the sense of "merit", the natural solution in the case of *A* IV 63ff discussed just before. But *dakṣiṇā*/*dakkhiṇā* primarily means the *gift* given to a person to be honoured,[58] originally to a priest as reward for his sacrificial service, but in Buddhism, of course, to the Buddha or to the Order or to monks. This being the case, it seems difficult to exclude *a priori* the possibility that, at least at an earlier stage, the expression *dakkhiṇaṃ ādis-* simply meant that a *gift*, though presented to monks, is *assigned* to divine beings (or deceased persons), the monks somehow acting as their representatives or as mediators.[59]

Among the Nikayic passages adduced as evidence for merit transfer to one's *deceased parents* or relatives is *Aṅguttaranikāya* III 43[60] (*petānaṃ kālaṅkatānaṃ dakkhiṇaṃ anuppadassati*), but once more it seems difficult to decide whether the passage means that the son will pass on or cede the reward for his gifts to the Order, that is, his *merit*, to his parents after they have died, or whether it has to be understood in the sense of the son's presenting or passing on *gifts* of *food*, etc., to his deceased parents as a recompense for what they have done for him when they were still alive.[61]

An interpretation in the latter sense seems to be definitely preferable in the case of *Aṅguttaranikāya* V 269ff.[62] This text asserts the possibility of feeding[63] only those deceased (*peta*) relatives who are reborn in the realm of the *manes*, i.e., as *pretas* in the sense of a specific class of living beings (hideous 'spirits' suffering from hunger, thirst and nakedness due to their bad karma[64]), and at the same time stresses that all offerings to the deceased, even if fruitless to them, are in any case fruitful to the donor (obviously because of his good intention). As has rightly been remarked by Gombrich,[65] the wording of this Sutta does not in any way express or indicate that there is any transference of merit but suggests a real transfer of food.[66] This is also—as has already been noticed by Stede[67]—the impression one gets from at least most of[68] the *Tirokuḍḍapetavatthu* (*Pv* I.5 (pp. 4f) = *Khp* VII) of which *A.* V 269ff may be a kind of doctrinal specification,[69] and according to *Kathāvatthu* VII.6 this same view seems to have been advocated by some non-Theravāda school(s).[70]

The question, however, is whether, as the first part of the *Tirokuḍḍapetavatthu* suggests, the *pretas* can by themselves take possession of food and drink (and clothes) presented to them, or whether they can obtain them only, in some mysterious way, through mediation of monks,[71] as seems to be implied in the second last verse of the same text, where it is stated that what will benefit the *pretas* for a long time and accrue to them at once is "a gift given, i.e., duly presented, to the Order"[72] (*dakkhiṇā dinnā saṅghamhi suppatiṭṭhitā*). The first pattern would correspond to the Brahmanical offering of rice-balls and water to the recently deceased (*preta* as well as to the *piṇḍapitṛyajña* where rice-balls, etc., are offered to the *manes* (*pitṛ*)[73] and directly eaten by them, whereas the second pattern reflects the situation of the Brahmanical *śrāddha* rite (the connection with which is explicit at *A.* V 269) where the rice-balls, water, clothes, etc., meant for the *manes* are at least partly consumed or taken by the *Brahmins* who act as their representatives.[74] As Gombrich[75] has shown, even in today's ritualized transfer of merit to the dead, the archaic stratum has survived in form of a little food being thrown outside and, of course, originally meant to be eaten by the *pretas* directly.

Thus there does not seem to exist in the four Nikāyas, any *unambiguous* evidence for merit transference to the *deceased*. The situation has, however, changed in the majority, though not in all,[76] of the tales of the *Petavatthu*.[77] Here, not only is the expression *dakkhiṇaṃ ādis-* frequently met with and the possibility of directly handing over a gift to a *preta* expressly denied,[78] but also the benefit accruing to the *pretas* is explicitly stated to be the fruit (*phala*) or ripening (*vipāka*) of the meritorious act performed by the donor.[79] In this way, the mysterious transition of food, etc., to the *pretas* through mediation of monks has come to be explained and, in a sense, rationalized in terms of merit transference. Yet, in these very passages, what accrues to the *pretas* through the merit transferred to them is still usually food, drink and clothes[80] though it may by far exceed, in quantity and quality, what has been presented to the Order by the donor.[81]

In several passages of the *Petavatthu*[82] we read that the *pretas* are worshipped or honored (*pūjita*) by the gift or merit transferred to them, and in some cases[83] the benefit acquired by the *preta* makes him shine (*sobhamāna*) with suprahuman power (*anubhāva, iddhi*). As both honor and glory (*yasa*) seem to be the typical benefit accruing to local deities in case a gift or merit is transferred to them,[84] there must be some connection between the two classes of beings. In fact, these local deities are not infrequently identified with the semi-divine, powerful (*mahiddhika*) *pretas* of the "flying mansions" (*vimāna*), or *yakkhas*,[85] whose lord is, by the way, Vessavaṇa.[86] Therefore, I doubt whether we are entitled to interpret, at least in the *Petavatthu*, such an acquisition of suprahuman power or of divine food and clothes, etc., as indicating that the *pretas* instantaneously obtain, by means of the merit transferred to them, rebirth in a heavenly existence, as suggested by Agasse[87] in the light of later explanations.[88] It is more probable that Stede[89] is right in assuming that they merely undergo a drastic change of status *within* their existence as *pretas* by being, through the gift, raised to the rank of powerful and blissful divine *pretas*.

A problem that needs further investigation is the question how and where the notion of merit transference was first developed. Was it in the context of gifts to deities or to *pretas*? Or did it develop outside both and was it only secondarily introduced into them as a convenient means of explanation? Actually, merit transference is, as is well known, not confined to these two cases, but can, even in Theravāda, at least in somewhat later texts, also be enacted with regard to other human beings even while they are still alive,[90] or even with regard to all living beings.[91] The benefit acquired, if specified, ranges from advantages in this life like health to better rebirth (especially in heaven) and occasionally, in accordance with tendencies making *Nirvāṇa* available for merit (see p. 207 above + n. 34), even final liberation.[92]

Some scholars have expressed the opinion that the Buddhist doctrine of merit transference arose in the context of the gifts to one's deceased parents or relatives.[93] On the other hand, H. Bechert,[94] though not denying this possibility, has suggested a doctrinal background of the *Mahāyāna* tenet of merit transfer to *all* living beings. According to him, this tenet is the result of a tension between the karma doctrine implying that one can only earn the fruit of what one has oneself done, and the fact that a disciple is enabled by the teaching of the Buddha to attain liberation although he is not yet mature in terms of his own karma, the tension being resolved by the assumption that the Buddha is able to transfer some of his surplus merit to the disciple. It will be clear from what has been said above (in III) that the presupposition of this explanation, namely, that liberation is due to good karma (merit), cannot be taken for granted as far as early Nikayic Buddhism is concerned. It would, however, seem plausible if we start from the situation to be observed in (somewhat later?) more popular or edificatory sources, according to which karma, obviously used in a broader sense, including even spiritual exercise, can fructify even in liberating insight and arhatship (see n. 34).

Yet, a quite similar tension is also obvious in the case of deities and especially of *pretas* receiving, from a donor, benefits or alleviation which they do not deserve on the basis of their own karma—benefits which, in the case of the *pretas*, even nullify bad karma. It seems to me much more probable that the notion of merit transfer as a kind of interpersonal balancing of karma was developed, or somehow adapted from Hinduism, in the context of integrating, into the framework of the karma doctrine, such deep-rooted popular practices as presenting gifts to protective deities or for the benefit of deceased relatives—attempts the Buddhist monks will have made not only because they may have found it profitable to replace the Brahmins who acted as mediators, but also, and perhaps primarily, because they must have been aware of the fact that ordinary Buddhist lay people not only continued to practise their heart-felt ancient religious customs and rites, but also expected the monks to participate in them and even to take a leading and active part. It thus appears natural that *in general* Buddhist monks not only tolerated popular religious customs and rites, but were also actively engaged in them, not only by participating in them or even practising them themselves,[95] but also by selecting, adapting, and interpreting them in accordance with Buddhist ethics and dogmatics. In this context, the notion of merit transference can easily be understood as an attempt to harmonize with the karma doctrine, the popular practice of presenting offerings to, or for the benefit of, local deities, and especially one's deceased relatives. After the notion of merit transference had once been developed or admitted in such special cases, there was virtually no reason to prevent it from operating in other cases, too, and, in view of the old practice of universal compassion and benevolence, its generalization would seem to be natural.

The hypothesis that the origin of the notion of merit transference should be sought in a more popular ambience seems to be supported by the fact that this notion (if the "karma balance hypothesis" is right) developed in the context of the karma doctrine, yet stands in conflict with the principle of strictly individual responsibility which seems to have been a basic feature of this doctrine at least in early Buddhism and Jainism. Yet in a more popular ambience it had to coexist with other views and practices stemming from other layers of religious history, and there was no need for complete systematical consistency. In popular religious practice and doctrine the notion of individual responsibility and the notion of merit transference could thus be *alternatively* emphasized according to the situation, without any conflict being felt.

But should we not expect that the conflict was obvious at least to specialists in dogmatics and philosophers? Why didn't they stop such a development? The Jainas in fact seem to have done so uncompromisingly and successfully, and the reason may be that the karma doctrine was the central element in their theory of bondage and liberation. In the core of early Buddhist spirituality, on the other hand, this does not seem to have been the case, and this fact may perhaps explain why Buddhists were, on the whole, less allergic to infringements of the principle of individual responsibility, provided that such infringements enhanced ethical conduct, or at least did not run counter to it. On these lines, at least in traditional Buddhism, transfer of demerit (bad karma) is not possible[97] as is also stated by Matthews.

A similar attitude seems to have obtained with regard to popular patterns of thought we would call *substantialist* or *magical*.[98] In popular texts merit is sometimes treated like a kind of merchandise[99] which can be bought or sold, or a kind of spiritual money. Its transference can be demanded or even extorted. Yet, in spite of such borderline cases, the non-magical ethics of Buddhism reasserts itself by the fact that transference of merit always seems to require, on the part of the transferer, the explicit intention to transfer and, on the part of the transferee, the thankful or joyous consent (*anumodanā*) to accept the transference[102] (see also Matthews, pp. 135-136).

This ethical concern must also have favored the retainment of the practice of offerings to one's deceased parents or relatives, because Buddhists could, and actually did, stress ethical aspects like thankfulness[103] or pity,[104] whereas the aspects of propitiation and expectation of gifts in return, prominent in Brahmanism, have receded into the background[105] (though they did not completely disappear[106]). As for protective deities, they were of course, like the Vedic gods, worshipped in order to be induced to confer some benefit upon the donor, and this is still palpable at *D* II 88. On the other hand, not only in Ceylon but also in other Buddhist countries, esp. in Tibet, deities have been given the rank of protectors of the Doctrine, and transference of merit to them becomes an ethical act of supporting the protectors of Buddhism.[107]

Yet, there are also attempts to re-interpret the doctrine of merit transference in such a way as to render it compatible with the principle of a strictly individual-bound retribution of karma. This principle is, for example, explicitly stressed at *Kathavatthu* VII.6,[108] where the possibility of feeding or clothing *pretas* by one's own act of giving—be it by somehow handing over to them these very gifts or by way of merit transference—is rejected, and, at least if we follow the commentary, the benefit gained by the *pretas* is attributed to *their own* joyful consent or rejoicing at the donor's merit (*anumodanā).*[109] This doctrine in which transference has been explained away in favor of a complete reassertion of the principle of strictly individual responsibility has become the orthodox view in Theravāda Buddhism up to the present day[110]. But in popular understanding the idea of a real transfer of merit, though inexplicit, continues to exist.[111]

Even in *Mahāyāna* it may be under the impact of the principle of individual-bound retribution of karma that, besides the idea of transference of merit to all living beings for the sake of *their* attainment of Supreme Awakening, we find, especially in philosophical texts, the view that a Bodhisattva dedicates (*pariṇāmanā*) his merit to his *own* Supreme Awakening[112] (which, on its part, is of course the basis for an effective activity for the sake of the salvation of all other living beings). Again, on the popular level, real merit transference is a matter of course at least in Tibetan Buddhism, as E. Dargyay amply shows for the Zanskar area. In the examples of merit-making described by Dargyay, merit transference entails, on the one hand, a kind of irradiation of meritorious performance on the whole community which is, however, itself as a whole somehow or other engaged in these performances. On the other hand, merit transfer has, here too, and not only in the frame of the dGe-tsha funeral rite, preserved its old aspect of transference of merit to the deceased, the benefit accruing to them being both better rebirth and *Nirvāṇa*.

An interesting development in the context of karma transference, or sharing another person's karma, is described in Yün-hua Jan's paper. According to Jan, prior to the spread of Buddhism in China there was a belief in the retribution of one's good and bad deeds but no rebirth doctrine. Therefore, retribution was considered to take effect either on oneself in this life or on one's family, especially on one's descendants. Such an idea of one's descendants having to pay for one's own deeds if one gets off free oneself, is, by the way, occasionally also found in Indian (Hindu) sources,[113] but it is of course contrary to the Buddhist ethics of individual responsibility and non-transferability of at least demerit. Thus, the negative aspect of the Chinese doctrine, namely, that one's evil deeds may fructify in one's family or descendants, if not the whole pattern of family retribution, was rejected by Chinese Buddhists quite early and supplanted by the doctrine of rebirth. In the popular short stories by Feng Meng-lung, however, both traditions, the old Chinese nese and the Buddhist, have been amalgamated: in the story "Esquire Kuei confessed when he had no place to go," Kuei could redeem himself by the confession of his misdeeds and by giving his daughter to the family towards which he had acted badly; but his wife and sons had to suffer from Kuei's deeds by being reborn as dogs.

Finally, it may be interesting to note that in Shinran's school of Pure Land Buddhism merit transfer, especially to the deceased, is rejected.[114] More precisely, there is only one efficacious transference of merit, namely, the one enacted by Amida through his Vow-power.[115] Transfer of one's own personal merit is as useless for salvation as is personal merit itself.

VI

Another problem to be discussed is the *philosophical framework* in which the theory of karma and rebirth is imbedded in Buddhism. According to Matthews (p. 125), early Buddhism radically changed the definition of karma "by introducing an anti-substance or *anatta* (no-self) doctrine" in the sense that it "denied that any personality or substance carried over the energy of karma into new life." This is not the right place to deal with the problem of self (*ātman*) or person (*pudgala*) in early Buddhism, which is still highly controversial,[116] and a satisfactory solution of which is, in my opinion, much hampered by the fact that most scholars still (or again) treat the Nikayic materials as largely homogeneous from the doctrinal point of view and try to force all of them into one coherent system instead of carefully distinguishing between different layers and tendencies. Besides, the problem requires systematical distinctions.[117] In the context of the problem of karma and rebirth, it may be sufficient to point out that the early Buddhist texts usually do not seem to feel any difficulty in speaking of a person (*puggala*), or man (purisa), or living being (*satta*), or oneself (*atta(n)* or *aham*)[118] in the ordinary, everyday sense of the words not reflected upon theoretically, and in using, without expressing any reserve, such words, or a pronoun representing them, as the subject, and frequently enough as the *identical* subject, or karmic activity as well as of dying (*cavati*,[119] etc.) and being reborn (*upapajjati*,[120] etc.).[121] Thus there does not seem to have been any ownership or identity problem for karma and its result in Nikayic

Buddhism except in a very few sūtras.[122] Moreover, as Matthews too indicates, at least certain strata of Nikayic Buddhism seem to regard mind (*viññāṇa*) as a kind of substratum wandering from one existence to another,[123] thus constituting an element of continuity between death and rebirth. I do not understand why Matthews considers this *viññāṇa* to be "not an entity." The only thing one can say is that it is not an *immutable* entity, thus not a (or the) Self in the specific sense implying permanence, blissfulness, and unchangeableness. This may also be the purpose of *M* I 256ff, though I admit that it is more probable that this Sūtra already polemicizes against the doctrine of *viññāṇa* as a transmigrating (though not immutable) entity as too substantialist a view.

VII

With the development, in most though not all[124] Hīnayāna schools, of a more or less consistent dogmatic antisubstantialism in the sense of a denial of real existence of permanent entities, especially of a permanent or perduring Self or Person, the problems of the ownership and retribution of karma were to become acute. The problem of how the act performed at a certain time can fructify at a much later time is, to be sure, not specific to Buddhism, similar problems occurring also in Vaiśeṣika,[125] Mīmāṃsā and Sāṃkya-Yoga[127]. But the systematization of antisubstantialist thought patterns in Buddhism may have been especially well-suited to bring it to the surface. Actually, in Buddhism speculation concerning this problem seems to have started quite early (cp. e.g., *Kathāvatthu* I.8; theory of the Kāśyaplīyas that karma, even when past, continues to exist up to the point of its fruition). Vasubandhu's *Karmasiddhiprakaraṇa* documents the existence of quite a number of different theories. The problem was also discussed by the Theravadins (cp., e.g., *VisM* XVII.174f), but Matthews does not enter into the issue. On the other hand, the whole of L. Dargyay's paper is devoted to this question, centering upon Tsong-kha-pa's solution.

Tsong-kha-pa's theory, as L. Dargyay points out, starts from certain passages in Candrakīrti. But the arguments of Candrakīrti Dargyay quotes will have to be understood as nothing but elements of a reductio ad absurdum (*prasaṅga*), demonstrating that the theory that decay has no cause (*vināśasyâhetukatvam*) contradicts both the proponent's own tenet of momentariness[128] and scriptural authority.[129] This is less obvious in the case of *Madhyamakāvatāra* VI.39-40[130] where Candrakīrti states that the future result can easily arise from the karmic act even if this act has ceased (*'gags (pa), niruddha*) a long time ago, because the act does not really (*svabhāvataḥ*) cease (to exist) owing to its having never really arisen (*MAv* 126, 14f). Thus the past act, not having ceased (*ma zhig pa, MAv* 126, 15), can produce the result. To my mind, the argument looks more like an eristic device which, similar to *MK* XVII.21cd (yasmāc ca tad anutpannaṃ, na tasmād vipraṇaśyati, significantly quoted in *MAv* 127, 1f), willfully contaminates the non-existence, in the absolute sense, of *all* (origination and) decay with the intramundane *special* notion of the non-decay (*avipraṇāśa*) of karma which has not yet produced its result.[131] According to Tsong-kha-pa, as L. Dargyay points out, the gap between the act and its future result is bridged by the cessation, or more precisely, the having ceased of the act (*las zhig pa*)[132] which according to Tsong-kha-pa has to be regarded as a thing or entity (*dngos po*). This qualification of cessation as an entity is, however, not an innovation introduced by Tsong-kha-pa, as L. Dargyay seems to assume, but it too is already found in Candrakīrti (*Pr* 174, 8f: nanv evaṃ sati. . .vināśo 'pi bhāvaḥ prāpnotîti ced, iṣyata evaîtat; vināśo hi svarūpāpekṣayā bhāvaḥ. . .). Yet, the combination of all these elements into a clear-cut theory of how the mechanism of karmic retribution works may be Tsong-kha-pa's own achievement, but I don't dare to be dogmatic on this.

It is, however, not easily intelligible how the cessation of the act (*las zhig pa*), even if it is an entity, can produce the future result. For as an entity (*bhāva, dngos po*), it too must be impermanent, momentary.[133] Therefore it too is no longer available at the time when the result is going to be produced. Tsong-kha-pa seems to be aware of this problem, for he elaborates his theory by obviously accepting a whole series of such cessations. For in his commentary on *MAv* VI.39, he says that the future origination of the result comes about through the cessation of the cessation of the act (*las zhig pa'i zhig pa*);[134] and in his commentary on *MK* XVII.21 he states that the continuum of a person (*gang zag gi rgyud*) with reference to which the notion of 'I' arises is the support of the cessation of the cessation of the act (*las zhig pa'i zhig pa*) which propagates itself in a homogeneous series (*rigs 'dra brgyud pa*), and that exactly this (series of cessations) is the basis for the connection of the result with the act.[135] Thus, Tsong-kha-pa seems to assume, as the connecting link between the act and its result, a whole series of entites, consisting in the cessation of the act, the cessation of this cessation, the cessation of this cessation-of-cessation, etc.

Yet it is not easy to see what makes these cessations specifically qualified to act as mediators between the act and its result. I for one cannot see in which way the cessation of the act, that is, its abstract negation, even if hypostasized into an entity, has any specific nature or property making it plausible that this cessation can somehow transmit a specific karmic impulse. The situation would be different if the connection between the act and result were established through the ceased act itself, in a concrete sense, taken to exist, as an entity, even after having ceased, that is, even as a past one.

This is what the Sarvāstivādins, especially the Kashmirian Vaibhāṣikas, had propounded. In the Kashmirian Vaibhāṣika system it is, as far as I can see, this existence even of the past act, and nothing else, that guarantees its capacity to fructify at a much later time. At least in texts up to the *Abhidharmakośabhāṣya* and the *Karmasiddhi*, other entities like "possession" (*prāpti*)[136] or "non-information" (*avijñapti*)[137] do not seem to have a function in this regard. "Possession" is responsible rather for the fact that a certain karma belongs to, and consequently fructifies in, one "stream of personality" (*santāna*) and not another,[138] or none at all. As for Candrakīrti's reference to "possession" in the context of the problem of the connection between the karmic act and its result pointed out by L. Dargyay (n. 6 of his paper), it is noteworthy that Tsong-kha-pa in his commentary on the passage (viz., *MAv* 126, 13) ascribes it, to be sure, to a group of the Vaibhāṣikas[139] (in the broader sense of Tibetan doxography, of course) but expressly states that the Kashmirian Vaibhāṣikas [are not this group because, it is true, they] accept "possession" [as an entity] but do not assume that what is taken possession of, that is, (in the present case) the two kinds of karma (viz., good and bad karma), *generates* a "possession" [of *itself* for the sake of future fructification].[140]

It is obvious that Tsong-kha-pa's theory of the cessation of the act (*las zhig pa*) as an entity mediating between act and result has, in spite of important differences, a significant affinity to the Kashmirian Vaibhāṣikas' theory of the continued existence of the past act, both theories subsisting on hypostatizing a negative term into an entity. Would it not be possible that Tsong-kha-pa somehow did not feel the two theories substantially distinct as far as the hypostasized negative entity is concerned? Could one not imagine that for him the difference between the cessation of the act and the act that has ceased, between the abstract and the concrete, was not as important and clear-cut as we may feel it to be? The more so in view of the fact that in the Tibetan language both categories can be expressed by the same expression, *las zhig pa* grammatically admitting of both interpretations, namely, cessation of the act as well as the ceased act. I could therefore imagine that Tsong-kha-pa, though developing his theory on the basis of Candrakīrti's remarks on cessation, yet felt his cessation of the act somewhat like the ceased act in a concrete sense (cp. Dargyay's term 'after-act') and that he thus had no plausibility problem. This is, admittedly, only a hypothetical suggestion. At any rate, Tsong-kha-pa expressly states that he admits that the past and the future are entities (*dngos po*).[141] Yet at the same time he also makes explicit the difference between his own position and that of the Vaibhāṣikas by pointing out that establishing the past and the future as entities is not possible when one takes them as really existing, by way of an independent essence of their own (*rang bzhin gyis grub pa*)[142] For Tsong-kha-pa as a Mādhyamika, on the other hand, neither the past and the future nor the present, neither the cessation of the act nor the act itself exist really by or in themselves, not even on the pragmatic level (*tha snyad du*).[143] And he states that it is precisely this view that entities (*dngos po*) do not exist by way of an independent essence of their own that allows one to accept even the ceased, or cessation, as an entity.[144]

Another point I should like to mention is the fact that, in addition to his theory of the cessation of the act (*las zhig pa*) as the connecting link between the karmic act and its later result, in his commentary on *MAv* VI.39, Tsong-kha-pa seems to admit also a theory in which the gap between the act and its result is bridged by residues (*bag chags vāsanā*)[145] the support of which is either the ego or the mind-series (*sems kyi rgyud*).[146] Unfortunately, Tsong-kha-pa does not comment in that passage on the systematic relation of this doctrine to that of the cessation of the act, and as it stands it gives the impression of a heterogeneous strand of thought evoked by certain remarks of Candrakīrti but not systematically synthesized with the other doctrine. But all this needs more comprehensive investigation. In another passage,[147] by the way, the theory that the karmic act is connected with its result by means of the residue (*bag chags*) it has left in the mind-series is—to be sure somewhat tentatively—ascribed by Tsong-kha-pa not only, as one might expect, to the Sautrāntikas but, curiously enough, also to the Kashmirian Vaibhāṣikas.

NOTES

I cordially thank my friends S.A. Srinivasan and A. Wezler for kindly reading the manuscript and making valuable suggestions with regard to both content and style. Needless to say, the responsibility for all shortcomings is mine. Abbreviations used in this paper are those of the *Critical Pāli Dictionary* (CPD), except the following:

AKBh	*Abhidharmakośabhāṣya of Vasubandhu*, ed. P. Pradhan, Patna 1967.
AKVy	*Abhidharmakośavyākhyā of Yaśomitra*, ed. U. Wogihara, Tokyo² 1971
AS	*Abhidharmasamuccaya of Asaṅga*, ed. P. Pradhan, Santiniketan 1950
ASBh	*Abhidharmasamuccayabhāṣya*, ed. N. Tatia, Patna 1976.
ASg	*A Manual of Abhidhamma* (Abhidhammattha Saṅgaha), ed. with Engl. transl. and notes by Nārada Mahā Thera, Kandy 1975.
G.Sh.K.	*Gō Shisō Kenkyū*, ed. Sh. Kumoi, Kyoto 1979.
I.B.St.	*Indological and Buddhist Studies* (Vol. in Honour of Prof. J.W. de Jong), ed. L.A. Hercus et al., Canberra 1982.
K.Reb.	*Karma and Rebirth in Classical Indian Traditions*, ed. W.D. O'Flaherty, Berkeley etc. 1980.
MAv	*Madhyamakāvatāa of Candrakīrti*, ed. de la Vallée Poussin St Petersbourg 1912.

MK	(*Mūla-*)*Madhyamakakārikās* of Nāgārjuna, ed. (with Candrakīrti's *Prasannapadā*) by L. de la Vallée Poussin, repr. Osnabrück 1970.
Pr	*Prasannapadā* (s. *MK*).
T	Taishō edition of the Chinese Tripiṭaka.
VisM	*Visuddhimagga of Buddhaghosa*, ed. Warren/Kosambi, Cambridge (Mass.) 1950.
Y	*Yogācārabhūmi*, ed. V. Bhattacharya, Calcutta 1957.

1. Just two examples: 1) On p. 129, Matthews says that the last cognitional process before death (*maraṇ*āsanna-javana-citta; Cp. *ASg* 266 (¶13): *maraṇāsannavīthiyaṃ*) "is 'registered' (*tadālambana*) by the final death-consciousness (*cuti-citta*)." Such a statement is not found in the text, nor in Nārada's comment where it is expressly stated that after the *javana* phase "the tadālambana consciousness. . .may or may not follow" for two moments. "After this occurs death consciousness (*cuti-citta*)" (*ASg* 273), the object of which is the same as that of the *bhavaṅgaviññāṇa*. Cp. also *VisM* XVII. 136:. . . tadārammaṇapariyosānāya javanavīthiyā anantaraṃ bhavaṅgavisayaṃ ārammaṇaṃ katvā cuticittaṃ uppajjati. 2) Another example is found a few lines later where Matthews asserts that "the 'rebirth consciousness'. . .takes as its object the *bhavaṅga*." *ASg* 265f (¶2) says that mind at the moment of rebirth arises "with reference to the object which has been apprehended in this way" (*tathāgahitaṃ ārammaṇam ārabbha*). It is clear from the next paragraph (¶3) of the text that this refers to the last cognitional process (*javana*) before death, as is confirmed by *VisM* XVII.136:. . .tad eva āpāthagataṃ kammaṃ vā kammanimittaṃ va arabbha. . .paṭisandhicittaṃ uppajjati. Cp. also *VisM* XIV.111-113. Thus, mind at the moment of rebirth has the same object as the last conscious or supraliminal mind process of the preceding life, and this same object is also kept by the *bhavaṅgaviññāṇa* of the new life whenever it occurs. This means that the *paṭisandhicitta* has the same object as the *bhavaṅga* (of the new life), but not that it has the *bhavaṅga* as its object.

2. Cp., e.g., Matthews' remark (p. 129) that "in 5.5.11, death is described as the decease of psychic life (*jīvitindriya*), heat (*usmā*) and consciousness . . . ." This is in Nārada's notes (*ASg* 269), but not in the text itself as Matthews' formulation suggests.

3. Cp. *Encycl. of Buddh.* (ed. Malalasekera) III.1 (Colombo, 1971), 19; L. de la Vallée Poussin, *Vijñaptimātratāsiddhi*, 196.

4. Cp. *VisM* XIV.114: paṭisandhiviññāṇe. . .niruddhe. . .tādisam eva bhavaṅgaviññāṇaṃ nāma pavattati.

5. Cp. *VisM* XIV.123: yaṃ sabbapacchimaṃ bhavaṅgacitaṃ, tam. . .cutī ti vuccati. Cp. also L.S. Cousins in *JPTS* 9/1981, 25.

6. Cp., e.g., *VisM* XIX.14.

7. Cp., e.g., the last three items of the ten bad ways of action (*akusalakammapatha*, e.g., *A V* 264ff), viz., *abbidhyā*, *vyāpāda*, and *mithyādṛṣṭi*, which are regarded as karma by the Dārṣṭāntikas (*AKBh* 237, 17 and 248, 10) and the Yogācāras (*Y* 182, 9ff; *ASBh* 63, 13f), but not by the Vaibhāṣikas (*AKBh* 248, 2-4), in order to avoid an amalgamation of karma and *kleśas* which was, in this special case, expressly admitted by the Dārṣṭāntikas (*AKBh* 237, 17ff; cp. D. Seyfort Ruegg in *JAOS* 87.2/1976, 164, n. 23).

8. Thus the usual rendering, according to *VisM* XVI.22; similar analysis *Vibhāṣā* (T vol. 27), p. 401 c 29, but not accepted. Another explanation is

"Truths of the Noble(s)": *VisM* XVI.21; *AKBh* 330, 16; *Vibhāṣā* 402 a 9f.

9. *S V* 421.

10. Cp. the material collected by Sh. Kumoi in *Bukkyō Shisō*, vol. 1: *Ai*, ed. H. Nakamura (Kyoto 1975), 40ff.

11. Cp., e.g., *AKBh* 333, 10 and 11-13.

12. Cp. in this connection, especially *Ch-Up* III.14.1 (yathākratur asmiṃ loke puruṣo bhavati, tathêtaḥ pretya bhavati) stating the quality of rebirth, or at least the state after death, to be dependent on one's desire or resolve (*kratu*, cp. *Śatapathabrāhmaṇa* IV.1.4.1: sa yad eva manasā kamayata 'idaṃ me syād, idaṃ kurvīya' iti, sa eva kratuḥ). See also F. Edgerton, "The Hour of Death," in *Annals of the Bhandarkar Institute* (Poona) 8/1927, 223; cp. also P. Horsch, "Vorstufen der indischen Seelenwanderungslehre," in *Asiatische Studien* 25/1971, 143f, 146 and 153f, pointing out, however, that the success of one's wish for rebirth may depend on one's ritual knowledge and activity.

13. Cp. *Mil* 51: *taṇhāpaccayā kammaṃ*. In the Nikāyas, however, such a formulation does not seem to occur (cp. I.B. Horner, *Milinda's Questions, I, p. XIV). See, however, Brh-Up* IV.4.5 (sa yathākāmo bhavati, tatkratur bhavati; yatkratur bhavati, tat karma kurute; yat karma kurute, tad abhisaṃpadyate). In this passage, which is obviously a development of *Ch-Up* III.14.1 (see n. 12), rebirth, or the state after death is, it is true, determined by karma, but karma itself is, through resolve (*kratu*), determined by desire (*kāma*).

14. *M* III 99ff.

15. Cp. the passages indicated by J.P. McDermott in *K.Reb.*, 177, n. 43, and 178, n. 45.

16. Cp. Edgerton, op. cit., 221.

17. For a different view in later, more popular Theravāda texts, see ibid., 233.

18. *M* III 99ff; *S* IV 302f. (cp. Edgerton, op. cit., 232).

19. *S* IV 168; It 12f.

20. *M* III 214. Cp. also *D* III 258ff.

21. Cp. also Edgerton, op. cit., 233f, and for similar views in other Buddhist traditions, ibid., 235f.

22. Cp. *Paramatthamañjūsā* (in *Visuddhimaggo*, ed. Rewatadhamma, Varanasi 1969), 1020 (ad *VisM* XIV.111): kammaṃ nāma. . .vipākadānāya laddhokāsaṃ.

23. Cp. ibid. kammanimittam kammāyūhanakkhaṇe cetanāya paccayabhūtaṃ deyyadhammādi (referring to one who is going to be reborn in the *kāma* sphere), and kammanimittam. . .ti pathavīkasiṇādikaṃ attano kammārammaṇam eva (referring to a person to be reborn in the *rūpa* or *arūpa* sphere).

24. Cp. ibid. gatinimittaṃ—yaṃ gatiṃ upapajjati, tappariyāpannaṃ rūpāyatanaṃ.

25. W. Gundert, *Japanische Religionsgeschichte* (Stuttgart 1943), 90.

26. Ibid., 90 and 95.

27. Cp. Sh. Kumoi, loc. cit., (see n.10).

28. Cp., e.g., the stereotyped detailed description of the path of liberation in *M* I 179ff, etc.

29. U. Schneider, *Einführung in den Buddhismus*, (Darmstadt 1980), 69f.

30. The Pāli text has: kāyena samvuto vācāya saṃvuto manasā saṃvuto,

sattannaṃ bodhipakkhiyānaṃ dhammānaṃ bhāvanam anvāya (*D* III 97). Only the first portion of it fits Schneider's thesis. Unfortunately, it is precisely this portion of the text that is missing in the two early Chinese versions (T vol. I, pp. 39 a 2, 676 c 15). At least the text as we have it speaks, at best, in favour of liberation through non-action or self-restraint in combination with spiritual exercise. I admit that in a strictly logical structure what would correspond to a theory of good and bad rebirth through good and bad action is a theory of liberation through non-action plus counter-karmic activity, if necessary. But other less logical but not self-contradictory combinations can hardly be said not to have existed. Especially if the karma theory was not fundamental in earliest Buddhist soteriology, it would be quite plausible that even when it was made use of in the explanation of rebirth it did not necessarily entail a revision of the doctrine of liberation but was easily combined with more or less suitable elements from the already available Buddhist stock. In *A* II 232, a brahmin pretends to have been told that the Buddha proclaims non-performance of all deeds (*sabbakammānaṃ akiriyā*) to be (conducive to) the annihilation of world(ly existence), but the Buddha's answer consists in the *Buddhicized* doctrine of liberation by means of anti-karmic karma of *M* No. 57 (see below).

31. E.g., *M* II 214ff; *A* I 220f; Cp. K. Fujita in *G.Sh.K.*, 139f, and J. Bronkhorst, *Two Traditions of Meditation in Ancient India* (unpublished manuscript), ch. II, n. 8.

32. *A* I 221 etc. Cp. Fujita, op. cit., 140f, and Bronkhorst, loc. cit.

33. Cp. also *A* II 230ff; *D* III 230.

34. J.P. McDermott, "Nibbāna as a reward for Kamma," in *JAOS* 93.3/1973, 344ff (referring to *Khuddakapāṭha* and *Milindapañha*); *Mūlasarvāstivādavinayavastu*, ed. N. Dutt (Gilgit Manuscripts III.1, Srinagar 1947), 18, 18-20 (*avadāna*-like context: previous good karma consisting in becoming a monk has resulted in seeing Truth); *Divyāvadāna*, ed. Vaidya, 33, 24ff (good karma consisting in recitation and spiritual exercise (!) finally results in Arhatship).

35. Cp., e.g., Long in *K.Reb.*, 41 and 51f; O'Flaherty, ibid., 25f.

36. Cp. also K. Fujita in *I.B.St.*, 151.

37. The latter statement has a positive parallel in the second part of the Sutta (*M* III 177f).

38. Cp., e.g., the verse *Sn* 650 referred to by both Matthews and Kawamura which, if interpreted from its immediate context (*Sn* 651-652 and 600-619 ' 648-649; 620-647 seems to be an intrusion of *Dhp* 396ff), must mean that one is not a brahmin by birth/caste but by *acting* like a Brahmin, i.e. by moral behaviour and spiritual effort. Cp. K. Fujita in *G.Sh.K.*, 134; McDermott in *K.Reb.*, 174f. The second level interpretation offered by McDermott (cp. also Fujita, ibid., 135) and seemingly followed by Kawamura, viz., that one is a Brahmin in this life due to one's past good deeds, does not seem to contrast well with being a Brahmin due to birth/caste (cp. also Fujita, loc. cit.) and is in my opinion hardly the original meaning of the verse, even if this would suit verses 653f which, however, do not appear homogeneous in the context. Of course, Fujita loc. cit. is right in stating that the first interpretation does *not* imply a denial of the karma doctrine; it merely wants to replace the social concept of Brahmin by a moral or spiritual one.

39. Cp. *CPD* II, 367.

40. My interpretation of *-parihāra* (PED: "being attacked by") follows Sheth, *Pāïa-sadda-mahaṇṇavo* ([2]1963), 568: *paribhog, āsevan*. The (Mūla-)Sarvāstivāda

tradition seems to have the lectio facilior *viṣamāparihāra* ("not avoiding what is unwholesome"): cp. *AKBh* 74, 12 quoting the *Prajñaptiśāstra* which mentions *viṣamāparihāra* (*AKVy* 169, 32: *atyaśanader viṣamasyâparihāreṇa*) as a cause of death (in which context, too, the Pāli tradition has *viṣamāparihāra* in *Mil* 302, 25) different from both exhaustion of life-span and exhaustion of merit. Cp. also *Y* 15, 13ff and (different context) 28, 9 and 29, 5.

41. *S* IV 230f (cp. also *A* II 87 and III 131). The importance of this passage has been stressed by W. Halbfass in *K.Reb.*, 295f. Cp. also Fujita in *G.Sh.K.*, 121f; id. in *I.B. St.*, 151f; McDermott in *JAOS* 97.4/1977, 465; Gomez in *Phew* 25, 82f. See also Matthews where, however, the matter is presented in a somewhat distorted way.

42. Cp. Halbfass in *K.Reb.*, 296.

43. *AKBh* 192, 4ff (see also L. Dargyay's paper). Cp. also *AS* 55, 11 (reconstruction, altered by myself): sādhāraṇaṃ karma katamat? yad bhājanaloka-vibhājakam(?) (gang snod kyi 'jig rten rnam par 'byed pa'o).

44. *AKBh* 179, 11f; *Y* 31, 4f and 36, 19f; *AS* 37, 8.

45. *AKBh* 179, 3f; *Y* 31, 1.

46. According to the Vaibhāṣikas (e.g., *AKBh* 94, 20-22) and Yogācāras (e.g., *ASBh* 42, 22), the external world is only a 'by-product' (*adhipati-phala*) of karma, not its main result (*vipāka*; on the distinction between *vipāka* and other effects of karma in *Theravāda* dogmatics see McDermott in *JAOS* 95.3/1975, 426). On the other hand, according to *Kv*(-a) VII.7 (cp. also Halbfass in *K.Reb.*, 296) the Andhakas advocated the opinion that the earth is *karma-vipāka*, possibly with special reference to the karma of the universal monarch (*cakravartin*) conducive to the *possession* of the earth. The same text also mentions the view that the whole external world is the *vipāka* of the common karma of all living beings (*Kv*-a 100, 31f), though this may be a distortion of the theory of the Vaibhāṣikas, etc., mentioned before.

47. *The Nine Ways of Bon* (London 1967), 12.

48. O'Flaherty in *K.Reb.*, 11ff and 28ff; M. Hara, "Transfer of Merit," in *The Adyar Library Bulletin* 31-32/1967-68, 382ff. Cp. also, for the Vedic period, P. Horsch, op. cit. (See n.12), 147f.

49. In *K.Reb.*, 235f.

50. McDermott in *K.Reb.*, 190; R. Gombrich, "'Merit Transference' in Sinhalese Buddhism," in *History of Religions* 11/1971, 203f; J.M. Agasse, "Le transfert de mérite dans le Bouddhisme Pāli classique," in *JA* 266/1978, 311.

51. See p. 211 and notes 54, 55 and 69.

52. McDermott in *K.Reb.*, 190f; Gombrich, op. cit., 207; Agasse, op. cit. 312ff; H. Bechert, "Buddha-Feld und Verdienstübertragung: Mahāyāna-Ideen im Theravāda-Buddhismus Ceylons," in *Académie royale de Belgique, Bulletin de la classe des lettres et des sciences morale et politiques*, 5e série, tome LXII, 1976, 39f.

53. See also *Pv* I.4.1-2 (p. 4).

54. As the text mentions a recitation of the *Pārāyana* it must be at least later than the reduction to literary form of this (admittedly fairly old) text. According to Akanuma's *Comparative Catalogue* there is no Chinese version of this Sutta.

55. According to A. Bareau in *L'Annuaire du Collège de France*, 74e année (resumé des cours de 1973-1974), 452ff, this passage is part of a later accretion.

56. Thus E. Waldschmidt, *Die Überlieferung vom Lebensende des Buddha*, I (Göttingen 1944), 58 n. 78 ("Übertragung *des Lohnes* guter Taten").

57. Tiracchānagate dānaṃ datvā sataguṇā dakkhiṇā pāṭikaṅkhitabbā, etc.; cp. *AKBh* 270,5f(. . . śataguṇo Vipākaḥ. . .).

58. See, e.g., *It* 19: datvā. . ..dakkhiṇeyyesu dakkhiṇaṃ.

59. Cp. also W. Stede, *Die Gespenstergeschichten des Peta Vatthu* (Leipzig 1914), 21. This would mean, in contrast with the Vedic *dakṣiṇā* which is something (especially a milk-giving cow) additionally presented to the officiating priests as a fee, at this stage of development the *dakṣiṇā*, the priests' fee, has, apart from being used for what is presented to Buddhist monks, come to be nothing but what originally was the priests' share in the *sacrificial food and drink* which above all was meant for the *gods*. By the way, the verb *ādiś-* is used already in *Śatapathabrāhmaṇa* I.1.4.24 in the sense of assigning a (burnt) offering (i.e., in a sense, an offering consumed by Agni as a representative or mediator of the gods) to a deity (ādiṣṭaṃ vā etad devatāyai havir bhavati; cp. ibid. I.6.2.7). Thus, it could easily have been used also when what was to be assigned to a deity was sacrificial food, etc., to be consumed by the *priests* as representatives of the gods or as mediators, and this food could have been termed *dakṣiṇā* when it was at the same time the priests' fee. For a detailed attempt to connect the Buddhist doctrine of merit transference with Vedic patterns, see B. Oguibenine in *I.B.St.*, 393ff.

60. Cp. also *D* III 189; *Divyāvadāna*, ed. Vaidya, 62, 22f.

61. Cp. *Pv* I.5.9 (= *Khp* VII.9; see n. 105). Cp. also *Pv* II.8.4 (p. 22) dassāmi dānaṃ pitunnaṃ.

62. There is a Chinese parallel in T Vol. II, p. 272b.

63. Cp. the reference to *āhāra* in the discussion of the different categories of deceased.

64. For details see Stede, op. cit., 21ff.

65. Gombrich, op. cit., 210f.

66. Cp. also *Pv* I.9.2 (p. 7) where we read that clothes presented to a certain *preta* all turn into something hideous or uncomfortable (*kiṭaka*, precise meaning not clear) due to that *preta*'s bad karma.

67. Stede, op. cit., 21. Cp. also Gombrich, op. cit., 212.

68. As for v. 11, see n. 72. In verse 9, petānaṃ dakkhiṇā (v.1 -ṇaṃ) dajjā pubbe kataṃ anussaraṃ, the *dakkhiṇā*(*s*?(!)) one should give to deceased relatives and friends (!) out of thankfulness would naturally be simply a gift of food, etc., presented to these *pretas* as recompense for the benefits received from them when they were still alive. In verse 12, merit (*puñña*) is, to be sure, expressly mentioned, but only as accruing to the donor, without any indication of its transference to the *pretas* (cp. also *Pv* I.1.2-3). Nor does the reference to the *monks* necessarily imply transfer of merit, as it can also be explained on the basis of their function as representatives or mediators in a transfer of *food*.

69. Cp. also the fact that a few verse fragments of the *Tirokuḍḍa-petavatthu* seem to have been incorporated into this text: cp. *A* V 271 dāyako pi anipphalo ≈ *Pv* 1.5.5d dāyakā ca anipphalā; *A* V 269 petānaṃ. . .upakappatu ≈ *Pv* 1.5.7f and 8d petānaṃ upakappati.

70. According to *Kv-a*: the Rājagiriyas and Siddhatthikas. McDermott (*JAOS* 95.3/1975, 431) insists that this view implies some doctrine of transfer of merit, because in the course of discussion the Rājagiriyas etc. "are made to agree that direct gifts to the *pretas* are not a possibility." Yet, this is exactly what the commentary takes their position to mean: the *pretas* "live on the *very same* clothes,

etc., that are given to them here" (yaṃ ito dinnaṃ cīvarādi ten' eva yāpenti). The wording of the *Kv* itself, viz., ito dinnena tattha yāpenti, is, it is true, less strict, but it too would be a rather strange way of expressing merit transfer. Wouldn't it be more natural to understand it in the sense of some mysterious, invisible handing over of food or clothes to the *pretas*, perhaps through mediation of monks?

71. For this distinction, cp. also Stede, op. cit., 21 and 51f.

72. Or: ". . .given (to the *pretas* by having been) duly presented to the Order"? I assume that *patiṭṭhita* is to be understood (as in *Pv* II.9.71, see below) as standing for *patiṭṭhāpita* (which may have the meaning presented to, conferred upon, according to PW s.v. *sthā* + *prati*, caus., 2, and W. Geiger, *Saṃyuttanikāya* transl., I (1930), 141, in spite of *Pv-a* 18f explaining it by having recourse to the field (*puññakkhetta*) metaphor. For there are quite a few passages (e.g., *D* I 51; *S* I 90; *A* II 68; *A* III 336; *Vv* 32) of the type, samaṇabrāhmaṇesu (or saṅghamhi, bhikkhusaṅghe) dakkhiṇaṃ patiṭṭhāpeti. The meaning of *dakkhiṇa* in these passages is clearly gift, as confirmed not only by the commentaries equating it with *dāna* (e.g., *Sp* I 160, 8 or *Sv* I 158, 5, and, for the passage under discussion, *Pv*-a 18, 28f) but also by *Pv* II.9.71 (p. 28) dānaṃ. . .dussīlesu patiṭṭhitaṃ. Yet, *saṅghamhi* can as well be connected with *dinnā*, for in these texts there is no difficulty in construing *dā*- with a locative: cp., e.g., *Vv* XXXIV.14ff (p. 31f) saṅghe dehi, saṅghe dinnam, saṅghe dānaṃ dassāmi, saṅghe dānāni datvāna. In the present passage, I therefore find it difficult to decide whether *saṅghamhi* is to be construed with *suppatiṭṭhitā*, *dinnā* ("given to the Order, and thus duly presented, or well-placed"), or both. The latter possibility seems to be supported by stylistic parallels like *Pv* IV.8.7 sīse tiṭṭhāmi matthake.

73. In Buddhism, *pretas* (in the specific sense) and *pitṛs* ("manes") are no longer distinguished: cp. Stede, op. cit., 32; Gombrich, op. cit., 208. Yet an analogous distinction comes in again by the fact that the (*ordinary*) *preta* is, by means of the gift or merit transferred to him, transformed into a divine *preta*, or *yakṣa*/ *yakkha* (see below).

74. J. Gonda, *Die Religionen Indiens* I (Stuttgart 1960), 135ff. Unlike O'Flaherty in *K.Reb.*, 11f, I should hesitate to call the process implied in the *piṇḍapitṛyajña* and *śrāddha* a transference of *merit*.

75. Op. cit., 208 and 212.

76. Cp., e.g., the *Tirokuḍḍa-petavatthu* discussed above.

77. Agasse, op. cit., 314.

78. E.g., *Pv* I.10.4 (p. 8) or II.4.7 (p. 17) and Stede, op. cit., 52.

79. E.g., *Pv* I.10.7f (p. 8); II.1.8f (p. 12); II.2.9 (p. 14); similarly *Mil* 294 (cp. McDermott in *JAOS* 97.4/1977, 462) synthesizing this view with the distinctions made in *A V* 269ff.

80. E.g., *Pv* I.10.7f (p. 8); II.1.9 and 15ff (pp. 12f); II.2.9 (p. 14).

81. E.g., *Pv* II.1.9 and 15ff (pp. 12f); III.2.12ff (pp. 36f); Stede, op. cit., 53. Cp. also the passage from the *Dhp*-a discussed by Gombrich, op. cit., 213, and Agasse, op. cit., 327.

82. E.g., *Pv* I.1.3 (p. 3); I.4.2 (p. 4; subject: *pretas* as well as local deities and World-Guardians!); I.5.5 and 12 (p. 4f); II.8.10 (p. 22).

83. *Pv* II.8.10f (pp. 22f); II.1.10ff (p. 12f).

84. Cp. *D* II 88; *Pv* I.4.2 (see n. 120); Agasse, op. cit., 327.

85. Stede, op. cit., 39ff.

86. Ibid., 43.

87. Agasse, op. cit., 327 n. 69.

88. Ibid., 327; Gombrich, op. cit., 213.

89. Stede, op. cit., 53.

90. Agasse, op. cit. 320. An assignment of the husband's merit to his wife is perhaps expressed in *Thī* v. 307f: cp. Agasse, op. cit., 314 n. 14, following *Thi*-a. But otherwise Norman, *Elder's verses* II, p. 32: "you [=the husband] should dedicate (my[=the wife's]) gift" (the explanations in square brackets are mine); however: to whom? Cp. also *Mil* 297 (McDermott in *JAOS* 97.4/1977, 463) where the possibility of sharing (*saṃvibhajituṃ*) one's good (karma) with whomever one wishes is expressed.

91. Bechert, op. cit. (See note 52), 44, referring to a passage from the *Buddhāpadāna* (vv. 44-48).

92. Agasse, op. cit., 326f; cp. also Schopen, "Two Problems in the History of Indian Buddhism: The Laymen/Monk Distinction and the Doctrine of the Transference of Merit," to be published in *Studien zur Indologie und Iranistik* 10/1984, ch. VIIIff.

93. Gombrich, op. cit., 206; McDermott in *K.Reb.*, 190; D. Schlingloff, *Die Religion des Buddhismus*, II (Berlin 1963), 21.

94. H. Bechert, Zur Frühgeschichte des Mahāyāna, in *ZDMG* 113 (1963), 532f. Cp. also: id., in *German Scholars on India*, I (Varanasi 1973), 15f.

95. As for donation for the sake of transference of merit to the deceased, there is not only inscriptional (Schopen, op. cit., ch. VIII-IX) but also literary evidence that it was not only practised by laymen but also by monks: cp., e.g., *Pv* II.2 (pp. 13f) or III.2 (pp. 35ff). Yet, in the *Pv*, instances of monks making donations for the benefit of *pretas* are in the minority, and no instance seems to occur in the Nikāyas. Moreover, the performance of this practice by monks seems to be secondary also on internal grounds; for a monk's gift of food, etc., to the Order, of which he himself is a member, is essentially nonsensical, and even impossible so long as he is really a *bhikkhu*, a beggar, unless carried out in a merely symbolical form by means of gifts of almost no value, as in *Pv* III.2.

96. A possible intermediate stage of development, viz., the notion of transference of merit not only to deceased relatives (or at least friends) but to any *preta* (as a suffering being), seems to be represented by *Pv* II.1 (pp. 12f), where a monk (Sāriputta) out of compassion donates a symbolic gift of food, cloth and water to the monks (*bhikkhūnaṃ*) and transfers the merit to a *pretī* who is in any case not expressly stated to be a relative or friend of his.

97. *Mil* 295, 7ff; cp. McDermott in *JAOS* 97.4/1977, 463.

98. Cp., in this context, the use of the magic of formulating a truth (*sacca kiriyā*) in texts like the *Jātaka*: cp. H. Luders, *Varuṇa*,II (Göttingen 1959), 487ff.

99. Agasee, op. cit., 325.

100. Gombrich, op. cit., 216f.

101. Agasse, op. cit., 323f.

102. Ibid., 315f and 328.

103. Ibid., 321 (referring to *Khp* VII.9 - *Pv* I.5.9).

104. *Pv* I.5.3 - *Khp* VII.3; cp. Stede, op. cit., 51.

105. Stede, op. cit., 39.

106. Cp., in this context, esp. the function of the powerful divine *pretas* *yakṣas* (Stede, op. cit., 39 and 42f).

107. Cp. Gombrich, op. cit., 207.

108. Cp. also *Kv* XVI.1, p. 525.

109. Gombrich, op. cit., 213; cp. Bechert, op. cit. (See note 52), 41.

110. Gombrich, op. cit., 213ff; Agasse, op. cit., 328ff; Bechert, op. cit., 38f. It is natural that especially (but perhaps not only) according to this doctrine the 'transferor' does not lose his merit but even gets more of it because transferring merit is itself a meritorious act.

111. Gombrich, op. cit., 216.

112. Har Dayal, *The Bodhisattva Doctrine in Buddhist Sanskrit Literature* (Repr. Delhi 1970), 192; cp. also Schopen in *IIJ* 21.2/1979, 7f and 12.

113. J.B. Long in *K.Reb.*, 43.

114. W. Gundert, op. cit. (See note 25), 93.

115. Ibid., 93f.

116. Cp., e.g., on the one hand: K. Bhattacharya, *L'ātman-braham dans le bouddhisme ancien*, Paris 1973, and J. Pérez-Remón, *Self and Non-self in Early Buddhism*, The Hague 1980; on the other: St. Collins, review of Pérez-Remón in *Numen* 29, 250ff; id., *Selfless Persons*, Cambridge 1982 (not yet seen); K.R. Norman, "A Note on atta in the Alagaddūpama-sutta," in *Studies in Indian Philosophy*, Ahmedabad 1981, 19ff.

117. For details see Claus Oetke, *"Ich" und das Ich. Analytische Untersuchungen zur buddhistisch-brahmanischen Atmankontroverse* (not yet published). Some of the following remarks are inspired by this book.

118. At least in the context of karma and rebirth, Pérez-Remón's (op. cit., 131ff) interpretation as "one's self" or "the self" instead of a simple reflexive pronoun is unacceptable in most if not all cases. See Collins, review, 256ff.

119. Lit. "moving away from, or being deprived of, [the previous existence]," as is clear from the fact that this verb is construed with the ablative; cp. also PW s. v. *cyu-* (2) and (4).

120. Lit. "approaching, or entering upon, [another existence]," as follows from the prevailing construction with the accusative; cp. *CPD* s. v. *upapajjati* (2); cp. also synonymous expressions as, e.g., in It p. 19: ito cutā manussattā saggaṃ *gacchanti* dāyakā.

121. Cp., e.g., *Dhp* 117: pāpaṃ ce *puriso* kayirā; 161: *attanā* hi kataṃ pāpaṃ; *M* III 203: idha. . .ekacco. . .*puriso*. . .pāṇāti-pātī hoti. . .; *so* tena kammena. . . paraṃ maraṇā. . .nirayaṃ upapajjati; I 403: ayaṃ. . .purisa*puggalo*. . .paraṃ maraṇā. . .nirayaṃ upapajjissati; I 22: *satte* passāmi cavamāne upapajjamane. . . yathākammūpage; ibid.: *so* tato cuto idh' ūpapanno; *D* I 17; III 147; II 286: cut' *ahaṃ* mānusā kāyā. . .puna devo bhavissāmi; cp. also passages like *S* I 133: ye. . .*sattā*. . .āgantāro punabbhavaṃ; *Sn* 729; *Thī* 434.

122. Cp. Pérez-Remón, op. cit., 137ff. In *M* III 19 (= *S* III 103), a monk's question as to which self deeds will affect if they are done by what is not the self (anattakatāni kammāni kam attānaṃ phusissanti), i.e., if the *skandhas* of the person by which they are done are not the self, is rejected as going beyond the Buddha's instruction. I for one cannot see that the passage expresses or indicates any distinction of a mundane level of karma and a supramundane level of non-self, and an exclusion of the former if in conflict with the latter, as Fujita in

I.B.St., 156f suggests. It only rejects the apparent dilemma that arises when the statement that one is oneself (*ātman* in the everyday sense) affected by what one has done (cp., e.g., *Dhp* 165) is, by way of systematizing but soteriologically valueless speculation, mixed up with the spiritually unrelated instruction that the *skandhas* are not the ātman, i.e., the (or a) self in a specific, metaphysical sense. Cp. also Pérez-Remón, op. cit., 253ff.

123. Cp., e.g., Frauwallner, *Geschichte der Indischen Philosophie* I (Salzburg, 1953), 204f.

124. The best known exceptions are, of course, the Vātsīputrīyas/Sāṃmitīyas whose position can perhaps be characterized as a dogmatization of the early canonical person (*puggala*), in the naive sense of everyday linguistic usage, into an entity, though not into an ātman in the specific sense of an altogether immutable entity.

125. Cp. Halbfass in *K.Reb.*, 286.

126. Cp. ibid., 274 and 275 n. 24.

127. Cp. Frauwallner, op. cit., 420f.

128. *Pr* 173, 8-10, quoted in n. 11 of L. Dargyay's paper.

129. *Pr* 173, 10f quoted in n. 15 of L. Dargyay's paper.

130. Cp. n. 13 of L. Dargyay's paper.

131. Cp. also *Rigs-pa'i rgya-mtsho* (1973) 308, 3ff (ad *MK* XVII.21 cd).

132. From the morphological point of view, *zhig pa* cannot be the past form of the transitive present *'jig pa*, to destroy, as Dargyay puts it (p. 172), but only of the intransitive *'jig pg*, to be ruined, to decay, (Jäschke).

133. Cp. *Pr* 173, 12.

134. *dGongs-pa rab-gsal* (1973) 231, 15f:. . .las zhig pa'i zhig pa las phyis kyi 'bras bu 'byung ba 'grub pas. . .; I have to thank Mr. Tsultrim Phuntsok for his most valuable advice regarding the interpretation of this and the following passage.

135. *Rigs-pa'i rgya-mtsho* 309, 19ff: las zhig pa'i zhig pa rigs 'dra brgyud pa'i rten ni nga'o synam pa gang la skye ba'i gang zag gi rgyud yin la de nyid las dang 'bras bu 'brel ba'i rten yang yin no.

136. McDermott in *K.Reb.*, pp. 186f. In spite of the references given by McDermott in n. 73, I have been unable to find any textual passage confirming his view that it is "through the mechanism of possession that latent. . .karma becomes effective" except in Saṅghabhadra (T vol. 29, p. 535 a 25 ff.; cp. also *AKVy* 148, 22f).

137. McDermott in *K.Reb.*, pp. 183f and 187. The same view, viz., that *avijñapti* has the function of connecting the act with its future result, has also been advocated by some Japanese scholars but has been contradicted by others and cogently been refuted by K. Mitomo, especially in his papers in *Ōsaki Gakuhō* 129/1976, 1ff, and in *Hokke Bunka Kenkyū* 3/1977, 179ff. Cp. also Genjun H. Sasaki, "Avijñapti—a Buddhist Moral Concept," in *Actes du XXIXe Congrès internationale des Orientalistes. . .*, Inde Ancienne, Vol. I (Paris 1976), 89ff, especially 95. *Avijñapti* can be described as an invisible material karmic event taking place when a person has intentionally set in motion a process through which additional merit or demerit accrues to him even when he is no longer mentally concerned with it. E.g., when a murder is committed that had previously been ordered by another person, this person commits or incurs an *avijñapti-karman* at the moment of the murder even if he has long forgotten his command (cp. *AKBh* 196, 16). Or when a gift is bestowed on monks, the donator

commits meritorious *avijñaptis* when the gift is, later on, used (*paribhuj-*) by the monks even if he does not know it (cp. ibid., 196, 12ff). Or when a person after having assumed the monastic vows automatically keeps to monastic discipline even when his mind is fixed on something else (*anyamanaska*), this is *avijñapti-karman* (ibid., 196, 24f). It is the reinterpretation of this notion by Vasubandhu (ibid., 197, 14ff) in terms of a special latent transformation of the stream-of-personality (*santāna-pariṇāma-viśeṣa*) that has obscured the distinction between *avijñapti* and the retributive mechanism and may have induced scholars to misinterpret *avijñapti* in the sense of the (or a) connecting link between the karmic act and its result. But the transformation of the stream-of-personality corresponding to *avijñapti* is not the automatic ripening process starting from *any* act and guaranteeing that there will be any result at all but rather a *specific* transformation conducive to a reinforcement or *increase* of the result (*bahutaraphalābhiniṣpattaye, AKBh* 197, 16f; cp. 198, 4f where *sā santatir* should be read instead of *samante 'pi*). For details on *avijñapti* see also J. van den Broeck, *La Saveur de l'Immortal* (La version chinoise de l'Amṛtarasa de Ghoṣaka), Lovain 1977, 30ff; St. Anacker, *Vasubandhu: Three Aspects* (Ph.D. thesis, Wisconsin 1970), 146ff.

138. Cp. *AKBh* 63, 14-16.

139. *dGongs-pa rab-gsal* 229,11.

140. *Dgongs-pa rab-gsal* 229, 13f: Kha che bas thob pa khas len kyang thob bya'i chos las gñis kyis thob pa skyed par mi 'dod la [/] 'dir ni de ltar 'dod pa zhig ste [/].

141. *Rigs-pa'i rgya-mtsho* 191, 17: . . .'das pa dngos por bzhed pa'i gnad kyis. . .ma 'ongs pa yang de dang 'dra ste.

142. Ibid., 191, 18f: 'das ma 'ongs kyi 'jog tshul 'di ni rang gi ngo bos grub pa la mi 'thad. . . .

143. Ibid., 191, 19f: rang bzhin de tha snyad du yang khas mi len pa'i lugs la sin tu 'thad pa. . . .

144. *dGongs-pa rab-gsal* 231, 17-19.

145. Ibid., 233, 14ff and 234, 14f.

146. Ibid., 234, 1ff.

147. Ibid., 229, 11-13.

III

The Western Context

CHAPTER THIRTEEN

In Search of Utopia: Karma and Rebirth in the Theosophical Movement

RONALD NEUFELDT

Introduction

Of the movements or societies preaching and teaching karma and rebirth in the modern Western world, certainly the Theosophical Society must rank as one of the first. Founded in the mid 1870's in New York City by Helena Blavatsky and Henry S. Olcott, the Society, according to Bruce F. Campbell, was born as an answer to the general religious controversy of the day, the discrediting of spiritualism and the cleavage between science and religion.[1] The claim of the movement from the beginning was that it was merely teaching an ancient wisdom tradition which had always been held to be true by all thinking men everywhere, but which had long been forgotten and shunned by the masses and those who formulated the thinking of the masses, particularly in the Western world. In the first instance, the concern of the Theosophical Society was merely to revive the ancient and universal truth about life, particularly in the sadly misled Western world.

The objectives of the Society, as stated frequently by Blavatsky, are three: to form the nucleus of a universal brotherhood without distinction of race, color, or creed; to promote the comparative study of ancient and modern systems of thought and scriptures, particularly the Aryan scriptures; to investigate the hidden laws of nature and the powers latent in man. Central to the fulfillment of these objectives is the belief in and teaching of karma and rebirth. Indeed these two ideas could be regarded as the two pillars upon which all of Theosophical teaching rests.

There is some question whether this was always the case from the beginning of the Society. Bruce Campbell, for example, takes the view that reincarnation appears to be absent from Blavatsky's first book *Isis Unveiled.*[2] A reading of *H.P. Blavatsky Collected Works* also points to controversy as early as 1882, concerning differences between the teachings of *Isis Unveiled* and *The Theosophist*. The view that *Isis Unveiled* does not teach that which is found in later theosophical writings, has, of course, been rejected by the Society in general, and Madame Blavatsky in particular. Indeed much effort was spent by her to discredit suggestions that there are any discrepancies or contradictions in her writings. A reading of the *Collected Writings* would suggest that the twin pillars of karma and rebirth are there in theosophical literature shortly after *Isis Unveiled* appears. In an 1879 article entitled "What is Theosophy," Blavatsky writes, "Theosophy believes also in the *Anastasis* or continued existence, and in transmigration (evolution) or a series of changes in the soul. . . ."[3] There is also some evidence to suggest that *Isis Unveiled* itself contains the ideas of karma and rebirth in substantially the same form as these ideas are found in Blavatsky's later works. To quote but one example:

> This philosophy teaches that nature never leaves her work unfinished; if baffled at the first attempt, she tries again. When she evolves a human embryo, the intention is that man shall be perfected— physically, intellectually, and spiritually. His body is to grow mature, wear out, and die; his mind unfold, ripen, and be harmoniously balanced; his divine spirit illuminate and blend easily with the *inner* man. No human being completes its grand cycle, or the "circle of necessity," until all these are accomplished.[4]

There is no reason to suggest that this quotation and others like it should not be read to mean that the eternal monad evolves through a series of human incarnations as well as other incarnations. The difficulty with Blavatsky's works lies not so much in radical shifts in her line of thinking. Rather it lies in an obviously sloppy use of terms or terminology and in the fact that in any given paragraph the discussion proceeds on two or more levels. Whether this was deliberate or not is difficult to say.

The concern of this paper is to analyze the teachings of karma and rebirth as found in the writings of H.P. Blavatsky. Originally the intent had been to look at these teachings throughout the history of the Theosophical Movement. That, however, is an ambitious project and will have to await further and certainly lengthier study. As the title indicates, my intent is to show that within the early writings of the Theosophical Movement, particularly the writings of H.P. Blavatsky, the teachings of karma and rebirth are essentially utopian in orientation. This will require a description of the teachings themselves as found in the writings of Blavatsky and an analysis of the utopian aspects of these teachings. Since this paper is included in the section dealing with the Western context of karma and rebirth, a brief justification for this placement is necessary.

THE WESTERN ORIENTATION OF H.P. BLAVATSKY

It might be argued that shortly after its beginning, the Theosophical Society became essentially Eastern in orientation. Such an argument, however, would have to be based almost entirely on two rather superficial elements—the establishment of the headquarters of the Society at Adyar in Madras, and the use of Eastern, particularly Hindu and Buddhist terminology.

Since this study is concerned with Blatavsky's writings, it is important to look at the basic tenor of her writings. In the first instance, the thrust of much of her writing is toward the Western and particularly Christian world which she perceives as peculiarly unenlightened, given to short-sighted notions of scientific materialism, decadent forms of spiritualism which teach reliance on the spirits of the deceased, and the pernicious teachings of Christianity which emphasize vicarious atonement and reliance on a God out-there rather than self-improvement and self-reliance. She writes therefore to a Western audience, perhaps an educated but confused elite. And most certainly she writes to cure this audience of the lack of hope, will, and vitality brought on by the false teachings prevalent in the Western world.

In the second instance, never does Blavatsky view her own teaching as Eastern. Clearly she views it as universal, that which lies at the heart of the teachings of all great teachers who ever lived. This is, of course, the meaning of the term occult, as used by her. It is simply a synonym for esoteric, referring to the true meaning, apart from the exoteric, of the scriptures of the world. Constant appeal is made to the esoteric meaning of passages of the Bible and other important writings of the Western world. One might argue that in Hindu and Buddhist terminology, Blavatsky merely discovers a convenient vehicle and happy justification for teachings which she has always regarded as true and universal. Indeed, she does not have to convince the Eastern audience, particularly the peasant, for in his heart of hearts, he already knows the truth about life. It is interesting to note in this respect that repeatedly, Blavatsky will appeal to esoteric interpretations of the New Testament as a justification for her teachings. Witness for example, the following interpretation of St. John:

> Christ, or the fourth Gospel at any rate, teaches reincarnation as also the annihilation of the personality, if you but forget the dead letter and hold to the esoteric Spirit. Remember verses 1 and 2 in chapter XV of St. John. What does the parable speak about if not the *upper triad* in man? *Atma* is the Husbandman—the Spiritual Ego or Buddhi (Christos) the Vine, while the animal and vital Soul, the *personality* is the branch.[5]

When she speaks of Eastern scriptures and traditions she does not speak of them in terms of having discovered something new, but always in terms of an ancient universal tradition which has been lost in the West and must be recovered.[6]

In addition to her appeal to a Western audience, there is also a concern to appear Western in the sense of being scientific, logical, and rational. In this respect there is a telling statement in the *Mahatma Letters*.

> Our philosophy falls under the definition of Hobbes. It is preeminently the science of effects by their causes and of causes by their effects, and since it is also the science of things deduced from first principle, as Bacon defines it, before we admit any such principle we must know it, and have no right to admit even its possibility.[7]

In her discussion of the theory of the periodic appearance of planetary chains, Blavatsky states that such a theory is more logical, probable, and philosophical than theories offered by Western scientists of the day.[8]

KARMA

The outline of the teaching concerning karma and rebirth is not particularly difficult or profound. Much more interesting, and perhaps important, are the claims made for the universality and significance of the teachings. However, a description of the outlines of belief is important, since by all accounts they played a central role in the teachings of the Society. Since the basic tenet of the Society was freedom of thought, belief in karma and rebirth was not required for membership in the Society. According to an 1879 article entitled "What is Theosophy?" the single "sin" for which one could be expelled was not rejection of particular doctrinal statements; rather it was dogmatism.

> We do not permit in it the shadow of dogmatism, whether of religion or of science. Each in his own particular branch does and acts as it seems good to him, but no one thinks of imposing his ideas on others in our general meetings. A member who would say to his

> "Brother" of another religion: "Believe as I do or you will be damned," or who would try to make him believe that he alone possessed truth, or who would insult his beliefs, would be immediately expelled from the society.[9]

While one merely had to take the position of a searcher for truth, wherever that search might lead, in order to be included in the Society, the teaching of karma and rebirth was regarded by the founders, and particularly by Blavatsky, to be the cornerstone of the esoteric teaching contained in all great philsophies[10] and to be of central importance in the education of the human race. It is a theme to which Blavatsky continually returns in her writings.

Simply stated, karma is the moral law of retribution, an immutable law which adjusts effects to causes according to the principle of universal harmony. It is to be distinguished from the general law of cause and effect or compensation which applies to all of life, inasmuch as the law of karma is a moral law implying moral responsibility and merit and demerit.[11] Properly, therefore, the discussion and application of karma applies to beings in the human realm; in other words, to the realm in which one finds the operation of consciousness and moral responsibility. Blavatsky, for example, makes a basic distinction between the human realm where one finds operative the law of karma and the animal realm where one thinks in terms of a general law of compensation:

> The law of *compensation* is also active in the animal world. A dog, that has to exercise its own sagacity to find food, will sooner develop psychical powers in that direction than one that does nothing but eat and sleep, and the individual or differentiated monad of the former will sooner reach the condition necessary to enter the human kingdom.[12]

There is then a general law of cause and effect which operates to effect both harmony and progress in the universe as such, and a moral law which is more properly thought of as retributive in nature, but which also effects both harmony and progress in the world of man.

In an 1889 article entitled "Thoughts on Karma and Reincarnation," karma is described in the context of the rejection of faulty Christian notions:

> Karma thus, is simply *action*, a concatenation of *causes* and *effects*. That which adjusts each effect to its direct cause; that which guides invisibly and as unerringly these effects to choose, as the field of their operation, the *right person in the right place*, is what we call

> *Karmic Law*. What is it? Shall we call it the hand of providence? We cannot do so, especially in Christian lands, because the term has been connected with, and interpreted theologically as, the *foresight* and *personal design* of a personal god; and because in the active laws of Karma—*absolute Equity*—based on the Universal Harmony, there is neither foresight nor desire; and because again, it is our own actions, thoughts and deeds which *guide that law*, instead of being guided by it.[13]

In this quotation one finds the ideas frequently associated with karma in Blavatsky's writings—the emphasis on cause and effect working unerringly, the application of moral responsibility to the individual, the affirmation of equity and harmony, and the rejection of providence, or a personal god who somehow guides and directs the life of the individual. Simply put, through the law of cause and effect we reap in a future life, the results of our thoughts and actions in this life. There is involved here a sense of punishment, but not punishment by a personal god; rather karma can be viewed as retribution or reward which we bring upon ourselves since all of our thoughts and actions bear results or consequences which are experienced by the actor. Blavatsky states:

> Hence Karma gives back to everyman the *actual consequences* of his own actions, without any regard to their moral character; but since he receives his due for *all*, it is obvious that he will be made to atone for all his sufferings which he caused, just as he will reap in joy and gladness the fruits of all the happiness and harmony he helped to produce.[14]

While we do not know the law of karma per se, we can, supposedly, describe quite accurately how it works. Thus one can say with certainty that the distinctions or differences one finds in life between classes and sexes, the inequalities one notices and experiences, are due to the working of the law of karma.[15] One finds here not only certainty in relating one's experiences to the functioning of the law of karma, but something approaching a karmic calculus in which one can relate specific recent historical incidents to specific actions which occurred centuries ago. The key here is of course the notion of a reincarnating monad which will suffer or be rewarded for the activities of its previous incarnations. The telling piece in this respect is an article entitled *Karmic Visions* which depicts the life and sufferings of Frederick III of Prussia who was supposedly the same individual who inhabited the body of Clovis, King of the Franks. It is a remarkable and moving story in which the throat disease of Frederick is attributed to the fact that Clovis pierced the throat of a witch in a fit of rage over her prophecy.[16] The explanation of this phenomenon is found in a clearly stated passage in *Key to Theosophy* in which human activity is compared to the ripples caused by a pebble thrown into the water:

> . . .*all* action, on every plane, produces disturbance in the balanced harmony of the Universe, and the vibrations so produced will continue to roll backwards and forwards, if its area is limited, till equilibrium is restored. But since each such disturbance starts from some particular point, it is clear that equilibrium and harmony can only be restored by the reconverging *to that same point* of all the forces which were set in motion from it. And here you have all the proof that the consequences of a man's deeds, thoughts, etc., must all react upon *himself* with the same force with which they were set in motion.[17]

Included in the understanding of karma are three key ideas—interdependence, harmony or equilibrium, and progress. The idea of interdependence allows for a wider application of the law of karma beyond just the individual. There is, according to Theosophy, such a thing as distributive karma, which means that the actions of individuals whether for good or ill have a wider effect than merely the life of the individual himself. It is here that Theosophy finds the answer to the question of societal or general suffering and its antidote. One can speak, in other words, of collective karma, aggregate karma, national karma, or even world karma, something which Blavatsky referred to as the "wider track" of karma in which "the aggregate of individual Karma becomes that of the nation to which those individuals belong, and. . .the sum total of National Karma is that of the World."[18] Speaking against the idea of separateness Blavatsky states:

> It is held as a truth among Theosophists that the interdependence of Humanity is the cause of what is called Distributive Karma, and it is this law which affords the solution to the great question of collective suffering and its relief. It is an occult law, moreover, that no man can rise superior to his individual failings, without lifting, be it ever so little, the whole body of which he is an integral part. In the same way, no one can sin, nor suffer the effects of sin alone.[19]

Further, the law of karma functions to restore harmony or equilibrium wherever that harmony has been disturbed. Since all action serves to disturb the balance or harmony of the universe, the law of karma works to restore that balance. In this sense karma is referred to as "an unfailing redresser of human injustice, and of all the failures of nature;

a stern adjuster of wrongs; a retributive law which rewards and punishes with equal impartiality."[20] According to Blavatsky, all pain and suffering is simply the result of a lack of harmony which in turn is caused by some form of selfishness which will eventually be removed through the functioning of the law of karma.

The movement toward the re-establishment of harmony must itself be understood as a progressive movement, or more accurately as evolution. According to Blavatsky, nature, under the influence of karma, moves ever forward.[21] This progress involves two aspects. On the one hand, the law of karma must be seen as a stern but wise and just taskmaster which educates the ego or the eternal monad through punishment or retribution. Thus the rebirth of the individual ego under the sway of the active law of karma is described as follows:

> It is at this moment that the future destiny of the now-rested Ego trembles on the scales of just Retribution, as *it* now falls once again under the sway of active Karmic law. It is this rebirth which is ready for *it*, a rebirth selected and prepared by this mysterious, inexorable, but in the equity and wisdom of its decrees infallible LAW, that the sins of the previous life of the Ego are punished.[22]

On the other hand, rebirth or reincarnation under the influence of the infallible karmic law is seen as necessary for the development of those qualities which allow the reincarnating ego to become more than human, or deity itself. This is described as a collecting or gathering process which results in the breaking out of a new form of life from a chrysalis:

> Collecting from every terrestrial personality, into which Karma forces it to incarnate, the nectar alone of the spiritual qualities and self-consciousness, it unites all these into one whole and emerges from its chrysalis as a glorified Dhyan Chohan.[23]

The individual ego must therefore be understood as a pilgrim moving forward in its attempt to regain a type of promised land, that is, the original status which it once had, the status of a god. Karma is the just, stern, and in the end, loving law under which this pilgrim ego moves forward. The mechanism through which this is made possible is of course rebirth, the second of the two pillars of Theosophy.

REBIRTH

As the discussion thus far, and particularly the quotations indicate, one cannot speak of karma without at the same time speaking of rebirth.

They are, in Blavatsky's writings, the twin principles on which all else hangs. For Blavatsky it is unthinkable that life should not be continuous. Rebirth is simply another term for continuity, and such continuity can supposedly be defended and buttressed by both philosophical and scientific arguments.

In spite of the appeal to both science and philosophy, there is very little of either scientific or philosophical argument for rebirth and karma. Usually in Blavatsky's writings both concepts are accepted as common-sense and self-evident realities which no thinking person would reject. There are, of course, the usual arguments from analogy. Witness for example the following analogy to a tree:

> Like a mighty tree that clothes itself every spring with a new foliage, to see it wither and die towards autumn, so the eternal Monad prevails through the series of smaller cycles, ever the same, yet ever changing and putting on, at each birth a new garment. The bud, that failed to open one year, will reappear in the next, the leaf that reached its maturity and died a natural death—can never be reborn on the same tree again.[24]

In addition to analogies, appeal is made to the testimony of seers, sages, and prophets from time immemorial, to the mass of inferential evidence and the universality and innateness of the belief in reincarnation. As is the case with the concept of karma, it is Blavatsky's contention that rebirth or reincarnation is taught by all major thinkers and scriptures, particularly Jesus in the New Testament. In the final analysis it is seen as a belief which makes eminently more sense than the belief that man is created by God for one brief span of life, a belief which is viewed as senseless and fiendish.[25] Such an idea is further seen as preposterous, since it refuses to recognize continuity for man's spiritual life when at the same time the principle of continuity is recognized for inorganic matter.[26] The idea of rebirth is therefore supported by persuasive rhetoric and analogies designed to convince by emotional impact rather than by close reasoned argumentation and detailed scientific data.

In the discussion of rebirth much attention was given by Blavatsky to the details of man's constitution. There are here two significant issues for early theosophical writing: what is man's constitution and with respect to this constitution what reincarnates and what happens to the reincarnating monad? Considerable controversy was raised concerning the division of man's constitution. In Blavatsky's writings, particularly the early writings, man's constitution was said in some instances to be threefold, and in other instances to be sevenfold. To the end Blavatsky claimed that there was no contradiction, but that the sevenfold constitution was merely a more detailed explanation or expansion of the three aspects of man, body, spirit, and soul. Most often then man was seen as having a septenary constitution. The number seven was apparently seen as a particularly auspicious occult number, and surfaced as well with respect to planets and cycles. Again, it is the contention of Blavatsky that the threefold constitution of man expanded into the sevenfold constitution is taught by ancient Greek philosophy, the New Testament, and the true Hindu and Buddhist scriptures and movements.

The basic division of man's constitution can be found in two almost identical charts, one found in an 1882 article and the other found in the later book, *The Key To Theosophy*.[27] In the first instance man can be seen as twofold. The lower quaternary, or the four principles which do not reincarnate, but are destined for annihilation, is made up of the physical body (*sthūla-śarīra* or *rūpa*), the life-principle (*prāṇa* or *jīva*), the astral body (*liṅga-śarīra*) and the seat of animal desires or passions (*kāma-rūpa*). The higher trinity, which is destined for reincarnation, is made up of mind or intelligence (*manas*), the spiritual soul (*buddhi*), and pure spirit (*ātma*). In the second instance these seven elements are seen as threefold: body made up of *sthūla-śarīra, jīva,* and *liṅga-śarīra*; soul made up of *kāma rūpa,* and *manas*; and spirit made up of *buddhi* and *ātma*.

It is in the explanation of these seven elements that the early theosophical view of reincarnation is found. The physical body or *sthūla-śarīra* is the vehicle of all other elements during life. *Prāṇa* or the life principle is necessary for the functioning of *sthūla-śarīra, liṅga-śarīra, kāma-rūpa,* and the lower *manas*. The *liṅga-śarīra* or astral body is merely the phantom double of the physical body. *Kāma-rūpa,* the seat of animal desires and passions is the line of demarcation between mortal and immortal man. *Manas* or mind links the eternal monad to mortal man during a life time. Strictly speaking, reincarnation does not at all apply to these principles except perhaps to *manas*. The first four which make up the lower quaternary are destined for annihilation after death. Whether anything of *manas* continues depends on whether it gravitates towards the animal passions or towards *buddhi*. In the latter case, the spiritual aspirations of *manas* will be absorbed by *buddhi* to form the ego which goes to a temporary state of bliss known as *devachan*.[28] Blavatsky states:

> The general and almost invariable rule is the merging of the personal into the individual or immortal consciousness of the Ego, a transformation or a divine transfiguration, and the entire annihilation only of the lower *quaternary*. Would you expect the man of flesh, or the *temporary* personality, his shadow, the "astral," his animal instincts and even physical life, to survive with the "spiritual

> Ego" and become sempiternal? Naturally all this ceases to exist, either at, or soon after corporeal death. It becomes in time entirely disintegrated and disappears from view, being annihilated as a whole.[29]

It is only the purer principles, *manas* if it tends toward *buddhi*, *buddhi* itself, and *ātma* which are guaranteed perpetuation through a series of lives. These are the purer portions of man, constituting his essential individuality.[30] In reality, however, it will not do to say that reincarnation applies to all three of these aspects. The dual nature of *manas* complicates matters. If it gravitates toward *buddhi*, it is absorbed by it and continues with *buddhi* and *ātma* to make up the three-fold ego of man. If *manas* gravitates to the animal passions, its link with the reincarnating ego is severed and it shares the fate of annihilation which awaits the lower quaternary.[31] Thus the *manas* does not always share in reincarnation. *Ātma* too, presents certain difficulties. Strictly speaking the *ātma* does not reincarnate since it is never really embodied in a physical vehicle. *Ātma* is pure universal spirit, a divine essence which is not the individual property of anyone, which never enters wholly into man but is only reflected through its vehicle, *buddhi*:

> It only overshadows the mortal; that which enters into him and pervades the whole body being only its omnipresent rays, or light, radiated through *Buddhi*, its vehicle and direct emanation. This is the secret meaning of the assertions of almost all the ancient philosophers, when they said that "the *rational* part of man's soul" never entered wholly into man, but only overshadowed him more or less through the *irrational* spiritual soul or *Buddhi*.[32]

Thus the presence of *ātma* in man is allowed only through radiation or emanation.

In answer to the query, What is reincarnated?, Blavatsky answers:

> The Spiritual thinking Ego, the permanent principle in man, or that which is the seat of *Manas*. It is not Atma, or even Atma-Buddhi, regarded as the dual *Monad*, which is the *individual*, or *divine* man, but Manas; for Atman is the Universal All, and becomes the Higher-Self of man only in conjunction with Buddhi, its vehicle, which links It to the individuality (or divine man). For it is the Buddhi-Manas which is called *Causal body*, (the United 5th and 6th Principles) and which is *Consciousness*, that connects it with every personality it inhabits on earth.[33]

Ātma according to Blavatsky is not an individual spirit, but is the universally diffused divine principle which shines on all like the sunshine, and *buddhi* is the vehicle of this principle. When these two are reflected in or united with *manas*, then *manas* becomes the thinking spiritual ego, the "real individuality" or the "divine man" which "having originally incarnated in the *senseless* human form animated by, but unconscious (since it had no consciousness) of, the presence in itself of the dual monad—made of that human-like form *a real man*."[34]

It is in the relationship of *ātma* to *buddhi* and *manas* that one sees the theosophical view of man's destiny. It is to move towards unity with *ātma*, an absorption with *ātma*, an achievement which is seen as an ascension to higher and higher forms of existence. This, however, is possible only through the process of rebirth in which one develops fully the various aspects and powers of his essential being through gathering together and unifying the essence of all experiences. One emerges as a purely spiritual or divine being. It is here where the analogy of the chrysalis becomes applicable. The spiritual ego is not pure enough to be one with *ātma*. Thus it must purify itself through a series of rebirths first in the lower kingdoms of life and then in the higher human planes.[35]

It is with reference to the spiritual ego that one also sees the relationship between karma and rebirth in theosophical thought. We have already seen that *buddhi* and *ātma* are not of any use on the human level unless united with consciousness of *manas*, which in conjunction with *ātma* and *buddhi* becomes the real individual or divine man. It is this *manas* which is said to be subject to karma and not *ātma* or *buddhi*. It is the theosophical position that "neither *atma* or buddhi are ever reached by karma."[36] At this point one arrives at a curious suggestion that *ātma* is the "highest aspect of Karma, *its working agent* of ITSELF."[37] Thus karma is a universal law but part and parcel of *ātma* itself. At any rate it is *manas* which is held responsible for the activities of each new personality.[38]

Further, karma affects the *manas* only during its time within a human body, not before or after the death of that body. Blavatsky looked with horror upon the idea that there was in some sense a hell or paradise in which one received either punishment or rewards for activities on earth. It was inconceivable to her that activities engaged in on earth would somehow receive their response in another world. They must be rewarded and punished in another earthly life.[39] Thus karma awaits the rebirth of the ego in order to function actively:

> After allowing the Soul, escaped from the pangs of personal life, a sufficient, aye, a hundredfold compensation, Karma, with its army of Skandhas, waits at the threshold of Devachan, when the *Ego* re-emerges to assume a new incarnation. It is at this moment that the future destiny of the now-rested Ego trembles on the scales of just Retribution, as *it* now falls once again under the sway of active Karmic law. It is this rebirth which is ready for *it*, a rebirth selected

> and prepared by this mysterious, inexorable, but in the equity and wisdom of its decrees infallible LAW, that the sins of the previous life of the Ego are punished.[40]

In order to make some sense of this, some attention must be given to Blavatsky's view of the fortunes of the individual ego in and between the rounds of rebirth. As has been stated the aspects of man which are in any sense permanent and infinite are *manas, buddhi,* and *ātma*. At the end of a human life all other aspects are destined for destruction. The more spiritualized aspects of *manas* are assimilated by *buddhi* when it follows *ātma* to a state of rest.[41] This Blavatsky refers to as the divine individuality, distinct from the finite personality made up of the lower *manas* and *kāma-rūpa*, in an effort to distinguish Theosophy from spiritists. She argues:

> There is a mighty difference in our Occult doctrine between an *impersonal* Individuality, and an individual *Personality*. C.C.M. will not be reincarnated; nor will he in his next birth be C.C.M., but quite a new being, born of the thoughts and deeds of C.C.M.: his own creation, the child and fruit of his present life, the effect of the *causes* he is now producing. Shall we say then with the spiritists that C.C.M., the man we know will be reborn again? No: but that his divine Monad will be clothed thousands of times yet before the end of the Grand Cycle, in various human forms, every one of them a *new* personality.[42]

The notion that the personal identity continues after death was also seen to be a result of corrupt teachings of the church.

Normally the spiritual monad is not immediately reborn upon death. This again is asserted against the Spiritists, who are seen as teaching the opposite.[43] The physical body, *sthūla-śarīra*, *prāṇa*, the life principle, and the *liṅga-śarīra* or astral body, dissolve immediately upon death. The remaining elements go on to *kāma-loka*. Thus according to Blavatsky man becomes a quintile just after death, made up of *ātma, buddhi,* two-fold *manas* and *kāma-rūpa*. *Kāma-loka* is supposedly a realm of existence surrounding the earth. Here one awaits a second death which involves the separation of the upper triad, *ātma-buddhi-manas* from *kāma-rūpa* and the lower or terrestrial aspect of *manas*. After a time, *kāma-rūpa* and the terrestrial aspect of *manas* disintegrate. According to Blavatsky, it is this part of man, bereft of *ātma, buddhi,* and higher *manas* which appears in the seance rooms of spiritists.[44]

Following the second death, the *ātma-buddhi-manas* complex moves on to *devachan* which one might describe as an existence of bliss in a paradise. Each incarnating ego earns the right to such a respite according the immutable law of justice and in accord with logic. In an emotional passage in which Blavatsky describes the lot of man on earth as more sinned against than sinning, she declares:

> Life is at best a heartless play, a stormy sea to cross, and a heavy burden often too difficult to bear. . . . And are we to believe that poor, helpless man, after being tossed about like a piece of rotten timber on the angry billows of life is, if he proves too weak to resist them, to be punished by a *sempiternity* of damnation, or even a temporary punishment? Never! Whether a great or average sinner, good or bad, guilty or innocent, once delivered of the burden of physical life, the tired and worn out *Manu* ("thinking Ego") has won the right to a period of absolute rest and bliss. The same unerringly wise and just rather than merciful Law, which inflicts upon the incarnated Ego the Karmic punishment for every sin committed during the preceding life on Earth, provided for the now disembodied Entity a long lease of mental rest, i.e., the entire oblivion of every sad event, aye, to the smallest painful thought, that took place in its last life as a personality, leaving in the soul-memory but the reminiscence of that which was bliss, or led to happiness.[45]

That this should take place is logical for Blavatsky in that the incarnating ego needs these periods of rest in order for it to be able to stand the stresses and strains of each incarnation. This period in *devachan* is also the work of karma and in this context Blavatsky refers to karma as the "tender mother, who heals the wounds inflicted by her during the preceding life."[46] With reference to one's terrestrial existence karma is a relentless punisher of sins committed in previous lives.

While life is seen by man as a burden, as unfair in many respects, according to the just law of karma, every suffering—whether mental or physical—is a consequence of activities of the incarnating ego in some previous existence. Although man does not sense or see this during life, there are two points at which this becomes very clear to the incarnating ego. The first is at the moment of death when the ego sees the justice of the whole chain of cause and effect up to that point. The second is the moment of rebirth when the ego has a prospective vision realizing all the causes which have led to the life he is about to undergo.[47]

Blavatsky speaks of one exception to this cycle of terrestrial activity followed by a period of bliss in *devachan*. In the case of an individual who has developed no spiritual qualities worth preserving, there is no devachanic bliss, but death is followed immediately by rebirth. Blavatsky likens this situation to sleeping through or missing a station along a railway.[48] In such a case nothing or little of the *manas* from the present life is preserved to be developed and enjoyed in *devachan*. The *manas* of such an individual perishes at death, and the divine monad is reborn grasping on to any faint traces of good karma from the previous life and the impressions of personalities from previous incarnations on the divine monad in order to build a new personality. The present "lost" life simply becomes a blank.[49]

The working of the law of karma in the final analysis results in real growth. Real growth according to Blavatsky is growth which progresses evenly. Man's tendency, however, is to cultivate uneven growth, that is, to pay inordinate attention to some aspects of his personality while neglecting others. The result is exaggerated growth in some areas and little or no growth in other areas. Karma evens things out, resulting in the growth of neglected aspects of the individual and real progress to higher states of existence.[50]

It should be clear from any analysis of Blavatsky's works that there is a single idea which ties her reflections on rebirth to her thoughts on karma. This is the idea of progress. One does not speak here merely of continuity, but of becoming or growth. Rebirth, just as karma, is essentially a mechanism for progress. Indeed, rebirth becomes the means whereby progress is achieved under the sway of the law of karma.

The most obvious instance in which the belief in progress is registered is in the rejection of the traditional Indian or Hindu teaching that regress from human to animal stages is possible through rebirth. For this reason the term reincarnation is used in preference to metempsychosis which Blavatsky takes to mean transmigration of a human soul into animal form. This is impossible according to Blavatsky for the simple reason that the course of nature is forward, the principle under which it operates is progress. While the possibility of momentary regression under the influence of karma is permitted, at least on the moral level, once the monad has reached the human level, it does not regress again to animal levels which are considered as lower levels of life.[51]

The belief in progress is seen further in the discussion of the fortunes of individuals who suddenly become despicable or criminal, to all appearances beyond redemption. While the *manas* or human soul of such an individual may indeed perish, and the rest afforded by the devachanic state may be lost for the moment, there is still a forward movement in that *ātma* and *buddhi* combine with the impressions of any good *karma* from the previous life, however faint, and the impressions left by the personalities of previous existences in order to form a new personality and physical form. Blavatsky likens the spiritual monad to a thread upon which are strung a series of personalities, and each personality leaves upon the divine ego its higher spiritual impressions. This is true even of the depraved individual. Undergirding this line of thought is an optimistic view of the human being which asserts that no human being, however criminal, is utterly depraved throughout his life. Again it is the principle of progress which asserts itself here. In discussing the depraved or useless individual Blavatsky states:

> Nature must always progress, and each fresh attempt is more successful than the previous one. This fresh evolution is due to the latent potentiality of life it has within itself. In the same manner, although one particular personality may be so depraved as to be entirely dissociated from the spiritual monad and go into the *eighth* sphere, where annihilation is its lot, yet the impressions of the previous personalities upon the higher Ego have in them potentiality enough to evolve a new physical Ego.[52]

The hallmark of nature then is growth, progress, or becoming, and man, as part of nature, is part of this becoming. And the travels of the divine ego through both terrestrial life and the post-mortem states of existence are designed to aid the ego in perfecting itself, in following undeviatingly its course to a final transformation in which it becomes a divine being. Even the loss of one's personality is seen by Blavatsky as a help in the progress of the individual.

Progress for Blavatsky is simply another term for evolution. One finds throughout her works repeated references to evolution. The emphasis however, is on spiritual rather than physical evolution, although the physical is not forgotten. Purely physical evolution, however, is rejected. Constant reference is made by Blavatsky to materialists, whom she finds as sinister as misguided Christians and spiritists, and who are viewed as the offspring of Charles Darwin. It is the search for man's divine self which is significant although the material is transformed through such a search or more correctly, through such an evolution. The goal in other words is to become a new more perfect man whose "capabilities and faculties will receive a corresponding increase in range and power, just as in the visible world. . .each stage in the evolutionary scale is marked by an increase of capacity."[53]

Behind the belief in evolution lies the belief in the involution of the Great Spirit, the primal unity which one finds so prevalent in modern interpretations of Advaita Vedānta. In the final analysis there is an evolutionary process, a progress toward the re-establishment of harmony only because the divine spirit or primal unity at some point became many. In a remarkable essay entitled "The Origin of Evil" Blavatsky states:

> Ancient wisdom alone solves the presence of the universal field in a satisfactory way. It attributes the birth of the Kosmos and the evolu-

> tion of life to the breaking asunder of primordial manifested Unity into plurality, or the great illusion of form.[54]

Evolution is merely the process of reconvergence to the point from which all vibrations began, to use the analogy of ripples caused by a stone thrown into water.

Evolution or progress is possible, indeed inevitable, only because the divine spirit is in everything, in the smallest particle of the universe. In this sense nature is eternal and uncreated. Deity for Blavatsky is not a personal, extra-cosmic, anthropomorphic entity but rather "the mysterious power of evolution and involution, the omnipresent, omnipotent, and even omniscient creative potentiality."[55] Thus the belief in involution and evolution is simply the belief in cycles, of the periodic appearance of the universe in the objective form in which we experience it.[56] It is the belief in passage from homogeneity to heterogeneity and back to homogeneity again. Karma and rebirth in turn are merely a part of this process applied to the realm of human affairs.

Blavatsky offers in *Isis Unveiled* an ingenious interpretation of the Genesis story on cyclical lines maintaining that Adam, an androgynous creature, a god-man, fell subject to the hints of the serpent-matter, thus breaking the androgynal union to form two separate entities. The movement back to the point of androgynal union, or the kingdom of the spirit can only be won through a long imprisonment in matter, in other words, evolution through numerous rebirths.[57] Darwin, it is said, merely shows that the highest forms (humans) evolve from the lowest, but has nothing to say about the travels of the monad through all the elements until the human level is reached and then beyond the human level.[58] *The Secret Doctrine* also echoes this cyclical view, but on a grander scale, when it says:

> . . .the one eternal Law unfolds everything in the (to be) manifested Nature on a sevenfold principle; among the rest, the countless circular chains of worlds, composed of seven globes, graduated on the four lower planes of the world of formation (the three others belonging to the Archetypal Universe). Out of these seven only *one, the lowest and most material* of these globes is within our plane or means of perception, the six others lying outside of it and being therefore invisible to the terrestrial eye. Every such chain of worlds is the progeny and creation of another, *lower* and *dead* chain—*its reincarnation,* so to say.[59].

CONCLUSION

The teaching of karma and rebirth in Blavatsky's writings is essentially a charter for the establishment of utopia and utopian hopes. The term utopia should not be understood to mean an unchanging resting place; rather it refers simply to the achievement of higher or better forms of existence in which the limitations and problems one experiences now are eliminated. I would argue that Blavatsky's concern is to establish the beliefs in karma and rebirth because of the benefits and advantages which she feels would result from the acceptance of these beliefs. Her concern is less with the details of the teachings and the scientific and philosophical evidence for the teachings than with spreading the good news of karma and rebirth. Detail that is given is often given only in response to charges of confusion, ambiguity, and contradiction. Throughout her writings one finds constant criticism of spiritists, Christians, and materialists who are regarded as spreaders of doom and gloom and blasphemers of the sacred. Against these she places theosophists who are preachers of truth, hope, and responsibility through their doctrines of karma and rebirth.[60]

The utopian character of these teachings becomes evident in a number of ways. The most obvious is in the belief in and the assertion of progress through karma and rebirth; in other words, in the evolutionary character of the teachings. Regression to lower physical and mental levels is rejected. The movement of life is always forward, with each new attempt better than the previous one. Life is seen as a pilgrimmage toward a re-establishment of the harmony and unity which existed before involution, toward the development of the divine being which man is in his true essence. It is, of course, a pilgrimmage which involves pain. All religions and philosophies, Blavatsky states, teach that true spiritual insight can only be had through a hard, painful, troublesome path, that man becomes a developed being through growth, but that this necessarily involves pain.[61]

The goal of this painful evolutionary process is a new man, in effect a divine being who realizes and lives according to the unity of all of life. He is a being more perfect than he is at present, one whose powers and capabilities have increased immeasurably. In effect he is one who has entered a higher plan of existence.[62] The belief in rebirth is essentially a belief in the ascension of life to higher and higher levels of existence, towards the unity from which all came or emanated in the first place. When Blavatsky speaks of the various aspects which make up the human being, she speaks of man as having three souls: the terrestrial or animal, the human, and the spiritual. The first, which includes the animal passions and desires, and the lower aspects of *manas*, is destined to oblivion. The second, or *manas*, survives in its higher or divine aspects, if not misused. The third, *buddhi*, "becomes *consciously* divine by the assimilation of the higher Manas."[63] This is the growth or evolution to higher forms of existence; it means to arrive at a point through the process of rebirth, where the spiritual ego or *buddhi* through assimilating that which is spiritual in the *manas* can manifest itself uninterruptedly.[64] This is what it means to become truly divine, conscious of one's unity with the divine All, the *ātma*. Blavatsky describes the belief in rebirth in the following way:

> It is a belief in a perpetual progress for each incarnating Ego, or divine soul, in an evolution from the outward into the inward, from the material to the spiritual, arriving at the end of each stage at absolute unity with the divine Principle. From strength to strength, from the beauty and perfection of one plane to the greater beauty and perfection of another, with accessions of new glory, of fresh knowledge and power in each cycle, such is the destiny of every Ego, which thus becomes its own Saviour in each world and incarnation.[65]

The utopian character of karma and rebirth is also seen in the effects which Blavatsky believes the teachings of Theosophy will have on mankind and on nations. In Blavatsky's mind, no other teachings are as conducive to goodness, beauty, and compassion. This is, of course, in keeping with one of the objectives of the Theosophical Society, the creation of a universal brotherhood without distinction of race, creed, or colour. The greatest truth which no theologian can surpass is, for Blavatsky, the teaching that "everything that is, is made of the same essence and substance, is animated by the same spirit, and that, consequently, everything in nature, whether physical or moral, is bound in solidarity."[66] This is a truth which one learns through the process of rebirth under the law of karma.

Repeatedly Blavatsky asserts in her writings that the teachings of Theosophy, if accepted, have the power to change life for the better and to counteract the insidious influence of teachers of falsehood, particularly Christians, spiritists, and materialists. Theosophy Blavatsky exclaims "develops in man a direct beholding. . .so that man thinks divine thoughts, views all things as they really are, and, finally, becomes recipient of the Soul of the World."[67] In true Theosophy, she asserts, there is no destructive bigotry but only a single-minded pursuit of truth wherever this might lead. Of the Society she says, "Day and night, we work in common for the spiritual regeneration of morally blind individuals, as well as for the elevation of the fallen nation."[68] Theosophy is regarded as the only cure for the selfishness of mankind, a selfishness which incidentally is attributed to the teachings of the Mosaic Bible which is seen as pandering to passions, conquest, annexation, and tyranny.[69] Selfishness and destructive passion are overcome by accepting as axiomatic the belief that everything in the universe is of one essence, and that therefore, by wronging one part of creation, man wrongs himself and the whole of humanity.[70]

Conversely, one who perfects himself cannot help but move mankind indeed the whole universe, forward on the path to perfection.[71]

Essentially Blavatsky calls for the inculcation in mankind of responsibility and compassion as well as hope. The development of these qualities would rest on the knowledge that man is not a separate being, that he is responsible for his own present condition as well as the present condition of his surroundings, that he is responsible for his own perfection as well as the perfection of mankind, and that this is achieved through the process of growth or evolution or rebirth under the law of karma. In rough terms these are the laws of nature which man must come to know. Blavatsky believes that it is knowledge of the laws of nature or Theosophy, the twin pillars of karma and rebirth which will create a society characterized by virtue. As proof for this assertion she appeals to a comparison of the religious civilizations of Ceylon and India and declares that according to the latest census one finds far less crime among the Buddhist populations of these countries than one finds among the Christians.[72] The reason for this is not far to seek. Buddhists rather than Christians have understood the laws of nature, particularly the keys to occult teaching, karma and rebirth, and have sought to live according to this understanding.

The utopian character of Blavatsky's teaching on karma and rebirth therefore points in two directions. On the one hand mankind can look forward to and strive for the achievement of ever higher states of existence in which the problems and limitations of the present are left behind. On the other hand, taking seriously the laws of karma and rebirth will result in the improvement of present society, the establishment of goodness, beauty, compassion, and unity, and the elimination of the basic human problem, selfishness.

NOTES

The author wishes to express his appreciation for helpful suggestions and responses from Mr. Ted Davy, General Secretary of the Canadian Theosophical Society.

1. Bruce F. Campbell, *Ancient Wisdom Revisited. A History of the Theosophical Movement* (Berkeley: University of California Press, 1980), p. 29.

2. Ibid., p. 39.

3. H.P. Blavatsky, *Collected Writings, Vol. II, 1879-1880* (Wheaton: The Theosophical Publishing House, n.d.), pp. 91-92.

4. H.P. Blavatsky, *Isis Unveiled, Vol. I* (Pasadena: Theosophical University Press, 1976), pp. 345-46.

5. H.P. Blavatsky, *The Key to Theosophy* (Pasadena: Theosophical University Press, 1946), pp. 186-87.

6. Robert S. Ellwood Jr. provides an interesting account of reasons for

Blavatsky's trip to India in *Alternate Altars, Unconventional and Eastern Spirituality in America* (Chicago: University of Chicago Press, 1979), pp. 104-35. He suggests that the trip was essentially a pilgrimmage in pursuit of a spiritual idea thought at that point to be more readily available in India than elsewhere.

7. *The Mahatma Letters to A.P. Sinnet*, compiled by A.T. Barker (London: T. Fischer Unwin Ltd., 1923), p. 52. There is of course disagreement over who wrote *The Mahatma Letters to A.P. Sinnet*. Whether Blavatsky wrote them or not, it is justifiable to use them as mirroring her own teachings in the volumes usually attributed to her.

8. H.P. Blavatsky, *The Secret Doctrine, Vol. I* (Pasadena: The Theosophical University Press, 1977), p. 154.

9. *Collected Writings, Vol. II*, p. 504.

10. H.P. Blavatsky, *Collected Writings, Vol. VII, 1886-1887* (Adyar: The Theosophical Publishing House, 1958), p. 177.

11. H.P. Blavatsky, *Collected Wrirings, Vol. VI, 1883-1884, 1885* (Los Angeles: Blavatsky Writings Publication Fund, 1954), pp. 236-37.

12. Ibid., p. 237.

13. H.P. Blavatsky, *Collected Writings, Vol. XI, 1889* (Wheaton: The Theosophical Publishing House, 1973), pp. 144-45.

14. *Key to Theosophy*, p. 207. An interesting comment of karma is found in *The Mahatma Letters to A.P. Sinnet*, p. 47 where karma is referred to as the great law of selection and life on earth as "the survival of the fittest."

15. Ibid., p. 202.

16. H.P. Blavatsky, *Collected Writings, Vol. IX, 1888* (Adyar: The Theosophical Publishing House, 1962), pp. 318-39.

17. *Key to Theosophy*, p. 206. *The Mahatma Letters to A.P. Sinnet*, p. 106 uses the analogy of the lamp. The Ego represents the wick and karma represents the oil. The quantity of oil depends on the difference in the duration of various karmas.

18. Ibid., p. 202.

19. Ibid., p. 203.

20. Ibid., p. 198. In *The Mahatma Letters to A.P. Sinnet*, p. 57 the source of evil is said to be the human intelligence or reason which dissociates man from Nature and exaggerates good under the influence of selfishness and greediness. But the greatest source of evil is religion, the sacerdotal castes, priests, and churches which enslave man.

21. *Collected Writings, Vol. XI*, p. 137.

22. *Key to Theosophy*, p. 141.

23. Ibid., p. 167.

24. H.P. Blavatsky, *Collected Writings, Vol. IV, 1882-1883* (Wheaton: The Theosophical Publishing House, 1969), p. 186.

25. *Key to Theosophy*, p. 111.

26. Joseph Head and S.L. Cranston (eds.), *Reincarnation: The Phoenix Fire Myster* (New York: Julian Press/Crown Publishers Inc., 1977), p. 502.

27. See "Reincarnation in Tibet" in *Collected Writings, Vol. IV*, p. 185, and *Key to Theosophy*, pp. 91-92.

28. *Key to Theosophy*, p. 92.

29. Ibid., p. 94.

30. *Collected Writings, Vol. IV,* p. 254
31. *Key to Theosophy,* pp. 103-4.
32. Ibid., pp. 101-2. See also *Collected Writings, Vol. II,* p. 94 where Blavatsky states: "The embodied soul and its never embodied spirit—the real self—are not separated from either the Universal Soul or other spirits by Space."
33. *Key to Theosophy,* p. 121.
34. Ibid., p. 136.
35. Ibid., pp. 183-84.
36. Ibid., p. 135.
37. Ibid.
38. Ibid., p. 136.
39. Ibid., p. 138. See also *The Mahatma Letters,* p. 68 where it is stated that those who propose an eternity of bliss or woe have not understood eternity nor the fact that nature operates according to the law of perfect justice and equilibrium.
40. Ibid., p. 141.
41. *Collected Writings, Vol. IV,* p. 185.
42. Ibid., p. 186. See also *The Mahatma Letters,* p. 114.
43. *Collected Writings, Vol. VII,* pp. 179-80.
44. *Key to Theosophy,* pp. 143-44. See also *The Mahatma Letters to A.P. Sinnet,* p. 48 where *Kāma-loka* is referred to as a tradition state for souls whose faculties and individuality lie dormant.
45. Ibid., pp. 139-40.
46. Ibid., p. 161.
47. Ibid., pp. 162-63.
48. Ibid., p. 170.
49. *Collected Writings, Vol. IV,* pp. 571-73.
50. *Collected Writings, Vol. VI,* pp. 332-33.
51. *Collected Writings, Vol. XI,* pp. 137-38.
52. *Collected Writings, Vol. IV,* p. 572.
53. *Collected Writings, Vol. VI,* pp. 332-33. *The Mahatma Letters,* pp. 66-70 and 93-94 include a detailed statement of the evolutionary process from one level of life to another and from globe to globe and provide the governing principle for this process: "Law in Nature is uniform and the conception, formation, birth, progress and development of a child differs from those of the globe only in magnitude" (p. 93).
54. H.P. Blavatsky, *Collected Writings, Vol. VIII, 1887* (Adyar: The Theosophical Publishing House, 1960), p. 110.
55. *Key to Theosophy,* p. 64.
56. For a discussion of the evolutionary process see *The Mahatma Letters,* pp. 94-98 and the lengthy but confusing discussion in *The Secret Doctrine, Vol. I,* pp. 152-91.
57. *Isis Unveiled, Vol. I,* p. 297. Equally ingenious is the interpretation of the "coats of skin," in Genesis 3, which are taken to mean the fleshy bodies with which the progenitors of our race become clothed in the progress of the cycles, in this case in the descending arc of the human cycle. See *Isis Unveiled, Vol. I,* pp. 310-11.
58. Ibid., p. 301.
59. *The Secret Doctrine, Vol. I,* p. 152.

60. *Collected Writings, Vol. XI,* pp. 186-202.
61. *Collected Writings, Vol. VI,* p. 331.
62. Ibid., pp. 332-33.
63. *Key to Theosophy,* pp. 121-22.
64. Ibid., p. 131.
65. Ibid., p. 155.
66. *Collected Writings, Vol. XI,* p. 128.
67. *Collected Writings, Vol. II,* p. 97.
68. Ibid., p. 502.
69. *Key to Theosophy,* pp. 40-42.
70. Ibid., p. 47.
71. Ibid., p. 203.
72. Ibid., pp. 73-74.

CHAPTER FOURTEEN

Karma and Rebirth in Western Psychology

HAROLD COWARD

Early in this century Western writers often pictured karma and rebirth as resulting in a callous fatalism. J.N. Farquhar, in his widely read, *The Crown of Hinduism*, portrayed the Indian experience of karma as follows:

> Since the sufferings of these people were justly measured requital of their past sins, no power on earth could save them from any part of their misery. Their *karma* was working itself out and would inevitably do so. Thus, Hindus not only shared the common conviction of the ancient world, that degraded tribes were like animals and could not be civilized. Their highest moral doctrine taught them that it was useless to attempt to help them in the slightest; for nothing could prevent their *karma* from bringing upon them their full tale of misery.[1]

It is not surprising then that karma and rebirth have often been understood in very negative and inhumane terms in Western thought. While it is possible to find karma equated with fate in Indian sources (e.g., in some Puranic materials), in other instances (e.g., the *Mahābhārata*) the forces of time and fate appear as non-karmic elements.[2] In Patañjali's *Yoga Sūtras* 2:12-14 and 4:7-9, karma, rather than being fatalistic or mechanistic, is understood as a memory trace or disposition from previous thought or action—an impulse which can either be acted upon and reinforced or negated by the exercise of free choice.[3] Wendy Doniger O'Flaherty has outlined the great variety of competing and contrasting understandings of karma within the Indian sources themselves.[4] Thus, it is clear that Farquhar's early presentation of karma and rebirth to the

West is unfairly one-sided. More recently the view of karma as a mental disposition which may carry over from one birth to the next has been picked up and given further development by some schools of thought in modern Western psychology. The aim of this essay is to examine the way in which karma and rebirth have been understood in modern Western psychology, and to identify the contribution these Indian concepts have made to recent psychological theory. The approach taken will be to examine the impact of karma and rebirth on Carl Jung and the currently influential school of Transpersonal Psychology.

I. KARMA AND REBIRTH IN CARL JUNG

There is no question that India had a major influence upon Jung's thought. Although many Hindu and Buddhist concepts fascinated him, it was the idea of karma and rebirth that continued to play a central role in the development of Jung's thinking to the end of his life.[5]

Jung's encounter with Eastern thought is complex, and in some respects can be described as a love/hate relationship.[6] After his break with Freud in 1910, and his 1912-1918 confrontation with the unconscious, one of the major sources Jung turned to for support and new insight was Eastern religion.[7] During the period 1920-1940, for example, the Upaniṣadic notion of *ātman* played a major role in the development of Jung's "Self" concept.[8] After 1940, and especially after his trip to India, Jung tended to turn his back on the East and adopt Western alchemy as his major source of inspiration. But the Eastern concept of karma and rebirth continued to reappear in Jung's thinking. In fact, careful analysis demonstrates that his attitude to karma and rebirth changed dramatically over the years. Throughout the last years his thinking came very close to the Indian perspective. For Jung the study of the Eastern ideas of karma and rebirth suggested that consciousness was wider than the typical modern Western fixation on the scientific intellect.[9] As we shall see these Indian ideas played a major role in the formation of Jung's archetype concept, and they continued to provoke Jung's thinking even after he had left other Eastern notions such as yogic meditation far behind.

The main basis of Jung's understanding of karma probably came from his in-depth study of Patañjali's *Yoga Sūtras*. Evidence of this comes from notes taken by Barbara Hannah at Jung's lectures given at the Eidenössische Technische Hochschule, Zürich, October 1938-June 1939. During this period Jung gave a detailed commentary on the *Yoga Sūtras* including a thorough discussion of karma in terms of *kleśas*, previous lives, and unconscious potentiality for this life.[10] Although Jung was acquainted with the more fatalistic interpretations of karma, it was the Yoga analysis of Patañjali and Vyāsa that strongly influenced his thinking.

Karma as Archetype

Although the archetype came to be Jung's most significant psychological postulate, it was an idea that evolved slowly in his mind interacting constantly with the Indian notion of karma. In the list of definitions attached to his 1921 publication *Psychological Types*, archetype is not listed, indicating that the concept was not yet formed.[11] Direct influence from Indian thought is evidenced in Jung's 1932 lectures on Kundalini Yoga. In Lecture One Jung states, "There is a rich world of archetypal images in the unconscious mind, and the archetypes are conditions, laws or categories of creative fantasy, and therefore might be called the psychological equivalent of the saṃskāra."[12] And at the end of the Fourth Lecture, in answer to the question "Are the saṃskāras archetypes?" Jung replies, "Yes, the first form of our existence is a life in archetypes."[13] Three years later in his *Psychological Commentary on "The Tibetan Book of the Dead,"* Jung is more explicit in his formulation of archetype in terms of karma theory:

> According to the Eastern view, *karma* implies a sort of psychic theory of heredity based on the hypothesis of reincarnation. . .we may cautionsly accept the idea of *karma* only if we understand it as *psychic heredity* in the very widest sense of the word. Psychic heredity does exist—that is to say, there is inheritance of psychic characteristics, such as predisposition to disease, traits of character, special gifts and so forth.[14]

By 1942, in writing his definitive work *The Psychology of the Unconscious*, Jung admits to a deliberate extension of the archetype notion by means of karmic theory. Karma, he says, is essential to a deeper understanding of the nature of the archetype.[15] The influence of karma theory of the *Yoga Sūtra* type is especially evident in the way Jung here described archetypes as at first latent (*bīja* or seed states) which later filled out or actualized (*saṃskāras* which have "sprouted and flowered").

> . . .the unconscious contains, as it were, two layers: the personal and the collective. The personal layer ends at the earliest memories of inhancy, but the collective layer comprises the pre-infantile period, that is, the residues of ancestral life. Whereas the memory-images of the personal unconscious are, as it were, filled out, because they are images personally experienced by the individual, the archetypes of the collective unconscious are not filled out because they are forms not personally experienced. On the other hand, when psychic energy regresses, going even beyond the period of early infancy, and breaks into the legacy of ancestral life, then mythological images are

awakened: these are the archetypes. An interior spiritual world whose existence we never suspected opens out and displays contents which seem to stand in sharpest contrast to all our former ideas.[16]

Although Jung himself clearly credits karma theory with the filling in of his notion of archetypes it is interesting to note that little recognition is given to this major Eastern influence by either Jacobi, Jung's systematizer, or Jungian scholars. Instead, Jacobi credits Plato's "idea and Bergson's *éternels incréés*" as sources of Jung's thought. Jacobi also cites analogies with Gestalt psychology and acknowledges Augustine as the source of the term archetype, but nowhere is mention made of karma.[17] This apparent attempt to hide or ignore the Eastern content in Jung's archetype may be an example of Western bias, or of a fear among the Jungians that such an admission would make their already suspect psychology even less acceptable to the mainstream of Western psychology. Whatever the reason, the obscuring of Jung's considerable debt to karma theory—a debt which he himself openly acknowledged—has veiled a significant impact that Eastern thought has had upon the modern West. For it is precisely the archetypal notions in Jung's psychology that have proven productive in the applications of Analytical Psychology to Western art, literature, and religion.[18]

Personal Karma, Collective Karma and Rebirth

Just as there are a variety of views in Indian thought as to the personal or collective nature of karma,[19] so also there is uncertainty over the matter in Jung's thinking. Jung seems to have been acquainted with only the Indian doctrine of personal karma, which, in his earlier writings he tended to distinguish from his own position of collective karma in the Collective Unconscious. For example, in a 1937 letter to Swami Devatmananda, Jung describes and rejects the Indian doctrine of karma as teaching retribution for each individual action and thus determining an individual's fate in his next life.[20] In a 1946 letter to Eleanor Bertine, Jung notes that our life is not made entirely by ourselves.

The main bulk of it is brought into existence out of sources that are hidden to us. Even complexes can start a century or more before a man is born. There is something like *karma*.[21]

A 1940 lecture entitled "Concerning Rebirth" cites the Buddha's experience of a long sequence of rebirths but then goes on to say, "it is by no means certain whether continuity of personality is guaranteed or not: there may only be a continuity of *karma*."[22]

The main statement of Jung's earlier position favoring collective rather than personal karma comes in his 1935 "Psychological Commentary on 'Tibetan Book of the Dead'." After characterizing the *Sidpa Bardo* as the fierce wind of karma which whirls the dead man along until he comes to the "womb-door," and the *Chonyid Bardo* as a state of karmic illusions resulting from the psychic residue of previous existences, Jung observes that neither scientific knowledge nor reason can accept the hypothesis of reincarnation assumed in the Tibetan Buddhist understanding of *Bardo* karma. But he allows that we may accept the idea of karma if we understand it as the psychic heredity of broad psychic characteristics such as traits of character, special gifts, and so forth. Just as we have inherited characteristics like eye and hair colour on the physical level, so on the psychic level there are the universal dispositions of the mind, the archetypes. These archetypes are "externally inherited forms and ideas which have at first no specific content. Their specific content only appears in the course of an individual's life, when personal existence is taken up in precisely these forms."[23] The source of the content of these inherited archetypes comes not from one's personal karma but from the collective karma of one's ancestors.[24] In a letter to E.L. Grant Watson, Jung clearly distinguishes his understanding of the personal experience of inherited karma from what he takes to be the Indian view.

> Inasmuch as *karma* means either a personal or at least individual inherited determinant of character and fate, it represents the individually differentiated manifestation of the instinctual behaviour pattern, i.e., the general archetypal disposition. *Karma* would express the individually modified archetypal inheritance represented by the collective unconscious in each individual. I avoid the term of *karma* because it includes metaphysical assumptions for which I have no evidence, i.e., that *karma* is a fate I have acquired in previous existence. . .[25]

In Jung's early thinking, therefore, there is no personal inherited karma as such, there is only the collective inherited karma of one's ancestors, the archetypes, which one creatively individuates in one's own personality development. A contemporary Jungian, Edward Edinger, proposes the Catholic image of a "treasury of merits" as helpful in understanding Jung's thinking: ". . .the psychological accomplishments of the individual leave some permanent spiritual residue that augments the cumulative collective treasury, a sort of positive collective *karma*."[26]

In a letter dated shortly before his death in 1961, Jung says that his continued wrestlings with the question of karma and rebirth has renewed his interest in the East, especially in Buddha.[27] During the last years prior to his death Jung seemed to soften his earlier rejection of the notion of personal karma and its psychological function in rebirth. The best insight into Jung's thought during this later period is found in the Chapter titled "On Life After Death" in his autobiography, *Memories, Dreams, Reflections*. Jung notes that the problem of karma and personal rebirth has remained obscure to him due to the lack of empirical evidence. But he then goes on to say,

> Recently, however, I observed in myself a series of dreams which would seem to describe the process of reincarnation. . .after this experience I view the problem of reincarnation with somewhat different eyes, though without being in a position to assert a definite opinion.[28]

Jung does not give any detailed analysis of the psychological processes which would be involved in personal reincarnation. However, he does offer a general speculation which brings him very close to traditional Indian thought.

> I could well imagine that I might have lived in former centuries and there encountered questions I was not yet able to answer; that I had to be born again because I had not fulfilled the task given to me. When I die, my deed will follow along with me—that is how I imagine it. I will bring with me what I have done.[29]

Karma as Motivation In This Life and The Next

In his later thought, Jung sees karma and rebirth in terms of a "motivation toward knowledge" which may be personal or impersonal in nature. Jung asks, "Is the *karma* I live the outcome of my past lives, or is it the achievement of my ancestors whose heritage comes together in me?"[30] He answers the question in terms of a psychological motivation toward knowledge—an approach to which Śaṃkara would surely have given his blessing. Jung perceives the meaning of his existence in terms of a question which life has addressed to him, a question which perhaps preoccupied him and/or his ancestors in a previous life, and which they could not answer. He admits that this question from the past could be the result of the collective karma of his ancestors or the result of his own karma acquired in a previous life. Either way it could be experienced today, suggests Jung, as "an impersonal archetype which presses hard on everyone and has taken particular hold on me—an archetype such as, for example, the development over the centuries of the divine triad and its confrontation with the feminine principle, or the still pending answer to the Gnostic question as to the origin of evil, or, to put it another way, the incompleteness of the Christian God-image."[31] Should Jung's way of posing the question or his answer prove unsatisfactory, then "someone who has my karma—or myself—would have to be reborn in order to give a more complete answer."[32] Thus the karmic motivation toward knowledge is the explanation for this life and the cause of the next.

Jung even goes so far as to entertain the Indian concept of release from *karma-saṃ*sāra via the path of knowledge. He says:

> It might happen that I would not be reborn again so long as the world needed no [more complete] answer, and that I would be entitled to several hundred years of peace until someone was once more needed who took an interest in these matters and could profitably tackle the task anew.[33]

Thus, for Jung, motivation for knowledge is the karma which leads from past lives into this life and on into future lives.

The notion of "an earned otherworldly peaceful pause" and the idea of "a determinant or motivation for rebirth" are both consistent with Indian theories of karma and rebirth. Jung even goes so far as to suggest that once a completeness of understanding was achieved, there would then no longer be a need for rebirth. The karmic goal of motivation for knowledge would have been realized.

> Then the soul would vanish from the three-dimensional world and attain what the Buddhists call *nirvana*. But if a *karma* still remains to be disposed of, then the soul relapses again into desires and returns to life once more, perhaps even doing so out of a realization that something remains to be completed.[34]

As to the exact motivation involved, Jung says that in his own case it must have been "a passionate urge toward understanding which brought about my birth."[35] He suggests that the psychological processes resulting in psychic dissociation illness (e.g., Schizophrenia) may provide an analogy for the understanding of life after death. Just as in a disturbed person a split-off complex can manifest itself as a projected personification, so rebirth might be conceived as a psychic projection. As evidence Jung offers one of his own dreams:

> I was walking along a little road through a hilly landscape; the sun was shining and I had a wide view in all directions. Then I came to a small wayside chapel. The door was ajar, and I went in. To my surprise, there was no image of the Virgin on the altar, and no cruci-

> fix either, but only a wonderful flower arrangement. But then I saw that on the floor sat a yogi—in lotus posture, in deep meditation. When I looked at him more closely, I realized that he had my face. I started in profound fright and awoke with the thought: "Aha, so he is the one who is meditating me. He has a dream, and I am it." I knew that when he awakened I would no longer be.[36]

In terms of analytical psychology, Jung's meditating yogi is the symbol or psychic projection of his unified Self from the other worldly reality of the archetypes. Thus, the empirical world is merely the projected karmic illusion and is characterized by an ego-conscious focus. The decisive question for man, says Jung, is: "Is he related to something infinite or not?"[37] The problem with the modern Western world is that its karma is too ego-centered. What is needed is a shift of the karmic center of gravity from the ego to the Self. For Jung this is the essence of transcendence in religious experience. In psychological terms it requires the successful individuation of the Self or God archetype. It is worth noting in passing that Jung's karmic understanding of the religious experience has had a significant impact on at least one contemporary Christian theologian, namely Paul Tillich.[38]

Empirical Evidence For Karma and Rebirth

Throughout his life Jung admitted his strong attraction to Indian karma and reincarnation theory, but its lack of empirical verification was the obstacle to its full acceptance. Most often he would classify the doctrine of reincarnation as a belief which, like the belief in God, did not admit of scientific proof.[39] Although he searched Western experience broadly, he could find only testimonies to personal experiences which could not be scientifically tested. One wonders how Jung would respond to the current studies of reincarnation by Ian Stevenson.[40] Later in life, however, Jung's dreams, which for him were empirical reality, gave him evidence pointing to his own reincarnation. It was the evidence of his own dreams, plus those of a close acquaintance, which led to a very positive assessment of Indian karma and rebirth theory in the last years before his death. To Jung, the Indian understanding seemed a great advance on the common Western view that a person's character is the particular admixture of blessings or curses which fate or the gods bestowed on the child at birth—the Western version of prenatal karma.[42]

II. Karma And Rebirth In Transpersonal Psychology

The most recent development in modern Western Psychology, Transpersonal Psychology, adopts a methodology which explicitly opens the way for influence from Hindu and Buddhist notions of karma and rebirth. Transpersonal Psychology radically widens the scope and methodologies of psychology. Modern scientific psychology is seen simply as one form of psychology amongst many others. Other psychologies can be found as part of religious traditions which are thousands of years old. Such traditions did not just act as receivers of religious experience, they also developed systematic psychological interpretations of their experiences. Transpersonal Psychology suggests that each of these traditional interpretations is as much a psychology as is the modern Western scientific interpretation. Consequently, the plural form of the term in the title of Charles Tart's book, *Transpersonal Psychologies*.[42] As Bregman puts it:

> Scriptures, and the meditative and devotional practices which are taught in these traditions, represent a distillation of generations of psychological expertise. This expertise has been based on a kind of experimentation, and represents a massive effort of reflection and systematizing. What is being claimed is that Buddhists, for example, are not only religious experiencers, but possessors of a coherent system of concepts and practices which is at least potentially comparable to a Western, modern psychological theory.[43]

Thus, through Transpersonal Psychology, the door is opened wide for the direct exposure of modern psychology to the major roles occupied by karma and rebirth in the traditional Eastern psychologies.

Karma and Rebirth as a Basic Paradigm

According to T.S. Kuhn in his *The Structure of Scientific Revolutions*, a paradigm is a theoretical formulation which interprets a wide variety of data into an internally consistent and coherent body of knowledge.[44] It quickly becomes a philosophical predisposition that directs and interprets the activity of the adherents to that paradigm. Rather than a tentatively held theory, a paradigm rapidly becomes "a dogma and defines the parameters within which researchers conduct their inquiries."[45] In this way a paradigm serves as a prism through which certain phenomena are included for inquiry while others are excluded. Until now, modern psychology has largely held to the Western Scientific paradigm. But with the recognition of the religious traditions as valid paradigms by the Transpersonal Psychologists, karma and rebirth, as a fundamental paradigm of the Eastern religions, is being given serious consideration. The karma and rebirth paradigm is extending boundaries for the understanding of human behavior in significant ways. The impact of this Eastern paradigm on theories of perception, cognition, motivation, self-regulation, and psychotherapy, may be considered as illustrative examples.

Karma Theory, Perception, Cognition and Motivation

The Eastern paradigm which sees karma functioning as a filtering device[46] has helped to focus attention on theories of constructive and/or reductive nature of cognition. Whereas modern scientific psychology has tended to adopt stimulus-response models which assume that we cognize what exists,[47] karma theories of the Jaina, Buddhist, and Hindu traditions presuppose that our ordinary awareness is a construction and not a mere registration of the external world. It is our past personal and cultural patterns of behavior that construct the karmic filters throught which our present experience is passed. In modern psychology this Eastern paradigm provided support for some philosophers and psychologists who saw the mind functioning as a reducing valve. Bergson's general proposal in this regard has been elaborated by C.D. Broad and popularized by Aldous Huxley. In *The Doors of Perception and Heaven and Hell*, Huxley quotes C.D. Broad as follows:

> [Bergson's] suggestion is that the function of the brain and nervous system and sense organs is in the main *eliminative* and not productive. Each person is at each moment capable of remembering all that has ever happened to him and of perceiving everything that is happening everywhere in the universe. The function of the brain and nervous system is to protect us from being overwhelmed and confused by this mass of largely useless and irrelevant knowledge, by shutting out most of what we should otherwise perceive or remember at any moment, and leaving only that very small and special selection which is likely to be practically useful.[48]

Huxley comments that accordingly each one of us is Mind-at-Large. But to make biological survival possible, the brain and sense organs act as a reducing valve for Mind-at-Large. "What comes out is a measly trickle of the kind of consciousness which will help us to stay alive on the surface of this particular planet."[49] Experimental studies, particularly on vision, support this view of perceptual and cognitive systems as reducers of information.[50] The eye, for example, responds to a limited range of stimuli, and once the sensory impulses reach the brain, different cells respond to different types of stimulation—certain cells detect edges and corners, others respond to movement on the retina, etc. Although sense organs have built-in ranges and limits of perception, our awareness and analysis of sense impulses is open to much construction or interpretation. Just as various computer programs can be created to sift input data, so the mind can create and change the cognitive programs by which the reported sensory stimuli are selected and acted upon. Within certain limitations we are able to reprogram and reconstruct our awareness in line with our motivations. Thus the reducing valve of the mind can be altered. Experimental work has begun to examine such mental programming activity. Karl Pribram, the neurophysiological psychologist, has demonstrated the mental filtering activity called habituation by which constancies in our environment are tuned out of awareness. For example, when we enter a room and a clock is ticking, we are aware of it for the first few minutes and then the sound is gradually tuned out. Any change in the loudness or speed of the ticking will immediately result in us hearing it again. Pribram pointed out an interesting example of this phenomenon. In New York a noisy train ran along Third Avenue at a certain time each night. When the train line was torn down people in the neighbourhood began calling the police to report strange things occuring late at night, noises, thieves, etc. These calls came at about the time of the former train. What they were hearing was the absence of the familiar noise of the train.[51] Such habituation programming forms an additional reducing valve behind the reducing valves of the senses. Jerome Bruner has conducted experiments verifying the constructive nature of our awareness. Rather than seeing reality as it is, we categorize it in the perception process. Stereotyped systems are learned through past experience for sorting out the input that reaches us. For example, when subjects were confronted with a red ace of spaces in a deck of cards they would mentally correct the image and perceive it as an ace of hearts.[52] Similarly, unless we are functioning as teachers in our correcting mode, we often miss typographical errors in what we read because as readers we do the mental correcting within ourselves under the category "correct English."

Karma theory not only provides supporting evidence and interpretation for such experiments, it suggests extrapolations which have not yet occurred to modern psychology. For example, if mental categorizing activity is learned from past behavior, then, under the theory of rebirth, the behavior of previous births, along with the behavior of this birth, helps produce the filtering categories of the mind. Karma suggests that the roots of habitual responses may be more deeply rooted in the psyche than modern psychology suspects. Much apparently pre-natal learning can be explained in terms of repeated karmic patterns. Thus our instincts, predispositions, and innate tendencies toward particular kinds of categorizations can be explained.

While the current work in American psychology parallels karma theory in understanding ordinary consciousness as a constructive process, the Eastern paradigm has clearly taken the lead in analyzing the ways in which the various filtering categories of the mind can be rendered inactive or perhaps even completely rooted out through the practise of meditation.

Karma, Meditation and the Opening-Up of Awareness

Without doubt, the strongest influence from karma theory via the Transpersonal psychologists to modern psychology has been focused on Eastern methods of meditation. The aim of the psychological techniques involving meditation is the opening-up or removal of the reducing-valve of the mind resulting in a corresponding expansion of awareness. The shutting down of the filtering activity of the mind is frequently accomplished through the repetition of the same karmic pattern over and over in the nervous system. The chanting of *mantras*, focusing upon a single visual image, regulating breathing and repeating the same body movement are all meditative tactics designed to disrupt the ordinary filtering activity of the mind and to open the way for new or fresh perception. In terms of Patañjali's Yoga, karmic patterns established in this and previous lives are being deconditioned and their filtering activity negated. *Yoga Sūtra* 2:52 states that the regulation of breathing removes the karma that covers discriminative awareness[53] and *Yoga Sūtra* 2:54 refers to "the withdrawal of senses" from their usual patterns of addiction to and perception of worldly objects.[54] In the karma and rebirth paradigm of the Eastern religions, such techniques are said to lead to a turning off of karmic filtering (i.e., habitual ways of perceiving and thinking of the external world) and a consequent opening up of a new state of awareness. The response of modern psychology to the meditation techniques of the karma paradigm have been of three general types: (1) empirical studies within the modern scientific paradigm aimed at verifying or discrediting the Eastern claims; (2) attempts at translating the esoteric meditation techniques into applications more in tune with modern technology, for example, biofeedback; and (3) applications in psychotherapy. We will briefly examine each of these responses.

In modern scientific psychology the impact of the karma paradigm has, among other things, stimulated an increasing number of empirical studies of meditation. These studies have been well summarized in the publications of Charles Tart[55] (*Altered States of Consciousness*, 1972) and Robert Ornstein[56] (*On the Psychology of Meditation*, 1973 and *The Psychology of Consciousness*, 1977) and will not be repeated here. Various laboratory conditions have been created to produce stabilized images—one-pointed visual meditation and sensory deprivation—the withdrawal of senses experience of Yoga. While the parallels are not exact, the laboratory results are not inconsistent with the proposals of karma theory. Ornstein summarizes as follows:

> It seems that a consequence of the structure of our central nervous system is that if awareness is restricted to one unchanging source of stimulation, a "turning off" of consciousness of the external world follows. . .
>
> Psychologically, continuous repetition of the same stimulus may be considered the equivalent of no stimulation at all. . .the void, the cloud of unknowing.[57]

Techniques for meditation, chanting, looking fixedly at an object, concentrating on a nonsensical question, repeating a prayer over and over, counting breaths, etc., are aids in focusing awareness on a single process, the continued recycling of the same subroutine through the brain and nervous system. In Patañjali's karma theory such repetition is described as a mental state (*citta-vṛtti*) leaving behind a memory trace (*saṃskāra*) leading again to the same mental state (*citta-vṛtti*) until a deeply rooted karmic pattern (*vāsanā*) is established (e.g., the visualization of a single image).[58] Although empirical studies support the claims of the karma paradigm that in meditation the usual filtering activity of the mind is greatly reduced or even turned off, scientific psychology has yet to examine the other side of the Eastern contention, namely, that once the filtering activity of the mind and sense organs is turned-off a corresponding expansion of awareness occurs. Does the turning-off action of meditative techniques simply plunge one into a dark void? Is the Buddhist emptiness (*śūnya*) truly empty, the nihilism that some Westerners have suspected all along? The fullness of expansion that comes after turning off has yet to be empirically demonstrated, however this may be mainly a problem of the measurement devices currently available being unable to register the content to be measured (e.g., *nirvicāra samādhi* or *prajñā*).

The only hint that scientific psychology has had to offer in this connection comes from Arthur Deikman's study of deautomatization. Deautomatization is defined as the undoing of automatization, presumably by reinvesting actions and percepts with attention.[59] Implied is deconditioning of learned aspects of perception and cognition which have come to be automatic in everyday functioning. Deikman's very simple study involved no empirical measurement and relied on introspection by the subjects.[60] After concentrating on a vase repeatedly they reported a shift in their perception of the vase to a deeper and more intense blue. Deikman likens deautomatization to the search of an artist to find a new expressive style by deautomatizing his perception so that a fresh, vivid, and significant experience may be regained. Ornstein regards deautomatization as a reduction of the normal filtering or selectivity of input so that the sensory stimulus is experienced differently, anew.[61] Thus, concludes Deikman, deautomatization is not a regression (as the Freudians would have us believe[62]) but an undoing of a pattern in order to permit a new and perhaps more advanced experience.[63]

Biofeedback represents the major attempt of psychology to translate the meditative techniques of the karmic paradigm into modern technology. The notion of biofeedback arose as a result of study of the ability of yogis voluntarily to control processes previously judged by psychology to involuntary (e.g., heart rate, blood pressure, EEG patterns, etc.). After working with the yogi Swami Rama at the Menninger Foundation, Elmer Green concluded: (1) that physiological states and mental-emotional states are directly connected so that a change in one results in a change in the other, and (2) that any physiological process that can be monitored, amplified, and made visible to an individual can be controlled by that individual.[64] Instrumentation was developed which would enable a person to perceive physiological activity that normally occurs below the threshold of awareness. After practice the individual is able to note correlations between physiological fluctuations and accompanying psychological states, usually in the form of a mental image to produce the physiological change at will. Success or failure is immediately registered by a physiological monitoring device—hence the term biofeedback. Since biofeedback is based on the mind-body connection, it has become a basic methodological tool for examining the long-standing problems of mind-body interaction and psychosomatic disorders. It has also provided the foundation for the new school of image therapy.[65]

In biofeedback stress is placed on an individual's internal states as the means for establishing voluntary control. Green notes, "In actuality there is no such thing as training in brain wave control, there is training only in the elicitation of certain subjective states. . .what are detected and manipulated (in some as yet unknown way) are subjective feelings, focus of attention, and thought processes."[66] The goal of biofeedback is in line with that of Yoga and is in marked contrast to that of psychological conditioning, whereas biofeedback, as a process of voluntary control, moves toward increased inner freedom, while conditioned control moves toward loss of freedom. Since most of the effort in modern Western psychology and psychiatry has been directed toward the kind of drug induced or conditioned control of behavior which promotes George Orwell's Big Brother Syndrome or the Doctor as God mentality, the introduction of a voluntary, patient-controlled approach from the karma paradigm via biofeedback marks a significant advance.

Biofeedback has been successfully applied to the field of psychotherapy in areas such as decreased systolic blood pressure control, correcting tachycardia, elimination of migraine headaches, treating of insomnia, reduction of free floating anxiety, relief for bronchial asthma, and deep relaxation prior to behavior modification training.[67] In such applications the appropriate physiological process, such as muscle tension in migraines, is monitored and amplified for the patient who then proceeds by trial and error to find the subjective state that effects control over that physiological process.[68] Once the connection has been learned the unhealthy processes can be controlled mentally, rather than through the use of drugs.

One researcher, Joe Kamiya, sees biofeedback as a short-cut towards an expansion of awareness that would take much longer by the traditional meditation methods. His extrapolition may however be a bit optimistic:

> In this age of technological sophistication, there seems to be no good reason why a beginning cannot be made toward courses in "physiological awareness, in which students are taught the subjective feel of changes in heart rate, EEG waves, sleep stages, electrodermal changes accompanying social stimuli, gastric contractions, etc. The dictum "Know Thyself" could be made easier to follow with techniques that make the covert internal processes of brain and body directly observable to the person.[69]

All this sounds rather close to a modern psychological version of the *savicāra samādhi* state of Patañjali's *Yoga Sūtras*.[70]

It is clear that by introducing the karma and rebirth paradigm into modern psychology, Transpersonal Psychology has prompted many important new developments. The major result would seem to be an extended concept of human consciousness,[71] and an approach to psychotherapy which emphasizes voluntary control and self-knowledge rather than manipulation by drugs or doctors. Thus karma theory is having a considerable impact on the way many modern psychologists are revising their basic concepts and assumptions relating to human nature. A notable factor in this regard is that since the karma paradigm has been introduced through the esoteric psychologies of the Eastern religions, the examination of spiritual experience is receiving more attention than is usual from modern psychology. For example, Ornstein's popular textbook, *The Psychology of Consciousness*, is structured around quotes from a Sufi source, "The Exploits of the Incomparable Mulla Nasrudin." It also includes a chapter, albeit brief, on the esoteric religious psychologies, while the companion book of readings includes some one hundred pages of traditional religious source materials.[72] Also featured are humanistic topics such as intuition and creativity, and psychologists such as

William James, Carl Jung, Michael Polanyi and Lama Govinda. If nothing else the impact of the karma paradigm is certainly expanding the consciousness of at least some modern psychologists and their students. The assumed conceptual filters of the scientific psychology paradigm are being broken down or at least partially suspended to allow room for many traditional karma and rebirth categories, often appearing in new guises. Whether the outcome will be a synthesis of the two paradigms in a new psychology, as the Transpersonalists predict, remains to be seen.[73]

IV. CONCLUSION

Our analysis of the impact of karma and rebirth upon modern psychology has come full circle. The Transpersonal psychologists, in opening the way for an expanded understanding of human nature, have returned with enthusiasm to the insights of Carl Jung and his openness to karma theory. Today, however, rather than through one isolated individual, karma theory is reaching out through the ever widening circles of Transpersonal Psychology to such diverse areas as neurophysiology, learning theory, perception, motivation, cognition, altered states of consciousness, psychotherapy, parapsychology, and psychology of religion. In effect some basic assumptions of modern scientific psychology ogy are being challenged by those of karma and rebirth.

NOTES

1. J.N. Farquhar, *The Crown of Hinduism*. New Delhi: Oriental Publishers Reprint Corporation, 1971, p. 142. (Originally published in 1913).

2. *Karma and Rebirth in Classical Indian Traditions*. ed. by Wendy Doniger O'Flaherty. Berkeley: University of California Press, 1980, p. xxiii.

3. See *The Yoga System of Patañjali* translated by J.H. Woods. Harvard Oriental Series, vol. 17. Delhi: Motilal Banarsidass, 1966.

4. *Karma and Rebirth in Classical Indian Traditions*, op. cit., pp. ix-xxv.

5. C.G. Jung, *Memories, Dreams, Reflections*, ed. by A. Jaffe. New York: Vintage Books, 1965, pp. 317-326.

6. Harold Coward, "Jung's Encounter with Yoga" in *The Journal of Analytical Psychology*, *23*, 1978, pp. 339-357.

7. *Memories, Dreams, Reflections*, op. cit. Cps. V, VI VII.

8. See C.G. Jung, *Psychological Types*, Collected Works (*CW*) 6, paras 188 & 189. Also Joseph L. Henderson, "The Self and Individuation" unpublished paper, 1975. All Jung's Collected Works (*CW*) are published by Princeton University Press.

9. "Jung's Encounter with Yoga", op. cit. p. 344.

10. Barbara Hannah, "The Process of Individuation: Notes on Lectures given at

the Eidgenössische Technische Hochschule, Zürich, by C.G. Jung," October, 1938 - June, 1939, unpublished.

11. C.G. Jung, *Psychological Types, C.W.*, 6, 1975.

12. C.G. Jung, "Psychological Commentary on Kundalini Yoga," *Spring*, 1975, p. 8.

13. C.G. Jung, "Psychological Commentary on Kundalini Yoga," *Spring*, 1976, p. 30.

14. C.G. Jung, *Psychological Commentary on "The Tibetan Book of the Dead", C.W.* 11, p. 517.

15. C.G. Jung, *The Psychology of the Unconscious, C.W.* 7, 1942, p. 76.

16. Ibid.

17. Jolande Jacobi, *The Psychology of C.G. Jung*. New Haven: Yale University Press, 1973. See also her *Complex, Archetype and Symbol in the Psychology of C.G. Jung*. New York: Bollingen, 1959.

18. See for example the writings of Robertson Davies, Northrop Frye, Paul Tillich.

19. See Wendy O'Flaherty's summary of the various Indian views in her "Introduction" to *Karma and Rebirth in Classical Indian Traditions*, op. cit. pp. ix-xxv.

20. *C.G. Jung: Letters*, op. cit., vol. I., p. 226-227.

21. Ibid., p. 436.

22. C.G. Jung, *Concerning Rebirth, C.W.* 9, Pt. 1, p. 113.

23. C.G. Jung, *Psychological Commentary on The Tibetan Book of the Dead", C.W.* 11, p. 518.

24. C.G. Jung, *Memories, Dreams, Reflections*, op. cit., p. 317.

25. *C.G. Jung: Letters*, op. cit., vol. 2, p. 289.

26. Edward F. Edinger, *Ego and Archetype*. Baltimore: Penquin Books, 1973, p. 220.

27. *C.G. Jung: Letters*, op. cit., vol. 2, p. 548.

28. *Memories, Dreams, Reflections*, op. cit., p. 319.

29. Ibid, p. 318.

30. Ibid, p. 317.

31. Ibid, p. 318.

32. Ibid, p. 319.

33. Ibid.

34. Ibid, pp. 321-322.

35. Ibid, p. 322.

36. Ibid, p. 323.

37. Ibid, p. 325.

38. See for example, Paul Tillich, *The Protestant Era*. Chicago: University of Chicago Press, 1957, p. xix.

39. *Memories, Dreams, Reflections*, op. cit., p. 319.

40. Ian Stevenson, "The Explanatory Value of the Idea of Reincarnation" in *The Journal of Nervous and Mental Disease, 164*, pp. 305-326.

41. C.G. Jung, *Mysterium Coniunctionis, C.W.* 14, p. 225.

42. Charles T. Tart (ed.) *Transpersonal Psychologies*. New York: Harper Colophon, 1977.

43. Lucy Bregman, "The Interpreter/Experiencer Split: Three Models in the

Psychology of Religion". *Journal of the American Academy of Religion, 56,* (Supplement), pp. 115-149.

44. T.S. Kuhn, *The Structure of Scientific Revolutions.* Chicago: University of Chicago Press, 1962.

45. K.R. Pellitier and C. Garfield, *Consciousness: East and West.* New York: Harper and Row, 1976, p. 5.

46. In Patañjali's *Yoga Sūtras,* for example, *karma* obscures reality. The purpose of yoga is to purge off the *karma* until bare reality stands fully revealed. See *Yoga Sūtras* I:1 & 2.

47. See for example, C.E. Osgood, *Method and Theory in Experimental Psychology.* New York: Oxford University Press, 1960.

48. Aldous Huxley, *The Doors of Perception and Heaven and Hell.* Harmondsworth Middlesex: Penguin, 1960, p. 21.

49. Ibid.

50. Some pertinent experimental studies are summarized by Robert Ornstein, *On the Psychology of Meditation.* New York: Viking Press, 1973, pp. 174-175.

51. Karl H. Pribram, "The Neurophysiology of Remembering," *Scientific American,* January, 1969, pp. 73-86.

52. Jerome Bruner, "On Perceptual Readiness," *Psychological Review, 64,* 1957, pp. 123-152.

53. *The Yoga-System of Patañjali* translated by J.H. Woods. Delhi: Motilal Banarsidass, 1966, *sutra* II:52, p. 196.

54. Ibid, *Yoga Sūtra* II:53, pp. 197-198.

55. *Altered States of Consciousness* ed. by Charles T. Tart. New York: Anchor, 1972.

56. Robert E. Ornstein, *The Psychology of Consciousness.* New York: Harcourt Brace Jovanovich, 1977.

57. Claudio Naranjo & Robert E. Ornstein, *On The Psychology of Meditation.*

58. *Yoga Sūtra,* op. cit., IV:7-9.

59. Arthur J. Deikman, "Deautomatization and the Mystic Experience," *Psychiatry, 29,* 1966, pp. 324-338.

60. Arthur J. Deikman, "Experimental Meditation," *Journal of Nervous and Mental Disorder, 136,* 1963, pp. 329-343.

61. Robert E. Ornstein, *The Psychology of Consciousness,* op. cit., pp. 182-183.

62. See for example, Raymon Prince and Charles Savage, "Mystical States and the Concept of Regression" in *The Highest State of Consciousness,* ed. by John White. New York: Anchor Books, 1972, pp. 114-134.

63. Deikman, "Experimental Meditation," op. cit., p. 342.

64. Elmer E. Green, A.M. Green & E.D. Walter, "Voluntary Control of Internal States: Psychological and Physiological," *Journal of Transpersonal Psychology, 2,* 1970, pp. 1-26.

65. "Towards a Transpersonal Psychotherapy" in *Consciousness: East and West,* op. cit., p. 257.

66. As quoted in *Consciousness: East and West,* op. cit., pp. 257-258.

67. Ibid, pp. 264-265.

68. Ibid, p. 264.

69. Joe Kamiya, "Conscious Control of Brain Waves," *Psychology Today*, April, 1968, p. 60.

70. *Yoga Sūtra* I:43.

71. See Cp. 11 "An Extended Concept of Human Consciousness" in *The Psychology of Consciousness*, op. cit., pp. 214-233.

72. *The Nature of Human Consciousness* ed. by R.E. Ornstein, San Francisco: W.H. Freeman, 1973.

73. See for example, *The Psychology of Consciousness*, op. cit., p. 216; and *Transpersonal Psychologies*, op. cit., p. 7.

CHAPTER FIFTEEN

Swami Bhaktivedanta: Karma, Rebirth and the Personal God

ROBERT D. BAIRD

Swami Bhaktivedanta, founder of the International Society for Kṛṣṇa Consciousness, does not present his views on karma and rebirth in either a systematic or an academic fashion. He sees himself as in the Vaiṣṇava tradition, resting firmly on the *Bhagavad-gītā*, *Śrīmad Bhāgavatam*, and the teachings of Śri Caitanya. He also presents himself as a bona fide spiritual master in disciplic succession from Śri Caitanya.

As such, although he has written several topical books, his views on karma and rebirth are largely to be found by examining his commentaries on the above-mentioned texts. There is no work or chapter in which he systematically develops these themes. Moreover, he disdains the work of academics who are labelled "mental speculators." He does not concern himself with comparing and contrasting his position with the position of other modern thinkers. Occasionally there is a stray reference, but only to indicate the errors that are engendered by not relying on a bona fide teacher. His purpose is not academic, nor does he follow academic procedures. Above all he seeks to lead all persons to spiritual realization.

When he speaks on karma and rebirth he does not present his teaching as containing novelty, only fidelity to the Vaiṣṇava tradition. His is, therefore, a decidedly theistic approach to the world, and this approach dominates the way he sees karma and rebirth. He has a strong view of the laws of nature and their inexorability. But, above and within those laws and the operation of karma is the guidance and control of God.

KARMA

The Realm of Karma

Swami Bhaktivedanta writes of the material world and the spiritual world. The human being is an eternal soul or living entity (*jīva*) within a material body which has a gross and subtle aspect. As long as the living entity is associated with a material body, that body is governed by the laws of material nature and karma.

From the smallest germ up to Indra, King of Heaven, all living beings are subject to the law of karma and suffer the results of attachment to their work.[1] Technically speaking, the soul is neither born nor does it die. It is the material body associated with it which is subject to birth and death. It is the body that is the locus of karma and reaps its harvest.[2]

There are 8,400,000 species of life into which the living entity can be born and a body is assigned according to one's karma.[3] These bodies may range from a demigod in one of the heavenly planets, to a human, animal, or vegetable form on this planet, to some form in a lower planet or hell. In each case a body is forced upon the living being by the laws of material nature and one's karma.[4] The living entity has no power to change the laws of material nature relating to the body which is acquired. If one is born as a dog or cat or hog, one must live like those animals.[5]

Karma, the results of fruitive activities, follows the living entity even when there is a dissolutionment of the world and a new creation. The same karma simply moves from actuality to potentiality to actuality again.[6]

Specific Karma

While Swami Bhaktivedanta does not attempt to give a complete account of specific acts which produce identifiable results, there are some specifics given and hints of a more general nature exist. To begin with, one's situation in the three *guṇas* has some generally predictable effects. Material bodies are dominated by one of the three *guṇas* of *prakṛti*. The mode of goodness (*sattva*) makes one wiser than others in the conditioned state.[7] Ideally, the *brāhmaṇa* is supposed to be situated in the mode of *sattva* and is more or less free from sinful reactions. By pious activities in the mode of goodness one is purified. One who dies in the mode of *sattva* is reborn in one of the higher planetary systems, enjoying godly happiness in Brahmaloka or Janaloka. While there are impurities in the material world regardless of which mode one is in, the mode of *sattva* is the purest form of existence and those who die there are "elevated to the planets where great sages and great devotees live."[8]

> There is an upper planetary system, consisting of the heavenly planets, where everyone is highly elevated. According to the degree of development of the mode of goodness, the living entity can be transferred to various planets in this system. The highest planet is Satyaloka, or Brahmaloka, where the prime person of this universe, Lord Brahmā, resides. We have already seen that we can hardly calculate the wondrous condition of life in Brahmaloka, but the highest condition of life, the mode of goodness, can bring us to this.[9]

Unfortunately, the mode of *sattva* is part of *prakṛti* and a person so situated may think of himself as advanced in knowledge and therefore superior to others. Even here, then, there is little likelihood of liberation or being transferred to the spiritual world.

> Repeatedly, one may become a philosopher, a scientist, or a poet, and, repeatedly, become entangled in the same disadvantages of birth and death. But, due to the illusion of the material energy, one thinks that that sort of life is pleasant.[10]

The mode of passion (*rajas*) is characterized by the attraction between man and woman. Modern society is dominated by the mode of *rajas*. Those predominantly in this mode want honor in society with a happy family and a nice house. Hence, in order to please wife, society, and keep up one's prestige, one has to work hard. But, "if there is no liberation for those in the mode of goodness, what of those who are entangled in the mode of passion?"[11]

> The mode of passion is mixed. It is in the middle, between the modes of goodness and ignorance. A person is not always pure, but even if he should be purely in the mode of passion, he will simply remain on this earth as a king or a rich man. But because there are mixtures, one can also go down. People on this earth, in the modes of passion or ignorance, cannot forcibly approach the higher planets by machine. In the mode of passion there is also the chance of becoming mad in the next life.[12]

A person who is predominantly in the mode of *tamas* or ignorance possesses little understanding. It should be obvious that all people will die, but one in the mode of *tamas* continues to seek the accumulation of money and is not much interested in spiritual advancement. Such people are lazy in spiritual things, and are inclined to sleep more than is required (six hours of sleep a night is sufficient). Such persons also appear to be dejected and are addicted to intoxicants. To fall into this mode is very risky since all that remain are subhuman forms.

> Beneath the human level there are eight million species of life: birds, beasts, reptiles, trees, etc., and, according to the development of the mode of ignorance, people are brought down to these abominable conditions. The word *tāmasāḥ* is very significant here. *Tāmasāḥ* indicates those who stay continually in the mode of ignorance without rising to a higher mode. Their future is very dark.[13]

Those in the lower modes of passion and ignorance can be elevated to the mode of goodness if they practice Kṛṣṇa consciousness. But, the ultimate goal is to achieve liberation through elevation above all the modes.[14]

There are some activities for which Bhaktivedanta is more specific. Killing animals for the eating of meat will result in the guilty person becoming an animal in a future life and in the animal having a body suitable to kill him.[15] Also, those who eat meat would seem to deserve birth in a body of those creatures who do such things.

> They are such fools that they do not know what will happen to them in their next life. Although they see varieties of living creatures eating abominable things—pigs eating stools, crocodiles eating all kinds of flesh, and so on—they do not realize that they themselves, because of their practice of eating all kinds of nonsense in this life, will be destined to eat the most abominable things in their next life.[16]

Killing on the battlefield or killing animals sacrificially, however, has a different effect since it is ordained.

> The animal sacrificed gets a human life immediately without undergoing the gradual evolutionary process from one form to another, and the *kṣatriyas* killed in the battlefield also attain the heavenly planets as do the *brāhmaṇas* who attain them by offering sacrifice.[17]

A woman is someone who was previously a man who was overly attached to his wife. If one is too attached to his wife, he thinks of her at the time of death and in his next life takes the body of a woman. But, if a woman thinks of her husband at the time of death, she becomes a man in the next life. While the bodies of men or women are merely one's bodily dress, it is easier to get out of the clutches of material nature from the body of a man. A woman is generally fond of household furnishings, ornaments and dresses, and children. Her attachment to the man is the result of his providing her with these things. Ideally, neither the man nor the woman should be attached to each other, but to the Lord.[18] The ideal is for the husband and wife to help each other advance in spiritual life. Sex and eating are both essential, but should be governed by this principle. Sex should be engaged in only in order to propagate Kṛṣṇa conscious children. Unfortunately, in this age, men and women unite for "unrestricted sexual enjoyment. Thus they are victimized, being obliged to take rebirth in the form of animals to fulfill their animalistic propensities."[19]

People who mock and jeer at Kṛṣṇa are born into lower and lower situations.

> Their destiny is certainly to take birth after birth in the species of atheistic and demoniac life. Perpetually, their real knowledge will remain under delusion, and gradually they will regress to the darkest region of creation.[20]

Inexorable Karma and Divine Control

There is a sense in which the results of fruitive actions are automatic and inevitable.

> Even in the present life, the body changes from childhood to boyhood, from boyhood to youth, and from youth to old age; similarly, when the body is too old to continue, the living being gives up his body and, by the laws of nature, *automatically* gets another body according to his fruitive activities, desires and ambitions. The laws of nature control this sequence, and therefore as long as the living entity is under the control of the external, material energy, the process of bodily change takes place *automatically*, according to one's fruitive activities.[21]

The laws of material nature are not to be contravened. Karma is fruitive action for which there is always a reaction, either good or bad.

Every fruitive activity must have its effect and cannot be nullified by some other activity. There would seem to be no place for counteractive karma. "A sinful activity cannot be counteracted by a pious activity."[22] So relentless is karma that attempts by philanthropists and social reformers to make significant changes in material conditions are doomed to failure. "Material conditions are already established by the superior administration according to one's *karma*."[23] One should not concern oneself with material conditions, but seek instead to raise people to Kṛṣṇa consciousness which results in transcending that material nature.

Swami Bhaktivedanta is interested in raising the living entity to Kṛṣṇa consciousness and bringing all beings "back to Godhead." He repeatedly castigates those who think they are the controllers or who think that somehow nature works without God. Although in one sense karma is inexorable, even to the extent of excluding counteractive karma, these laws do not operate independently. The material nature is the Lord's external energy and both the laws of nature as well as the effects of karma are controlled and administered by the Lord. "Therefore victory and defeat come according to the result of one's *karma*, and the judgment is given by the Supreme Lord."[24] On several occasions Swami Bhaktivedanta counters what he takes to be the materialistic position of the *karma mīmāṃsā* in which karma is the cause of everything, even to binding the Supreme Controller to act in a given way.[25] Karma is not the original cause of one's position. Behind it all is the hand of God, who administers his justice with the help of his agents, the demigods.

Is determinism, then, merely raised from the level of material nature to the level of divine control? There are statements that would seem to suggest that.

> Since we act under the control of the Supreme according to our *karma*, no one is independent, from Brahmā down to the insignificant ant. Whether we are defeated or victorious, the Supreme Lord is always victorious because everyone acts under his directions.[26]
>
> Victory is always with the Supreme Personality of Godhead. As for the subordinant living entities, they fight under the arrangement of the Supreme Personality of Godhead. Victory or defeat is not actually theirs; it is an arrangement by the Lord through the agency of material nature.[27]

Swami Bhaktivedanta cannot countenance a view of the world that omits reference to the Supreme Controller. To grant that there is anything that is not in the control of Kṛṣṇa would be to admit that some things happen on their own. But neither is he interested in affirming a determinism that diminishes human responsibility. So, although Kṛṣṇa is the "ultimate doer" of everything, He is not thereby responsible for the plight of the living souls.

> Although the Supreme Personality of Godhead is the ultimate doer of everything, in His original transcendental existence He is not responsible for the happiness and distress, or bondage and liberation, of the conditioned souls. These are due to the results of the fruitive activities of the living entities within this material world.[28]

There is a hierarchy of causes for every act. Although nothing is without its cause, human beings are responsible for their actions within the context of those causes. The supreme cause of all is the Lord. But, the Lord works through material nature and the karma of the living entity.

> In the material creations, the Lord is the only supreme cause. The immediate cause is material nature by which the cosmic manifestation is visible. The created beings are of many varieties, such as the demigods, human beings and lower animals, and all of them are subject to the reactions of their own past good or bad activities. The Lord only gives them the proper facilities for such activities and the regulations of the modes of nature, but He is never responsible for their past and present activities.[29]

The Lord does not create the particular situations into which living entities are placed. Rather, they desire to be placed into these situations, and impartial as He is, the Lord grants all such desires. But, He does not interfere with the desires of independent living beings.[30]

It has been observed that the Lord controls the working of karma which is not set loose to operate on its own.[31] It has also been seen that the Lord is impartial to all. Yet there are instances where the Lord is free to change the results of actions.[32] Swami Bhaktivedanta explicitly denies that the Lord, as Lord of karma, is bound to its results.

> We must always remember that the Lord is the supreme will, and He is not bound by any law. Generally the law of *karma* is that one is awarded the results of one's own actions, but in special cases, by the will of the Lord, such resultant actions are changed also. But this change can be effected by the will of the Lord only, and no other. . . the Supreme Will is absolutely free to do whatever He likes; and because He is all-perfect, there is no mistake in any of His actions or reactions. These changes of resultant actions are especially rendered by the Lord when a pure devotee is involved.[33]

Since the Lord is impartial and not arbitrary, and since the laws of material nature and of karma itself are due to Him, before one concludes that the Lord sometimes acts in such a way as to set aside such laws one should remember that the intellectual capabilities of the living entity are not sufficient to understand the workings of the infinite.

> The activities of the Lord are always inconceivable to the tiny brain of the living entities. Nothing is impossible for the Supreme Lord,

> but all His actions are wonderful for us, and thus He is always beyond the range of our conceivable limits.[34]

Therefore, what might appear to be contrary to karma or the laws of material nature might be quite reasonable within the divine intelligence.

Karma and the Devotee

A devotee of the Lord is not under the laws of karma and cannot be punished for past karma. We will see later that this involves transcending the sphere of karma rather than interfering with it from within. For example, only the foolish would think that one's life could be extended beyond one's karmically determined time.[35] But the Lord can extend the duration of the devotees' time and in effect nullify the results of his karma.

> When one becomes a devotee, however, he is not destined to die according to a limited duration of life. Everyone has a limited duration of life, but a devotee's lifetime can be extended by the mercy of the Supreme Lord, who is able to nullify the results of one's karma. . . . A devotee is not under the laws of karma.[36]

A devotee who is less than a pure devotee is still capable of misusing his position and thereby having to be born in a lower form. But, the punishment is different than it is for ordinary materialistic persons. By the grace of the Lord the devotee is punished in such a way that his desire to achieve Kṛṣṇa consciousness is increased which enables him to achieve liberation during his next lifetime.[37] Swami Bhaktivedanta comments on the case of Bharata Mahārāja, who due to his compassion for a young deer was compelled to take the body of a deer for a short time to rectify that mistake.

> He was very anxious to get out of his deer body, and this indicates that his affection for devotional services was intensified, so much so that he was quickly to attain perfection in a *brāhmaṇa* body in the next life.[38]

But, "such punishment is only for a short period, and it is not due to past *karma*. It may appear to be due to past *karma*, but it is offered to rectify the devotee and bring him to pure devotional service."[39] The devotee is also aware that whatever punishment is given him is to bring him to the right path.[40]

In the theism of Bhaktivedanta, then, the Lord is in complete control as the ultimate cause of all the laws of material nature and of karma.

Nothing takes place outside of His will or knowledge. But the living entity is still free and thereby responsible for his destiny. And, one should not lightly think that the Lord sets aside His karmic laws.

TRANSMIGRATION

Transmigration, like karma, applies only to the world of material nature. The original nature of the living entity is spiritual and that is the destiny to which it should return. Hence, although the various bodies with which the living entity is associated differ widely, one's ultimate goal is to transcend them all and return to a spiritual existence. Being caught in the cycles of birth and death is the result of desire. How this gets started is described by Swami Bhaktivedanta as follows.

> Originally the living entity is a spiritual being, but when he actually desires to enjoy this material world, he comes down. . . . The living entity first accepts a body that is human in form, but gradually, due to his degraded activities, he falls into lower forms of life—into the animal, plant and aquatic forms. By the gradual process of evolution, the living entity again attains the body of a human being and is given another chance to get out of the process of transmigration. If he again misses his chance in the human form to understand his position, he is again placed in the cycle of birth and death in various types of bodies.[41]

Bodies are arranged according to a gradual evolution from the lower species of life to the higher or human forms. Humans are distinguished from the lower vegetable forms in that they have consciousness, and from animal forms in that the animal cannot control itself and has no sense of decency.[42] The living being passes through a natural evolutionary process until it reaches a human body at which time the will becomes significant for future progress. Only in human life is liberation possible.[43]

If one wastes one's human years in sense gratification, one will transmigrate in the next life to the body of an animal such as a dog, cat, or hog.[44] One may even take the form of a tree.[45] Swami Bhaktivedanta parts with theosophical thought in believing that one can be born in a subhuman form after having attained the human level. He also sees Darwin's theory as incomplete because although it describes evolution from ape to man, it does not take into account the reverse condition as a possibility.[46] If one misuses the opportunity provided by the human body one will slip to subhuman forms, but if one utilizes the human opportunity one will be elevated to higher planetary systems in the next life.

Not only, then, does the living entity transmigrate from one life to another on earth, but rebirth takes place on planets above and below our present planetary system.[47] Life on the higher planets is more pleasurable and of longer duration. Each of the higher planets is ruled over by a demigod whose life span is immense. Lord Brahmā, who rules over Brahmaloka, the highest planet in the system, lives for a very long time. But, unlike Kṛṣṇa, even Brahmā is subject to death. Living entities who are born in one of the upper planetary systems are usually reborn later as humans. It is even possible to be born as a demigod and thereby become a further purified devotee and return to Godhead.[48] By worshipping the demigod who presides over it, one goes to that planet at death.[49] But all of these planets are part of the material universe and unless one transcends them to the spiritual universe of Vaikuṇṭha one will never escape the rounds of birth and death.[50]

> In the higher planets of the material world, the *yogīs* can enjoy more comfortable and more pleasant lives for hundreds and thousands of years, but life in those higher planets is not eternal. Those who desire eternal life enter into the anti-material universe through mystic powers at certain opportune moments that are created by the demigod administrators.[51]

One of these heavenly planets is the moon. One who goes there still possesses some material desire.[52] When that is entirely gone one travels to Kṛṣṇa's abode which is the spiritual world of Vaikuṇṭha.

The Material Body

The living entity transmigrates through a variety of bodies until it is finally liberated and returns in its spiritual body to Godhead. During that time, the bodies that it inhabits are composed of a variety of elements. There is the gross body that is visible to the eye and which is composed of the five elements of material nature: earth, water, fire, air and sky. There is also the subtle body, unperceived by the material senses, which is composed of the three subtle elements: mind, intelligence, and ego.[53]

At the time of death it is the gross body that is burned in cremation.[54] However, unless the living entity is liberated, the subtle body remains and carries the soul to its next gross body.[55] Throughout life and even at the moment of death the gross body acts to form the disposition of the subtle body. After death, the subtle body continues and is responsible for the determination of the next gross body.[56]

If, at the time of sex, the secretions of the mother are more profuse, the child will receive a female body, while if the secretions of the father are more profuse, the body will be male. These are the laws of nature, but they act according to desire. Hence the gross body is determined by the subtle body. The way to change this situation is to change the subtle body.

> If a human being is taught to change his subtle body by developing a consciousness of Kṛṣṇa, at the time of death the subtle body will create a gross body in which he will be a devotee of Kṛṣṇa, or if he is still more perfect, he will not take another material body but will immediately get a spiritual body and thus return home, back to Godhead.[57]

The subtle body continues in the womb even though the gross body is not fully developed.[58] Even after birth it takes some time for the effects of one's karma to manifest themselves in the gross body. Hence, although small children may appear to be innocent, this should not be confused with the state of liberation. The effects of one's fruitive activities are simply held in reservation in the subtle body to appear at a later stage in development.[59]

In dreams, the living entity, encased in the subtle body, is able to leave the gross body for a time.[60] When we sleep we forget the identity of the gross body, and when we awaken we forget the identity of the subtle body.[61] It is possible to experience things in a dream which have never been seen or heard of in this life because they have been experienced in previous lives. And novelty may result from combining experiences.[62] The stage of development of the senses may also influence the subtle body and one's dreams.

> In a dream a young man may experience the presence of a young woman because at that time the senses are active. Because of undeveloped senses, a child or boy will not see a young woman in his dreams. The senses are active in youth even when one dreams, and although there may be no young woman present, the senses may act and there may be a seminal discharge (nocturnal emission). The activities of the subtle and gross bodies depend on how developed conditions are.[63]

Usually one does not remember previous lives nor know the type of body one will have next. However, there are exceptions. If one has come to the end of the usefulness of his present gross body and knows that the next one will be a step down, one may want to retain the one that he has. While the forces of nature are too strong to counteract, this desire for retention may cause one to lie in a coma for an extended period before death occurs.[64]

If one is overly attracted to one's life situation, one is not given another gross body and is forced to remain as a ghost in a subtle body without a gross body.[65] Such a one is a disturbance to others in society since ghosts seek a body to inhabit.[66]

It is said repeatedly that the living entity who is not liberated is forced to take another material body according to the laws of material nature and one's karma. But as before, we see that the Supreme Personality of Godhead has a hand in the formation of the material body. Not only are the laws of material nature and karma determined by Him, but material nature is His external energy. In addition, one has not only a subtle and gross body and a living soul (*jīva*), but is endowed with a Supersoul. This Supersoul is a form of the Supreme which resides within the individual. It transmigrates from body to body along with the original soul and reflects the divine guidance of the whole procedure. The Lord remains the ultimate cause in control of the universe and uses mediate causes to accomplish His purpose.

> The Supersoul is said to be friendly because the Supreme Personality of Godhead is so kind to the original soul that when the original soul transmigrates from one body to another, the Lord goes with him. Furthermore, according to the desire and *karma* of the individual soul, the Lord, through the agency of *māyā*, creates another body for him.[67]

At the appropriate time, then, the next body is prepared and the individual soul and the Supersoul transfer to that "particular bodily machine."[68] There is a close connection between saying that material nature forces one to take a particular body and saying that the Lord prepares a particular body.[69] Actually the Lord works in an orderly fashion according to the laws of material nature which He guides.

> At the time of death, according to his mental condition, the living being is carried by the subtle body, consisting of mind, intelligence and ego, to another gross body. When higher authorities have decided what kind of gross body the living entity will have, he is forced to enter such a body, and thus he automatically gives up his previous body.[70]

But the moment of death is more specifically sketched out.

Death

Death always comes at the right time.[71] There is even a gracious and timely element to capital punishment. If a murderer were permitted to live he might commit future murders and have to suffer the inevitable karmic results of such activities.[72]

At death the gross body divides and the gross elements go back to their source. After the destruction of the gross body, the soul and Supersoul remain.[73] In cremation it is the gross body that is destroyed and if there is no more desire for material enjoyment the subtle body is also ended.[74] If, however, further transmigration is required, attachment to the old body makes cremation desirable.[75]

At death one might transmigrate to higher planets or to Vaikuṇṭha. Or, one may go to Yamarāja, the controller of sinful activities.[76] In the latter case, the messengers of Yamarāja, the Yamadūtas, punish the living entity. To an extent that the living entity is able to tolerate, he must suffer the consequences of sense gratification. While passing from this planet to the planet of Yamarāja, the culprit meets many dogs who bark and bite to remind him of his criminal activities of sense gratification.[77] He passes a vast distance in a few moments. In this passage,

> The subtle body is covered by the constables so that the living entity can pass such a long distance quickly and at the same time tolerate the suffering. This covering, although material, is of such fine elements that material scientists cannot discover what the coverings are made of. To pass 792,000 miles within a few minutes seems wonderful to the modern space travellers. They have so far travelled at the speed of 18,000 miles per hour, but here we see that a criminal passes 792,000 miles within a few seconds only, although the process is not spiritual but material.[78]

It should be understood that Yamarāja is not a fictitious character. He is truly the king of his abode, Pitṛloka. He is appointed by the Supreme Personality of Godhead to see that human beings do not violate His regulations.[79] The punishment inflicted on the planet of Pitṛloka is intended as remedial, but those so punished often continue to follow their sensual ways.

> The conditioned souls, who have come to this material world for sense gratification, are allowed to enjoy their senses under certain regulative principles. If they violate these regulations, they are judged and punished by Yamarāja. He brings them to the hellish planets and properly chastises them to bring them back to Kṛṣṇa consciousness. By the influence of māyā, however, the conditioned souls remain infatuated with the mode of ignorance. Thus in spite of repeated punishment by Yamarāja, they do not come to their senses, but continue to live within the material condition, committing sinful activities again and again.[80]

The concentration of the mind at the moment of death determines one's next destination. "Whatever state of being one remembers when he quits his body, that state he will attain without fail."[81] It is not a magical moment, however, since one is bound to act characteristically. The point is that "whatever we do in life will be tested at the time of death."[82] Mahārāja Bharata thought of a deer and became one in his next life. If one has had no thoughts other than how to maintain his family throughout life, he will think of them at the moment of death. He may even in his last words ask that someone look after his family. Such a one will surely be reborn.[83]

The ultimate goal of one's life will be reached if one is able to remember the Lord at the moment of death. One way to do this is to chant the *mahāmantra*. But even this is not possible for the person who has not practised Kṛṣṇa consciousness throughout life.

> Anyone who quits his body in Kṛṣṇa consciousness is at once transferred to the transcendental abode of the Supreme Lord. The word smaran (remembering) is important. Remembering of Kṛṣṇa is not possible for the impure soul who has not practised Kṛṣṇa consciousness in devotional service. To remember Kṛṣṇa one should chant the mahāmantra. . . .[84]

The significance of this has to do with the importance of the subtle body in forming the next gross body and the formative influence of the mind in the process. At the time of death the mind and intelligence create the subtle form of the body for the next life. If the thought is not congenial, the next life will be unfavorable. But if one thinks of Kṛṣṇa one is translated to His abode. If one is worshipping one of the demigods one will be transferred to their planet. But that will entail future rebirths.[85]

In death as in life, one should understand that the process is not purely naturalistic. There are laws which determine death and the transfer to another body. But these are governed by the Lord. For "Lord Viṣṇu is even the Supreme Lord of death. . . ."[86] The living entity generally does not remember his previous life and hence forgets where he was in the process of God realization. However, the Lord in the form of Paramātman is present in the transmigration and supplies the remembrance which enables the living entity to renew his work where the last life ended.[87] The whole process of death is neither accidental nor wholly explained through natural law. For that law is under the control of the Supreme Personality of Godhead.

Birth and Life in the Womb

The birth of the human being's body takes place as the result of a mixture of semen and ovum, but that mixture does not always produce pregnancy.[88] Unless the soul enters the mixture there is no pregnancy. Therefore, it is important to note that the father and mother, while agents in the production of the material body, do not create the living entity which is put into the semen according to its karma.[89] One should not even say that the semen creates the living entity, for the soul merely, "takes shelter in a particle of semina and is then pushed into the womb of a woman."[90] The soul is transferred to the semen of a man who is karmically suitable to become the material father.[91]

Death usually involves being in a trance for seven months. When at the end of seven months the being awakens from the trance and finds himself in the womb he feels confined. In this condition he often prays to the Lord to liberate him from his condition.[92] The miserable condition of material existence, then, is felt not only when one emerges from the womb, but when one is confined within. But once one is born, *māyā* conceals from the living entity the miserable condition of material existence. It is possible within the womb to understand one's relationship to Vasudeva, and such a one has his liberation assured.[93] The existence of the child in the womb is a precarious one. "On one side of where the child is floating there is the heat of gastric fire, and on the other side there is urine, stool, blood and discharges."[94] Not only does the child pray to the Lord for deliverance from the womb, but, knowing that one forgets his relationship to the Lord after birth, sometimes prays to remain in the womb.

> It is said that Śukadeva Gosvāmī, on this consideration, remained for sixteen years within the womb of his mother; he did not want to be entangled in false bodily identification. After cultivating such knowledge within the womb of his mother, he came out at the end of sixteen years and immediately left home so that he might not be captured by the influence of *māyā*.[95]

It is possible, within the womb, to be conscious of one's situation, to pray, and to be constantly absorbed in Kṛṣṇa consciousness.[96]

As we have seen before, this process operates according to the laws of material nature and one's karma. But that is not the final explanation. In the ultimate sense, the body is created by the Lord who is the original cause.[97]

> Whether the body is of *sattva-guṇa, rajo-guṇa* or *tamoguṇa*, everything is done by the direction of the Supreme Lord through the agency

of the external energy (*pṛthak sva-māyayā*). In this way, in different types of bodies, the Lord (*Īśvara*) gives directions as Paramātma, and again, to destroy the body, He employs the *tamo-guṇa*. This is the way the living entities receive different types of bodies.[98]

LIBERATION

One usually achieves liberation only after many births.[99] However, if one surrenders to the Lord, it can happen earlier.[100]

> After many, many births, and after attaining the platform of transcendental knowledge, one becomes perfect when he surrenders unto the Lord. This is the general procedure. But one who surrenders at the very beginning. . .at once surpasses all stages simply by adopting the devotional attitude.[101]

If "unalloyed devotion is the ultimate goal of life,"[102] it is because it issues in liberation or ultimate freedom in a transcendental or spiritual world. The material spheres have three divisions of planets. But no matter how high one is elevated in the material planets, one is always subject to birth and death. Liberation involves transcending the material universe and entering one of the spiritual planets.[103] There is nothing superior to Goloka Vṛndāvan, Kṛṣṇa's spiritual abode, which is one's ultimate destination.[104] True liberation is above the three *guṇas* of *prakṛti* and is called Kṛṣṇa consciousness.[105] This ultimate abode is uncompromisingly spiritual.[106] When in liberation one transcends the material worlds one also receives a spiritual body.[107] This spiritual body is one's original state before contamination by the material world.

> The result of perfection in Kṛṣṇa consciousness is that after giving up one's material body, one is immediately transferred to the spiritual world in one's original spiritual body to become an associate of the Supreme Personality of Godhead. Some devotees go to Vaikuṇṭhaloka, and others go to Goloka Vṛndāvana to become associates of Kṛṣṇa.[108]

This ultimate freedom does not mean the loss of the individual identity of the soul. Just as there is variegatedness in the material world, so is this true of the spiritual world in which there are eternal distinctions. To be born in this spiritual world also means that one is no longer affected by the creation and destruction of the material world in the day and night of Brahmā.[109] Liberation means that one learns that all living beings are merely part and parcel of the Lord and that their bodily existence that induces them to think of themselves as independent is *māyā*.[110] "Liberation means to be situated in one's constitutional position as the eternal servitor of Kṛṣṇa (Kṛṣṇa consciousness)."[111] And, since all of the material world is nothing more than the Lord's external energy, the one who is Kṛṣṇa conscious understands the situation of the living entity and the process of karma and rebirth as well.

In the final analysis full illumination and death are simultaneous.

> And in due course of time, when a pure devotee is completely prepared, all of a sudden the change of body occurs which is commonly called death. And for the pure devotee such a change takes place exactly like lightning, and illumination follows simultaneously. That is to say that a devottee simultaneously changes his material body and develops a spiritual body by the will of the Supreme.[112]

However, "even before death, a pure devotee has no material affection due to his body being spiritualized like a red-hot iron in contact with fire."[113] Although one can be involved in the practice of Kṛṣṇa consciousness and fall into material desire, the pure devotee is already spiritualized during his life.

> One who is always busy serving Kṛṣṇa, in whatever condition he may live, is understood to be liberated even in this life. Such a person, who is a pure devotee, does not need to change his body; indeed, he does not possess a material body, for his body has already been spiritualized. An iron rod kept constantly within a fire will ultimately become fire, and whatever it touches will burn. Similarly, the pure devotee is in the fire of spiritual existence, and therefore his body is *cin-maya*; that is, it is spiritual, not material, because the pure devotee has no desire but the transcendental desire to serve the Lord.[114]

It is for this reason that the pure devotee is said to be unaffected by karma. He is living above it. The devotee lives transcendentally and not on the material level as it might appear.[115]

The impersonal experience of *advaita* is only preliminary to the final liberation which has three stages.

> Brahman is the beginning of transcendental realization. Paramātmā, the Supersoul, is the middle, the second stage in transcendental realization, and the Supreme Personality of Godhead is the ultimate realization of the Absolute Truth. Therefore, both Paramātmā and the impersonal Brahman are within the Supreme Person.[116]

The person who is fully engaged in Kṛṣṇa consciousness is no longer engaged in sense gratification,[117] for he knows that he is not the body, but a "fragmental portion of the Supreme Personality of Godhead."[118]

To be liberated, then, is to live above the realm of material nature and the karma that operates there. It is also to cease to be reborn since one is elevated to a spiritual planet from which one does not return.[119]

Means to Liberation

One must begin by pointing out that one cannot reach liberation by worshipping the demigods.[120] Nor is *jñāna* sufficient for liberation.[121] *Jñāna* and karma yoga both ultimately lead to bhakti which is the supreme yoga.[122] One is not able to engage in counteractive karma to cancel out past karma and achieve liberation. Instead it is necessary to be raised above the level of karma to a transcendental level.

> One has to *act* in the status of spirit soul, otherwise there is no escape from material bondage. Action in Kṛṣṇa consciousness is not, however, action on the fruitive platform. Activities performed in full knowledge strengthen one's advancement in real knowledge. Without Kṛṣṇa consciousness, mere renunciation of fruitive activities does not actually purify the heart of a conditioned soul. As long as the heart is not purified, one has to work on the fruitive platform. But action in Kṛṣṇa consciousness automatically helps one escape the result of fruitive action so that one need not descend to the material platform[123]

Swami Bhaktivedanta sometimes talks of cleansing all sinful reaction, or of burning up reactions.[124] But in addition to having reactions to one's work burned up through Kṛṣṇa consciousness, one's existence is raised to the transcendental level. The means that are used, then, should not be seen as "good" karma as over against "bad" karma. They are actions which, rather than counteracting karma, raise one above its sphere until one's very material body is "spiritualized."

It should not be surprising, then, to learn that no matter what one does, it is not sufficient apart from the grace of the Lord. For, whatever one does is done on the level of material nature. Only the Lord who lives above this plane and is untouched by it can raise one above it.[125] "Therefore He is the Supreme, and only He can deliver the conditioned soul from the onslaught of material nature. . . ."[126]

The Lord rescues living entities by His causeless or uncompelled nature.[127] But, the Lord is not arbitrary. Although His mercy is causeless and cannot be forced, He does respond to surrender and devotional service. Personal striving is on the level of desire. But the pure devotee does not even desire promotion to the spiritual world.[128] This is why the pure devotee receives liberation and elevation to the spiritual planet at death. He is surrendered entirely to the Lord which is the only way to be liberated. "That supreme abode can be achieved only by surrender and by no other means."[129]

This position that liberation is the result of the causeless mercy of the Lord does not mean that there is nothing that the individual can do. Indeed, the causeles mercy of the Lord is commonly given to those who surrender to Him and who engage in devotional service,

> . . .which consists of nine different activities: hearing, chanting, remembering, serving, worshipping, praying, obeying, maintaining friendship and surrendering everything. By the practice of these nine elements of devotional service one is elevated to spiritual consciousness, Kṛṣṇa consciousness.[130]

Devotional service is so pure that once one has started it, one is dragged eventually to ultimate success.[131] For devotional service is above mundane causes and cannot be affected by them.[132] Devotional service, "being transcendental in nature, it frees one from reaction."[133] Rather than being merely a form of counteractive karma, devotional service seems to raise one above both good and bad reactions to a transcendental level.[134] The more one is engaged in devotional service, the more is one fixed on that transcendental plane.[135] The soul is cleansed from material contamination and one rises to the level of *sattva* and then finally to Kṛṣṇa's abode.

The gracious ingredient of liberation is further seen in the fact that when the devotee surrenders to Kṛṣṇa, Kṛṣṇa takes away all sinful reactions of the devotee. Likewise the spiritual master, as the eternal manifestation of Kṛṣṇa, takes on the sinful reactions of the disciples that he initiates.

> As Kṛṣṇa takes away all the sinful reactions of a person immediately upon his surrender unto Him, similarly the external manifestation of Kṛṣṇa, the representative of Kṛṣṇa who acts as the mercy of the Supreme Personality of Godhead, takes all the resultant actions of the sinful life of the disciple immediately after the disciple's initiation.[136]

When a spiritual master gets sick, or has bad dreams, it is not the result of his karma, but of that of his disciples.[137] It is for this reason that Śri Caitanya urged not to make many disciples. But, in the process of preaching, for Bhaktivedanta, that became a necessary risk. But even here, grace is operative. Only the Supreme Personality of Godhead Himself is powerful enough to neutralize fully the reactions of sinful deeds.

But if the spiritual master becomes overloaded with his disciples' sinful reactions, Kṛṣṇa neutralizes those for his servant as well.

> No one but the Supreme Personality of Godhead is able to neutralize the reactions of sinful deeds, whether one's own or those of others. Sometimes the spiritual master, after accepting a disciple, must take charge of that disciple's sinful past activities and, being overloaded, must sometimes suffer—if not fully, then partially—for the sinful acts of the disciple. . . .The poor spiritual master is kind and merciful enough to accept a disciple and partially suffer for that disciple's sinful activities, but Kṛṣṇa, being merciful to His servant, neutralizes the reactions of sinful deeds for the servant who engages in preaching His glories.[138]

Even karma is a form of grace when one realizes that the laws of material nature and karma are the external energy of the Lord. It is through this, and His residence within as Supersoul, and His role as spiritual master that the Lord seeks to reclaim conditioned souls.

> This means that the conditioned souls are being reclaimed by the Lord both ways, namely by the process of punishment by the external energy of the Lord, and by Himself as the spiritual master within and without. Within the heart of every living being the Lord Himself as the Supersoul Paramātmā becomes the spiritual master in the shape of scriptures, saints and initiator spiritual master.[139]

Swami Bhaktivedanta does not present a full range of logical arguments for karma and rebirth. He speaks with confidence while denouncing the views of materialists, mental speculators, advaitins, academics and others who are caught in the web of ignorance. Nor does he claim to be innovative or to modify a teaching in the light of modern academic knowledge. For, a bona fide teacher in disciplic succession merely passes on an authentic and ancient truth. A proper response is not to challenge but to submit.

But, while Swami Bhaktivedanta's understanding is not novel in terms of his tradition, in the light of other contemporary approaches to karma and rebirth it stands out decisively as a view that consistently interprets these doctrines within the control of a personalized God. Material laws and karma can not be circumvented. But this is not because material nature runs on its own or is out of God's control, but because both immanently (in His external energy and as Supersoul) and transcendentally (as the Supreme Personality of Godhead), Kṛṣṇa guides every aspect of the universe. And, if one finally transcends these material rounds of birth and death in a spiritual planet and existence, that too is the result of the Supreme Lord.

NOTES

The author wishes to express his appreciation to Subhanandadasa, Senior Editor of The Bhaktivedanta Book Trust, for reading this manuscript and making several valuable suggestions.

1. A.C. Bhaktivedanta Swami Prabhupāda, *Śrīmad-Bhāgavatam* (Los Angeles: The Bhaktivedanta Book Trust, 1972), I, 1, 305. (Bhaktivedanta's 29 volumes of this set were published from 1972 to 1980. The roman numeral refers to the *Canto,* the first number thereafter refers to the *Part,* and the last number to the *page.* Hereafter, references to this set will simply read *Ś.B.*)
2. A.C. Bhaktivedanta Swami Prabhupāda, *Bhagavad-gītā As It Is* (New York: Collier Books, 1972), p. 99. (Hereafter referred to simply as *Bhagavad-gītā*).
3. *Bhagavad-gītā,* p. 112.
4. *Ś.B.,* IV, 1, 371.
5. *Bhagavad-gītā,* p. 646.
6. *Ś.B.,* IV, 1, 311.
7. *Bhagavad-gītā,* p. 699ff.
8. Ibid., p. 677.
9. Ibid., p. 682.
10. Ibid., p. 670.
11. Ibid., p. 671.
12. Ibid., p. 682.
13. Ibid.
14. Ibid., pp. 682-683.
15. Ibid., p. 679.
16. *Ś.B.,* VII, 2, 254.
17. *Bhagavad-gītā,* p. 114.
18. *Ś.B.,* III, 4, 1358.
19. *Ś.B.,* VII, 3, 112.
20. *Bhagavad-gītā,* p. 463.
21. *Ś.B.,* X, 1, 64-65; (*emphasis mine*).
22. A.C. Bhaktivedanta Swami Prabhupāda, *The Nectar of Instruction* (Los Angeles: The Bhaktivedanta Book Trust, 1975), p. 3.
23. *Ś.B.,* V, 1, 279.
24. *Ś.B.,* VI, 2, 223.
25. *Ś.B.,* VI, 3, 44.
26. *Ś.B.,* VI, 2, 223.
27. *Ś.B.,* VI, 2, 222.
28. *Ś.B.,* VI, 3, 189.
29. *Bhagavad-gītā,* p. 237.
30. Ibid., p. 288.
31. *Ś.B.,* IV, 1, 371 and VI, 2, 223.
32. *Ś.B.,* I, 3, 712-713.

33. Ibid.
34. *Ś.B.*, I, 2, 389.
35. *Bhagavad-gītā*, p. 737.
36. *Ś.B.*, VII, 2, 313.
37. *Ś.B.*, V, 1, 300.
38. *Ś.B.*, V, 1, 295.
39. *Ś.B.*, V, 1, 295-296.
40. *Ś.B.*, VIII, 3, 160.
41. *Ś.B.*, IV, 4, 1376.
42. *Ś.B.*, III, 4, 1334.
43. A.C. Bhaktivedanta Swami Prabhupāda, *Śrī Īśopaniṣad*, (Los Angeles: The Bhaktivedanta Book Trust, 1969), pp. 108-109.
44. *Ś.B.*, VII, 2, 3-12.
45. *Ś.B.*, VIII, 2, 225-226.
46. *Ś.B.*, VII, 3, 109.
47. *Ś.B.*, III, 3, 1360.
48. *Ś.B.*, X, 2, 197.
49. *Śrī Īśopaniṣad*, pp. 65, 70.
50. Ibid., p. 83.
51. A.C. Bhaktivedanta Swami Prabhupāda, *Easy Journey to Other Planets* (Los Angeles: The Bhaktivedanta Book Trust, 1970), p. 31.
52. *Bhagavad-gītā*, pp. 127-128.
53. *Ś.B.*, VI, 3, 83.
54. *Ś.B.*, IX, 1, 214.
55. *Ś.B.*, X, 1, 66.
56. *Ś.B.*, VI, 1, 76.
57. Ibid.
58. *Ś.B.*, IV, 4, 1462.
59. *Ś.B.*, IV, 4, 1463.
60. *Ś.B.*, IV, 4, 1446.
61. *Ś.B.*, IV, 4, 1461.
62. *Ś.B.*, IV, 4, 1456.
63. *Ś.B.*, IV, 4, 1462.
64. *Ś.B.*, IV, 4, 1468.
65. *Ś.B.*, IV, 4, 1468-1469.
66. *Ś.B.*, X, 2, 51.
67. *Ś.B.*, VI, 1, 46-47.
68. *Ś.B.*, VI, 1, 47.
69. *Bhagavad-gītā*, p. 656.
70. *Ś.B.*, X, 1, 66.
71. *Ś.B.*, V, 1, 314.
72. *Ś.B.*, IV, 1, 189.
73. *Bhagavad-gītā*, p. 654.
74. *Ś.B.*, IX, 1, 124.
75. *Ś.B.*, VII, 1, 96.
76. *Ś.B.*, III, 4, 1298.
77. *Ś.B.*, III, 4, 1300.
78. *Ś.B.*, III, 4, 1302.

79. *Ś.B.*, V, 2, 439.
80. Ibid.
81. *Bhagavad-gītā*, 8.6.
82. Ibid., p. 411.
83. *Ś.B.*, III, 4, 1297.
84. *Bhagavad-gītā*, p. 415.
85. *The Nectar of Devotion*, p. 74.
86. *Ś.B.*, V, 2, 279.
87. *Bhagavad-gītā*, p. 713.
88. *Ś.B.*, VII, 2, 59.
89. *Ś.B.*, VI, 2, 228.
90. *Ś.B.*, III, 4, 1314.
91. Ibid.
92. *Ś.B.*, I, 2, 616.
93. *Ś.B.*, III, 4, 1325.
94. *Ś.B.*, III, 4, 1331.
95. *Ś.B.*, III, 4, 1336.
96. *Ś.B.*, III, 4, 1338.
97. *Ś.B.*, VI, 2, 228.
98. *Ś.B.*, VII, 1, 17.
99. *Bhagavad-gītā*, pp. 349, 390; *Śrī Īśopaniṣad*, p. 36.
100. *Bhagavad-gītā*, p. 158.
101. *Śrī Īśopaniṣad*, p. 109.
102. *Ś.B.*, I, 2, 426.
103. *Śrī Īśopaniṣad*, p. 83.
104. *Bhagavad-gītā*, p. 431.
105. Ibid., p. 379.
106. Ibid., p. 432.
107. Ibid., pp. 703-704.
108. *Ś.B.*, VI, 1, 133.
109. *Bhagavad-gītā*, p. 665.
110. Ibid., p. 261.
111. Ibid., p. 262.
112. *Ś.B.*, I, 1, 304.
113. Ibid.
114. *Ś.B.*, X, 1, 103.
115. *Ś.B.*, VIII, 3, 151.
116. *Bhagavad-gītā*, p. 690. See also p. 139.
117. Ibid., p. 312.
118. Ibid., p. 294.
119. *Ś.B.*, VI, 1, 272.
120. *Śrī Īśopaniṣad*, pp. 65 & 70.
121. *Bhagavad-gītā*, p. 274.
122. Ibid., p. 359.
123. Ibid., p. 274.
124. Ibid., pp. 242-243; 263.
125. Ibid., p. 253.
126. *Ś.B.*, VII, 2, 217.

127. *Ś.B.*, I, 1, 295-296.
128. *Bhagavad-gītā*, p. 424.
129. Ibid., p. 702.
130. Ibid., p. 443.
131. *The Nectar of Instruction*, p. 36.
132. Ibid., p. 37.
133. *Bhagavad-gītā*, p. 272.
134. Ibid., p. 135.
135. *Ś.B.*, I, 1, 110.
136. *Ś.B.*, IV, 3, 851.
137. *Perfect Questions Perfect Answers* (Los Angeles: The Bhaktivedanta Book Trust, 1977), pp. 59-60.
138. *Ś.B.*, IX, 2, 6.
139. *Ś.B.*, I, 1, 323.

CHAPTER SIXTEEN

Teachings on Karma and Rebirth: Social and Spiritual Role in the Rajneesh Neo-Saṃnyāsin Movement

ROBERT E. GUSSNER
(Sw. Anand Jina)

Because it is scarcely a dozen years old, the Rahneesh movement represents the most recent post-classical development concerning teachings on karma and rebirth to be considered in this volume. In this movement we find a trend to prune traditional doctrines on karma and rebirth of aspects (1) that legitimate the present social order East or West, (2) that recommend ways to manage karma tending to leave power in the hands of priests, parents or others with official system-roles in the society, (3) that teach ways to repress yourself, or, (4) that instill fear about punishment in the next life or in the interval between lives.

We shall also see that in the Rajneesh movement the connection between unawareness and karma is strong, and the connection between unawareness and rebirth is strong, but that any link between karma and rebirth is remarkably muted. Or put another way, one post-classical development at work in the Rajneesh movement is to insist that the basic polarity in regard to any subject whatsoever is between awareness and unawareness (*avidyā* and *vidyā*). Thus, of the root afflictions (*kleśas*) in Patanjala yoga, *avidyā* alone is emphasized; of all the links (*nidānas*) in the chain of conditioned co-production (*pratītyasamutpada*), *avidyā* is stressed in preference to *saṃskāras* (subliminal-activators, or karmic substratum-deposits). In part, this severing of karma from rebirth and society may be due to Rajneesh's upbringing in the Jain community and to his Buddhist leanings, but even more so it is due to two other factors: his view that societal repression of the individual has rendered him so inauthentic that he cannot progress in the spiritual life unless he becomes real, and that this requires an approach of allowing emotional, sexual and inter-personal genuineness as the prerequisite to healing the mind-body split in modern man. This is preliminary to any spiritual life because only the united energies of mind and body are powerful enough to carry you beyond into the spiritual. Thus, Rajneesh's teachings on karma and rebirth are largely determined by his views on the spiritual path—an illustration of the way in which Indian philosophy is "path philosophy," according to Karl Potter. His particular path requires authenticity and cathartic release of repressions at the outset, and a de-focal expressive mode of meditation further on. Beyond this, Rajneesh's teachings also seem to presuppose a kind of "second coming of age" in man's evolution—a new maturity that frees him from the need of society's moral tutelage even more radically than did man's first coming of age in humanism and secularism. Of this, more in my conclusions. Throughout the paper I trace how Rajneesh's teachings on karma and rebirth are fashioned in such a way that if you are aware (to be defined later) you can be real, even apparently immoral, and not fear that you are incurring bad karma thereby, or an unfortunate birth in another life. Before turning to these teachings, however, a brief orientation to the Rajneesh movement may be helpful for those unfamiliar with its brief but controversial history.

THE RAJNEESH MOVEMENT

Rajneesh Chandra Mohan was born into a Jain family near Jabalpur in Central India in 1931, and is said to have experienced full enlightenment in March, 1953. He took an M.A. in philosophy in 1957 and taught in two universities until 1966, when he resigned and began to tour India, speaking and searching for spiritual co-workers. As Ācārya Rajneesh he was a controversial guru who experimented with physically active styles of meditation and taught a spiritual progression from sex to love to prayer to transcendence. In 1970 he settled in Bombay, gradually accepted Western disciples, and soon declared himself Bhagwan Shree Rajneesh. Bhagwan, he says, simply means, "the blessed one." In 1974, under the aegis of the newly incorporated Rajneesh Foundation, he established an ashram in Poona, and introduced numerous types of Western therapy and growth groups into the Ashram routine as part of the preparatory path in the spiritual life. Freedom of expression in the ashram soon made it the largest growth center in the world and aroused much Indian oposition. In May of 1981, after ten years of daily discourses, Rajneesh entered into a final, silent period of his work, and shortly thereafter moved to the United States. Most of the key ashram workers followed him to the United States.

Today the movement claims 250,000 initiated neo-*saṃnyāsins* with followers most numerous in the Netherlands, W. Germany, and the United Kingdom. Although the movement is less visible in the U.S., its headquarters are now in the newly incorporated town of Rajneesh-puram in

Oregon, situated on a 64,000 acre ranch where Bhagwan is now in residence. The projected growth of this center is between two and ten thousand people. Other major centers exist in Texas, Massachusetts, New Jersey and California.

Detailed descriptions of life in the Poona ashram are available in Satya Bharti's *Death Comes Dancing* (Kegan Paul), or *Drunk on the Divine* (Grove Press). Harper and Row has Bernard Gunther's *Dying for Enlightenment: Living with Bhagwan Shree Rajneesh,* and Grove Press has verbatim *darśana* accounts in their publication, *Hammer on the Rock,* and a new *Rajneesh Reader.*

SOURCES OF THIS STUDY

A word about the sources I have used is in order to underline the limitations of this study. Bhagwan's discourses run to 336 volumes, besides some unpublished tape recordings. No index of this material exists, although a beginning has been made. For this study, I have read in only about sixty books and heard another score of tapes. His editors have directed me to five places where Rajneesh discusses karma and rebirth, and I have checked the five places where he discusses karma in his ten volume commentary on Patanjala yoga. The study, therefore, is a sample of his thought on karma and rebirth, and cannot claim to be exhaustive. I hope I have found the central thrust of his teachings on these topics, but he may have other points to emphasize about karma and rebirth which I have totally missed.

KARMA THEORY: AWARENESS VS. CULTIVATION OF GOOD KARMA

The most substantial and systematic references to karma in Rajneesh's works are to be found in his ten volume commentary on the *Yoga Sūtras* of Patañjali. In those *sūtras,* karma as a word occurs on five occasions (I.24, II.12, III.22, IV.7 and IV.30). Rajneesh accepts without qualification the existence of the three traditional types of karma—*sañcita, prārabdha,* and *kriyāman.*[1] *Sañcita* karma is the total accumulated karma from all of your past lives. *Prārabdha* karma is that portion of the total that you have to work out, or fulfill in this life—what you will act out, realize, suffer, and pass through. *Kriyāman* karma is the even smaller day-to-day portion of the *prārabdha* karma. Each moment one is presented with a chance to do something in reaction or not to do something. The correct way to work out karma, according to Rajneesh, is not to attempt a good reaction rather than a bad one, but rather not to react at all. One can *observe* the reaction within the mind to an insult and allow it to be, but unexpressed. Expressed, more *kriyāman* karma again falls into the *sañcita* karma, accumulated for future lives. If you don't react to an insult by a person (whom you may have insulted previously) then the account is closed and a past karma is fulfilled.[2] An aware person will be able to detect a subtle inner freeing and he will be happy.[3]

Rajneesh identifies *kriyāman* karma with the conscious domain of the mind; in psychological terms the *prārabdha* domain is the subconscious. Below that is the even deeper area of the *sañcita*, which he calls the unconscious.[4] His strategy for working with karma is to bring awareness to the surface realm first, and then, progressively, to the two deeper layers. One starts by becoming aware of day-to-day activities like eating or walking, remaining focused on the activity, instead of mentally wandering here and there like a zombie.[5] And whatever you are saying can be said with full alertness. This he equates with the modern ideal of being here-now.[6] After practice of this first step, you can move to the subconscious, and you will not only become aware when you have become angry, you will be immediately aware when you have been insulted that a very small, subtle wave has begun to move in your subconscious. Awareness of subtle nuances and shades of emotions is awareness of *prārabdha* karma. The more you grow in this ability to sense, the more you can grow in awareness of the *sañcita* karma. When you completely bring the light of consciousness into the deepest core of your being, and nothing is dark, you become a Buddha.[7]

In the above views, the centrality of the notions of awareness and unawareness is already apparent. In one sense awareness means alert mindfulness in the Theravadin sense of *satipatthana*, noting what is going on in your mind, in your movements and in your surroundings. In a second and deeper sense, it means cognizance of your own subjective presence as a crystalized witness, which arises as a shadow-reflex of mindfulness practice carried on without slack or strain, and which has a quality of deep silence in it. For those who are familiar with Gurdjieff/Ouspensky terminology, this second sense of the word awareness is equivalent to self-remembering with its double-arrowed consciousness and peculiar sense of "I am here." Rajneesh also uses the word awareness (or consciousness) to mean fully enlightened and liberated consciousness. In what follows, the context will usually suggest which sense is intended.

The notion of awareness, even in its first and minimal sense, is central to Rajneesh's concept of what an act is and what karma is. He holds that "whatever you do in unawareness (identification) becomes a karma."[8] A simple mechanical reaction is the usual example, and this is contrasted with a response which is total, spontaneous, and centered. A response is not an action, for Rajneesh, and leaves no trace (*saṃskāra*) on the mind-stuff. Any such action is complete in itself, and this is not an action. Thus, the crucial differentia of a karma which leaves a subliminal-activator deposit is its incompleteness. That defines the category of action for Rajneesh.[9] In terms of *Yoga Sūtra* I.3, Rajneesh seems to hold that every thought and every act leaves a mark only so long as you are in a state of being identified (*sārūpyam*) with the mental fluctuation (*vṛtti*), but not when there is a standing, witness-like, in your own nature (*svarūpine 'vasthānam*). He says this can happen momentarily whenever the observing-self briefly cognizes the object-self.

As an aside, I might note that mindful responses, not being acts, tend to complete two types of karma without adding karma. Thus, such responses are *nivṛtti,* not in the sense that a response is not motivated by desire and need (it is, as are all doings prior to enlightenment), and not in the sense that one need be outside of householder social structures to perform the act, but in the simple sense that it is a turning in, a turning down, into awareness of mind and of *kriyāman* and *prārabdha* karma in the sense discussed above. As such, it is the opposite of *pravṛtti,* mind-fluctuations going outward in unconscious reactions with a mechanical identification with the *vṛtti* (mind fluctuation) and the production of karma. *Pravṛtti* is outward going in the sense that it takes you further way from the last observing act that will finish off your last residue of *sañcita* karma, and *nivṛtti* is inward turning in the sense that it is homeward bound, is a return into your nature and ground as enlightened. The concepts seem essentially directional in nature.

Elsewhere, in commentary on *Yoga Sūtra* II.10-14, central concepts in Rajneesh's presentation of karma theory are developed differently. They are repetition, the self-energizing action of habit, the ego's rationalization of its freedom, and ultimate slavery to karma. These form four stages in an ontological descent into skid row. The way out of karmic entrapment lies in (1) realizing your rationalization, (2) seeing deeply into the fact that you alone are absolutely responsible for all your misery and dissatisfaction, and, (3) most importantly, undertaking the process of *pratiprasava*, or flowing back to the cause.

The first point to note is that Rajneesh is not saying that whatever you repeat becomes a habit. Rather, he says, "Whatsoever you do creates its own repetition."[10] This, says Rajneesh, is the heart of the theory of karma. "Each action has its own way of persisting. If you were angry the day before yesterday, you created a certain potentiality to be angry yesterday."[11] The act creates a channel into your being and the energy coming from the First Principle will run into readily available channels. The channel being there it will deepen itself. This view of karma articulates with Raymond Panikkar's characterization of karma as "the act that acts,"[12] but here in a double sense.

The way the habit grows is that this channel "starts absorbing energy from your Being, from you."[13] According to Rajneesh this absorbing may be subconscious; moreover it can occur after the anger has gone away and you think that you are not angry any longer. When the mood of anger has gone, nothing basic has happened, the wheel of the mind has only moved and the spoke that was up has gone down.[14] If, on the other hand, you should still be conscious of lingering anger and attempt to suppress it, the anger will suffuse throughout your being. The indirect attention of avoidance also feeds the channel. So the persistence and deepening of the channel is not something for which the ego need give itself credit. The channel automatically and mechanically deepens itself, by and large. As the channel gathers energy it will sooner or later achieve the status of a habit, it will become second nature. In fact, says Rajneesh, it becomes your first nature; your real nature as pure, free consciousness becomes an appendix, a footnote in the book, and habit (character) becomes the main body of the book.[15] Eventually you end up in the grip of the habit; you live through the habit, or rather the habit lives through you. It finally takes enough energy so that it becomes the master and you become just the servant, a kind of shadow in the situation. The habit will give the order and you will be the obedient servant coming and going from the background somewhere.

At this point the third step in the descent occurs—the ego must rationalize the habit. You must befool yourself that you are doing it. The ego goes on thinking that you are still the boss. It may say, "I had to be angry, otherwise the children would go astray, or the office would go into chaos, or the wife would get out of place."[16] This is a deception because, says Rajneesh, the anger was only apparently forced by outer circumstances, but, fundamentally, the reaction or the mood boiled up from within. True, something may have pushed your button, as it were, but consider well. If you had been in an all-wants-supplied isolation chamber, in perfect conditions and completely apart from human stimulation, you would still move through all the moods that you have in relationships—euphoria, sadness, anger. Basically something comes from within and you hang it on someone else. It surfaces mechanically as response to stimulus, but it comes from within. If you do not realize this, you lock yourself behind the double door of the two-fold rationalization: I am really the boss, and something did it to me. Then one is blind to the mechanism of imprisonment and to the fact of imprisonment; consequently, one has no reason to seek release, or even to suspect that escape is necessary. Here one may live on and on.

This brings us to the nadir of the karmic situation, and the beginning of the way out. Escape happens in three deep insights: (1) seeing that reactions come from within; (2) realizing that you (as higher self and also as witnessing lower self) are absolutely responsible for whatsoever happens to you; (3) reliving the root cause of the reaction in the clear light of consciousness and healing the wound or impressions. This is the step of *pratiprasava* (return to the original state).

The point about responsibility is probably the most problematic, so I shall begin there and end with a word on *pratiprasava* as rebirthing.

As I understand Rajneesh, there are at least three senses in which one is responsible. First, you allowed the channel formation in the first place by being unaware and so engaging in identified action. Secondly, you are responsible because you make your experience what it is by how you construe and interpret it. Finally, in your nature as witness (*draṣṭṛ*) you can respond in such a way as to eliminate the pattern. If the root cause is some initial wound, you can heal that wound with the light of awareness in *pratiprasava*.

Let us consider this process as it is promulgated in the Rajneesh movement, for it is the basis of primal scream work, encounter groups, and so on. Says Rajneesh, notice, for example, when your wife is nasty to you. Perhaps you are reading the paper and she calls you insensitive, ugly, unsuccessful, unfaithful, etc. You alone are responsible for your experience of being hurt. The wound that was touched is in you; how you construe the exchange—as an insult or whatever—is also your doing.

If you actually achieve the insight that this is so, you may be depressed and frustrated at first. You are helpless and debarred from doing the things you usually do in this situation—reasoning or trying to change the other (the most unfulfilled wish in human life, according to Rajneesh). To change another is to try to change their marks and the turning of their wheel, and they are largely unconscious about this. So we usually try to get a sleepy person to wake up. It seldom happens.

Instead, you can see that your wife, in the last analysis, is nasty because of her own inner mechanism and channels. The habit of complaining, with its energy, is coming up as the wheel turns for her. In a sense, she is not nasty with you in any very specific way; if you were not there she would have been grumpy with the child, irritated with the plates or impatient with the radio. She had to do something. You were available at the wrong moment. She is responsible for her being and her behavior.

But so are you. Probably you have to react in anger. But once this happens you can go back from this effect to the cause, a wound perhaps from a previous life. By trying to go back within yourself, you take the first step, to stop throwing the responsibility outward. You stop trying to find out why your wife is nasty. Instead, you find out why you are hurt by the nastiness.

The method of *pratiprasava* is to relax, then penetrate into the anger until you feel it intensely inside. Then let this aroused energy help move you back toward the past, closer to the basic wounds in your memory. The wound may be one big one, or several small ones. Whatever the case, the point is to unroll the spool of film backwards to the root cause. Consciously feeling the wound, not in remembering, which is an impotent process, but in an intense reliving, where you become the child again, heals the wound.

The real secret of this healing, according to Rajneesh, is that consciousness is the healing force; "just the light of consciousness heals."[17] But the observing must be done without judgment or condemnation, otherwise the mind will close the wound and the ego will hide it. Then the mind becomes divided; you create a basement of the mind, and the disastrous modern dissociation begins.

Successfully done, witnessing keeps the mind in a oneness, deeply heals the karmic mark (anything you can complete, you are free from), and releases the mind from the past, making it available for a present-centered mode of experiencing. If there are dated emotions, or unfinished business from the past, says Rajneesh, then the present moment in your life will be just a fleeting passage from the past to the future. You will miss going deeply into the now-moment concealed in the vanishing present, and hence miss the vertical dimension which the now-moment is. Notice that for Rajneesh, the degree of solid contact with the now-moment is the exact measure of the degree of freedom operating vis-a-vis karmic bondage. It is the test of how much freedom you have. Solid contact, of course, is synonymous with awareness in its first sense.

By daily practice of the art of going backwards, re-experiencing the events of the day every evening, you will become proficient at *pratiprasava* and be able to open many deep and remote karmic wounds rapidly. You need only see them. No overt doing is required. This daily practice will also largely prevent burdening the mind with new karma, since anything re-experienced with sufficient intensity eliminates the impression on the mind. As we have seen, for Rajneeesh this is a very fundamental law.

> Any experience that is complete, you are finished with it. It leaves no trace—not even footprints. It simply disappears, evaporates. It leaves no karma, it creates no karma. This can happen in primal scream therapy.[18]

Here I should remark parenthetically, since this is a discussion of post-classical developments in karma-theory, that the use of Western growth groups such as Primal Scream workshops surely represents a development in the processing of karma, if not in its theory.

Let us now assess what Rajneesh accepts and what he rejects in classical karma theory. Clearly he accepts most of its essentials—the law of repetition, the three types of karma, its near-terrifying power to enslave.

For him, only the power of awareness, the mysterious expression of one's very self, is stronger. Only this saves man from a complete psychological subjugation and Rajneesh's position from philosophical determinism.

But what does he reject? Most popular applications of karma theory to social life, the effort to build good karma (in the form of good habits and good character), and, finally, the linking of karma to *jāti* (rebirth-species) and to *āyus* (length of future life). He does not, however, refuse to link karma to *bhoga* (experiences of life that you will meet). Let us consider this briefly.

Rajneesh's acceptance of a karma/*bhoga* link and his rejection of a karma/*jāti* link and a karma/*āyus* link occur in his commentary on *Yoga Sūtra* II.13. Pointedly ignoring the *jāti/āyus* portion of the total *sūtra*, which reads, "When root karma exists, it will ripen in species of birth, length of life, and types of experiences," he speaks only of types of experiences. Seeds, he says, that are unfinished will be fulfilled in millions of ways as you see situations and opportunities to complete them. The main result of karma seems to be the creation of character, or disposition, which finds situations attractive, challenging or baffling. This seems to be the sense of this commentary on sutra II.13.

> In this life you may be rich, but you are a miser and live the life of a poor man. That is karma. You have riches but you cannot live those riches, thinking perhaps that it is not religious. . . . On the other hand you may be a beggar and yet live like a rich man and worry about nothing. You have nothing to lose and enjoy yourself. This man carries the seeds of a rich life from his past and will find situations and opportunities to enjoy himself. Wherever you are it will not make much difference. You will have to live through your past.[19]

Rajneesh seems to side with those Indians who say that Karma is not so much what happens to you (e.g., getting hit by a truck), as your reaction to what happens to you (being cheerful, having a nervous breakdown, etc.). In any event, he is silent about any nexus between caste, karma and *guṇa* or the like, such as we find Kṛṣṇa expressing in the *Bhagavad-gītā*.

Let us turn to those aspects of popular karma doctrine that Rajneesh surely rejects. In one passage he says, "This is one of my most fundamental ideas that you have to understand: I am against the whole idea of karma."[20] Here he means its popular and priestly applications. His indictment is lengthy. Karma theory is a strategy of the mind to throw responsibility for misery on an unchangeable past; it makes people feel like helpless victims and needlessly ruins their lives. Again, it is an invention of the priests to keep people in poverty, yet content and causing no trouble for the *status quo*. It has prevented revolution through all of Indian history, has created a conformist mind about accepting whatsoever is, and this mind led to the disappearance of Buddhism from India. It gives the feeling that to take money or land from the rich is a sin that goes against God, and a horrible thing to do, like breaking the walls of a prison and letting the prisoners escape.[21] He ridicules karma as the theory which says, "Put your hand in the fire now, and you will get burned in the next life."[22] Clearly the result of an act is not some future event for Rajneesh, but the wound-mark in the mind which life always gives immediately.[23]

More basic is his rejection of attempts to balance bad karma with good acts. He distinguishes two general attitudes in India toward what should be done with the karmic burden—one is that of Patañjali and the other is that of Mahāvira, the last *tīrthaṅkāra* of the Jain community. "Mahāvira says, if you have done wrong you have to right it, otherwise you will suffer. Do good to the world."[24] This standpoint is concerned with actions, morality, "shoulds and shouldnots."[25] It addresses what to do, not how to be. Patañjali, on the other hand, stresses bringing the energy of awareness to your past; it is consciousness-oriented, not action-oriented. Not surprisingly, Rajneesh says, "I am all in favor of Patañjali."[26]

This approach negates the whole Brahmanical panoply of procedures for accumulating good karma through doing your duty in the social order called the *varnāśramadharma* system, as well as merit accumulation through study, penance, austerities and the like. More, it is an expression of an underlying repudiation of the cultivation of good habits, and, in fact, of all cultivation, as such. Consideration of the topics "habit" and "cultivation" will reveal what actuates Rajneesh's rejection of selected aspects of karmic teachings. His is an opting for the needs of the individual to throw off repression as a first step toward God-realization rather than opting for the needs of society for good individuals. Let me document this briefly from Rajneesh's discussion of karma in connection with *Yoga Sūtra* IV.7, where he interprets the aphorism, "The yogi's karmas are neither pure nor impure because they come out of original mind."

His discussion here centers on habits. The basic problem is that habits cannot be dropped in any simple sense because of the overriding power of karma. There are only two ways to deal with them.[27] One is to substitute another habit for the one you have. This is cutting another channel for the water of your being to flow into. It is changing one problem for another. Even if I develop a habit of helping others and doing saintly acts, then desires will arise to do more good, and if all my associates are away, I will feel restless to find someone to help. All habits are bad from the standpoint of God-realization, though not from society's standpoint. If the habit to do good becomes second nature, then when you want to drop it, that will not be easy. "Never," Rajneesh says, "try to change a bad habit into a good one." The temptation is great, of course, because of social pressure. If you begin going to church every day instead of the pub, you become moral, and once you are moral society is not bothered with you. It is finished with you except to cheer you and garland you with respect. You are a very good man. "But," says Rajneesh, "you yourself have yet long to go. The journey is not complete yet."[28] Habit as such is against your original nature.[29]

Here we see Rajneesh's basic concern to create a *saṅgha* as a transformative example outside of an official *dharmic* social order. We might explain this as due only to his being a Jain with Buddhist sympathies, and because he is overwhelmingly concerned with enlightenment, not life in Hindu society. But from the general emphasis of his works as a whole, the decisive motivation seems to be compassion for modern man everywhere, whom he sees as suffering from sealed-in repression of anger, sadness, loneliness, distancing from his real feelings.

This is reflected in his advice to deal with habits by awareness. Awareness "is the fire that burns the past."[30] Don't worry about dropping the habit, he counsels. "Whenever you repeat the habit, become aware." Repeat it, but with a witnessing, an alertness, an awareness. That makes you separate from the habit and the energy that was going in the habit channel and cutting the groove deeper doesn't go there any more. The energy you were giving the habit unknowingly doesn't go anywhere, doesn't make a new groove. It accumulates in your being against the day of a final explosion in realization. And by and by the habit will shrink.

This brings us very close to the heart of Rajneesh's stance on karma, namely that he rejects any view of karma and any application of karma theory to cultivate character. In fact, for him, *to cultivate anything is to become "pseudo."*[31] It means "you are creating something around you which you are not."[32] It means creating a split between your organismic reality/flow and your facade. "Then you live in a camouflage."[33] Cultivation creates holier-than-thou attitudes, gives the ego satisfactions; it does not create true morality (which comes from contacting Being within and is an overflow of love), it creates only ugly puritans.[34] His opposition to cultivation is many-sided and poly-dimensional. It puts you in a prison when you cultivate because, deep down, you create its opposite. What you suppress suffuses your being, and you have to fight its emergence and can never really relax. And you will feel one thing and show another, you will say one thing and do another. It will make you diplomatic (one of the most pejorative buzz words within the Rajneesh movement) and infect you with the most basic of diseases, the disease of seriousness, another buzz word in the movement, used in contrast to sincerity (being what you are at the moment). Cultivation cripples, divides energy, results in mankind dragging at low levels of vitality, creates deadness, and prevents morality. Real morality, he holds, is not to be cultivated, but comes as a shadow of being aware, consciousness. The way to this state is to begin by being aware of your neutral habits—walking eating, talking, feeling the wind, the coolness of the sheets in your bed at night, etc. One should be conscious of doing one's good habits and finally try and move to awareness of one's bad habits as they are being done. "Once you have become aware of your whole habitual pattern, that habitual pattern is your mind. Any day the shift will happen. Suddenly you will be in no-mind."[35]

We can now summarize the decisive role of awareness in Rajneesh's karma theory. An act is an act only if done with identification and unawareness. Only this kind of act creates a channel. If a channel is made, it will have to be completed. If a channel exists in the mind you will meet situations that activate that channel, and it will be self-active too. So, on one side of his theory are the elements unawareness-act-channel-incompleteness, and, on the other side, the elements awareness, a non-act, no channel creation, and a completeness of that unit of experience. So completeness can be obtained either by never creating the mark in the mind in the first instance, or by living it through in balancing of accounts through many lives and innumerable experiences (Mahāvira), or by awareness of habits that shrink and silt-up the channel (Patañjali as interpreted by Rajneesh). This summary of his position on karma should clarify what I said at the beginning about it being pruned of elements that connect it to society and morality, and it being decisively shaped by Rajneesh's espousal of the awareness path in spiritual life and his general sense that modern man need no longer be a ward of society. We shall see the same position operating in his presentation of death, the *bardo* state, and rebirth.

REBIRTH

Rajneesh accepts the fact of transmigration in Buddhist terms: there is transmigration but no transmigrants. The idea behind the device of teaching many lives, and the significance of the original message, was this:

> Remember that you have been living in the same rotten way over and over again. Can't you see it? You are moving in a wheel, going in circles. Are you not bored yet? Can't you see the futility of desiring the same thing; succeeding and failing and dying every time? Can't you see that something more is needed? This world won't do; you have to transcend it.[36]

What really happened was something totally different, just the opposite. The unconscious mind interpreted the whole purport of the message to be, "There is no hurry, we will think of God in old age or in the next life."[37] The devices created by conscious minds harm, not help. Nectar from the Buddhas becomes poison by the time it reaches you.

Similarly, in the West the idea behind teaching only one life on the part of Moses and others, who knew better, according to Rajneesh, was this:

> Time is short, so don't waste it on non-essential things, material things, trivial things, accumulating money and gadgets. This of the essential, not the accidental and superficial.[38]

But people turned it completely upside down so that they became interested in the non-essential. They began to say:

> There is not much time, so eat, drink and be merry. You are not coming again—who knows about God, heaven and the other world—so enjoy this life as much as you can; squeeze every moment to your heart's content.[39]

This is the conclusion that prevailed in the West. The hurry of having only one life, he says, begets a pressure and an ability to do everything quickly and skillfully. The mind is well developed. There is not a lot of thought about where you are going, but the speed with which you go and do is nearly perfected. In India, on the other hand, everything from the government to the mind to technology became 'lousy' because time to improve was endless. The general ability to do declined and speed was less than ideal. The conclusion Rajneesh draws from all of this is that a new universal mind is needed. This mind will not think in terms of one life, or many lives, but only in terms of consciousness.[40] All thought of hemispheres East and West, all thought of tradition as a basic category, all thought of race, blood and nationality must go, and only the familiar emphasis upon the difference between awareness and sleep is stressed.

Although *bardo* states (between-life intervals) and rebirth are secondary topics for Rajneesh, he teaches them as a fact on the authority of his own conscious death, *bardo* state, and rebirth. And there is much lore in the movement about the past lives of present disciples, and a strong sense that they work together recurringly down through the centuries.

In his discussions on rebirth, Rajneesh discusses four principal subjects: the importance of remembering past lives, vegetarianism, the nature of the interval state between bodies, and the free rebirth of conscious souls, and in each case the discussion is dominated by the theme of awareness.

Remembering past lives is important for Rajneesh because it saves time and energy in the practical matter of progress in the spiritual life. As animals don't evolve because of lack of communication, and each monkey must start his learning all over at the level that his father began, so a soul may merely repeat the building of the foundation of his house over and over again. By searching out your past lives you will start from where you left off, and not be only a repetition. The knowledge can produce a spiritual revolution in you.[41]

In remembering past lives, techniques of regression are the least difficult thing. Harder is the courage to remain undisturbed and centered in the midst of difficult memories which come to you, not in installments, but in their painful entirety. The lightness of mind and fluid ability to receive imagery is also hard to come by. And the key to this is vegetarianism, says Rajneesh. It is no coincidence that all the vegetarian religions (Hinduism, Jainism, Buddhism) believe in transmigration, and Western ones do not.

> When a person is utterly vegetarian he can easily remember his past lives. His clarity is such that he can look into his past lives. He is not gross, his energy is not blocked, his energy moves easily. His river of consciousness can penetrate to the ancientmost times; he can go backwards as much as he wants. The consciousness of the non-vegetarian is blocked, he has been absorbing gross matter in himself. That gross matter functions as a barrier. That's why all three religions that were born outside of India, and have remained non-vegetarian could not come to the idea of reincarnation. They could not experience it.[42]

Disagreeing on many other things, Indian religions could not disagree on rebirth because of their experience of past lives. This comes out of deeper meditation, which, in turn is aided by vegetarianism. Eating meat and meditating, says Rajneesh, is like climbing a mountain carrying big rocks—it can be done, but it is more difficult. Vegetarianism is advocated as an aesthetic and spiritual matter, not a moral and religious one.

Let us now take up the complex, and for Rajneesh, relatively unimportant subject of the nature of the state between bodies, the interval state. Here we find a tremendous potpourri of points to sort out. I shall present them as a series of questions, or issues.

a. *The issue of the nature of Bardo experience.* Whatever experiences can be had in the interval will be such as can be had without a body:[43] a few can meditate, a few can explore by psychic capacities, most are in a dream-like state. As dreams are experiences from seeds in memory, so interval experiences are, too. As in a dream there is little doubt about the reality of those experiences, so here, too. As in a dream impossible transformations don't appear impossible, so here, too. In the interval things can seem even more vividly real than in a body, because while awake in a body there is room for doubt about the "realisticalness" of happenings.[44] Demons seem absolutely real, as do heavenly damsels.

b. *The issue of heaven and hell.* Heaven and hell are just deep dream lives. A dream might be only of heaven, or only of hell, or mixed. Descriptions of heaven and hell differ, as the persons with faint memories of the dream have different mental states.[45] Newborns generally remember the dream for six months, very sensitive people a little longer, up to five years.[46]

c. *The issue of finding a new womb.* There are three types of souls. A minority are *pretas.* They are evil and for them it is difficult to find another birth because the wombs with which they fit are a microscopic minority. Existence is like a bell-curve in this regard. Similarly some are *devas,* serene calm beings, who also find wombs scarce. We shall consider the rebirth prospects of the would-be *bodhisattva* separately when discussing Rajneesh's rebirth experience. The third type of soul, the average majority, have some differences of character and so of interval-experiences, but are all essentially of the same type. Some can be psychic and aware in the interval, but most go into a coma and are reborn immediately or within a few years.[47] They may even be dying and entering the womb of a couple having intercourse simultaneously.[48]

d. *The issue of time-sense.* The length of time passed between lives is not clearly measured in the memory of the disembodied. As a dream may seem like eight hours and be only five minutes, so when dead you would not know if your dream night had been lengthened to eight years. During the interval there is no clear awareness of the duration of time.[49]

e. *The issue of movement.* The question as to whether the dead are stationary or in a movement condition does not apply. These depend upon a body and its sense of time and space, but these are absent. The boundaries of time and space, within which movement or non-movement is observed by the person, do not exist during that interval.[50]

f. *The issue of space.* The dead are right here, so to speak. As in this room space is filled by different things that do not conflict, so with souls. This space can have an aroma of incense, it can have air waves of sound, it can have radio waves, and they do not interfere with each other; so the subtle matter of the mind can be right here.[51]

g. *The issue of spirit-possession*. Since there is no movement on the part of disembodied souls, it is not right to say that souls will enter a body. This is a linguistic fallacy. It is better to say that some body may behave in such a way that it will cause a soul to enter. Two types of living persons are in a state of deep receptivity to souls: those in great fear, and those in a deeply prayerful moment. In both, the soul contracts and vacates parts of bodily space. Souls that are in misery and agony enter empty bodily space within the fearful, who are like ditches that catch downward moving things. In the same way, higher souls enter the prayerful, induced by the many techniques of invocation and invitation existing in all religions.[52]

h. *The issue of communication*. Communication is not possible for souls with each other in their dream state. It is like a roomful of sleeping people. It is only possible to communicate if a soul can enter someone's body. Then communication is possible between the entering soul and the soul existing in the body. So the Vedas were communicated to the *ṛṣis* via auditory experiences. Two souls can communicate with each other if they both take bodies. Ordinarily, communication requires body and brain. But people who have developed ESP and can communicate without the brain routing, may succeed, while bodiless, in establishing relationships with *preta* and *deva* spirits. Few have that capacity; however, information about the spiritual world has been given to us only by such souls.[53] It is like twenty drunks in a room. One, by practice, can stay conscious a bit longer and can tell us about the experiences of being drunk. The others could not tell because they become unconscious before knowing anything.[54] Those dying with no ESP capabilities cannot recognize, communicate with others, nor possess a living person's body. They die in a coma, deeply unconscious, awaiting a new birth. A kind of natural anaesthesia happens.

i. *The issue of development*. There is no development of any type whatsoever during the interval state, even if it is a hundred years. You begin your new birth right from where you left off. All development is blocked; even the gods can't reach liberation while in heaven.[55] However, in the moments-of-death, when the body might be technically dead, but not subtly so, when one is semi-deceased in Tibetan terms, some development is possible. One can recognize all the high levels of one's being, and Tibetan *bardo* work is actually a training to create a dream sequence in this semi-deceased state, where one still has a body in a certain sense. Once past this state, when actual death comes, there is a gap until one begins re-entry into the world and into a body. In that gap ninety-nine percent are simply unconscious.[56]

j. *The issue of knowing your approaching death*. The hour before you fall asleep and the hour just after you awaken have a certain quality of "dream-smoke." This time is traditionally called the *sandhyakāla*, the twilight time. It is not necessarily at the junction of day and night. It is the hour before you go to sleep and the hour after you awaken, which might or might not coincide with the dawn and dusk. If you utilize that hour properly in meditation and prayer you can know exactly your time of death six months before your death because that quality which was previously coming for only one hour will remain continuous and steady through those last six months.[57] Also six months before death the eyes become "loose" and begin to roll up; one will not be able to see the tip of one's nose any longer. Nine months before death, Rajneesh also asserts, a sensitive person can feel a click in the abdominal region, in the *hara*. Further, a person able to make a *samyāma*, an act of absorption, will be able to look at his *prārabdha* karma-room and see that only a little is left in one corner, so that this life cannot last much longer.[58]

To make the point about the absence of connection in Rajneesh's presentations between karma and the circumstances of rebirth, I shall quote one typical answer to a question that illustrates, at the same time, the inevitable connection in his thought between consciousness/awareness and rebirth.

A *saṃnyāsin asked, "In my pre-sannyas period, my life with my family* was unhappy. Why did I choose an unhappy family to be born into?" Probably the questioner had in mind some penalty for being evil in a past life implying a theory of karma of punishment for being naughty and the whole image of an infantile humanity implied in that.

The answer, however, ignores that and comes swiftly to an even more devastating point: "You didn't choose; if you could have you wouldn't have chosen this family. You moved into the womb robotlike."[59] This is saying, on the basis of our preceding classification of souls, that the questioner is in the average majority. The answer continues:

> You died unconsciously and entered the womb unconsciously. Death is the condensed moment of life. If you have been unconscious in life, the moment of death will be a tremendously condensed unconsciousness. Millions of people are making love all over the world. Many wombs are ready. They are unconscious as you are unconscious. They don't know what is happening. They are making love out of unawareness, not out of awareness. If a couple who has exactly the same kind of unawareness that you have is making love, then immediately you will enter into that womb. That fits with you. You did not choose to be born into an unhappy family; you could not have

> done otherwise. You have done it many times, and beware or you will do it again. You can choose only when you are aware.[60]

It should be clear, I think, that compared to this overwhelming emphasis on the connection between consciousness and rebirth, that Rajneesh's infrequent and unelaborated connections between karma and rebirth can only be said to be unimportant. This, surely, is a striking shift of emphasis from anything we find in classical times.

We should turn now to what may be a post-classical development about the rebirth of *bodhisattvas*. Rajneesh teaches about this in relation to his own present incarnation, and has something new to say, I think.

Rajneesh was not completely enlightened in his last life, he says, and came only with "near-about" full knowledge, that is, twelve of the fourteen steps (*guṇasthānas*) in the Jain reckoning completed. He had not skipped over any steps; he had intact the *tīrthaṅkāra bandha*, or desire to be a teacher. Situated at step twelve there is only a curtain between you and reality, and you can lift it. Lifting it is the thirteenth step and going completely beyond is the fourteenth. After the twelve steps, he says, the last steps can be stretched out from one to three births. Here we have a Jain version of the Buddhist *bodhisattva* teaching being unfolded. If, however, you go beyond the curtain, at most one more birth is possible.[61]

If you stay on this side of the curtain, where no walls separate you from seeing Reality, you have the possibility to set aside the last two steps. This certainly is the *bodhisattva*'s turning back.

Buddha and Mahāvira did not use the opportunity to stop at stage twelve because their circumstances were different. They had many advanced students and one life was enough to teach them, and to entrust to special ones the left over work with the circle of disciples in question. And, says Rajneesh, in Mahāvira's time, eight fully realized people were at work in the state of Bihar alone.[62] There were many "near-about" people to whom the work of finishing could be entrusted.

Now, however, in Rajneesh's case the situation is completely different. As always, full knowledge can be taught only to very advanced students, but now developed *sādhakas* are practically nil.[63] So it is very hard to find a birth to take. Suitable parents are a problem. Rajneesh says he was previously born about 700 years ago, reckoned by seeing in this life that one of his disciples with whom he was working in his last life had taken ten births. During the interval that a high level person has to wait to take births, which is getting to be a thousand years nowadays,[64] the persons with whom he was working get ten layers of new problems in ten lives.[65] There are more impediments needing cutting through. So future teachers will have to work for many births to complete the work.

To make matters worse, the deteriorating times leave the would-be teacher bereft of adepts able to finish his work. So, before taking a birth, an illumined soul, or a *bodhisattva*, has two considerations to weigh: the fear that his labor may go to waste, and the fear that he may actually harm you. This last seems strange, but Rajneesh's argument goes like this: in one birth it is not possible to do much; a compassionate person needs to take something away from you and then give you something in replacement; you need to be able to receive what he gives in replacement for stability, otherwise you will be destabilized and disoriented. You will be in danger, not able to see what you could see before.[66] The *bodhisattva* will feel that taking away alone is not good, unless you are able to show something as well. This is just how a compassionate person is.[67] In this situation, Rajneesh feels it is good that he did not attain enlightenment (being stabbed three days before his fast was to end in enlightenment) because now he can still take yet another birth. "Whether I take another birth," he says, "depends on whether I feel it will be useful."[68]

We hear much about the degenerate age of the *dharma* in Buddhist literature. Here, I think, we have the novel glimpse of a discussion of that as it affects the rebirth choices of *bodhisattvas* and those who attain enlightenment in this life. It is something new in the tradition and worth further investigation by scholars.

CONCLUSION

Indians who oppose Rajneesh, and those who don't, tend to agree that he is traditional in what he teaches, but untraditional in his methods and disciplines. As we have seen, he is not entirely traditional in his teachings, yet is substantially so. It may be well to try to specify more exactly where he is traditional and not.

On karma, Rajneesh's exposition is similar to tradition at many points: channel theory echoes much about *praṇāla* and *śrota* noted by J. Bruce Long in the *Mahābhārata*.[69] It also echoes Jain doctrine, where "karma is not in any sense considered to *impel* the soul; it functions, rather, to direct the motive force which is already present."[70] And Rajneesh certainly selects for emphasis a point found in the *Caraka Saṃhitā*, namely, that the root ill (*doṣa*) in all deeds comes from their being done *prajñā-'parādha*, that is, lacking in the wisdom and concentration associated with centered awareness.[71] Finally, the heart of what Rajneesh has to say about karma management articulates with the Theravadin recognition, mentioned by James McDermott, that there is a clas of deeds which leads to neither dark, light or mixed results, but which, rather, consumes past karma, because it is non-purposive action, choicelessness,[72] or selflessness. These are the principal elements played up in his discussion of karma, always stressing that it can be mastered by awareness, and always downplaying any mastering of it by the gradual paths of duty, conformity to codes, and so on. If we ask what is common to emphasizing consciousness and de-emphasizing morality, the answer is consistency with the *sādhana* of mindfulness and awareness, what Rajneesh calls the *via negativa*. Of this, more later.

On rebirth, we hear echoes of the Jain view of *samaya*, that the soul moves into another body in a single instant after death, as discussed by Padmanabh S. Jaini.[73] On the other hand, he also accepts an interval-state of a being (*antarā bhava*) similar to the Vaibāṣika theory of the *gandharva/gandhabba* studied by both McDermott and Jaini.[74] Apparently, Rajneesh tries to reconcile these two seemingly contradictory positions by saying that between embodiments the time-sense is unclear and so people with any memory of the interval will give conflicting recollections of it, and by saying that some persons do, in fact, go into immediate rebirth and others not, depending upon variables of ability to stay aware. This ability harkens back, I think, to the Jain teaching on *upayoga*, or scale of awareness doctrine, noted by P.S. Jaini.[75]

Throughout this essay I have been arguing that it is Rajneesh's choice of spiritual path more than his Jain background that determines his doctrine. Now it may be the time to contrast the two paths that he sees in order to make this point clear. Rajneesh contrasts a *via positiva* with a *via negativa* and endorses the latter. The awareness path is the *via negativa*, and some may call it non-traditional merely because it is non-Hindu. It is not non-Indian except in its expressive, cathartic preamble.

The awareness path is also called the path of surrender, and the path of the let-go. It is expressive, and contrasts with the path of striving, of the warrior, of concentration, of control, of holding on, of struggle and fighting to advance. It is de-focal (takes no one object of meditation in order to focus on it) and flowing. It has no preferences. But, the warrior path is the *via affirmativa* because it says yes to society, family, morality, cultivation of character. It is a training, a "yang" path; you have much to do in the way of exercises, *ascesis*. You advance gradually. There is a technology and clearly defined steps and stages of progress. It is technique-centered and so requires time to prepare, learn, improve. It is a path that can be explained, and is quite orderly and scientific. It begins with morality and moves to awareness. It respects scriptures as authorities, legitimates system-roles and gives them a spiritual direction; its saints tend to be advisors to the religious and political powers-that-be. Usually it is a path of prayer, devotion, God. It is the way of mainstream Christianity, Hinduism, Judaism, Islam. It affirms positive values in society, affirms doing, rising step by step, effort.[76] It articulates with creating good karma.

The *via negativa*, of course, is the opposite at every point. This is what Rajneesh mostly teaches and this determines what he says about karma and rebirth, and what he omits or de-emphasizes, too. This path is the path of the rebels like Lao Tzu, Bodhidharma, Nāgārjuna, Buddha, Krishnamurti, and so on. It simply witnesses the body and mind, without particular effort to change things. It is waiting, not seeking. It is "yin" receptivity, watching. "It is where you have exactly nothing to do."[77] So it is a mysterious path, no technology, no steps, no clear stages and explanations. It doesn't care much for the opinions of society, of ordinary ego-mind, scriptures, traditions, social leaders. It is the way of the Tantric adept, of the Baul mystic, of the Taoists; meditation not action.[78]

And, of course, karma theory has to do with action and the effects of action and the use of action to improve. To the path of choicelessness, the idea of improving implies preference, and hence, is the antithesis of choicelessness. It is along these lines, I think, that we must look if we want to interpret why he skips over developing good karma and good habits so lightly. But, even here, Rajneesh's mode of discourse is not without precedent in India.

In yet other ways, Rajneesh seems traditionally Indian. For example, J. Bruce Long in his study of the *Mokṣadharmaparvan* portion of the *Mahābhārata* notes that the work "puts the spotlight on the nature of the path to enlightenment."[79] And aspects of the doctrines of karma and rebirth are developed "rather curiously."[80] They function only as a springboard to the more elaborate articulation of the nature of liberation and ways of achieving it. In particular it deals with the cancelling and creating of karmic debts "until the embodied self achieves a true knowledge of the duties required by that contemplation which leads to liberation."[81] Rajneesh obviously shares the text's concern for enlightenment. And the text seems to view doing good (building good habits) only as a means for coming to the real understanding that is needed on how to manage karma, namely what one comes to know in and through contemplation. Rajneesh's presentation differs from that of the *Mahābhārata* only by telling you that the preliminaries of good work are just that, and that the preliminaries are not really needed. He moves directly in his discussion to the essential subject of contemplation. Again, this may be non-Hindu, but it is not on that account non-Indian.

Let me try to summarize and position Rajneesh in the larger history of karma and rebirth thought. In classical times, tribal ideas of a routine rebirth were changed. They were linked to the performance of good deeds as socially defined by the great tradition that was replacing, or supplementing, the little traditions. Individual ethics began to supersede tribal *mores* and the calculations of omens, divination, and augury as guides to the correct actions that would please the spirits. Better actions resulted in a better birth in the social system, and improving your karma and your rebirth was linked to doing your duties in the social structure. Then, with the rise of the Buddhist *saṅgha*, karma-attenuation by contemplation apart from roles and duties in the society appeared. The individual withdrew from society; he managed his reconstruction his way, while society continued to enjoin the doing of good deeds upon its members. The *saṅgha* drew apart, but did not seek to assimilate the society to itself, nor to abolish society's strategem. Society and *saṅgha* ran in two parallel lines, intermixed to some extent, to be sure. With Rajneesh we see, I think, an offensive from the side of the *saṅgha* against the social tyranny of "the good," as seen in his position on cultivation of character. It is as if times have changed in two ways: society is more repressive to the point of crippling spiritual growth; and the individual is more mature as a separate ego. Being a mature ego, the individual, although less spiritual than the giants of the past, is ready to assume responsibility for his spiritual growth basically free of the domination of the super-ego. The super-ego may have been appropriate in the past, but modern man finds it toxic now. Whether this is in fact true or not, I shall not argue. Rather, my point is that interpreting the significance of Rajneesh's position on karma and rebirth seems to require the conclusion that he thinks it is true.

NOTES

1. Bhagwan Shree Rajneesh, *Yoga: The Alpha and the Omega*, VIII (Poona: Rajneesh Foundation, 1977), 10.
2. Ibid., p. 11.
3. Ibid.,
4. Ibid., p. 20.
5. Rajneesh, *Yoga: The Alpha and the Omega*, X (Poona: Rajneesh Foundation, 1978), 70.
6. Rajneesh, *Yoga*, VIII, 21.
7. Ibid., p. 21.
8. Ibid., p. 11.
9. Ibid.,
10. Rajneesh, *Yoga: The Alpha and the Omega*, IV (Poona: Rajneesh Foundation, 1976), 163.
11. Ibid., *Yoga*, IV, 163.
12. Raymond Ranikkar, "The Law Of Karma and the Historical Dimension of Man," *Philosophy East and West*, XXII, No. 1 (1972), 32.
13. Rajneesh, *Yoga*, IV, 163.
14. Ibid., p. 163.
15. Ibid., p. 164.
16. Ibid., p. 165.
17. Ibid., p. 169.
18. Bhagwan Shree Rajneesh, *Philosophia Perennis* II (Antelope, Oregon: Rejneesh Foundation International, 1981), 201-2.
19. Rajneesh, *Yoga*, IV, 182.

20. Bhagwan Shree Rajneesh, *The Book of Wisdom*, Cassette recording, Rajneesh Foundation, Tape #18.
21. Ibid.
22. Rajneesh, *Be Still and Know*, Cassette Recording, Rajneesh Foundation, Tape #4.
23. Rajneesh, *Book of Wisdom*, Tape #18.
24. Rajneesh, *Yoga*, IV, 185.
25. Ibid.
26. Ibid.
27. Rajneesh, *Yoga*, X, 69.
28. Ibid.
29. Ibid.
30. Rajneesh, *Yoga*, IV, 185.
31. Rajneesh, *Philosophia Perennis*, p. 339.
32. Ibid.
33. Ibid.
34. Ibid.
35. Rajneesh, *Yoga*, X, 71.
36. Rajneesh, *The Book of the Books*, IV, Cassette Recording #18.
37. Ibid.
38. Ibid.
39. Ibid.
40. Ibid.
41. Rajneesh, *Dimensions Beyond the Known* (Los Angeles, California: Wisdom Garden Books, 1975), p. 58.
42. Rajneesh, *Philosophia Perennis*, pp. 194-5.
43. Rajneesh, *Dimensions*, p. 127.
44. Ibid.
45. Ibid., p. 109.
46. Ibid., p. 111.
47. Ibid., pp. 1089.
48. Bhagwan Shree Rajneesh, *The White Lotus* (Poona: The Rajneesh Foundation, 1981), p. 196.
49. Rajneesh, *Dimensions*, p. 110.
50. Ibid., pp. 123-5.
51. Ibid., pp. 129-30.
52. Ibid.
53. Ibid., p. 139.
54. Ibid.
55. Bhagwan Shree Rajneesh, *The Great Challenge: A Rajneesh Reader* (New York: The Grove Press, Inc., 1982), p. 209.
56. Rajneesh, *Yoga*, VIII, 9.
57. Rajneesh, *Dimensions*, p. 113.
58. Rajneesh, *Yoga*, VIII, 18.
59. Rajneesh, *The Book of Books*, Cassette Recording, IV, #18.
60. Ibid.
61. Rajneesh, *Dimensions*, p. 71.
62. Ibid., p. 72.

63. Ibid., p. 73.
64. Ibid.
65. Ibid.
66. Ibid.
67. Ibid.
68. Ibid.
69. J. Bruce Long, "Human Action and Rebirth in the Mahābhārata," in *Karma and Rebirth in Classical Indian Traditions*, ed. by Wendy Doniger O'Flaherty (Berkeley, California: University of California Press, 1980), p. 58.
70. Padmanabh S. Jaini, "Karma and the Problem of Rebirth in Jainism," in *Karma and Rebirth in Classical Indian Traditions*, p. 230.
71. Mitchell G. Weiss, "Caraka Samhitā on the Doctrine of Karma," in *Karma and Rebirth in Classical Indian Traditions*, p. 115.
72. James P. McMDermott, "Karma and Rebirth in Early Buddhism," in *Karma and Rebirth in Classical Indian Traditions*, pp. 180-81.
73. Jaini in *Karma and Rebirth in Classical Indian Traditions*, p. 221.
74. McDermott in *Karma and Rebirth in Classical Indian Traditions*, pp. 171 and p. 229.
75. Jaini in *Karma and Rebirth in Classical Indian Traditions*, p. 233.
76. Bhagwan Shree Rajneesh, *Tao: The Pathless Path* I (Poona: The Rajneesh Foundation, 1979), 231-36.
77. Ibid., p. 232.
78. Ibid.
79. Long in *Karma and Rebirth in Classical Indian Traditions*, p. 60.
80. Ibid.
81. Ibid.

CHAPTER SEVENTEEN

Karma and Rebirth In The Land of the Earth-Eaters

CHARLES PREBISH

It has been nearly a decade since scholarly works on the Buddhist tradition in America began to appear in the appropriate journals with some regularity, and by the mid-1970s, full length volumes were beginning to emerge as well. There was little precedent for these landmark studies, and no more than a bare handful of models as well. While Buddhism had appeared in the West well over a century before the publication of Emma McCloy Layman's *Buddhism in America* in 1976, it had previously merited no more than a minimal chapter or two in works like Heinrich Dumoulin and John Maraldo's *Buddhism in the Modern World* or Jacob Needleman's *The New Religions*. The problem seemed to center around the fact that proper Buddhologists did not consider the study of Buddhism in America part of their professional mission, while specialists in American religion, even those purporting to emphasize new (or marginal) religious movements, had little facility, expertise, or interest in transplanted Oriental traditions. It is perhaps to the credit of the history of religion methodology that its exponents fared significantly better in approaching this new religious phenomenon, as witnessed by the publication of works like Robert S. Ellwood's *The Eagle and the Rising Sun*. Nevertheless, apart from Christmas Humphreys' *Sixty Years of Buddhism in England (1907-1967)*, published in 1968, and Louise Hunter's interesting but overly restrictive (and now outdated) *Buddhism in Hawaii*, there was little in the way of guidelines for the would-be investigator.

As a result of the above circumstance, initial studies of the Buddhist tradition in America[1] shared some common features which undermined the scope of their respective inquiries and limited their findings. In the first place, it was necessary for these works to catalogue rather than comment and to arrange rather than assess. Without a common foundation of data, there was little for the reader to utilize in guiding his application of the research presented. As a further complicating factor, many of the authors presented their materials in a somewhat slanted, even didactic fashion, reflecting their *personal* commitment to the very tradition they were exploring in a seemingly impartial fashion. Although this problem is more subtly handled today, it nevertheless persists.[2] Finally, some of the works published were case specific for a particular tradition, making no attempt to integrate the resulting conclusions into a wider, overarching perspective on the Buddhist movement in America.

With this in mind, it is necessary to make a few statements about the manner in which the doctrine of karma and its implications will be considered here. For our purposes, the threefold division of karma into *kuśala* (positive), *akuśala* (negative), and *avyākṛta* (indeterminate) will be employed. Karmic activities will be measured in terms of volition (*cetanā*), as is traditional, and with regard to ultimate resultant (*vipāka*). For the most part, we will focus on karmic activity in the phenomenal, ordinary realm (*saṃvṛti*) as expressed by the divisions of *sahetuka* karma. In other words, actions based on greed, hatred, and delusion (*rāga, dveṣa, moha*) yield *akuśala* karma, while actions based on an absence of greed, hatred, and delusion yield *kuśala* karma. In each case, the resultant is *duḥkha*. Consequently, although it is more difficult to explore, the goal for American as well as Asian Buddhists is to produce *ahetuka* karma or that which is not based on craving (*tṛṣṇā*). In so doing, karmic activity becomes ultimate or *paramārtha*. Common sense tells us, then, that in this paper we shall be more concerned with the moral dimension of American Buddhism as it applies to the karmic categories of traditional Buddhism.

Throughout its early history in various Asian countries, one of Buddhism's strongest attractions has been its profoundly rigorous ethical dimension. On the monastic level, fully one third of the Buddhist Tripiṭaka is devoted to the promotion and maintenance of a proper ethical framework in which the religious professional can integrate exemplary conduct into his general and overarching quest for salvation. Perhaps the highest expression of this concern is found in one of the introductory verses of the *Mahāsāṃghika-Lokottaravādin Prātimokṣa-sūtra*:

> The Śramaṇa who is intent upon *śīla* crosses over;
> The Brāhmaṇa who is intent upon *śīla* crosses over.
> One who is intent upon *śīla* is worthy of worship by men and gods;
> There is Prātimokṣa for one intent upon *śīla*.[3]

Here it is not just *Vinaya*, or the disciplinary code for the monastic, that is being praised, but rather *śīla*, a difficult word to explicate, but which refers to the *internally* enforced ethical framework by which the monk or nun structures his or her life. Thus, Buddhist ethical life operates under the double balance of the *externally* enforced monastic code, exemplified by Prātimokṣa, and the *internally* enforced guideline of *śīla*. The monastic codes, however, were canonized quite early in Buddhist history, leaving the commentarial tradition as the sole means for amending or altering the ethical dimension of Buddhist monastic life. For quite some time, Buddhism had an active, vibrant commentarial tradition, but in recent centuries this tradition has slackened, resulting in the fossilization of this aspect of the Buddhist tradition. On the lay level as well, ethical life is governed by the traditional five vows and their explication in a few key texts that are over two thousand years old. Now all this is not to say that the ethical tradition in Buddhism does not demand a high degree of moral behavior. Quite the contrary is true. Nevertheless, until quite recently, Buddhism's lack of willingness to confront modernity, its lack of willingness to redefine itself in the context of rapid social change, had led to serious problems in its homeland. The situation is no less difficult for Buddhism in America. Faced with the task of applying a somewhat outdated and outmoded ethical tradition to modern circumstances or innovating a genuinely new framework which integrates appropriate aspects of its once rich tradition (as Asian Buddhists are now doing), American Buddhists have vacillated. While Christians have taken a long, hard look at the changing face of modern society, and offered to confront the chief ethical issues directly and forthrightly, if not altogether effectively, Buddhists have done neither.

In their pursuit of positive karmic conduct, American Buddhists have been limited in at least two major ways. First, Asian Buddhism, or at least the Buddhism of the prescribed ethical lifestyle, was an essentially rural movement. Ethical conduct was anticipated in a way of life that was uncluttered by the sorts of demands that city dwelling imposes. This does not mean to say that the ethical conduct mandated by the earliest tradition *cannot* be entertained in the city, but it does recognize an entirely different set of circumstances and living requirements. In another context I said, with regard to many American Buddhists, that

> Some of these practitioners simply rejected the evils of city life; others seemed to be motivated by a concern for the preservation of a sane ecological environment; and a goodly number were naively pursuing a "back to nature" style of life. Many American Buddhists had been blindly seduced by the rural settings of monastic institutions in Asia or the rustic settings of Japanese landscape painting and were convinced that Buddhism could *only* be practiced in the pristine wilds. In any case, these Buddhist practitioners searched for

> a peaceful spot in which, they were certain, it would be much easier to "actualize themselves." Most have returned to the city, but they do not seem to know why.[4]

Perhaps they *still* do not know why, but the answer is certainly clear enough: *American Buddhism is a city movement,* and that both imposes and requires an entirely different approach to the issue of karmic responsibility. The second limiting factor in American Buddhists' pursuit of karmic propriety is that Asian Buddhism, although numbered by mainly lay practitioners, anticipated monastic conduct as the proper mode of behavior for all—if not in this life, then the next. In other words, positive karmic responsibility on the part of the laity, in this life, was anticipated as a prelude to a potentialy monastic way of life in the next. Such an ideal holds throughout the Theravāda tradition at least, and most other *nikāyas* as well. It is in the Mahāyāna and Vajrayāna traditions that this notion changes somewhat, but we shall say more about these two traditions later. American Buddhism is almost completely a lay movement, and although we do see some evidence of a monastic tradition emerging, it is unlikely that such an approach will prosper on the American soil. As a result, karmic responsibility on the part of the American Buddhist must be considered from the lay standpoint, and this means a consideration of the five traditional vows of the laity.

In the wildly chaotic decade of the 1960s, Buddhists, like other Americans, were caught in the midst of the Free Speech Movement, the Sexual Freedom Movement, the era of assassination, the terror of urban blight, the Peace Movement, the proliferation of psychoactive drugs, and a host of other polarizing forces. In many ways, Buddhists' infant community life in America was more seriously disrupted than were those of more established communities in the mainstream of American culture. Consequently, through its association with the counter-culture, Buddhist community life was to some extent a hotbed of current or defunct radicals practicing everything from do-it-yourself macrobiotics to various forms of multilateral marriage. In reaction to these elements in Buddhism, some Buddhist teachers in the 1970s have returned to the traditional mode of instruction for laymen, that is, emphasis on non-harming, abstention from theft, false speech, intoxicants and drugs of any kind, and illicit sexual behavior. In so doing, these teachers began to realize that the traditional mode was generally outdated (and consequently, rendered ineffective or unbelievable) or ill-suited to modern America. In their attempt to extemporize meaningfully and responsibly, Buddhists are learning, for example, that some drugs, although psychoactive, are valuable therapeutic tools when utilized by a trained and licensed professional. In addition, Buddhists are learning that some forms of premarital (and perhaps even extramarital) relationships that include sexuality may provide valuable personal growth rather than social and emotional harm. The whole dimension of the emphasis on non-harming is being rearranged for American Buddhists by the more stirring developments in medical ethics. These problems are certainly not distinct to Buddhists. Nevertheless, in confronting them directly, Buddhists squarely face not only the immediate problems in the ethical domain, but the greater problem of American identity. For struggling as Americans with critical issues in American life, Buddhists in this country are able to emphasize their sameness rather than their separateness. Further, in beginning to alter the traditional patterns of Buddhist ethics, they are for the first time creatively dealing with their plight in the modern world.

What we are saying above, and rather bluntly too, is that the traditional five layman's vows, as generaly explicated, may well be at variance with the value orientation of many Americans who are now calling themselves Buddhists. They are difficult, demanding, and exact an abiding commitment to moral perfection, at least in the Buddhist context, that even many Buddhists cannot or will not make. In the preparation of my own volume on American Buddhism published in 1979, my travels took me to many centers of American Buddhism, and while I generally found that American Buddhists had little difficulty adhering to the precepts requiring non-harming, abstention from falsehood, and non-theft, the requirements forbidding illicit sexuality and the taking of intoxicants were almost universally ignored or abused to some significant extent. In some Buddhist communities, indulgence in alcohol and sexuality seemed to be almost encouraged and justified as a learning device for novices struggling with ego problems. If the five additional precepts of the monastic are added (not to eat at the wrong times, to avoid dancing, singing, and stage plays, to abstain from using garlands, perfumes, and ornaments, to abstain from sitting on high seats, and not to accept gold and silver), the situation becomes even more muddled, for many of the things to be expressly avoided are an integral part of the life of average Americans, from which the Buddhist membership is drawn. Is the American Buddhist to avoid all concerts, or theater presentations, or money? Do we shun Shakespeare, Mozart, and E.F. Hutton? The newly initiated American Buddhist is at once trapped between the proverbial rock and the hard place. One can adhere solidly to all of the layman's precepts, maintaining religious integrity, but paying the price in social seclusion, or one can selectively ignore (or reinterpret) certain precepts for the sake of acculturation and social identity, accruing unsatisfactory karma in the process. Who can choose?

Fortunately, there are other guidelines for the aspiring layman that make karmic responsibility easier to deal with, even in the American context. The Theravadin *Sigālovāda Sutta,* for example, outlines the proper mode of behavior in a variety of relationships including children and parents, husband and wife, teacher and pupil, servants and work-people, and friends. What makes these bits of counsel so valuable is that they are truly transcultural; no impact is lost in the transition to the American context. Of equal impact, on the American scene as well as in Asia, are two other basic Buddhist notions which are emphasized throughout the Buddhist tradition. The first of these is the famous "three refuges" which goes hand in hand with the five vows of the laity. In fact, Holmes Welch even suggested in *The Practice of Chinese Buddhism 1900-1950*, that the only true measure of a Buddhist was positive commitment to *both* the five layman's vows and the three refuges. And just as we earlier learned that the five layman's vows were generally ignored or practiced in truncated fashion in America, so also the three refuges, despite widespread acceptance on the part of most American Buddhists, are for the most part either misunderstood or taken in a perfunctory manner. It is probably fair to say that the refuge ceremony is the most widespread Buddhist ritual practiced in America, yet few realize its full implication. To be sure, Americans have little difficulty understanding the first two refuges (i.e., Buddha, *dharma*). It is the third refuge, that of the *saṅgha*, that is misunderstood. As a result, serious problems ensue which have implications for the notion of karma as practiced in American Buddhism. There are two traditional terms for referring to the *saṅgha* in Buddhism: *āryasaṅgha* and *samvṛtisaṅgha*. The former is comprised of all those Buddhists who have attained the status of *āryapudgala*, that is, those who have at least entered the stream and become *srotāpannas*. In the *āryasaṅgha* there is no distinction between monastic and lay vocation. In other words, a member of the laity may well have attained status in the *āryasaṅgha* while a *bhikṣu* or *bhikṣuṇī* may not. The *samvṛtisaṅgha*, on the other hand, is comprised of only *bhikṣus* and *bhikṣuṇīs*. No *upāsakas* or *upāsikās* are counted as members. What most American Buddhists do not know, simply because they have not been told, is that it is the *āryasaṅgha* and not the *samvṛtisaṅgha* that one affirms in the refuge ceremony. The reason for affirming the *āryasaṅgha* in the refuge ceremony is obvious: one puts their faith in those who have realized the essence of the Buddha's teaching and are in the process of actualizing it societally. To make matters worse, most American Buddhists also do not know that the laity is not included in the *samvṛtisaṅgha*, so they think they are affirming *themselves*, as the *saṅgha*, in the refuge ceremony. In so doing, they are sanctioning the least correct karmic actors rather than the most efficient and proper functionaries.

Winston King, in his classic book *In the Hope of Nibbana* (pp. 186-201) offers four descriptions of why the *saṅgha* might be considered the ideal community. These include regulation of the community through the rules of the *Vinaya*, community functionality through democratic government, religious instruction through a proper teacher of *dharma*, and institutionalized utilization of the *saṅgha* as a moral counsellor. At the very core of each of these four aspects of the *saṅgha* is proper karmic activity. Unfortunately, with few exceptions, the American Buddhist community has little regard for the *Vinaya*, at least to the extent that its maxims are essentially ignored. The community is generally run by an authoritative head, or in some cases, by a board of advanced students chosen by the head to implement his or her injunctions. The *dharma* teacher too is often less than exemplary in personal conduct and behavior, and the community has virtually no counselling service, moral or otherwise. Thus, the American Buddhist community has little opportunity to fulfill its karmic responsibility, collectively or individually.

The other basic Buddhist notion which might well be useful from a karmic standpoint is that portion of the fourth noble truth devoted to *śīla*: right speech (*samyak vācā*), right action (*samyak karmānta*), and right livelihood (*samyak ājīva*). With regard to the first of these, H. Saddhatissa points out that by practicing right speech, "we create a connecting link between thought and action. One, moreover, which is characterized by wisdom and kindness."[5] Right action, of course, reinforces the practice of the five vows of the laity. Right livelihood insists on an occupation that brings no harm to others, traditionally excluding trades that sell weapons, living beings, flesh, intoxicating drinks, and poisons. Needless to say, time and circumstance has lent a host of new meanings and interpretations to that list, each of which has karmic implications for American Buddhists. It must also be noted that, "*Śīla* or morality is not placed lowest in the scale of values because it is inferior to other values, but because it is fundamental and foundational to them."[6] Nonetheless, despite being the lowest level, few get beyond it, in Asia or America. It need not be so. Winston King states very clearly that, "*Experientially speaking the very materials of one's daily Śīla-life may become the materials of meditational contemplation.* Moral action becomes meditative theme and meditative theme becomes action."[7] This notion is no doubt of profound impact for Buddhism in general, but on the American scene it is radically trivialized. American Buddhists seem to have little patience for slow and gradual religious development, so they tend to (1) flock to traditions emphasizing sudden enlightenment (such as Zen or Tibetan Buddhism), often not realizing that the so-called sudden experience only comes after countless years, or even lives, of preparation, and (2) define *nirvāṇa* in purely psychological terms, omitting the ethical and other aspects of salvation. It is no doubt possible to view meditation itself as a good karmic act,[8] but when this particular activity is emphasized at the gross exclusion of all other karmically positive behavior, then the salvific act itself becomes prostituted in a grievous fashion, undermining the very intent of the tradition. In a culture that is almost consumed with intent for the production of "instant" products such as fast-foods, self-developing photographic film, and expedient no-fault divorces, it is understandable how this mind-set spills over into the religious domain, but it nevertheless limits the degree to which the Buddhist tradition can thrive on American soil.

In recent years, only two volumes have appeared that purport to deal with the question of Buddhist ethics: Tachibana's *The Ethics of Buddhism* and Saddhatissa's *Buddhist Ethics*. Unfortunately, neither truly confronts the question. Only Winston King's *In the Hope of Nibbana* provides a responsible, serious treatment of the topic. King's work, however, apart from being somewhat dated (1964), is really specific only for Burma. Admittedly, King's initial two chapters ("The Framework of Self-Perfection" and "The Self: Kamma and Rebirth") are brilliant in their attempt to find the contextual locus of the ethical tradition in Buddhism. As we progress through the volume, though, we discover that in King's application of rather rigid Western categories (at least as he utilizes them) to the Theravāda tradition in Burma, he does justice to neither the Theravāda nor Western situation. To grant the Buddhist parity with the Westerner in pursuing individual perfection, as King does, only tells a partial story, for it ignores the aspect of social ethics in Buddhism. Of course King will not admit that Buddhism has social ethics at all, and it is here that he misses the point altogether. Recently, Harvey Aronson, in his *Love and Sympathy in Theravāda Buddhism*, has made the same point. He says,

> Two modern Western scholars, Winston King and Melford Spiro, have asserted that the normative ethic of Theravāda Buddhism is one of withdrawal from society and abstention from social involvement. According to King and Spiro's view, the current situation of diminished monastic social involvement reflects a supposed ethical norm established in the discourses and their commentaries. However, a rigorous analysis of the specific instructions on social concern—namely, the teachings on love, sympathy, and the sublime attitudes—indicates this is not the case. Furthermore, the historical records indicate that up to the modern period the Buddhist monastic community has been actively involved in improving the community life of the societies where it has flourished.[9]

To some degree, Buddhism in America has sought to advance karmic propriety through implementing a series of community activities that could easily fall under the category of social ethics. No American Buddhist group, for example, has done more in this area than the San Francisco Zen Center. Located in the now rather seedy "Fillmore District" of San

Francisco, the Zen Center launched the "Neighborhood Foundation" in 1975, in an attempt to upgrade the area to its once beautiful setting. Consistent with that effort they opened a grocery store ("Green Gulch Greengrocer") in 1975, providing a market outlet for the fresh produce yielded by their farm. They have also operated a stitchery, study center, and other similar concerns. The bottom line is that everyone profits: Zen center, disciples, and the community. And it might well be anticipated that other American Buddhist groups will advance the cause led by San Francisco Zen Center.

Earlier we suggested that the Mahāyāna and Vajrayāna schools of Buddhism did not emphasize the monastic ideal to the extent that the so-called Hīnayāna schools did. In other words, a fuller and more complete role in the tradition was afforded to the ordinary disciple. This is partly because, in the Mahāyāna and Vajrayāna traditions, there is a full pantheon of celestial Buddhas and Bodhisattvas, each of whom, through the notion of "transference of merit,"[10] can provide aid to the Buddhist practitioner. Consequently, each American Buddhist in one of these traditions has an array of supernormal beings to assist in his quest. Not only are these celestial patrons significant through their offering a good merit to the practitioner, but also because they engender, by their example, a prototypic behavior that is founded on exemplary moral comportment. Thus, American Buddhists are reminded to structure the ethical dimension of their own lives around the cardinal practices of love, compassion, sympathetic joy, and equanimity, therefore enhancing their own progress on the *bodhisattva* path. The transformative function of these practices must not be underestimated, yielding a profoundly beneficial impact on society as well. In a culture beset with so much moral uncertainty, these supernormal helpers provide American Buddhists with an oasis amidst despair and confusion, and by inculcating the values they symbolize, the entire course of American Buddhism is advanced.

In addition to the obvious supernormal helpers, Buddhism is assisted by the tradition known as *lineage*. Each of the various Buddhist traditions maintains a rich literature regarding the various and famous recipients of the teaching, and it matters little, from a pragmatic viewpoint, whether the *dharma* is transmitted from teacher to disciple (as in the Zen tradition) or effected through an incarnation system (as in Tibetan Buddhism). It could even be argued that edifying tales concerning famous, accomplished *theras* and *therīs* in the Theravāda traditions function in the same fashion as more proper lineages. Nonetheless, these bastions of the various Buddhist traditions establish, through the lineage, not only a living reminder of the efficacy of the respective teachings, but also present a means by which it is possible, in each successive generation, to maintain a link to Buddhist orthodoxy. In this way, Buddhism is able to renew itself continually, while maintaining bonds with an increasingly authoritative historical tradition. In studying and practicing with an American Buddhist teacher who is in the *dharma* line of a Dōgen or a Tsong-kha-pa, each disciple shares in the religious power of that lineage, and draws on it freely in pursuing his own experience of the Buddhist tradition. We have a few cases of *dharma* transmission to American Buddhists already, and it is not unreasonable to project, in the near future, an unbroken lineage of American Buddhist masters in the various traditions. I suspect that such an American lineage will have a profound effect on the assimilation of the Buddhist tradition in America. It will also be instrumental in making the proper karmic conduct manageable in the same environment.

When we try to collect the data that we have presented, and interpret it with an eye towards offering suggestions which might advance the Buddhist cause in America as well as refocus the perspective in which the doctrine of karma can be meaningfully shaped to the American ethical landscape, several issues become immediately apparent. In the first place, American Buddhists would do well to reconsider those virtues that have dominated the Buddhist ideal lifestyle for century after century. Tachibana devotes about two thirds of his 1926 volume *The Ethics of Buddhism* to just these items. Such an enterprise would include a careful consideration of self-restraint, abstinence, temperance, contentment, patience, purity humility, benevolence, liberality, tolerance, reverence, gratitude, veracity, and other applicable moral traits, all to be welded together into a mode of action that makes the attainment of *paramārtha* karma possible.

In addition, Buddhism in America appears to need, on the one hand, a revitalized ethical system, emphasizing the laity, and informed by modern advances in the human and physical sciences. I have in mind here a return to the practices known as the *Brahma-vihāras* or the "divine abodes." These four practices, usually identified as love (*maitrī*), compassion (*karuṇā*), sympathetic joy (*muditā*), and equanimity (*upekṣā*), when explicated in their totality, are the highest expression of the Buddhist ethical domain. And they have a clear application to American religious experience. On the other hand, Buddhism in America might reawaken the long silent commentarial tradition, in order to address from the American perspective, the critical issues prevalent today. Only a few Buddhist groups have begun to reassess and reassert Buddhist ethics on the American scene, and their effort to date has been modest; but like all pioneering attempts, it will take time. In spite of its unobtrusive beginning, the new emphasis on Buddhist ethics is starting to make some impact on the various American Buddhist communities.

Since the great preponderance of Buddhists in America belong to either Mahāyāna or Vajrayāna groups, it must also be emphasized that a renewed commitment to positive karmic responsibility requires a genuine attempt to engage in those practices known as *pāramitās* or "perfections." These include the traditional six of giving (*dāna*), morality (*śīla*), patience (*kṣānti*), vigor (*vīrya*), meditation (*samādhi*), and wisdom (*prajñā*). Many of the Buddhist groups now operative on the American scene stress the importance of the seventh (in the alternate schema of ten *pāramitās*) perfection: skill-in-means (*upāya*). They indicate that it is essential that it is critical to know just how to act in each prospective circumstance. They should be reminded that *upāya* emerges out of *prajñā*, and that one of these *pāramitās* without the other is a hopeless enterprise. Further, quite as many American Buddhists are now taking *bodhisattva* vows as previously took refuge, and it seems that they understand the implications of these vows quite as little as they understood the refuge ceremony. When one vows "to gain complete, perfect enlightenment for the sake of all sentient beings," this cannot be an expression of radical chic Buddhism. Indeed, these would-be *bodhisattvas* seem not to understand that the "thought of enlightenment" (or *Bodhicitta*), a prime prerequisite of entry onto the *bodhisattva* path, cannot be purchased like a *zafu* by all who have the ten dollar price. In other words, Buddhist ethical behavior and karmic responsibility must be based on basic education and understanding of the Buddhist tradition.

As American and world culture continues to make monumental advances in all aspects of technology, Buddhists addressing the issue of karma and rebirth must learn to finally confront science and modernity. When Harold K. Schilling argues in defense of complexity in "In Celebration of Complexity,"[11] American Buddhists might at least acknowledge that matters are significantly more complicated than they have admitted. While American Buddhists vainly chase the simplicity that they *think* Buddhism represents, they fail to recognize that the *context* has changed. Thus, as Americans consider the potential abandonment of their dream of the "innocent Adam," American Buddhists might do well to abandon their dream of the "innocent Buddha." Although the innocent Buddha may be transmuted into a cybernetic version of the HAL computer in Space Oddysey: 2001, or Michael Crichton's "terminal man," Buddhists in America would find it advantageous to end their silence on the relationship between Buddhism and science (or end their *simplistic* approach to the relationship), and in the proces, assert their sameness with the American mission rather than their separateness.

While it is generally true that Buddhism in this country is more modern than its Asian counterpart, this fact is more a product of American culture than Buddhist endeavor. The greatest advances have been made in the area of *human sciences*, particularly psychology. The reason is obvious: Buddhism has had throughout its history a deep concern for the mind and its function, as evidenced by the Abhidharma tradition and the meditative systems that grew out of it (some of which militated against it). It is commonplace for American Buddhist teachers to utilize more than a liberal sprinkling of psychological terminology and jargon in their public lectures and seminars, as well as in private instruction. Unfortunately, many of these teachers have little more than a layman's knowledge of formal psychology, doing it as much injustice as most Western psychologists do in treating Buddhist psychology. More complete knowledge of each of these traditions would certainly benefit the other, but this is not now (with few exceptions) being done. To be sure, the problem is quite as difficult in the other human sciences. In the physical sciences, Buddhism has lagged severely. I suspect that this is less due to Buddhism's inability than it is to Buddhism's apologetic position. There is much in modern physics, for example, that has a deep resonance with Buddhist tenets. This has only been superficially explored. The same is true in such fields as chemistry, biology, and the like. Nevertheless, Buddhism attempts to *appear* scientific. American Buddhists tend to shy away from the tradition of reason and logic in Buddhist thought, although it represents the most significant strata of Buddhist philosophy. Indeed, one could go on and on. Perhaps the solution to the problem lies in a twofold approach. Needless to say, the first necessary step is the *decision to change*. The second step would enable Buddhism to exploit the simple fact that in this country its adherents are an extremely literate group, quite often including professionals from virtually all the scientific fields. The high level of educational training, as well as the professional positions of these American Buddhists, might be utilized to some degree in addressing problems common to Buddhism and science. As a corollary of this last issue, the question of Buddhism and vocation comes directly to the forefront. It appears that the time is ripe for American Buddhist teachers to emphasize more firmly education and career to their students, and to encourage those with scientific background and leaning to pursue these studies further, but in a way consonant with American Buddhist needs and requirements. In so doing, Buddhism could forthrightly confront science and modernity in a more profound fashion than their predecessors. Technology, societal complexity, medicine, and the like will simply not wait for advancement until American Buddhists suddenly experience a collective "eureka." And the longer Buddhists wait to pursue these avenues of research, the more difficult the problem becomes. The experiential lag that Buddhists are seeking to correct in their everyday lives through religious training rests on the verge of becoming a cultural lag that escalates the difficulty exponentially.

In summarizing, it must be said that while Americans are still rather eager to profess their steadfast commitment to the Buddhist tradition, and in growing numbers, they bring to their new religion neither the intellectual understanding of its history, doctrines, and practices nor the personal ability to take its teachings on karma and rebirth seriously. In an environment in which entrapment in perpetual rebirth means simply another round of HBO or ESPN, a few more lines of cocaine, and perhaps another herpes scare, it is difficult to worry too much about *nirvāṇa* in a soteriological context. Until karmic resultants can be understood in terms of poverty, terminal illness, and a life of psychological despair, karma is something to read about and espouse vigorously, but not to do. For my money, I'll take my stand with Winston King when he says,

> The present moment, the psychological "now," is the key point in moral progress and discipline. Its proper use contains the hope of ethical perfection and ultimate liberation in Nibbana. The past cannot be altered, for Kamma carries every thought, word, or deed to its ultimate fruition, good or bad; and to a great extent my present existence is filled with and determined by my past. Yet each moment is also new and contains elements of freedom with that newness. The present moment indeed is the *only* moment in which karmic process can be directed or ultimately escaped. And since all past Kamma was once present Kamma, every man has the power to achieve his own perfection lying within his control for the full length of his life as a human being; every new moment of existence presents a new opportunity to build a good future kamma.[12]

NOTES

1. See, for example, Gyomay Kubose, *American Buddhism. A New Direction* (Chicago: The Dharma House, 1976), or Kashima Tetsuden, *Buddhism in America: The Social Organization of an Ethnic Religious Organization* (Westport, Conn.: Greenwood Press, 1977).

2. See, Rick Fields, *How the Swans Came to the Lake: A Narrative History of Buddhism in America* (Boulder: Shambahala, 1981). This fine book is nonetheless written by an author who has been more or less associated with Chögyam Trungpa, Rinpoche.

3. Charles S. Prebish, *Buddhist Monastic Discipline: The Sanskrit Prātimokṣa Sūtras of the Mahāsāṃghikas and Mūlasarvāstivādins* (University Park: Pennsylvania State University Press, 1975), p. 42.

4. Charles Prebish, *American Buddhism* (North Scituate, Mass.: Duxbury Press, 1979), p. 38.

5. H. Saddhatissa, *Buddhist Ethics* (New York: George Braziller, 1970), p. 71.

6. Winston King, *In the Hope of Nibbana* (LaSalle, Illinois: Open Court, 1964), p. 171.

7. Ibid., p. 172.

8. Many point this out. See, for example, King, *In the Hope of Nibbana*, p. 172.

9. Harvey Aronson, *Love and Sympathy in Theravāda Buddhism* (Delhi: Motilal Banarsidass, 1980), p. 2.

10. There is also a suggestion of transference of merit in the Theravāda tradition. It is simply not considered here.

11. Harold K. Schilling, "In Celebration of Complexity," *Union Seminary Quarterly Review*, 30, 2-4 (Winter-Summer, 1975), pp. 85-93.

12. King, *In the Hope of Nibbana*, p. 19.

CHAPTER EIGHTEEN

Critical Response

TERENCE PENELHUM

I write these comments as a Western analytical philosopher in particular, with no formal training in religious scholarship, and/no first-hand knowledge of the Eastern religious traditions. As a result, it is best that I should say at the outset what I take the term karma to signify, and comment on some of the problems that doctrines involving this notion present to many Western hearers. I shall then use these reflections as a base for comment on the preceding five papers.

Prior to the interesting revelations this occasion has offered for understanding recent developments in karmic teaching, I have always had an understanding of the doctrine of karma that is close to what Professor Potter has called the Classical Karma Theory of India. That is, I have assumed that someone who believes in karma believes that certain fundamental features of our lives, such as our general psychological predispositions, our social status, our susceptibility to this or that disease, are not, as most of us think, sheer brute facts which we find when we enter the world, or good or bad events which merely happen to us, but are to be understood instead as outcomes of actions and choices of our own. This alleged fact about our condition is not, it seems, offered as itself a discovery or revelation of any one of the religious traditions that teach it; it is rather something each of them takes for granted as a self-evident fact of nature, to which each of the traditions offers a response. By saying it is a fact of nature, I mean that it is thought of as more akin to such general principles as the Laws of Thermodynamics or Gravitation, than to such intrinsically religious principles as that of Providence or Original Sin.

This is a feature of the doctrine of karma which has always made it hard for Westerners to take it with full seriousness, especially in modern times. This is not because they espouse a different cosmic principle that competes with it; but because they do not, or at least think that they do not, espouse any such principle at all.

For the doctrine of karma contains within it an inescapable core of *evaluation*, and it is the received wisdom of Western culture that no evaluative elements belong in the understanding of the way the natural world is structured. Westerners see karmic doctrine as telling us that the natural order contains within its structure a pervasive sort of *justice*, and in particular a built-in strand of retribution: an answer, however general and vague, to questions of the form "Why does X, rather than Y, live out his life in the particular circumstances in which he finds himself"? But they themselves think that no true account of the way the natural world is, can contain evaluative elements of this sort; that science can only contain talk about causes, not reasons or justifications. In philosophical terms, they would see the doctrine of karma as one which confuses descriptive and prescriptive laws: laws which tell us how things are, and laws which tell us what to do—the former being discovered, and the latter legislated. Not only do they believe in the ultimacy of this distinction; they are vain about it, and think of it as a major achievement of Western civilization to have recognised it, and to have compartmentalized its thinking and its professional activities to match that recognition.

I am not arguing here that this received Western opinion is right. Historically it is not right; at least it has taken a very long time for the concept of natural law to be purged of its evaluative content. When we first encounter it, for example, in the reported teachings of Anaximander, we find it expressed in the language of justice.[1] He explains the succession of the seasons as due to the fact that in summer the hot and dry principles dominate over their opposites, the cold and wet principles, and that this creates an injustice for which they have to make amends by yielding their place for a time. Of course, once the profound innovation of transfering the concept of law from the realm of social relationships to that of natural understanding has been made, many questions arise. They are questions about how far the original implications of the concept of law remain with it when it has been thus reapplied. Do natural, as opposed to social, laws have sanctions attached? Can they, in fact, ever be broken? Are they laid down by anyone? Can they be changed? Over the centuries these questions have been answered in many different ways, but in spite of the fact that major figures like Plato, who wished to identify the objects of moral and scientific thought rather than to separate them, have argued otherwise, the most widespread consensus by modern times is that natural law is a matter of sheer given sequence, with no evaluative component within it. (The greatest single intellectual influence in this direction has been Hume.) Even those who have believed that the natural order has a purpose and direction hold that the purpose and direction come from a divine mind external to the order he has created, who bends it to his purpose by special intervention.

I incline to think that this is the major barrier in the way of a more ready reception for karmic teaching in Western circles. Other common objections, if taken without it, seem confused or arbitrary. To dismiss rebirth and pre-existence as absurd, when post-mortem survival is at worst thought to be contingently false, seems arbitrary. To dismiss the doctrine of karma as fatalist seems confused, since it is of its essence to maintain that our future circumstances issue from past and present choices. But these objections have greater weight if one sees that the rejected doctrines themselves are logical consequences of an understanding of the cosmic order as an intrinsically retributive one. For in a culture where the exclusion of such possibilities from the understanding of nature is synonymous with enlightenment in the thinking of so many, doctrines which express and depend upon it are bound to meet with the deepest resistance.

If there is any truth in this, we would expect to find that Western adoption of the doctrine of karma is accompanied by a lack of clear understanding of it, or by attempts to domesticate it and represent it in the thought-forms of contemporary psychology, or Christian theology. I approached the five papers on which I was asked to comment, wondering whether this would turn out to be so. The essays divided in an obvious way. Those by Professors Prebish, Gussner, and Baird are about movements which have gained a notable degree of acceptance among Westerners, and I think they do illustrate predictable doctrinal modifications which help to explain some of this acceptance. (In making this comment, I have no wish to deny that Western adherents of these movements are drawn by their radical *differences* from traditions familiar to them; only to assert that there are likely to be more deep-seated intellectual obstacles to their capacity for adaptation than they suppose.) The two papers by Professors Coward and Neufeldt deal with Western thinkers who have mined Eastern traditions for sources of enlightenment in intellectual and personal quests which never lose their Western character. Since these quests consist in part of attempts to undermine dominant Western scientific and metaphysical assumptions, the degree of intellectual assimilation of key Eastern doctrines seems to me to be greater, even though there is less ostensible identification with the traditions from which these doctrines are absorbed. I have no moral to draw from this, except to note the obvious fact that the influence of Jung and Blavatsky is always likely to be restricted.

Professor Prebish's paper does not address itself centrally to questions of interpretation of the doctrines of karma and rebirth in the way the others in this collection do. Since his theme is the cultural problems of North American Buddhism, he concentrates upon the special features of Buddhist practice as these are understood (or misunderstood) on this continent, and, to a lesser extent, the effect of North American culture on the supposed place of meditation in the Buddhist way.

As I first thought about it, it appeared to me that there was a conflict in the paper between two claims: first, the claim that traditional Buddhist precepts are not readily adaptable to the conditions of American life; second, the claim that American Buddhists lack, and should try to acquire (or recover) the original meaning of the precepts they follow and the practices in which they engage. It seemed to me that although this latter is obviously desirable in itself, it is not something guaranteed to lessen, but something which is quite likely to worsen, the problem of non-adaptation. This would certainly not be the first time in which a religious movement has grown through the misunderstanding of its meaning, and it would not be the last time in which understanding had weakened commitment instead of strengthening it. But there is a partial answer in the paper to this criticism. It consists in the recommendation that American Buddhists try to create a common framework of thought with their scientifically-oriented contemporaries, by exploring the analogies that Professor Prebish says exist between Buddhist teaching and natural science. He only gives hints of how this could proceed, but it would presumably have to include the examination of the question of how far traditional Buddhist understandings of karma can be related to psychology, biology (including, no doubt, genetics) and physics. I have already given general reasons for thinking that this is a formidable task. But of course it is the formidable things that are most worthwhile.

The most striking fact that emerges from Professor Gussner's fascinating account of Rajneesh's teachings on rebirth (and it is a fact which he notes) is the separation that results in it between what Rajneesh says about rebirth and what he says about karma. I speculate that this will have something to do with the appeal he has far Westerners.

As I understand it, Rajneesh says that karma has its hold upon us through improper consciousness, incomplete or distorted attention; to avoid it one must avoid such distortions (or self-deceptions) in one's ongoing experience, and to gain release from its consequences one must try to revive earlier experiences hitherto corrupted by them. It is easy to say that the appeal of this to Western hearers is due to the rejection of conventional ethical paths towards release. But might it not be due at least as much to the fact that one can hold this perception of karma in a way which does not entail regarding it as more than a psychological liability of this one life; without, that is, having to take very seriously the view that there are pre-existent misperceptions from earlier lives that have to be reversed also? For all the luxuriance of the talk about rebirths, it seems to be there for reasons which are essentially independent of what is said about karma. That there is not much explicit talk of karma would seem to confirm this suspicion, and indicate that the connection of it to the idea of rebirth does not have much real use. By this I do not suggest that Rajneesh does not adhere to doctrines of rebirth, but that what he says about karma does not connect very tightly with it. This would have the effect that karmic teaching would present itself to the Westerner as psychology and psychotherapy, not metaphysics, and would appeal more immediately for that very reason.

It is clear from Professor Baird's lucid and well-documented account of them, that Swami Bhaktivedanta's teachings involve no conscious compromise or adaptation designed to make them more palatable to the Western mind. Certainly karma does not emerge here as a force which is explicable merely in psychological terms. But it is also clear that his system of thought is full of obvious analogues of key doctrines in Christian theology, and that these must serve to make that system readily accessible to the intellect and imaginations of those familiar with it. To say that karma is subject to the Lord's will but is normally allowed to take its course is similar to saying that God permits us, in the unregenerate world, to live out the consequences of one another's choices; and to say that surrender to the Lord leads to release is similar to saying the salvation can come through the grace of God if one turns to God in faith and does not rely on one's merits. So even though the doctrine of karma is not altered in any fundamental way, it is presented within a framework in which the dominant element is the grace of a Lord whose will is distinct from the karmic system, and who can and will lift one out of it if one surrenders. So the justice, the retribution, and the grace that rescues us from them, have their source in a being who transcends the natural order; all this in spite of the pantheistic aspects of the Vaiṣṇavite system.

If these brief reflections on three essays point to any conclusion, it is to the unsurprising one that traditions embodying the doctrines of karma and rebirth are prone to be misunderstood by Westerners, even those who seek to espouse them, and will gain acceptance in part at least because of special features which make them seem less unfamiliar at the cost of changing their personal and doctrinal significance—or because of simple misunderstanding.

I shall take the two parts of Professor Coward's paper in the reverse order to his. In describing the influence of the idea of karma on those influenced by Transpersonal Psychology, he is informing us of the many ways in which an awareness of this concept has enabled some Western investigators to widen the theoretical frameworks of their studies. While I incline to think this falls far short of the adoption of a new paradigm in Kuhn's sense, it certainly manifests an important imaginative emancipation from the restrictions more orthodox Western psychologists have been eager to impose on themselves. While the interpretation of commonsense consciousness as a filter in Western thought is due, in my opinion, neither to awareness of Eastern thinking nor to Bergson, but to Kant—the radical view that it might be liberating (indeed that it might be possible) to have a form of consciousness that is not so filtered is due to these sources, and is in principle a major advance. Similarly, the study of the increase in one's repertoire of direct actions through biofeedback seems to be an important development that has direct links with the recognition of the power of techniques known first in the context of karmic theory. I contest none of this, but remark only that these examples seem to me to be cases of the best kind of plagiarism, where thinkers working in one tradition seek to enlarge its scope by recognising ways in which another has yielded incontestable results. This does not show that the adoption of the theoretical assumptions of the other tradition is either implied or desirable, even if the assumptions of one's own tradition have genuinely precluded these results, and cannot be patched up to accommodate them.

With Jung, however, one is much closer to the deep absorption of the Eastern metaphysical substructure (as one is, as Professor Coward says, in the case of Tillich). In common with others, I had for a long time imagined that the theory of the collective unconscious was a vague misapplication of the concept of the *ātman*, but this is clearly a mistake. Jung wishes to explain certain common intellectual predispositions in terms of psychic (rather than physical) inheritance, which he construes as collective karma, through which we inherit dispositions from our ancestors. If Jung inched towards acceptance of an individual karma doctrine also, it is hard to see that this would be necessary to explain the same phenomena, whatever other explanatory power it might have. Individual karma is surely a doctrine that serves to explain differences between peoples' circumstances, and what Jung is anxious to account for in the doctrine of archetypes is the widespread *similarity* between us in certain respects which cannot be traced to individual experience after birth (hence the common assimilation to Plato's doctrine of Reminiscence). The only difficulty is that the idea of psychical inheritance seems to lack very clear content. Individual karma works between the successive lives of one individual, not between ancestors and descendants, and the related doctrines of the subtle body, bardo-states, and the rest, provide a mechanism, independent of the biological mechanisms of heredity, to make the process intelligible. But if collective karma accounts for our inheriting predispositions from our ancestors, rather than from earlier phases of ourselves, the mechanism of individual karma will not serve to carry it. On the other hand, the mechanism of biological heredity, that is, that of genetics, would appear to be as adequate to carry this form of inheritance as it is to carry others. So a distinct form of psychical heredity looks to be unnecessary, in addition to having been left without detailed content.

In spite of these difficulties, Jung remains the only major psychological thinker who has wrestled with the problems of assimilating the doctrine of karma itself into his thought, rather than finding stimulus in the tradition from which it comes.

I turn finally to Professor Neufeldt's account of Theosophy. In spite of her animadversions on Christianity, there are clear signs of its influence on Blavatsky's system (if that is the word for it). It seems to be an amalgamation of karma-rebirth theory and a non-rigorous, universalist doctrine of salvation that derives in obvious ways from Christian eschatology. For what Professor Neufeldt calls the Utopianism of the system is the proclamation of an inevitably positive outcome to the series of rebirths; a sort of benign predestinarianism without God. It is strikingly a theory which treats the workings of karma as facts of nature; but it changes the understanding of these workings to emphasise their benevolence as well as their justice, choosing benevolence over justice when the two seem to conflict. It is interesting to compare this amalgamation of two traditions with the fusion attempted recently by John Hick.[2] While I find his more successful, he achieves it (and incorporates the expectation of universal salvation within it) by retaining a theistic base for it. Without that, the claim of Theosophy to offer us a universally acceptable blend of religious insights faces a difficulty with which my comments began: what ground is there, at least for the skeptical Western mind, to suppose that the workings of the natural order, as distinct from the workings of the mind of a personal God, incorporate any moral attitude at all, whether it be justice or benevolence?

NOTES

1. For a standard account of Anaximander see John Burnet, *Early Greek Philosophy*, (Adam and Charles Black: London) 1952, pp. 50-71.

2. See his *Death and Eternal Life*, (Collins: London) 1976.

Contributors Notes

ROBERT D. BAIRD is Professor in the History of Religion at the School of Religion, University of Iowa, Iowa City, Iowa. In addition to numerous articles he has published *Category Formation and the History of Religion*, The Hague: Mouton and Co., 1971; and edited *Religion in Modern India*, Colombia: South Asia Books, 1982.

HAROLD G. COWARD is Professor of Religious Studies and Director of the Humanities Institute at University of Calgary, Calgary, Alberta. Among his numerous articles and books are *Religious Pluralism and the World Religions*, Madras: University of Madras Press, 1982; *Sphoṭa Theory of Language*, Delhi: Motilal Banarsidass, 1980; and *Jung and Eastern Thought*, 1984.

AUSTIN B. CREEL is Chairman of the Department of Religion, University of Florida, Gainsville, Florida. His many publications on religion in India include *Dharma in Hindu Ethics*, Columbia, Mo: South Asia Books, 1977.

EVA K. DARGYAY is Associate Professor of Buddhist Studies in the Religious Studies Department, University of Calgary, Calgary, Alberta. She has numerous books and articles on Tibetan culture to her credit including *Tibetan Village Communities - Structure and Change*, Warminster, England: Aris & Phillips, 1982.

L. DARGYAY is Research Scholar, Institute of Indian Studies (Ladakh Project), University of Munich, Munich, Germany, and Fellow in The Humanities Institute, The University of Calgary, Calgary, Alberta. His many articles on Tibetan Buddhism include "The View of Bodhicitta in Tibetan Buddhism" appearing in *The*

The Bodhisattva Doctrine in Buddhism ed. by Leslie S. Kawamura, Waterloo: Wilfrid Laurier University Press, 1981.

ROBERT E. GUSSNER is Assistant Professor of Comparative Religion at the University of Vermont, Burlington, Vermont. His published articles include "A Stylometric Study of the Authorship of Seventeen Sanskrit Hymns Attributed to Sankara," *Journal of the American Oriental Society*, Vol. 96, No. 2, March-June 1976.

YÜN-HUA JAN is Professor of Religious Studies at McMaster University, Hamilton, Ontario. His many published papers have appeared in international journals including *T'opung Pao, History of Religions, Philosophy East and West, Journal of Chinese Philosophy, Oriens Extremus, Indian Historical Quarterly*.

LESLIE S. KAWAMARA is Professor of Buddhist Studies and Head of the Religious Studies Department, University of Calgary, Calgary, Alberta. His many publications include *The Bodhisattva Doctrine in Buddhism*, proceedings of the Calgary Buddhism Conference, Waterloo: Wilfrid Laurier University Press, 1981.

KLAUS K. KLOSTERMAIER is Professor of Religious Studies in the Department of Religion, University of Manitoba, Winnipeg, Manitoba. The most recent of his many publications on religion in India is *Mythologies and Philosophies of Salvation in Theistic Traditions of India*, Waterloo: Wilfrid Laurier University Press, 1984.

V. BRUCE MATTHEWS is Associate Professor of Religious Studies at Acadia University, Nova Scotia. He is currently Associate Editor of *The Review/Revue* of the Canadian Asian Studies Association and has published a number of articles on Buddhism in Sri Lanka.

DAVID M. MILLER is Associate Professor of Religious Studies at Concordia University, Montreal, Quebec. His publications include *Hindu Monastic Life: The Monks and Monasteries of Bhubaneswar* (with Dorothy Wertz), Montreal: McGill-Queen's University Press, 1976, and a number of articles on religion in modern India.

ROBERT N. MINOR is Associate Professor of Religious Studies, University of Kansas, Lawrence, Kansas. His many publications on religion in modern India include *The Bhagavad-gītā: An Exegetical Commentary*, Columbia, Mo: South Asia Books, 1981.

RONALD W. NEUFELDT is Associate Professor of Religious Studies, University of Calgary, Calgary, Alberta. His publications on religion in modern India include *F. Max Müller and The Rig Veda*, Columbia, Mo: South Asia Books, 1980.

TERENCE M. PENELHUM is Professor of Religious Studies, University of Calgary, Calgary, Alberta. Among his numerous publications in philosophy and religion his most recent is *God and Skepticism: A Study in Skepticism and Fideism*, Dordrecht: Reidel, 1983.

KARL H. POTTER is Professor of Philosophy and South Asian Studies at the University of Washington, Seattle, Washington. His numerous publications on Indian Philosophy include *Indian Theories of Logic and Cosmology: The Philosophy of Nyāya-Vaiesika*; and *Advaita Vedānta up to Śaṃkara and His Pupils*, Vols. 2 and 3 of the *Encyclopedia of Indian Philosophies*, Delhi: Motilal Banarsidass and Princeton: Princeton University Press, 1978 and 1981.

CHARLES S. PREBISH is Associate Professor in the Department of Religious Studies, Pennsylvania State University, University Park, Pennsylvania. Among his many publications are *American Buddhism*, Belmont, California: Wadsworth Publishing Company, Inc., 1979; and *Buddhism: A Modern Perspective*, University Park: The Pennsylvania State University Press, 1975.

LAMBERT SCHMITHAUSEN is Professor in the Seminar für Kultur und Geschichte Indiens, at the University of Hamburg. His numerous publications in Buddhist studies include *Der Nirvāna Abschnitt in der Viniścayasamgrahaṇī der Yogacarabhūmiḥ*, Vienna: Austrian Academy of Science and Liberal Arts, 1969; and "Philologische Bemerkergen zum Ratnagotravibhāga," *Vienner Zeitschrift für die Kunde Südasiens*, Vol. 15, 197, 123-177.

GEORGE M. WILLIAMS is Professor in the History of Religions at California State University, Chico, California. His publications include the authoritative study on Vivekananda, *The Quest for Meaning of Svāmī Vivekānanda: A Study of Religious Change*, Chico: New Horizons Press, 1974.

INDEX